ALFRED ADLER:

HIS INFLUENCE ON PSYCHOLOGY TODAY

ALFRED ADLER: HIS INFLUENCE ON PSYCHOLOGY TODAY

Edited by Harold H. Mosak

NOYES PRESS

Park Ridge, New Jersey

Published in the United States by
NOYES PRESS
Noyes Building
Park Ridge, New Jersey 07656

PREFACE

The commemoration of the centennial of Alfred Adler's birth has recently ended. The celebrations have been held, the eulogies spoken, and the papers written. The psychological world, Adlerian and non-Adlerian as well, recalled Adler's contributions to psychological thought and practice. While it is difficult, and to the Adlerian superfluous, to establish primacy, it was recalled that Adler constructed a theory that was holistic, social, teleological, and phenomenological. He perceived man as an actor rather than a victim of drives, instincts, heredity or environment. Man was a "becoming" individual who strived to give meaning both to himself and to life. To understand man in this framework Adler introduced the concept of the life style, the study of family constellation (which some psychologists erroneously equate with birth order and ordinal position), and the interpretation of early recollections, the "grand-daddy" of projective techniques.

Others recalled Adler's contributions to psychological practice. His establishment of community outreach programs (1898) and his introduction of family therapy (1922) may be cited as two major contributions. A field theorist, Adler felt that man could not be understood except as a social being. Consequently, throughout his career he addressed himself to problems of man in relationship to the life tasks. The catholicity of his interests encouraged him to write on such topics as war, religion, education, social relations, and group psychology.

Life was problem solving, a movement toward goals which each individual set in accordance with his apperceptive framework and which he felt would give him a place in the world. The highest ideal was social interest, a multi-dimensional construct which acknowledged that because we live in a social world, we are *responsible* for our fellowman. Man must not merely adjust to society; he is obligated to change it in the interest of the common weal.

Since Adler's death in 1937, those who identify with his philosophy have continued the tradition which he and his followers had begun to develop in Vienna. Accretions to and modifications of theory were elaborated. In practice, various Adlerians introduced group therapy into private practice, developed multiple psychotherapy, established family education centers, and conducted parent study groups.

This is where Adlerians have been. However, Adlerians are more interested in what people are moving toward than in looking backward. For this, among other reasons, the American Society of Adlerian Psychology authorized the publication of the present volume. The included papers provide an overview of the current interests of the Adlerian practitioner. Contributions reflect concern with personality theory, psychotherapy, the social sciences, the humanities, and applications. While the reader may deduce from these papers the directions which Adlerian psychology is taking, he should be reminded of Adler's admonition concerning the unreliability and precariousness of prognosis. Prediction is by definition probabilistic but Adler's declaration that "We cannot escape from the net of our own relatedness. Our sole safety is to assume the logic of our communal existence upon this planet as an ultimate absolute truth. . . ." clearly suggests that Adlerians will be engaged in the future as they have in the past in creating a society of fellowmen.

The contributed papers were read by Dr. Kurt A. Adler, Dr. Heinz L. Ansbacher, Mr. Maurice Bullard, Ms. Danica Deutsch, and Dr. Bernard H. Shulman. Their devotion to the Society's ideals has earned them the gratitude of the Society as well as that of the Editor. Since the Society is unaware until this moment of her tremendous contribution, I must express my own thanks to my wife, Birdie, whose encouragement, organizing, filing, typing, letter writing, and providing coffee to keep me awake during the late hours prevented me from requiring the psychological services of my colleagues.

Harold H. Mosak

Chicago, Illinois
September 10, 1973

CONTENTS

Contents

MEMORIAL TO DR. ALFRED ADLER

Willard and Marguerite Beecher

The tallest measure of a man is the effect that he has on the lives of others. And the deepest measure of his value lies in what they learn from him in terms of enduring wisdom—the kind that helps them when critical forks-in-the-road confront them. In the few years that we were fortunate enough to share with Alfred Adler before he died he revealed some monumental truths to us. He gave us a view of the comprehensive as well as the particular aspects of human behavior. The greatest honor we can pay him at this time is to share with others that which he helped us to see through his vision. It is our hope that it will not die with us and that it may be of some help to others.

We learned from him essentially:

1. That the individual's approach to life is a result of early self-training due to his interpretation of his situation. He can change it in later years only if he realizes that his disturbing, conditioned responses are nothing more than inappropriate, inadequate holdovers from childhood. The adult is expected to replace such behavior with more useful responses to be a help and not a burden. He should realize it is useless to try to escape the pain he creates for himself trying to solve adult problems with a child's tricks and evasions, since problems are only situations for which we have not trained ourselves.

2. That the problems of behavior, which make us feel and act like inferior second-class passengers in life, are no more than the results of our failure to develop the habit of both emotional and physical self-reliance. We retain from childhood the mistaken expectation that others should "hold up our pants" for us emotionally and physically and be interested in as well as responsible for our welfare.

3. That leaning on others emotionally or physically is a child's way of life. We should not permit this habit to follow us into adult life, *since dependency is the root of all feelings of inferiority.* Dependency generates the feeling of second-class citizenship. Out of this grows the habit of competition, envy, making comparisons and similar mistaken compensatory strivings we create in our effort to assuage the pain of feeling second class in relation to others. Humiliating feelings of inferiority produce the gnawing, distracting, disruptive, destructive craving for personal recognition and prestige, with its inescapable fear of failure.

1

4. That unhappiness, loneliness, neurotic symptoms, crime and similar distresses arise directly from this unresolved process of leaning and depending on others whom we try to control, rule, dominate or exploit for our own benefit, since we cannot otherwise support ourselves physically and emotionally.

5. That only those who are self-reliant emotionally and physically can function as *adult* human beings able to cooperate with other adults, because life demands that we be useful and productive or, as Adler said, to "be a help and not a burden."

6. That the inadequate responses of envy, greed, competition and sabotage—with which we try to solve confronting problems of life—are only reactions *which would not arise in the first place* if we were in the habit of standing on our own feet and were not always trying to find someone on whom to lean and exploit; whom we demand prop us up and hold us there.

7. That defects of self-reliance and the *inescapable pain* that accompanies them can be changed only when we *fully realize* that the pain we suffer is but the other-end-of-the-stick of our leaning, dependent, subaltern habits of mind. Our problems do not have mysterious, hidden sources in some hypothetical "Id." We do not have to look far or deep to find the source; we keep stumbling, tripping and falling over it all day long, even though *we refuse to identify it as our own childishness.*

8. That all human beings are the product of evolution, and that we share the inheritance of all human potentialities and are each equally based in evolution. Each can evoke his store of potentialities to shape them into his *own creation* and discover his own reality. Each is his own architect. Whatever one human being has done can be done by others. Creation is a built-in attribute of each of us. It waits, however, for the awakening touch of self-reliance to shape its parts and aspects.[1]

In addition to the comprehensive view of human behavior pictured above, he gave us the most specific and particular way of seeing things directly as they unfold before us. He encouraged us to TRUST ONLY MOVEMENT! He revealed that each of us puts the whole meaning we are presently giving to life in whatever we happen to be doing at any current moment. He made us look at the immediate confrontation and blocked escape into alibis, self-pity or recriminations about the situation.

Adler taught us that living is a process which takes place in the *here-and-now* and that any relationship one makes is a process of self-revelation. In other words, an individual reveals himself in everything he does. From Adler we learned that behavior is not some dead thing which is a mere result of inner or outside compulsions from the self, the environment, or the past. He urged us to watch not only the relationships a person makes but to avoid getting trapped into some imputed or hypothetical "why" of things. He stressed that the unfolding behavior in a situation reveals its own explicit dynamics.

Adler made clear that the way an individual can alter the mistakes of his own personality—his own behavior—is to see with the impartial, uncritical eye of a camera. He must see himself to discover his own "law of movement" when coping with confronting situations. He must view this approach non-judgmentally without evasion or aversion so that he does not shift blame on anyone or anything outside himself. He must be able to see that no one is destroyed from "causes" outside himself. And, when he has learned to see himself in his law of movement, he can see others through their eyes and help them to a similar self-discovery. Thus no one needs to live indefinitely blinded by his own mistaken certainties, illusions or wishful thinking.

If we confine ourselves to watching the behavior of individuals in coping with situations, we can understand the challenging and exciting phenomenon we call behavior. Contrary to common belief, our behavior does not have a cause which is reaching out of our past, driving us to do what we do. Behavior is a response to a challenge arising in the here-and-now. It is something we create to achieve security in the confronting present. We alone select our behavior and are responsible for what we are doing at any moment. Each chooses whatever he estimates will resolve the encounter or get him out of it. Or, as in neurosis, bring someone to his side to solve the problem for him.

Much of our behavior is made up of old habits which are only conditioning-with-a-purpose. Habit never rests and it persists until we choose to alter it to serve another purpose. Habits are forms of behavior we have invented and tested repeatedly in the past. We like our habits, *both those we label good and especially those we label bad.* The habits we retain for current use are like old friends on whom we lean for our comfort and security—as the alcoholic lovingly hugs his bottle! We hide our admiration of our vices—a fact we quickly discover when someone brings pressure on us to get rid of them; we defend them against all opposition.

Habits operate much like a satellite in orbit. As long as a person finds them useful to his way of life, he keeps them in orbit. (Certainly, he is not the helpless victim of habits, although it might be flattering to believe this.) Once we launch habits in orbit, they remain of their own momentum until we alter the purpose they serve for us or use them to serve a different goal. Habits do not rule an individual at any time in any way as he would like to pretend they do. They are his obedient servants all the way.

It is not necessary to know or investigate the past of an individual to change his behavior. It makes no difference how he got the way he is. All that it is important to know is that he is holding on to his present behavior because it suits his purpose. He may wish to escape the side effects of some of his old habits but these penalties are unavoidable unless he gives up the habit itself that is at the root of his pain. The pain lies in resisting pain. A problem is only a situation for which a person has not trained himself and he *resists the situation* instead of facing it. Thus, he remains in pain.

3

Pain, then, is not the result of something in the past. It lies in our present refusal to meet a confronting situation on its own demands. We are trying to face it with old habits, traditions, attitudes and prejudices; in short, with wishful thinking!

Analysis of the past does not recondition behavior or change our goals and is not essential for anyone who wants to get rid of his own disturbing behavior. An individual may like to believe that behavior has causes rising out of the past and that he is a blameless victim so that he can escape personal responsibility for what he is doing now (by blaming it on the past). This explains the popularity of psychoanalysis which allows the individual to continue his old behavior without feeling responsible for it in the present.

Emotional difficulties arise only in those areas of life in which one still leans and depends on people or things outside himself rather than on the innate power of his own mind. The mind is a product of evolution and is millions of years old. It works properly only when it is free of all outside dependence. Under such conditions, it works spontaneously; it is on constant alert and sees directly into situations without any dithering, anxieties or confusion. When dependency exists, the Wishful Mind grasps for something outside itself such as authority figures, traditions, deals, habits and beliefs in which to wrap itself for support. But the mind is not able to function when caught in such a bind as it cannot serve the self and an outside authority *at the same time*. The wish to do both simultaneously becomes a double bind—or "chasing two rabbits at once," thus catching neither. Such an hestitating attitude (a step forward and a step backward) results in a dither so that, actually, one stands still in fear.

One does not achieve freedom of the mind by any form of discipline, effort or mind-developing, mind-expanding exercises or drugs. Nothing can be added to the mind in any way; one can only liberate it from clinging dependencies that thwart its spontaneity. When the last crutch has been eliminated and an individual stands alone, the mind is no longer under any outside pressures of conformity. At that moment it assumes its natural contours.

The solution of emotional problems, as Adler said, is to increase self-reliance in areas where an individual is dependent and thus in pain. When he becomes non-attached, the mind can "let go and walk on." The center of gravity is no longer placed on those around him and on crutches outside himself on which he has leaned. He brings the center of gravity back into the self and stands on his own two feet. Only under such conditions may he function as a wholly adequate and self-reliant being. This is the natural heritage granted to each of us who claims his heritage.

This, then, is Alfred Adler as we experienced him. Others will see him differently. And that is as it ought to be as there are multiple facets to his great genius. He needs no adulation since his work speaks for him to each of us differently in a language of its own.

1. Indentations 1 through 8 are excerpted by permission of The Julian Press from Beecher and Beecher (1).

REFERENCES

1. Beecher, W. & Beecher, Marguerite. *Beyond Success and Failure.* New York, Julian Press, 1966.

MOTIVATION AND THE WILL

Vytautas J. Bieliauskas

One of the most significant differences between continental European psychology and American psychology can be seen in the apparent gap existing between philosophy and psychology in the U.S.A. and the much smaller difficulty in dealing with the same problem overseas. The need to view science and philosophy in terms of dichotomies which is so prevalent here, has hardly been in existence in Europe. This may be the reason why we are experiencing tensions between science and philosophy, and psychology and philosophy here, while there are fewer signs of such a tension in Europe. As a matter of fact many European psychologists readily admit that their theories had deep roots in philosophy. Probably the best example to illustrate this point is Alfred Adler whose theories concerning human behavior are as philosophical as they are psychological. Only Adler could have the courage and the background to speak about the causality in the psychic life without being misunderstood by psychologists and philosophers (1). Adler wrote for his European audience and would not tolerate the difficulty of dichotomies which very frequently exist in the U.S.A.

In an earlier publication this author (6) has attempted to show the futility of dichotomous thinking, which leads to no solutions and to unintended, but factual, departures from proper understanding of reality. While there seems to be no difficulty in accepting the fallacy of dichotomous thinking in science, there seems to be a serious difficulty in trying to avoid it in dealing with borderline questions which include both philosophy and science. Modern psychology is considered as a branch of the behavioral sciences. However, because of its need to deal with human behavior, psychology often cannot and should not avoid theoretical and philosophical questions (12, 30). Therefore psychology, more than any other branch of science, is in a position where it must deal with concepts which are only partially within its own province, and where it is forced to seek a bridging of the gap between science and philosophy. As indicated in my previous publications (5, 6), I consider

6

that this bridging of the gap between science and philosophy can be accomplished, not in dichotomous, but in continuum thinking. The attempt to study the concepts of motivation and the will, as proposed by this paper, is aimed at offering another method of bringing science and philosophy to a better understanding of each other or, in Ruth Benedict's terminology, in establishing a "synergy" between them (3, 22, 26). This will be done through examining their differences and similarities, with the hope that clear views of the differences will provide for better understanding.

The problem we want to consider as an example of borderline questions between psychology and philosophy is the "why" of human behavior. Why do human beings act the way they do? We propose to look for an answer to this question through a study of two concepts very frequently used nowadays: motivation and the will.

Scientific Determinism vs. Philosophical Indeterminism

In his desire to study the causality of events, a scientist finds himself most comfortable in accepting the principle of determinism. In studying human behavior, the scientist, as a rule would prefer to assume that human actions are caused, determined by various factors over which man has no control. These factors are usually called motives, and it is thought that motives force us to act. Therefore to study and understand human behavior one would just have to study and understand motives. This deterministic approach, regardless of its philosophical validity, enables the scientific psychologist to approach human behavior by using the scientific model. He thus becomes concerned with prediction of behavior. If human actions are determined by motives, and if one knows all the motives and the effect which they have upon this particular individual, one can predict how he will act. However, if one introduces the concept of free choice on the part of the individual, he is introducing the unknown which tends to contaminate the study of his behavior and puts a "monkey wrench" into the scientific model of thinking. Therefore as Boring (7) points out, scientists as scientists do not like such concepts as freedom. They prefer hard-core determinism. There is no doubt that such an approach has been shared by some philosophers, especially by English empiricists. However, many other philosophers, especially the scholasticists, find the scientific model unacceptable and do not share the enthusiasm of some human behavior scientists who, in accepting hard determinism, insist that they can predict human actions. The scholastic model of thinking considers that man can make a free choice and that he can determine his own actions. This model of thinking puts a pessimistic note on prediction of behavior, but it adds a special quality to the behavior subject, namely, freedom. However, this concept of freedom of choice could not be accepted by scholastic philosophers as a "causeless" behavior. Therefore, in adhering to the traditional Aristotelian causal thinking, the scholasticists introduced the concept of the will which, in fact, can be considered as a power which determines behavior. The only difference is that the will is something which cannot be studied through the use of empirical methods. Or can it?

With this we have approached the core of our problem—an examination of the scientific knowledge concerning the "why" of human behavior. After a presentation of a summary of scientific-psychological facts and theories concerning causes of behavior, we will turn to the philosophy of the will, with an effort to examine its relationship to scientific findings. Then we will turn to the freedom of human behavior, examining the implications of modern psychological findings upon individual responsibility.

Determinants of Behavior

As Cofer and Appley (10, p. 22) point out, the problem of how conduct may be understood has been approached from many points of view. Most of these explanations have motivational implications and they include "cognition, instinct, knowledge, will and free will, unconscious factors, hedonism, and conceptions of human nature and its motives." It would be very interesting to explore all these approaches and evaluate their contributions to an understanding of the determinants of human behavior. However, our scope is limited to an examination of the primary factors which constitute a basic knowledge about human nature and its motives.

1. Definition of Motive and Motivation

There seems to be some difficulty in exactly defining motive. Therefore, I would like to select the road used by many psychologists, providing a description rather than a definition. Motive, in general, is that which causes behavior. There are three main sources which can give origin to motivational causation of behavior: 1) *environment,* something which is outside the organism and which makes it act in a certain way; 2) *internal experiences,* such as drives, needs, desires, emotions, feelings, etc; and 3) the *incentives, goals* or *object values* which may attract or repel the organism. Thus there are extrinsic and intrinsic forces which may work upon the organism and produce activity in it. This fact is quite clearly accepted by most modern psychologists. We have added also a third force which could be explained through a combination of the intrinsic and extrinsic forces, but which has specific characteristics, namely, goals and values.

The concept of motivation, then, would include arousing of an action, and sustaining, and direction of the activity (31). This is a very general description, but as Cofer and Appley correctly remark, "there is no one set of phenomena, or conditions under which behavioral phenomena occur, with which all motivational theorists are concerned" (10, p. 9). Therefore, any definition or description must be so general that it would include the basic concepts used by various theorists. There is also an interesting phenomenon which may have been observed or which may have been overlooked by some. Off and on I have been speaking about the organism, and referring to motives which can produce behavior in the organism.

This was not an accident. It was done intentionally. When psychologists speak about motives and motivation, they speak about behavior of man and animal alike and do not intend to limit their discussions primarily to man. Since motivation is a very complex and somewhat nebulous aspect of behavior, they contend that its study requires at first a basic science approach which has as its starting point the lower organisms. Many laws and principles concerning motivation have been, and are being, established as "basic science" principles on the animal level. I believe that this is a very important observation which we should keep in mind lest we succumb to a common error. Many unsuspecting readers of psychological theories consider that when psychologists speak about motivation they mean primarily *human* motivation and that the concept of motivation includes the concept of the will and the like. This is a fallacy which can be illustrated by the following example. A psychologist teaches a hungry rat to abstain from satisfying hunger and reaching for the food in a spot where it cannot be reached without the rat having to walk over an electrically-charged grid which produces severe pain. Therefore, if he is not starving for food, he will stand back and will not attempt to reach for food. Technically speaking, through reinforcement, the avoidance (of pain) has reached a more prominent valence than the approach (food), and it is now working as a motivating force. In non-technical terms we can say: "There is no danger, but the rat has learned to control himself," or (to make things look even more controversial), we can say that the rat has developed a strong "will power." Thus, after a simple experiment we have reached far-reaching conclusions which are not really included in our experiment. The process of reductionism has been put in reverse. Such a process, as we know, is a fallacy. Therefore, one has to be very careful not to over-extend the conclusion and include the behavior of higher species, when the experiments are conducted on lower species. Of course this does not mean that animal experiments dealing with motivation are not useful for humans. They can be useful, if properly understood and interpreted.

2. *The Organism and its Motives: Needs, Drives and Desires.*

Having clarified the meaning of motivation, we would like to present briefly some theories concerning the internal and external forces modifying and motivating the behavior of the organism. Of course I hate to speak about the human being as an organism—I prefer to use the word person—but since the term person may or may not fit what I want to discuss, I will stick with the concept of the organism. After all, Adler (1, p. 27) was able to discuss the concept of the organism and the organ in the chapter entitled "The Soul," and therefore it seems to be reasonable to assume the opposite approach for the purpose of discussion.

There is a group of instigators of behavior which are inherent in each organism to greater or lesser extent, depending upon the level of its complexity. These are certain needs which are basic for survival of the individual or for the survival of the species, and they must be satisfied in order for the organism to remain alive. A few examples are: need for water, need for food, need for air, need for rest, need for elimination, and the need for procreation. These needs are produced by lack of something in the organism or by certain chemical changes in the body which may endanger the welfare of the organism. The presence of a need produces a drive in the organism which initiates activity leading to or searching for elimination of that need. Since the needs are basically inherent in the organism and therefore must follow the physiological patterns of the organism, the drives, too, depend upon relatively stable and essentially innate patterns of behavior. While the psychologists prefer to use the concept of drive, the physiologists and especially the ethologists consider much of drive behavior to be instinct. Regardless of whether we want to call such behavior drive or instinct, the fact remains that such behavior is determined by the inner forces of the organism and therefore it leaves hardly any room for choice. Since drives and needs primarily depend upon bodily conditions, it would follow that various bodily conditions determine the behavior of the organism.

In addition to the above-mentioned needs such as hunger, thirst, etc., the psychologists tend to explain, on the drive basis, such behavior forms as nesting, sucking, hoarding, homing and migration, and maternal care of the young. Harlow and Zimmerman (17) added to this the need for soft body contact in maternal-filial behavior. Some of this behavior is controlled·by internal changes in the organism and some of it can be directly related to hormonal changes. Cannon (9), in observing the physiological processes of the organism, came to the conclusion that the organism has a natural balance. He called this physiological equilibrium-seeking tendency "homeostasis." Since Cannon, many workers in the field of motivations have been using the homeostasic construct for explanation of various forms of behavior. Probably the best example to illustrate the point is the description of the behavior of the drug addict. At first the organism may react against a drug as an undesirable foreign agent. However, if the drug is supplied consistently, it may become a part of the body's physiological equilibrium, so that if an attempt is then made to withdraw the drug, the organism will respond with extreme craving for the drug which, many times, will express itself as an uncontrollable drive.

In addition to needs and drives, psychologists also speak about desires which, if used in organismic terms, are a somewhat weaker expression of that which is called drive. Desire refers more to a conscious striving for a goal. However, the striving itself involves less intensity than is the case in the drive. In general, desires would include behavior which is needed, not for simple survival of the organism, but for a more comfortable, more pleasant survival. Desire can be attached or super-imposed over a drive. In such a case it would tend to produce more discrimination in the drive, such as eating not merely to satisfy hunger, but to enjoy the pleasure associated with food and digestion.

The concept of desire becomes even more useful in describing the regulatory behavior which is associated with the so-called social needs such as the need for success, recognition, security, etc. (cf. 1, 12). While these needs and goals involve more and more conscious goal-directed participation on the part of the individual, it nevertheless includes many stable, determining factors.

3. *The Environment Motives*

While the drives depend to the greatest extent upon inner motivat-ing forces, they are by no means the only factors determining the be-havior of the organism. Even the primary needs and drives many times can be enhanced by the presence of an adequate outside stimulus when they would otherwise be dormant. Therefore, there is no difficulty in demonstrating the old Stimulus-Response (S-R) element involved in most motivational theories. Royce (25) attempted to diminish the im-pact of the S-R deterministic approach which represents a dominant trend in our experimental psychology. He used the S-O-R formula whereby the stimulus is only partially a determining factor in regard to the outcome. He placed the organism as the intervening variable. How-ever, this was an attempt to rationalize the S-R psychologists out of their dilemma without much success or appreciation. For the S-R psy-chologists nowadays there are many outside forces determining behavior. They assume that almost every stimulus determines the response and therefore they think that our perception already determines our be-havior. Or could it be said that the perceived goal determines behavior? (cf. 12).

In addition to the S-R formula of motivation, there are a few inter-esting observations which require our attention. Some of these observa-tions are very recent, and they are mostly related to space research. One phenomenon which has been discovered by the scientists prepar-ing people for space flight is the fact that the organism has an inherent need to be stimulated. Several studies dealing with stimulus depriva-tion (cf. 19, 24, 28, 29) suggest that the organism needs stimulation and that stimulus deprivation can serve as a motivational force to activity. If no activity is possible, some studies show, hallucinatory experiences will occur. (cf. 18). Self reports of stimulus-deprived subjects indicate that, if they have an opportunity, they will try to stimulate themselves through such activities as pinching, touching, rotating their position, etc.

Another observation worth mentioning is the need for exploration and activity. Harlow, Harlow, and Mayer (15) reported that their mon-keys did not need any other reward for assembling a mechanical puzzle than just the opportunity to do so. Other research reports suggest that the organism tends to respond with greater interest to an environment with a variety of stimuli rather than to a monotonous environment. This seems to provide some support to the theory that there is a need for establishing contact with the environment and that there is a stable pattern requiring the organism to recognize its environment.

A third fact which we need to mention here is the observation by most research workers that motivation and learning have a strong interdependency. Through manipulation of drives, needs, and desires, motivation for the learning of new forms of behavior can be produced. As a matter of fact, most research on learning deals with reward or punishment as reinforcers of behavior. Our example of the "will power" in the rat implies the use of fear of pain as a deterrent which superimposes itself over the need for food. Recent studies add the just-mentioned motivational approaches including stimulus deprivation, varying stimulation, etc. All observations show that learning can increase motivation and that the motivation can be controlled by manipulating the needs (cf. 8).

4. Incentives, Goals, and Values

As we mentioned in the beginning, besides internal motivational forces and external environmental forces, there is a third source of motivation, namely, the combination of both, with special attention given to the organism. This motivational source includes, primarily, conscious behavior. It involves the organism inasmuch as it has to make a choice between the responses. Some authors call this alternating behavior, some use a fancier term like decision-making. Probably the best term for this behavior is that of choice behavior. Dember (11) and his co-workers observed such choice behavior in studying the behavior of rats in a maze. They found that some animals made their choice as to what alternative pathway to take, not just by chance, but in following a stable pattern. Dember did not come up with the answer for the reason of the choice, but nevertheless he raised some interesting questions concerning motivation and its determining factors.

Since the advent of cybernetics, the model of information feedback has been used in studying motivation. It is quite well known that not only the specially constructed machines, but each organism provides a feedback concerning the applicability of its response and thus provides possibility for adjustment and improvement of response. This feedback includes a continuous alertness on the part of the organism and it gives a much greater importance to its role in behavior than other previous explanations, based upon drive and need. Goodwin (13) considers that the feedback theory of action clearly demonstrates that determinism is no longer a useful concept in studying motivation. The organism has its chance to change the response, and therefore it contributes to the response more than just the uncontrollable forces from within or from outside. While this opens new avenues for studying motives in all organisms, this approach is of special interest to those studying human motivational behavior. While we don't want to be oversold on the idea and think that now we have a solution to a better understanding of human behavior, nevertheless we are inclined to think that Goodwin and Immergluck are bringing a refreshing look to the study of motivation in humans. If we would accept the concept of the organism in a broader sense, as Adler (1) did, we could very easily arrive at the concept of "soft" determinism of human behavior proposed by the Adlerians whereby behavior, no matter how much it is controlled from the outside, can be determined at least to some extent by the individual.

Values, Choice and the Will

The brief summary of motivation research in psychology, which hardly does justice to the subject and which should be taken as a point of departure rather than a full answer to the problem, left us with some feeling of lack or deficit, speaking in behavioral terms. We considered the motivation of the organism and did not pay much attention to human beings. As I mentioned before, I do not think of the human being as just an organism. To me, a human being is a person, a bearer of value and dignity (cf. 2). Therefore an organism approach to motivation answers only half of the problem. Let us now take our interest to the "why" of human behavior. The human being is an organism and therefore the principles developed about organismic motivation will fit the human being as well. However, the human being is more than an organism. One could easily agree with Maslow (22) that it could be possible to imagine that all organismic needs of a human being could be fulfilled, including primary and secondary needs. But then, so it would seem, an individual would have to stop living, because there would be no purpose to living. Most people still want to live even after fulfilling all their needs, because they have other motives than those described in terms of the organismic language. The human being has an additional dimension in dealing with self and the environment, namely, an intellect, which organisms per se do not have. Therefore a man is not only stimulated by his environment, not only subject to internal physiological forces, but he also can approach the environment from the abstract point of view or as Maslow (23) says, he can transcend his organismic needs. We can think. *Thinking* is a new dimension which cannot be eliminated when we speak about human motivation. Through thinking we recognize new horizons and learn new facts about the environment (cf. 27). One of the things which we learn through thinking is the realm of *values*. Values are usually abstractions, and without intellectual knowledge we would not be able to know about them. However, having the facility to use thinking, we learn about values and desire them. Thus the knowledge of values may act also as a motivational force in the human being. Knowing about a value would enable me to choose it, but in order to pattern my life according to the values I know, I may have to suppress my motivational forces. And so, as a human being I have an intellect, which not only helps me acquire knowledge, but also provides me with the intellectual control of my drives, needs, and desires. When I use this control, I choose to act or not to act in a certain way or I make the way free to reach the values which I desire. Is this what the scholasticists call "the will"? I believe it is, but let me be a psychologist and call it the intellectual control which also serves as a motivational force in human beings.

Semantics is of some importance. However, the real acid test is not in semantics, but in what we really mean by the words we use. What you *call* the element of personality, which selects, chooses, and acts—will, intellectual control, or something else—is not as imporant as understanding what it *does*. From what we mentioned above, the characteristic of the human being is his ability to recognize values and to pattern his behavior according to these values. The question is, to what extent is this possible, or do we always have a free choice? If we observe concrete individuals we will find that the fact that they are organisms is not an abstraction but a concrete reality. We will find that human behavior is not always directed by free choice. Humans are also affected by influences other than self-determination. There is no doubt that we are greatly influenced by our drives, needs, and desires. And, no doubt, there are many human beings who are not familiar with values and whose choice is consequently limited or even impossible. There are many whose drives are so strong that they are unable to make any other than organismic choices. The hypothesis of the will has never advocated the ideal human nature in which the right choices would be easy and always present. Therefore, while we agree that we can choose values, we have to remember that this may not always be possible.

The "Transcending" Individual

While I believe that thus far we can find an agreement between the philosopher and the psychologist, I would like to turn to my psychology and try to apply some of the principles to the understanding of human behavior. I believe that to understand the reasons for human behavior I cannot use only the organismic approach, nor can I use only the idealistic approach. If I assume that the human being has no self-determination, then I must assume that he should be controlled by others. But when I say that he or they should be controlled, I naturally do not include myself and I believe that nobody would think differently about himself. On the other hand, If I assume that I can always make a free choice, I am dealing with an illusion, and it will not help me to understand man better.

The assumption that man is always a free agent can be very harmful. Take, for example, a moralist who is dealing with an individual, a man, who tends to lie under duress. He tells this individual to shape up and learn how to tell the truth. The individual tries, and he is finally hospitalized with a nervous breakdown. A psychologist or a psychiatrist, dealing with the same individual, works with him and discovers that this individual has tremendous anxiety or fear of being punished and therefore lies to protect himself. The psychologist works with this individual and helps him to gain insight and to become free of undue fear. Once this happens, the individual can make his choice. There are many basic needs which interfere with individual freedom and undermine intellectual control. The understanding of motivational forces may help one to reduce their importance in human life. The human individual is also subject to learning and establishing habits. He learns not only on the intellectual level, but also on the conditioning level. Many times we teach humans on the organismic level and expect to produce good human behavior. For example, if you use a punishment and reward method to train a child to attend church, you will succeed in conditioning a good church-attender. However, whether such an individual will be a good Christian has very little to do with the technique. Human training should emphasize the values on the intellectual level. Values are human goals and we will not be able to train people to reach them by using dog-training methods.

There is so much talk about will power. Even some serious people think that so-called will power can be increased by certain physical exercises, such as push-ups, cold showers, food deprivation, etc. As Lindworsky (21) pointed out, the concept of will power is a useless concept because it really has nothing to do with either the will or with power. It really is a concept which suggests a motivational approach to human training and education. While it may sound ridiculous, the experiment with the rat which was mentioned earlier could be considered as describing the concept of will power. What is necessary is not an organismic will power approach to motivation, but a training towards an intellectual understanding of values. A human being who is subject primarily to organismic motives cannot be considered as free to make choices, as being responsible. It is quite understandable therefore that many times people inflicted with mental or emotional disorders may not be sufficiently free to make the right choice and therefore this may even have moral implications. I consider that the work of a clinical psychologist is to help the individual become free from motivational forces, thus preparing him for making a choice.

Of course, choosing includes the concept of freedom. Only a person who feels free can choose. Sometimes such a person may live under the illusion of personal freedom, but as Immergluck (20) says, "this is a necessary illusion." To reduce the illusion to reality, it is necessary to prepare people, starting from childhood, for freedom and responsibility. And this cannot be done and will not be done through a rigid, punitive, and organismic approach to education. Modern psychology may not have contributed to better knowledge about the will and its functions, but it certainly has made extensive contributions in terms of what actions do not belong to the will. And though it may be negative, this is an important contribution.

The concept of will, especially free will, is really not a psychological, but a philosophical concept. Science will neither prove nor disprove the freedom of the will, as it will neither prove nor disprove freedom itself. However, science, and especially the science of psychology, can provide considerable information concerning values, and how people go about selecting them. While there may be some difficulties in reconciling some philosophical points of view, it seems to me that there is no difficulty in dealing with facts which are the same to the psychologist, philosopher, and theologian. Psychology has made considerable advancements towards a better understanding of motivation. Consequently, I believe that it is all but impossible for anyone dealing with or judging human conduct to be effective, unless he includes the basic principles of the psychology of motivation in his background.

Summary and Conclusions

Motivation and the will are two different concepts, and while they are not contradictory, they do differ in their content and in the consideration of the level of reality. We described several motivational theories of modern psychology and pointed out that these theories deal primarily with the organismic aspects of behavior. The alternation and decision behavior theories led us to discussions of choice and its specific implications in humans. We gave special attention to the feedback construct in the description of motivation. The interaction between the will and motivation was considered, and the various differences and interferences were pointed out. While hard-core determinism was rejected, I feel that a soft determinism or moderate indeterminism is an inevitable fact for those dealing with human behavior. Freedom is related to individual responsibility, and there is a real need for changing educational methods to encourage human rather than organismic motivation. While there is a tendency among people to doubt the freedom of human behavior, one thing is certain. I do not doubt that I am free. Freedom should not be considered as a negative concept, but rather as a reality which can be fused successfully with social responsibilities. There is the possibility of seeing a "high synergy" between the individual freedom and his need to do something for others. There is also the possibility of seeing a positive fusing between organismic motivational forces and intellectual control under the overall concept of "the good of the individual." It is not necessary to assume that drives, needs and desires must always be in contradiction to values and value choices. It is quite possible that they could be fused into a positive continuum. Of course, how this can be done is a question which neither psychology nor philosophy can answer at the present. However, research in motivation to date is providing the plan from which future researchers will try to answer the question concerning the "why" of human motivation. Chances are that they will have to discover some new concepts to explain their findings. It is also quite possible that at that time the concept of the will will be much more palatable to the taste of a hard-core scientist. And if we attempt to speak in Adlerian terms, we may expect that the concept of the will is the only way to understand *responsibility* in human behavior.

REFERENCES

1. Adler, A., *Understanding Human Nature*. Greenwich, Conn., Premier Books, 1954.
2. Adler, A., *What Life Should Mean to You*. New York, Capricorn Books, 1958.
3. Benedict, Ruth, *Patterns of Culture*. Boston, Houghton Mifflin, 1934.
4. Bieliauskas, V. J., "Choice Behavior and Freedom." *Bull. Albertus Magnus Guild,* 196, 14, No. 1, pp. 1-7.
5. Bieliauskas, V. J., "Science, Philosophy and Psychology," in F. L. Ruch, ed., *Psychology and Life*. Chicago, Scott, Foresman, 1964, pp. 575-579.
6. Bieliauskas, V. J., ed. "Science and Philosophy," in R. W. Russell, gen. ed., *Frontiers in Psychology*. Chicago, Scott, Foresman, 1964, pp. 1-24.
7. Boring, E. G., "When is Human Behavior Predetermined?" *The Scientific Monthly,* 87(1957), pp. 189-196.
8. Brownfield, C. A., *Isolation: Clinical and Experimental Approaches*. New York, Random House, 1965.
9. Cannon, W. B., *The Wisdom of the Body*. New York, Norton, 1939.
10. Cofer, C. N. and Appley, M. H., *Motivation: Theory and Research*. New York, John Wiley, 1964.
11. Dember, W. N., "The New Look in Motivation." *Amer. Scientist,* 53(4), (1965), pp. 409-427.
12. Dreikurs, R., *Fundamentals of Adlerian Psychology*. Chicago, Alfred Adler Inst., 1950.
13. Goodwin, L. "Using the Feedback Theory of Action to Reshape the Freedom-Determinism Controversy." *Amer. Psychologist,* 20(1954), pp. 234-235.
14. Harlow, H. F., "Learning and Satiation of Response in Intrinsically Motivated Complex Puzzle Performance by Monkeys," *J. Compar. Physiol. Psychol.,* 43(1960), pp. 289-294.
15. Harlow, H. F., Harlow, Margaret K., and Meyer, D. R., "Learning Motivated by a Manipulation Drive." *J. of Exper. Psychol.* 40(1950), pp. 228-234.

16. Harlow, H. F. and McClearn, G. E., "Object Discrimination Learned by Monkeys on the Basis of Manipulation Motives." *J. Compar. Physiol. Psychol.*, 47(1954), pp. 73-76.

17. Harlow, H. P. and Zimmerman, R. R., "Affectional Responses in the Infant Monkey." *Science*, 130(1965), pp. 421-432.

18. Heron, W., Deane, B. K. and Scott, T. H., "Visual Disturbances after Prolonged Perceptual Isolation." *Canad. J. Psychol.*, 10(1965), pp. 12-16.

19. Holland, J. G., "Human Vigilance." *Science*, 128(1958), pp. 61-67.

20. Immergluck, L., "Determinism-Freedom in Contemporary Psychology: An Ancient Problem Revisited." *Amer. Psychologist*, 19(1964), pp. 270-281.

21. Lindworsky, J., *The Training of the Will*. Milwaukee, Wis., Bruce, 1929.

22. Maslow, A. H., "Synergy in the Society and the Individual." *J. Indiv. Psychol.*, 20(1964), pp. 153-164.

23. Maslow, A. H., *Toward a Psychology of Being*. Princeton, N. J., Van Nostrand, 1962.

24. Rohrer, J. H., "Human Adjustment to Antarctic Isolation." *Nav. Res. Rev. O N R*, June, 1959, pp. 1-5.

25. Royce, J. E., *Man and His Nature*. New York, McGraw-Hill, 1961.

26. Seif, L., "Zur Synergie der Gegensatze." Int. Z. Indiv. Psychol., 9(1931), pp. 269-274.

27. Simon, Y., *Prevoir et Savoir*. Montreal, Editions de L'Arbre, 1944.

28. Solomon, P., Kubzansky, P. E., Laiderman, P. H., Mendelson, J. H., Trumbull, R., and Wexler, D., eds. *Sensory Deprivation: A Symposium at Harvard Medical School*. Cambridge, Harvard University Press, 1961.

29. Solomon, P., Leiderman, P. H., Mendelson, J. and Wexler, D., "Perceptual and Sensory Deprivation—a Review." *Amer. J. of Psychiat.* 114(1957), pp. 357-363.

30. Wolfe, B., *Nervous Breakdown*. London, Routledge & Kegan Paul, 1934.

31. Young, P. T., *Motivation and Emotion*. New York, Wiley, 1961.

THE PRIVATE LOGIC

Rudolf Dreikurs

The term, "private logic," is familiar to all Adlerians. It is widely used in the literature, but as with many other concepts they accept, Adlerians differ in their understanding and interpretation of private logic. Such differences in the definition of concepts are often subtle. Terms like "life style," "goals," and "private logic" are used as if there were consensus about their meaning. The Ansbachers (5, 6, 7), in their endeavor to present Adler's ideas, have brought to light many of the different meanings which Adler himself gave to his concepts. No wonder that many of his followers express their own preferences in the use of many of his basic concepts.

Let us take the term, "private logic." Since Adler used the term in different ways, each of us must choose which meaning he will give to this concept. My first formulation of the meaning of this concept appeared in 1933 (10). Whatever modifications I have since made refer more to the content than to the meaning of the term.

What is Private Logic?

At times Adler spoke of "private logic" as being interchangeable with "private sense," "private intelligence," "private world," "private intelligence map," "personal intelligence," and "isolated intelligence." All are opposed to what Adler called "common sense" or reason. In his conception he followed the concepts developed by Kant. Ansbacher (5) shows the identity of Adler's concepts with that of Kant, who considered the unique private sense of reasoning which he called the *sensus privatus* as underlying all mental disorders. The latter are characterized by a loss of common sense, called *sensus communis*. The distinction between the terms becomes even clearer when one considers the original German terms. Common sense for Kant is *Gemeinsinn,* or reason, while *sensus privatus* is *Eigensinn*. *Eigensinn* means stubbornness, unreasonableness. A person with whom one cannot reason, who is impervious to reasoning, is called *eigensinnig*. He is either sick, maladjusted, or at least,

19

unapproachable.

Similarly, Adler first considered the private logic of a person as an indication of abnormality and maladjustment. The neurotic knows the demands of life and of social living; however, he does not use his common sense, but acts according to his own private logic. The normal, socially-adjusted person acts in line with logic and reason, while the neurotic uses a private frame of reference (6). The neurotic does not see life in the light of objectivity and common sense but according to his private logic. He solves his problems in a self-centered, private sense, rather than in a task-centered, common sense, fashion (6).

Adler emphasized time and again this crucial difference between private logic and common sense. He contended that the private map is developed in childhood and that it remains the fictive world of the neurotic (7). Common sense is the highest development of reason. It is only possible when the individual has a high degree of social interest (4) which prevents him from deceiving himself (7). The private intelligence is a "mistaken reason" (7).

Adler's identification of private logic with anti-social intentions can be seen in the following quotation:

> We must distinguish between "private intelligence" and "common sense," and must understand reason as being connected with common sense—sense that can be shared. According to private intelligence, an individual may attempt, through a personal, private view of the world, to assert himself and enhance his own sense of superiority by injuring that of someone else. Private intelligence is at work whenever a person tries, unfairly, to turn to his own advantage the social contribution of another person. But . . . the injury inflicted is not deliberately intentional (7, p. 253).

Bottome (8) used the term, private sense, in a much broader way, including in it all of Adler's schema of apperception, the normal as well as the abnormal. One year earlier, in 1933, I had arrived at the same conclusion. According to the Ansbachers (6), Adler moved in the same direction. During the period between 1920-30 he developed a criterion of normality with which he could rewrite his motivational theory in terms of the normal. The normal individual has an optimum amount of social interest. Even when he has a goal of superiority, it still includes the welfare of others. His goal of superiority is less accentuated, less dogmatized. The motivation of the neurotic stems from his greater inferiority feelings.

Thus Adler revised his opinion about the neurotic who now appears as the average contemporary man caught in the vise of a competitive society. In his *The Neurotic Constitution* (2), Adler does not describe the neurotic but modern man. Today we are inclined to consider neurosis as an acute faulty response to life's demands and not characteristic for a person as such. As a matter of fact, it seems that everyone can, under certain circumstances, develop a neurosis. In recent years, Ellis (14) continued the original concept of Adler as if biased apperception were characteristic for the "irrational" concepts and convictions of a sick person. Adlerian psychology holds that *everyone* grows up with a distorted picture of life.

Biased Apperception and Fictive Goals

To what extent are distortions of reality a sign of personal maladjustment? Are they perhaps intrinsic in human existence? Today we can accept such a possibility, while at the time of Kant, it was intolerable if a person acted according to his own private logic. He *had* to behave as he was told to; that was proper and reasonable. Authorities decided what was right and wrong. Adler, in his rather derogatory attitude toward the socially maladjusted individual, referred to him as "neurotic," one who operates only on the basis of his own self-interest. Despite his realization that man lives, as we say today, within his phenomenological field, in accordance with his subjective perception of reality, he still favored objectivity over subjectivity. Only later did Adler consider social interest as the basis of normality, regardless of the person's perception of reality. True enough, the neurotic's concept is a negative distortion, assuming dangers and defeats which exist only in his subjective world, but the well-adjusted and "normal" person may equally misinterpret reality but not in a hostile and defensive way. With the disappearance of an autocratic society the concept of absolute truth disappeared, and the question is not whether one can see what life really is, but in which direction one is lead by one's distorted apperception. Biased apperception became a fundamental Adlerian concept— we can perceive reality only in line with our intentions.

The neurotic is not alone in trying to make his life conform to fiction. The healthy person also needs fictions for his orientation in the world to guide him. These fictions assume very definite shape and find expression in one's opinions, beliefs and ideals (12). They are efficient ways of solving difficult problems. Generalizations, abstractions, concepts and ideas are all necessary fictions.

In his formative years, the child develops his own ideas about the way in which he can find a place within his family. While he possesses keen observation, his ability to interpret observable events correctly is limited. The conclusions which he draws from his observations are the basis of his life style. He develops his character traits in line with the goal which he has set for himself as a means toward attaining personal significance. Adler called this final goal of a person as fictitious; it is usually a fictional goal of superiority erected in childhood (6). "All feelings of uncertainty and inferiority give rise to a need for an objective to guide, reassure, and make life bearable" (12, p. 47). Even normal children want to be tall and strong and take command "like father," and this final goal influences their behavior.

21

> If we wish to preserve mistaken ideas about life and ourselves which we formed as children we have to regard everything we see and all our experiences from the biased point of view *(Tendenziöse Entstellung)*. The private logic which each person evolves appears to justify his mistaken behavior and prevents him from seeing that most of the difficulty and disappointments in life are the logical consequences of mistakes in his life plan. We "make" our experiences according to our "biased apperception" and can learn by experience only if no personal bias is involved (12, p. 48).

In my opinion such a biased apperception is an intrinsic human feature. Subjectivity and objectivity are a continuum, are complimentary modes of functioning. Together they permit apperception and movement on the social plane (13, p. 121).

We come now to the crucial question—can the fictitious goal of the life style ever be founded on an accurate perception of life? In my mind, it cannot, even under optimal conditions. The life style with its fictitious goal is always based upon a misinterpretation of life. Why?

There is first the fact that the life style always represents a generalization. It expresses a person's convictions under which conditions he can have a place. This "striving for significance, for worthwhileness," is in itself based upon a mistake, upon the assumption that an individual would be worthless and insignificant unless . . . In the second phase of Adler's writing, this striving for power and superiority was regarded as indispensable and "normal," since he assumed that inferiority feelings are the prime motivating factors in life, leading to the "will to power." Only in the last phase of his writings did Adler recognize the striving for power and superiority as a neurotic motivation in contrast to social interest, the realization of having a place for oneself, the desire to belong (4). When one feels belonging as he is, he acts on the basis of his social interest, without the need for personal superiority. "People can develop their capacity for cooperation only if they feel that in spite of all external dissimilarities they are not fundamentally different from other people—if they feel belonging" (12, p. 5).

This feeling of belonging is possible for everyone, regardless of his style of life. However, certain life styles are more prone to lead to maladjustment than others; some are broader, some more narrow. But even under the most mistaken assumptions, neurotic or other abnormal conditions can be avoided if the individual is fortunate enough not to encounter situations which he cannot meet with his particular life style.

A young girl may grow up with the conviction that she is small, cannot take care of herself and, therefore, always needs the protection and service of a strong person, particularly of a man. As long as she is the favorite of father, has a brother who looks after her, or a husband—or eventually a son, she can function adequately, even with a very mistaken concept of herself. Her dilemma would only occur if and when she would be obliged to take care of herself. Conversely, even the most useful and constructive self-concept can sometimes lead to maladjustment. A girl who grows up with the conviction that she can have a place only if she can please, will—in most instances—be able to get along well. However, if she runs into a situation where people are not pleased with her, she may feel completely lost and worthless, with all its consequences. Or, a man grows up with the assumption that he can always find his place through useful contributions, a goal which obviously is far removed from Adler's concept of a neurotic character. And yet, he may break down when he cannot contribute, either because of sickness, unemployment or because of other circumstances over which he has no control. There is no connection—as far as I can see—between psychopathology and life style, contrary to what many Adlerians seem to believe.

In one study judges were presented with life style information of thirty people, ten of whom were supposedly healthy and normal, ten neurotic and ten psychotic. None of the judges was able to identify the person's adjustment or maladjustment on the basis of life style (15). This means that everyone, regardless of his personality structure and life style, has the ability to function in a normal, healthy and useful way, to become neurotic in certain crisis situations, or even to have a psychotic breakdown when he completely severs his connection with the rest of mankind. One can only say that the more narrow the life style is, the more vulnerable is the person, the greater the probability of a breakdown.

The crisis situation arises whenever a specific life style prevents a person from meeting the demands of the situation. Our competitive social structure facilitates a breakdown due to increased inferiority feelings and limited individual feelings of belonging. At present, the guiding lines which a child sets for himself are usually in line with a desire for superiority and, therefore, entail the constant threat of failure and defeat.

The Significance of Goals

It seems to be intrinsic in human nature that we cannot be aware of our goals. Our goals are always hidden and unconscious. "The individual is largely unaware of his goals . . . it is a hidden or unconscious goal, a goal which the individual does not understand. It is the true nature of the individual's hidden goal which constitutes the essential content of the unconscious" (6, p. 89).

According to Vaihinger, thought processes, including the fictional activity, are fundamentally "carried out in the darkness of the unconscious" (17). This is one of the most important foundations of the nature of "private logic," as I understand it.

Why do most psychological processes remain below the threshold of the consciousness? It seems that the organization of our mental functions is such, that they have to escape full conscious awareness, mainly on the basis of an economic principle. We know clearly and consciously only what we need or what we want to know. Most of our mental activities are so organized that they function best without conscious interference. We strive for our goals best when we do not interfere through introspection. One cannot be actor and observer at the same time. This is one of the reasons why a great deal of the present so-called "sensitivity training" is ill-advised and often dangerous because it is devoted to helping people become aware of their emotions. What people need to know, if they wish to improve their functioning, is their intentions and goals. We are concerned with their actions and not with their feelings. To help people change their emotions is a difficult task, particularly if nobody helps them to understand the purpose. In contrast, it is often amazingly easy to make people aware of their intentions and ideas, of their private logic and hidden reasons. By themselves, people cannot know their own bias because full awareness would not permit their continuation.

There are different kinds of goals which can be distinguished. The most important are the long-range goals of the life style. The life style is the unifying principle upon which a person acts in life; it permits an understanding of the whole person in his movement through life. His fictive goals and guiding lines by which he tries to find his place remain unchanged throughout his life, if they are not disclosed to him. Making a person aware of his goals gives him an opportunity to reconsider them and to seek alternatives which are better suited to solve his problems.

We owe Adler a tremendous debt for having given us a rather simple technique for understanding the life style easily, quickly and reliably. Two sets of investigations permit the recognition of the wholeness and uniqueness of each person. The first is the exploration of the family constellation, of his transactions with brothers, sisters and parents during the formative years of early childhood. In these transactions no child is a victim of others, since each actively participates in establishing his own role which he plays in his family and which then becomes the basis for his style of life. The sociogram of the early family permits a clear picture of the movement of each child within the family. Even parents do not exert, as is generally assumed, the decisive influence on the child's personality development. They are usually more influenced by each child than they themselves influence him. The parents do not cause the child's development; they merely make it possible through their reinforcement of the role which each child chooses for himself. By their reaction, they make the "good one" better and the "bad one" worse. Each child is characterized by his personality traits which he has developed in coordination with those of his brothers and sisters. The person who affects any child's personality development the most is the brother or sister who is most different in character, abilities, traits and interests. Whatever the children of a given family have in common re-

flects the atmosphere and values of the family; the individual differences are the result of the competition within the family. Each of two
competitors will succeed where the other fails, or become deficient
where the other develops special skills. This intense competition in our
competitive families is most pronounced between the first two siblings.
In a family without competition all children are more or less alike in
their strengths and weaknesses, in line with the pattern of the family.

While one can understand the role of each child within the family
merely by observing the character differences between them, the most
reliable information about each one's outlook on life, developed in the
transaction within the family, are the early recollections. Pointing to
the significance and importance of the early recollections is probably
Adler's greatest single contribution to psychology (1). If one knows
what a person remembers from the multitude of experiences in his early
childhood, then one knows how he looks at life, his concepts about himself and life and the goals which he has set for himself. The early recollections are a reliable projective test (16). It requires some skill to elicit
the proper information and to evaluate each detail remembered. Knowing the incidents which he remembers, one knows the private logic according to which he functions in life.

There are some who assume that the fictive goals of the life style are
the only goals on which a person operates, the only goals which are
worth recognizing, and the only ones to be changed when a person is
disturbed in his functioning. Adler himself gave some indication that
there are partial or sub-goals. He states, for instance, "While all psychological movements derive their direction from a pre-determined
goal, all the preliminary separate goals, after a short existence in the
psychological development of the child, come under the dominance of
the fictitional, final goal" (6, p. 94). It is self-evident that all separate
goals are "under the dominance" of the life goals. The term "preliminary" would indicate that Adler considered partial goals only before the
life style is firmly established. In our experience, partial or sub-goals
exist throughout a person's life, indicating his response and his interpretation of the situation in which he finds himself.

Adler speaks about the special scheme or what he calls "psychological
complex" which has to be understood by a person's relations to the
tasks presented by the environment. "They are derivatives of the directive power of the final goal—simplifications, schematizations. Schematizations may exist in thousands of variations. The perspective grown
from such schematization is the basis of what one calls a complex. The
complex characterizes a number of movements which, in a meaningful
manner, strive in the same direction. It is not understood by its bearer,
yet it is used by him. One finds this in everybody. There is no person
whose attitude cannot be resolved into complexes. This is true to some
extent within the approximately normal range, to a larger extent with-

in the abnormal. Therefore, it is an interesting and valuable application to study people with regard to their complexes. This offers the psychologist and psychiatrist a suitable, practical, valuable prospect because he can gain far-reaching calculations from these complexes" (7, p. 72).

Adler enumerates a great variety of such complexes. It is not always clear whether they refer to the basic life pattern of an individual, or to his reaction to an immediate situation. He once described one of these complexes found in a child which clearly indicates a power conflict between the child and his mother. Impressing the mother with his power is one of the immediate goals which I observed and defined in young children, characterizing their way of dealing with adults (9).

The four goals of a disturbing child which I have described (9) can all be found in Adler's writing. I merely systematized them, making the child's behavior understandable. I often encounter opposition to my having "pigeonholed" children's behavior and tried to force them into one or the other of these four goals. Actually I did not put them there; I found them there—and in Adler's writings. These four goals are examples of the many ways a child can choose to make himself significant and have a place. The four goals—attention, power, revenge, and withdrawal—are all mistaken ideas of the child who has become discouraged and does not believe in his ability to find his place through useful contribution. The same goals can be found also in adolescents and in adults, but with them, they are not exclusive as they are with the young child.

The opposition to the recognition of the four goals as motivational factors comes from many quarters. There are those who regard them as insignificant and superficial, because they look for "deeper causes" of maladjustment, not recognizing that behavior indicates the way a person seeks significance. We also encounter the objections of some Adlerians who recognize only the goals of the life style, but not the sub-goals. While the latter have to be understood within the framework of the life style, the recognition of immediate goals has far-reaching effects on counseling and therapy.

If one ignores or fails to recognize a person's immediate goals and directs all corrective efforts only toward a change in the life style, then one not only fails to be aware of the person's movement at the moment but also ignores the possibility of considerable improvement without changing the patient's life style. Freedom of movement exists within the given life style. The four goals of disturbing behavior are only one example. Parents or teachers who are not aware of the child's immediate goals will reinforce his mistaken assumptions instead of correcting them. In turn, every mother can learn to become a more effective mother without any need to change her whole personality structure. She can find better alternative reactions to the child's behavior which then enables her to influence him. The same holds true in many other forms of counseling, in marital counseling, vocational counseling, and educational counseling.

Psychotherapy, directed toward change in the long-range goals of the life style, is only indicated when the whole pattern of a person needs to be changed. Even then, it is often a mistake to start with establishing a person's life style before his immediate goals are recognized. For example, a student therapist who was treating a woman patient with psychotherapy for her various physical symptoms and complaints, began by trying to ascertain her life style. He was not aware of the fact that she was trying to prevent her husband from being sent to Vietnam by her "illness." What chance can psychotherapy have under these circumstances? In any case, the movement of the patient in the present field of action has to be ascertained and understood first. It indicates the patient's immediate goal which Adler called "a complex." In any given situation, it is up to the individual to decide how he wants to react to the problems he faces. His reactions usually show a certain pattern, which is why Adler calls them complexes.

We have described the four goals of disturbing behavior in young children. There are many ways a young child can and will find his place through constructive means as long as he is not discouraged. He may use charm, cuteness, smartness, affection and considerateness or anything else that brings him the desired results. The question is whether such behavior patterns express the fundamental outlook of the child, his style of life, or his interpretation of and reaction to his immediate situation.

While we accept as very probable that the life style of a person is well established in his formative years between the ages of four and six, at this age we are more prominently confronted with his immediate goals, or with the benefits which he derives from being good. For this reason, we concern ourselves usually with the life style of a child only after the age of ten, when early recollections permit a reliable diagnosis. By and large, we can see that the goals of the life style characterize the unique personality in all its distinctions from others, while the immediate goals are usually typical for a great variety of children and of their behavior patterns.

Reactions to Disclosures

We have discussed before that all goals, be they long-range goals of the life style or the short-range goals of the immediate situation, do not reach the level of consciousness and awareness. Nobody knows why he acts in a certain way unless his goals are brought to his attention. The reaction to this disclosure is different when the confrontation concerns the goals of the life style or goals of the immediate situation. But before we can go further in exploring these characteristic differences, we have

27

to recognize yet another aspect of the private logic. This aspect of the private logic is not connected with any specific goal, but with the rationale which one uses to justify one's behavior. This rationalization can be considered as "the hidden reason" for a person's particular behavior or statement.

When a person says or does something which is unusual, he is not aware why he did or said it. This fact is so constant that one must consider it as axiomatic. So far, we have not found any case where the person, asked for his reasons, did not either say that he did not know, or gave some plausible rationalization which proved to be incorrect. Then one must guess what was in his mind at the time. Before Adler, guessing, as a method of investigation, was not considered permissible. When Adler trained his students in the art of guessing, he was fifty years ahead of his time. Today, guessing has become quite acceptable (11), since the use of stochastic processes became a legitimate form of "scientific" investigation. An understanding of the "hidden reason" is impossible without guessing. One must discover the exact words that the patient had in his mind at the time.

The reaction to this kind of disclosure is quite different from that obtained from a confrontation with the goals of the life style and that of the immediate goals. Each of the three forms of providing "insight" evokes a different and characteristic response. Let us take some examples of each group. First some summaries of life styles.

1. The martyr—"Life is ugly and dangerous. I have to be good, but even then my reward will be evil, particularly from men who are not trustworthy. I look down on those who abuse me." (Moral superiority).

2. The baby—"Life is dangerous, and I am weak and cannot take care of myself. I need the protection of others."

3. The angel—"I have to be good, otherwise horrible things will happen to me."

4. The hero—"I am strong and have to be a hero among men. Nobody can stop me, but intellectually I cannot depend on myself."

5. The passive tyrant—"I am small. People take advantage of me but I can outsmart them. I have my way with them, and punish them if they do not do what I want. One does not have to be considerate of others, especially of women whom I can use for excitement or pleasure."

There is an unending variation of life styles, although certain patterns recur with only subtle differences. The typical reaction to the disclosure of the life style is one of concern. Certain interpretations are easily and readily accepted; others take time to "sink in." The strongest resistance is found in people who must be good or right, and, therefore, cannot accept that they are neither. It is usually easy to make patients aware of their goals; they can recognize them when they are presented to them, and often feel satisfied, even from painful explanations, since they suddenly begin to understand themselves and their actions, and particularly their predicaments. It is more difficult to convince them that their self-evaluation is mistaken and that they do not have to continue in the same way but can change their self-concept and goals.

The situation is quite different in a disclosure of immediate goals. We have described the so-called "recognition reflex" obtained from children when their goal is correctly explained. They do not respond to a wrong guess, and sometimes have to think it over for a few seconds before they begin to "see" their intentions. The same peculiar "knowing" smile can also be obtained when the immediate goal is revealed to adolescents and to adults, but perhaps not as readily as in children. In adults, the "poker face" reaction or outright denial is more frequent, although a variation in the description of what they are doing to others may eventually, too, lead to a typical facial expression of insight. What are some of the immediate goals in adolescents? First there is a whole series of goals serving the enhancement of status, the achievement of "importance." There is a striving for pleasure as the only worthwhile enterprise in life, as an expression of "independence." In adults many forms of disturbing behavior and neurotic symptoms are directed toward immediate goals; making the patient aware of them often leads to the display of the recognition reflex.

The situation is completely different with hidden reasons. The patient's reaction to guessing what went on in his mind when he did or said something "peculiar" is quite startling and surprising. We have found that his response is absolutely reliable, regardless of the relationship to the therapist or his personality. When the subject rejects a guess about hidden reasons, one can be absolutely sure that the guess was incorrect. When one comes close to what the patient thought, he will respond with a "maybe." But his reaction is most dramatic when one makes the correct guess, using the exact words which had been in his mind. He will, almost compulsively, exclaim, "Yes, you are right." The same response can be obtained from normal healthy individuals as well as from neurotic or otherwise disturbed people, including juvenile delinquents and psychotics. What is most amazing is the change in the whole bearing and attitude of difficult patients who suddenly feel "understood." In this sense, this procedure has special significance for the initial stage of counseling and psychotherapy, since it establishes—more than anything else—deep trust and confidence.

The technique we use is rather simple. Its outstanding feature is the fact that one can make any guess about hidden reasons without risking a detrimental effect. If one makes a wrong guess, then all that happens is that one does not get any confirmation. Then one can keep on guessing until the proper response is achieved. Sometimes one fails to make the right guess and no harm is done, either. One merely proceeds, waiting for another occasion when a specific behavior of the client provides another opportunity to guess his "hidden reason." This technique lends itself to teaching diagnostic sensitivity, particularly if such instruction takes place in a group setting. It is quite impressive when every student has to make a guess to see the various reactions of the client, either rejecting the guess, considering its approximation or fully accepting it. It opens a new avenue for becoming sensitive to what goes on in a client. Here are a few examples:

A fourteen year old black girl was in violent rebellion at home and in school. While she constantly misbehaved, she always felt abused. She could only talk about what wrongs other people did to her. We asked her whether she wanted help, and she vehemently replied, "No." Then we had to ask why she shouted "No."

Here is the point where many trained students will run into difficulties. Until now they have been taught not to look for logical explanations of behavior, but for psychological understanding of goals. And here we are not concerning ourselves with any goals of the patient but only with his "logic," although it is his private logic. There are many possible psychological interpretations of the girl's reaction, and many are probably even correct. Perhaps she was pessimistic and did not think anybody could help her. Perhaps she wanted to continue her rebellion and her desire to punish others, to be defiant in order to show her independence. All these are psychological explanations, worth investigating and revealing to her. But one can be sure that none of these thoughts were on her mind when she rejected help. She, herself, could not say why she said it. Then each student in the class tried to figure out what was on her mind. After many futile suggestions, one guessed it. She was thinking, "I don't need help, the others do." Not only did she agree to that, but immediately her facial expression changed, and she became accessible and receptive.

Another case seemed to be similar. It was also a fourteen year old black girl who sat quietly and seemingly withdrawn while her case was discussed with her parents and the social worker. When she was asked something, she refused to answer. We aried to find out why she did not answer. Again one can explain her behavior psychologically, e.g., that she was in a power conflict, in rebellion. I thought it would be quite easy to guess what went on in her mind when she refused to answer. In many similar cases it would be, "Leave me alone, I don't want to have anything to do with you." I was almost sure that I gussed right when I told her this. Her whole behavior, her posture, her blank facial expression would support such a guess. But it was wrong. She simply said, "No." Then one of the students made the correct guess. "I can't say anything. I am dumb." This was it.

A female patient could not get along with people, provoked abuse, made constant mistakes. Her psychological motivation was to provoke people in order to look down on them. She was an over-ambitious pessimist who did not expect to get anywhere in life, and she was always upset when she did something wrong. This did not explain what went on in her mind when she made a mistake. Many guesses were made in the class. None of the "psychological" explanations got any results; a patient does not think about himself in psychological terms. A more possible guess was perhaps she felt "weak" or, "unable," to do anything right. This would be a rather frequent "hidden reason" for people who cannot live up to their own expectations. But that was not true in her case. The explanation to which she immediately responded was, "I am condemned to do things wrong." In this moment all reserve was gone and she felt understood.

Another example may show how careful one has to be in finding the *exact words* which the patient had in mind. A young man had been very spoiled by an indulgent mother and grandmother, both of whom supported his insistence upon doing whatever he wanted. But one day he brought up a problem which puzzled him. His employer asked him to do something which was rather unpleasant, and he refused to do it. He knew he should have done it, and he could not understand what hindered him. We tried to figure out what was going on in his mind. Perhaps he thought, "I won't do anything unpleasant." This he denied; he often performed tasks which were not pleasant. Then came the correct guess, "I am willing to do anything, but only if I feel like doing it." The first guess was very close, but it was not exactly what he thought.

The ability to guess what is going on in a client's mind is essential if one wants to understand him and give him the feeling that he is understood. But most professionals are not yet trained to this approach, and thereby fail to understand the "reasons" for their clients' behavior and, what is even more tragic, are perplexed by the reactions they get to their own reasoning. To illustrate, a young Negro belonged to a Pentecostal sect in which each member was a Saint of Christ. The social worker tried to explain to him that he was a Christian, which the man emphatically denied. "I am not a Christian; I am a Saint of Christ," he insisted. The social worker couldn't understand that this man did not know what Christians were, and attributed his "ignorance" to his "cultural deprivation." She simply did not understand what he meant. Our guess proved to be correct. He did not consider himself to be like the rest; he was something special, something different, he was not like the other "Christians." Not understanding him, the social worker had tried to deprive him of the only area of significance and superiority which he had ever experienced.

Summary

The private logic, as I see it, comprises all unconscious ideas, concepts, intentions and goals upon which the individual acts. We can distinguish three psychological processes as part of the private logic. They are the long-range goals of the life style, the immediate goals within the given situation, and the hidden reasons which justify a person's actions, deeds and thoughts. The disclosure of each of them evokes different characteristic responses.

REFERENCES

1. Adler, A., "Erste Kindheitserrinerungen" *Int. Z. Indiv. Psychol.*, 11(1933), pp. 81-90.
2. Adler, A., *The Neurotic Constitution.* New York, Dodd, Mead, 1926.
3. Adler, A., "The Significance of Early Recollections." *Int. J. Indiv. Psychol.*, 3(4), (1937), pp. 283-287.
4. Adler, A., *Social Interest* (1930). New York, Capricorn, 1964.
5. Ansbacher, H. L., "Sensus Privatus Versus Sensus Communis." *J. Indiv. Psychol.*, 21(1965), pp. 48-50.
6. Ansbacher, H. L. and Rowena, eds., *The Individual Psychology of Alfred Adler* (1956). New York, Harper Torchbooks, 1964.
7. Ansbacher, H. L. and Rowena, eds., *Superiority and Social Interest.* Evanston, Ill., Northwestern Univ. Press, 1964.
8. Bottome, Phyllis, *Alfred Adler: Apostle of Freedom.* London, Faber & Faber, 1939.
9. Dreikurs, R., *The Challenge of Parenthood.* New York, Duell, Sloan & Pearce, 1948.
10. Dreikurs, R., *Einfuhrung in die Individualpsychologie.* Leipzig, S. Hirzel, 1933.
11. Dreikurs, R., "Guiding, Teaching and Demonstrating: An Adlerian Autobiography." *J. Indiv. Psychol.*, 23(1967), pp. 145-157.
12. Dreikurs, R., *Fundamentals of Adlerian Psychology.* Chicago, Alfred Adler Inst., 1950.
13. Dreikurs, R., *Psychodynamics, Psychotherapy, and Counseling: Collected Papers.* Chicago, Alfred Adler Inst., 1950.
14. Ellis, A., *Reason and Emotion in Psychotherapy.* New York, Lyle Stuart.
15. Ferguson, Eva D., "The Use of Early Recollections in Assessing Life Style and Diagnosing Psychopathology." *J. Proj. Tech.*, 28(1964), pp. 402-412.
16. Mosak, H. H., "Early Recollections as a Projective Technique." *J. Proj. Tech.*, 22(1958), pp. 302-311.
17. Vaihinger, H., *The Philosophy of "As If".* New York, Harcourt, Brace, 1925.

DISTANCE:
ANTECEDENT OF ALIENATION

Paul Rom

The protagonist of a modern novel by Bigiaretti muses about a convention of Public Relations Officers thus:

> In fact, everything Figari said, as with gorged complacence he kept repeating the word 'alienation,' let me leap a step ahead of him. I recalled the numerous articles and essays I'd read recently on the subject. Figari's most brilliant observations on the need for reintegration of man in the mechanical world of automation were literally borrowed from books by Friedman, Mumford, Whyte, and other sociologists ... Poor Figari seemed to be unaware that his pronouncements on the subject of alienation had by now become so familiar and been so vulgarized that even the novelists were making use of them (7, p. 104).

This passage illuminates the present use of the term "alienation" by people of the western world who are enjoying the freedom of competition, restricted only by the anonymous, alienated authority of conformism (15, p. 152).

Freud and Alienation

Weiss, a neo-Freudian, writes, "The age of hysteria was followed by the age of psychosomatics, in which anxiety and conflict are mainly expressed in physical symptoms. In our time, this has been followed by the age of alienation" (26, p. 463). Many Freudians and neo-Freudians now speak of "alienation," a term which Freud himself did not use. The founder of psychoanalysis left the term to lawyers for whom it meant "the loss of property or ownership to another person" and for whom an alien was a man with the passport of another country; also to the psychiatric profession who referred to themselves as "alienists." While he did not employ the term, "alienation," he did in one of his letters refer to an *Entfremdungsgefühl*, a feeling of alienation or derealization, which he experienced while standing on the Acropolis. In an open letter to Romain Rolland, written in January, 1936, on the occasion of the novelist's seventieth birthday, Freud shared his conviction that "derealizations are remarkable phenomena which are still little understood" (13, p. 244). He distinguished "derealization" *(Entfremdung),* in which a piece of reality is strange to man, from "depersonalization," in which "a piece of his own self is strange to him," but they both serve a purpose of defence; they aim at keeping something away from the ego (13, p. 245).

While the phrase, "a piece of his own self," reflects his division of the "psychic apparatus" into three "provinces," the phrase, "keeping something away from the ego," leans toward the Adlerian concepts of holism, of purposiveness, and of distance. However, for Freud, the term, "ego," never came to mean "the I, the self, the whole person, one and indivisible." It remained a portion of the psychic apparatus.[1]

American Freudians, Neo-Freudians, and Alienation

It is interesting that when they discuss alienation, several American Freudians also use the term "distance" explicitly. Schachtel, for example, sees distance as an interpersonal phenomenon. "The I that feels that I am this or that, in doing so distances itself from the very same reified object attribute which it experiences as determining its identity" (19, p. 78).

Weiss: Weiss, a follower of Horney, moves beyond Freud and toward Adler in conceiving the responsible, whole person. He states, "The image of man as an id harboring only libidinous, aggressive, and destructive forces; as a superego, functioning as an inner police force, not as a healthy human conscience; and as a more or less passive ego, which reminds one of a rather sick self—such an image of man in itself appears fragmented and alienated" (26, p. 472). He continues with a criticism of orthodox Freudian therapy, remarking that "the concept of a doctor-patient relationship which is seen as determined by the transference of a neurotic past but which disregards the constructive impact of the creative 'meeting' (Hans Trueb) in the present, is in itself alienating. Instead of lessening the patient's alienation, it is likely to prolong it" (26, pp. 472-473).

It would seem that until the recent introduction of social emphases into psychoanalytic theory, little attention was devoted to the process of alienation which had resulted since the Industrial Revolution increasingly mechanized all people so that they became "strangers" (8) in a world they no longer could understand. Weiss offers a countering view of how therapy should proceed to avoid prolonging the patient's alienation:

> Making the unconscious conscious is not, in itself, therapeutically effective. To know, for example, that I harbor strong, compulsive dependency needs, may increase rather than lessen my self-alienation. Self-knowledge becomes therapeutically active only when it is experientially owned, and generates the emotional shock which is inherent in the pro-

cess of self-confrontation. Only such experience has the power to lead to change, choice, and commitment (26, p. 473).

Except for Weiss' phraseology, the above statement echoes Adler, who would have written "discouragement and withdrawal" for "self-alienation." Since Adler also distinguished between knowledge and understanding, he would have understood "self-confrontation" as referring to the self, the individual, confronting life with its tasks of friendship, work, and sex. Weiss' goal of leading the patient to "commitment" is reminiscent of Adler's focus upon individual responsibility and courage.

Fromm: During the fifties, Fromm began to remind his readers of Marx's findings and their relationship to psychology. The works of Karl Marx help us "to understand the essential connections between private property, greed, the separation of labor, capital and land, exchange and competition, value and the devaluation of men, monopoly, and competition—between the whole system of alienation and the money system" (16, p. 94). Those interested in contributing to "The Sane Society" (15) are reminded by Fromm that today most people feel they are in many cases not human beings, but degraded to mere numbers and objects of an anonymous machinery, the workings of which they fail to understand. Increasingly people are becoming aware of the state of alienation in which they live—men, dehumanized, estranged creatures, enmeshed in barren conventions and money relationships, unfree, and unproductive of human values.

Marx described the ideal image of free human beings as follows:

> Assume *man* as *man*, and his relation to the world as a human one, and you can exchange love only for love, confidence for confidence, etc. If you wish to enjoy art, you must be an artistically trained person; if you wish to have influence on other people, you must be a person who has really stimulating and furthering influence on the other people. Every one of your relationships to man and to nature must be a definite expression of your *real, individual* life corresponding to the object of your will. If you love without calling forth love, that is, if your love as such does not produce love, if by means of an *expression of life* as a loving person you do not make of yourself a *loved person,* then your love is impotent, a misfortune (15, p. 132).

As a humanistic psychoanalyst, Fromm sees our situation thus:

> Man regresses to a receptive and marketing orientation and ceases to be productive; he loses his sense of self, becomes dependent on approval, hence tends to conform and yet to feel insecure; he is dissatisfied, bored, and anxious, and spends most of his energy in the attempt to compensate for, or just cover up, this anxiety. His intelligence is excellent, his reason deteriorates, and in view of his technical powers he is seriously endangering the existence of civilization, and even of the human race (15, pp. 270-271).

Fromm then shifts from humanistic psychoanalyst to humanistic socialist as he argues:

> Because alienation has reached a point where it borders on insanity in the whole industrialized world, undermining and destroying its religious,

spiritual, and political traditions and threatening general destruction through nuclear war, many are better able to see that Marx had recognized the central issue of modern man's sickness; that he had not only seen, as Feuerbach and Kierkegaard had, this "sickness", but that he had shown that contemporary idolatry is rooted in the contemporary mode of production and can be changed only by the complete change of the economic-social constellation together with the spiritual liberation of man (14, p. 59).

Vranicki, like Fromm a humanistic socialist, points out that

the historical process thus far has consisted just as much of a process of the creation of various forms of alienation as of a process of dealienation . . . (16, p. 278). Certain forms of alienation have been of historically progressive significance under certain historical circumstances . . . Even today many theoreticians of socialism consider alienation to be incompatible with socialism, as though socialism were immune by nature to this disease . . . The problem of alienation is the central problem of socialism (16, p. 281).

It is, in the form of distance, also a central concern of Individual Psychology; but Adler, although in his Vienna days politically active, concentrated his efforts upon understanding and helping individuals who were erring in their immediate interpersonal relationships. He never excluded the interpretation of socio-economic influence nor did he fail to encourage his patients to contribute to its transformation. Like Marx, he held that we not only are the products of our circumstances, but also their creators, and therefore can contribute to the modification and amelioration of social conditions. Moreover, he perceived that whatever particular conditions of alienation prevail in a given society, a discouraged person may tend to use "tricks," e.g., psychopathologic symptomatology (2), in order to create distance between himself and the pressing social obligations. In behaving neurotically he does not lose his self-esteem as long as the people with whom he comes in contact are "strangers" who take his symptoms to be part of a "disease" rather than as the creation of one who is pursuing invalid social goals. Adler also taught that in counteracting the economic-political alienation process in society, men may develop their social interest and put it into action. "De-alienation" would mean for the Adlerian that on the basis of mutual respect every man becomes accepted as an equal.

A British View

Laing: Laing, himself an "existentialist-phenomenological psychiatrist," believes that "The mad things said and done by the schizophrenic will remain essentially a closed book, if one does not understand their existential context"[2] (17, p. 17). He formulates the problem of the psychiatrist engaged in therapy in a manner similar to Weiss. "How can I go straight to the patient if the psychiatric words at my disposal keep the patient at a distance from me?" Explaining schizophrenia in the literal sense of the word, he expresses a holistic view when he says, "We cannot give an adequate account of the existential splits unless we can begin from the concept of the *unitary whole*, and no such concept exists, nor can any such concept be expressed within the current language of psychiatry or psychoanalysis" (17, p. 19). Reminiscent of Adler's statement that in order to understand another, "We must be able to see with his eyes and listen with his ears" (4, p. 57), Laing demands "that we look at the extraordinary behavior of the psychotic from his own point of view" (17, pp. 160-161).

One is reminded of Ferenczi's deviation from Freud (13, p. 229) when one reads in Laing's book, "The main agent in uniting the patient, in allowing the pieces to come together and cohere, is the physician's *love*, a love that recognizes the patient's total being, and accepts it with no strings attached" (17, p. 165). This goes beyond Freud's authoritarian attitude toward his patients. It also differs from Adler's democratic cooperation of helper and helped (4, p. 56). When Laing then says, "The self has lost contact with realness, and cannot feel itself real or alive" (17, p. 165), he expresses most simply the problem of the alienated person, who is successfully using the neurotic technique of creating distance from the tasks of life (12). He feels and acts as an alien, as one who is in "enemy country" (Adler), where he is afraid of everything. Eventually, he may increase the distance from the real world and its inhabitants to the extreme by creating the fictitious world of psychosis, where he is the only citizen.

Adler and the Problem of Distance

While a spatial or temporary distance can be measured, and while a social distance in a class society can be felt "on both sides of the barricade," distance in Adler's sense can not be measured. It can be interpreted as the non-understood arrangement of a person lacking in self-confidence and courage. Instead of a progressive movement towards achievement in all spheres of life, we may find in people's behavior four ways of distance-creating:

1. A retrogressive movement. Adler saw it expressed in suicide and its attempts, in agoraphobia, and in various compulsions. "Anxiety and falling dreams, as well as criminal ones, are frequent and indicate what exaggerated precautions are at work—the fear of what might conceivably happen" (1, p. 104).
2. The standing still of a person whom one would expect to make progress and achieve something. This can give the impression that he finds himself in a magic circle which hinders him "from coming into closer contact with the facts of life by confronting truth face to face; to stand a test of his worth or of taking a decision" (1, p. 105). Dreams of being confined or of being examined are common with these persons.
3. Doubt, expressed in undue hesitation and oscillation in thoughts

37

and actions, which are reflected in dreams by to and fro movements and tardiness. This secures a distance from the decision or action, admitted to be necessary but deemed dangerous.

4. Construction of obstacles and their mastery. For instance, a normal person facing an examination will do the necessary work of preparation without fuss. If he "arranges" to have headaches, and a lack of concentration, he may be successful in spite of these symptoms and thus feel added glory in having succeeded. Should he fail, he has the good excuse that only his affliction prevented his triumph[3].

Other Adlerian Writers on Distance and Alienation

Sperber: In the early thirties, Manes Sperber, the youngest amongst Adler's earliest students and friends, became personally estranged from his teacher and later on acutely realized the cruel alienation prevailing in the Moscow-oriented communist parties. In a powerful novel trilogy, many passages name and graphically describe the phenomenon of alienation in a party machine where man becomes a mere means to an end, and where each comrade is a stranger to the other (21, 22, 23).

Sperber had already found his way back from Stalinism to Humanism when, in 1937, he wrote a penetrating essay on the "calamity *Unglück* of being gifted" (24). Having in the first section dealt with giftedness *(Begabung)* in the light of Adler's insights into "compensation and overcompensation," he studies in the second part " the problem of distance" as it concerns the gifted person, or the genius, and illustrates it with historical cases: Moses, Saint-Just, Jesus, as well as two writers who were his patients in Berlin. He arrives at the following conclusions:

1. Between the gifted peron and other people there is unavoidably a distance *(Distanz)*.
2. The lengthening or shortening of this distance produces in the gifted one, according to his life style, a tension which constitutes most important creative forces.
3. Disturbances in the balance of this tension lead to disturbances in the creativity of the gifted one. These tensions are due to, and correspond to, a contradictory effort upon all his relationships.
4. The superiority of the gifted one inevitably gives him feelings of insecurity and distrust and is thus a cause for his alienation *(Entfremdung)* from his contemporaries. This superiority attracts others as long as they accept it and identify themselves with the superior one. It alienates those who negate it as being unbearable, for it threatens their self-esteem.
5. This distance also explains why the gifted one usually overestimates the strength of the other's attachment to him, and why he must again and again suffer the bitter experience of feeling betrayed.

The following sections on the problem of value and that of society indicate how an alienated gifted one might overcome the "calamity" arising from his distance to others. But even though under an imaginable new social order, which would encourage each one and thus allow him to develop all his human potentialities, many more people would appear to be "gifted," the distance between overcompensating and merely compensating persons, between leaders and followers, pioneers and conservers, may always remain.

I[4] have often regretted that Adler, having died the year before, could not read this volume of 1938. This might have resolved the estrangement between the two men. Agreeing with Goethe that "If you do not commit errors, you will not become wise. If you wish to become a man, do it on your own responsibility," Adler would have liked the quoted essay as much as the other one "Concerning the Analysis of Tyranny." These essays as well as Sperber's later novels illustrate splendidly what Adler expressed more simply as far back as 1918, when he stated that the fate of Bolshevism was sealed since its rule was based upon the possession of power (Cf. 18, pp. 100-103).[5]

Shulman: Shulman introduces his "Essays on Schizophrenia" with the statement that "the schizophrenic feels more estranged from his fellows than any other category of person met by the psychiatrist" (20, p. 2).

He attributes the following thoughts to the person who starts on this erroneous way: "Life is hard for me and unsatisfactory. I had better keep my *distance* from life" (20, p. 29), and classifying the twelve signs occurring in schizophrenia in four groups, he puts in the first one "symptoms with the purpose of permitting and facilitating withdrawal from social integration" (20, p. 50). Consequently, the general goal of individual therapy is formulated as "a better rapprochement with Life" (20, p. 84)."

Amongst the various techniques which can be applied to develop "a common logic and language" with the patient, figures also that of "teaching common words to describe 'strange' subjective experiences" (20 p. 98).

Having quoted Freud's and Sullivan's view on the "uncanny," Shulman writes:

> The ability to feel like a stranger in a strange environment may certainly have been part of our infantile experiences, but no one ever loses the ability to perceive something as *alien* and *inimical*. It is true that people are more likely to feel this way if they have a tendency to be distrustful and suspicious of the world and tend to feel inadequate to cope with it as it comes . . . The schizophrenic has had at least a few, and perhaps many, impressive experiences where he felt "strange" or felt that the world was "strange." Having "gone out into left field," he finds himself bewildered and frightened. Uncanny sensations are actually the consequence of feeling alienated, not the cause of it. In their essence, all feelings of strangeness and feelings of loneliness are actually subjective *variations in the feeling of not belonging, the absence of Gemeinschaftsgefühl*, the state of alienation (20, p. 99).

From that follows the therapeutic insight that

> whenever we can turn a strange experience into a consensually familiar one, we have done two things for the patient. (1) We have helped him to find his bearings and (2) we have helped him to use common sense rather than private sense (and thereby made him less psychotic, since common sense is a device which binds people to consensuality and a common reality) (20, p. 99).

The Beechers: The Beechers use both terms, "alienation" and "distance" in their description of illusions as "alienation from the now" (6, p. 154). They hold that "our degree of alienation—or distance from the living now—is in direct ratio to our habit of wishful thinking" (7, p. 155).

Ansbacher: Ansbacher (5, pp. 483-484) found that the "alienation syndrome" as formulated by Davids (9) corresponds to Adler's concept of "distance." Davids and Murray (11) administered to Harvard students an affect questionnaire which measured eight critical dispositions of personality: three positive ones, i.e., sociocentricity, optimism, and trust; and five negative ones, i.e., egocentricity, pessimism, distrust, anxiety, and resentment. Analyzing the results statistically, they called the syndrome composed of the five negative dispositions "alienation."

This research, though not idiographic like a life style interpretation, is certainly more concrete than the scholasticism of last century's abstract classical psychology. Perceiving the link between these findings and Adler's concept under discussion, Ansbacher gave a quotation from Adler's writings, inserting the descriptive terms from Davids so as to show the striking agreement between them. It reads:

> Once a person has acquired the attitude of running away from the difficulties of life (i.e. creating a distance), this attitude may be greatly strengthened and safeguarded by the addition of anxiety (Davids' anxiety) . . . It embitters (Davids' resentment) his life to a marked degree, renders him quite unsuited for making contacts, and thus also for laying the basis for a peaceful life and for fruitful accomplishments . . .
> We shall meet again the well-known type who feels himself forced by necessity to think more of himself and consequently has little left for his fellow man (Davids' egocentricity). As though in confirmation of this view, one often finds that such people are inclined to think of the past or of death, which has about the same effect . . . Or they emphasize that all is vanity, after all, that this life is short, and one cannot know what will happen (Davids' pessimism) (5, p. 483).

As for the here absent effect of distrust, Ansbacher points out that this is implied in Adler's notion of "oversensitivity," characteristic of the neurotically disposed person. Indeed, Adler wrote, "Distrust in his own strength which awakens doubt about everything; distrust in others which is socially disturbing and disrupts every group—these at times characterize the oversensitive patient" (5, p. 483).

In a note replying to Ansbacher's observations, Davids acknowledged the "real value" of the observations and says in his last paragraph,

If we had taken as our point of departure the theoretical notions and statements advanced by Adler, and had designed our researches specifically to tent propositions derived from his theory, we would have confirmed them in a well-controlled laboratory investigation employing modern statistical procedures (11, p. 486).

Summary

The concern of many present-day writers with the concept of alienation reflects its importance. The concept of alienation can be traced via Marx to Hegel and ultimately to Calvin. Yet, in its very conception, it is so difficult a concept that numerous books have been written about it. On the other hand, the concept of distance is a more descriptive, simpler, and more operational term and therefore would deserve preference over alienation. Alienation describes a state of being, while Adler's *Distanzierung* (distance creating), which underlies all asocial and antisocial behavior in every society, reflects the individual's law of movement.

FOOTNOTES

1. I am grateful to Prof. Heinz Ansbacher for his many helpful suggestions in the preparation of this paper.
2. Binswanger, one of the founders of existential psychology, when using the term, "existence" *(Dasein),* inserted parenthetically, "formerly one would have said 'life' " [noted by Ansbacher in his editorial, "A Key to Existence," *J. Indiv. Psychol.,* 15(1959), pp. 141-142].
3. Mosak describes this method for protecting one's self-esteem regardless of what happens as "buying insurance."
4. This "I" is not in conformity with the usage of "the writer" in such papers. But is placing the third person in the place of the first not a sign of alienation between the writer and the reader?
5. To celebrate the centenary of his teacher's and friend's birth, Manes Sperber published a profound book *"Alfred Adler oder des Elend der Psychologie"* (Wien: Molden, 1970).

REFERENCES

1. Adler, A., *The Practice and Theory of Individual Psychology* (1925). Paterson, N. J., Littlefield, Adams, 1963.
2. Adler, A., "Trick and Neurosis." *Int. J. Indiv. Psychol.,* 2(2), (1936), pp. 3-10.
3. Adler, A., *Understanding Human Nature* (1927). Greenwich, Conn., Premier Books, 1954.
4. Adler, A., *What Life Should Mean to You* (1931). London, Unwin Books, 1962.
5. Ansbacher, H. L., "The Alienation Syndrome and Adler's Concept of Distance." *J. Consult. Psychol.,* 20(1956), pp. 483-484.
6. Beecher, W. and Beecher, Marguerite, *Beyond Success and Failure.*

New York, Julian Press, 1966.

7. Bigiaretti, L., *The Convention*. London, Macmillan, 1965.

8. Camus, A., *L'Etranger*. Paris, Gallimard, 1942.

9. Davids, A., "Alienation, Social Perception and Ego Structure." *J. Consult. Psychol.*, 19(1955), pp. 21-27.

10. Davids, A., "Some Comments on Ansbacher's Note on the 'Alienation Syndrome' and Adler's Concept of 'Distance'." *J. Consult. Psychol.* 20(1956), pp. 485-486.

11. Davids, A., and Murray, H. A., "Preliminary Appraisal of an Auditory Projective Technique for Studying Personality and Cognition." *Amer, J. Orthopsychiat.*, 25(1955), pp. 543-554.

12. Dreikurs, R. and Mosak, H. H., "The Tasks of Life: i.e. Adler's Three Tasks." *Indiv. Psychologist*, 4(1966), pp. 18-22.

13. Freud, S., *Complete Works*. Vol. 22. London, Hogarth Press, 1964.

14. Fromm, E., *Beyond the Chains of Illusion: My Encounter with Marx and Freud*. New York, Simon & Schuster, 1962.

15. Fromm, E., *The Sane Society*. London, Routledge & Kegan Paul, 1956.

16. Fromm, E., ed., *Socialist Humanism: An International Symposium*. New York, Doubleday, 1965.

17. Laing, R. D., *The Divided Self: An Existential Study in Sanity* (1960). London, Pelican Books, 1965.

18. Rom, P., *Alfred Adler und die wissenschaftliche Menschenkenntnis*. Frankfurt-am-Main, Kramer, 1966.

19. Schachtel, E. G., "On Alienated Concepts of Identity," *Amer. J. Psychoanal.*, 21(1961), pp. 120-131.

20. Shulman, B. H., *Essays in Schizophrenia*. Baltimore, Williams & Wilkins, 1968.

21. Sperber, M., *The Lost Bay*. London, Wingate, 1956.

22. Sperber, M., *To Dusty Death*. London, Wingate, 1952.

23. Sperber, M., *The Wind and the Flame*. London, Wingate, 1951.

24. Sperber, M., *Zur Analyse der Tyrannis. Das Unglück, begabt zu sein: Zwei Spezialpsychologische Essais*. Paris, Science et Littérature, 1938.

25. Vranicki, P., "Socialism and the Problem of Alienation." In E. Fromm, ed., *Socialist Humanism: An International Symposium*. New York, Doubleday, 1965.

26. Weiss, F. A., "Self-alienation: Dynamics and Therapy." *Amer. J. Psychoanal.*, 2(1961), pp. 207-218.

THE CONTROLLER—A SOCIAL INTERPRETATION OF THE ANAL CHARACTER

Harold H. Mosak

The possibility of translating a psychoanalytic character description based upon libido into social terms has been demonstrated in a previous paper on the "oral character" (13). Similarly the "anal character" may be described in social terms as the controlling personality.

When one thinks about controlling, generally our first associations center about the active forms of controlling. We perhaps think about mastery or dominance or the manipulation of the environment. While the controlling individual certainly engages in such activities, there are controllers who do not endeavor to control actively; they are merely unwilling to permit life and others to control them.

Control through Use of the Intellect

The active forms of control vary from individual to individual depending upon their perceptions, and ultimately their convictions as to what will give them a place. Some controllers, having learned that "knowledge is power," rely upon intellect. Have a party, and they are off in a corner leading a discussion, a discussion about some topic they know well. If you become engaged in the discussion, they resort to intellectualization to advertise their superiority and to defeat you. This can be accomplished in two ways, first by definition of terms, what one newspaper columnist calls "antics with semantics." Ask a person whether he has ever been in love and he answers, "Yes," "No," "Many times," "I thought I was but it was only puppy love." The controller meets your question with the response, "What is love?"

The second method is talking beside the point. An old joke illustrates this maneuver well. "Should olives be eaten with the fingers?" "No, the fingers should be eaten separately." One receives the impression that the controller understands your communication quite well al-

43

though his answer seems to negate such comprehension.

Controlling through Right

Other controllers place their faith in the right. When coupled with reliance upon intellect, these opinionated and argumentative people inform you, as one joke has it, "I'm not always right but I'm *never* wrong." Controlling through being right generally involves creating an orderly world where the credo for living is "Everything in its place and a place for everything." These people are organized, methodical, and orderly. Punctuality is exalted. Since a person who wants to be right must know his duty and then do it, the controller customarily practices over-conscientiousness. In the words of the television commercials, the good housewife controls dirt. She does it from morning to night. Parenthetically, the overconscientious controller, as hard as he may work, never permits himself to complete all of his tasks. If he should, there would be nothing left to control tomorrow. He is always behind schedule and consequently he must push himself to do more, work faster, and not take time off. He is always busy catching up. If his alarm clock fails to go off one morning, he is not merely fifteen minutes behind in his schedule. It is catastrophic; his entire day lies in ruins. Routine and schedules appeal to the controller. He brags about eating the same lunch every day at the same restaurant for the past twenty years. Frequently, although there are exceptions, as Adler takes care to explain in *The Case of Mrs. A* (1), the controller is overconcerned with his appearance, being super-neatly groomed, immaculately dressed, scrupulously clean, and having every hair in place. After all, if "cleanliness is next to godliness," is it not only right that one should keep oneself clean?

The insistence upon being and doing right creates dilemmas, subjective conflict, and malaise, for not to be right is to be wrong, and to be wrong leads to drastic consequences. Therefore where his assurance of being right is not guaranteed, he must assume a posture of caution. As one of my patients remarked, "Nothing ventured, nothing lost." Another patient lamented, "They'll engrave on my tombstone, 'She never did any thing wrong . . . because she never did anything.' " Chronic doubt afflicts the controller. Sometimes he doesn't know what the right is; how can he then do it? Sometimes he is confronted with the choice between two rights, e.g. between personal interest and social interest. Worse yet, he may feel required to choose between two evils, and then his movement is paralyzed indeed, for the "lesser of two evils" does not fall within the realm of possible solutions for the person who has to be right. If only there were guidelines for everything so that one could always know what was right. He cannot tolerate ambiguity. This hesitating attitude toward life, marked by pronounced overcautiousness, is seen in exaggerated form in the neurotic controller, the obsessive-compulsive, who not only feels compelled to do the right thing but attaches the direst consequences to his failure to execute it, e.g. "I must say this three times or someone will die." While subjectively the controller exhibits doubt, ambivalence, and indecisiveness (in terms of movement, these are all one step forward and one step backward; the net effect is to remain in the same place) (5), he does not realize that he creates these feelings in order not to make a decision because in doing so, he might be wrong. The goal of perfection is, of course, transparent.

The "Ruling Type"

A third group of controllers are what Adler called "the ruling type" (4, 8, 9), many of whom develop attributes of leadership and some of ruthlessness, and others of non-amenability to authority. They speak with authority and perform with apparent confidence. There are parents and teachers who command children, "Do it because I tell you to." To reinforce authority and control, they resort to intimidation, threat, and violence. The teacher threatens, "If you don't do this, you'll go to the principal's office." The mother threatens, "Eat your spinach or no dessert for you." The university student admonishes the administration, "Acquiesce to our demands or we'll take over the university." The militant black encourages others to carry guns in their confrontations with the honkie. The child throws himself on the floor, holds his breath, or yells, screams and kicks in the hope that his parents will succumb. If parents can resist this form of control, the child can still conquer them utilizing the light artillery of "I don't love you" or the heavy artillery of "that just proves that you don't love me." The controlling wife, having been raised in a culture and by an educational system which emphasizes reward and punishment as motivating forces (11), uses sex as a motivater. We might also observe that the redhead is born with a license to intimidate, and if you're fortunate enough to be Irish, you are entitled to have an Irish temper.

Threat, violence, intimidation, temper, tyranny are repugnant to many individuals, controllers and otherwise. The controller who feels compelled to do the right thing finds these methods especially repulsive. Opposed to these methods, some people control through the use of money. "Money talks." It buys things. "Everyone has a price." Through generosity one may acquire the positive regard of others. Moreover, it may make them obligated to you. Others may rely instead upon charm and try to wind people around their fingers. Youngest children and girls often have a head start in training for such a role.

So-called passive methods constitute another resource for the ruling controller. Consider the shy child who hides behind his mother and makes you coax him out. Or the Victorian lady who fainted when she wished to control the situation. Or the wife, in imitation of her Victorian counterpart, who turns on the tears and makes her husband succumb. These devices are popularly considered to be signs of weakness, delicate nerves, a hypersensitive nature. Adlerians, interpreting these and all other behavior in terms of movement, consider them oppositely. Adler calls this utilization of crying, "water power" (3, 8). Weakness is nevertheless not excluded from the armamentarium of control. Some examples are the Goal IV child (10), the woman who has headaches at bedtime and the patients who use various forms of symptoms. An interesting use of weakness characterizes those who lose control, using active or passive means, in order to preserve control. People who fly off the handle, have emotional "fits," and behave with emotional instability lose control in order to gain control.

As any actor knows, the voice constitutes another vehicle for control. Speak in a low tone, and people either will bend forward, the better to hear you, or will lose interest in listening. Speak rapidly or slowly and you may grab your listener by the lapels. Speak seductively and you enchant. Thunder and you intimidate. Speak monotonously and you *arrange* to bore.

In the ruling type the crucial issue is to make others behave in the manner one desires. "I made you" represents the essence of control. We can observe it in a children's playground game. One child obtains the attention of another child, points in the direction behind the other child's back, and exclaims, "Look!" The second child turns and sees nothing there whereupon the first child chants tauntingly, "Ha, ha! I made you look! I made you look! I made you buy a penny book!" Similar observations can be made among adults. For example, when a man gets a girl to do what he wants, he is said to have "made" her. Thus, where the getting personality is "on the take," the controlling personality is "on the make." His emphasis upon who can make whom do what leads to the perception of others as potential antagonists and the ruling controller must constantly be vigilant, perhaps even suspicious, since others are potential adversaries. Because he perceives the world as populated by enemies, his feeling of hostility toward the world is appropriate from his frame of reference. His posture, based upon his self image and his evaluation of the environment, is one of defensiveness in the face of the hostility from others. Only the external observer regards his assumption of hostility from others as the controller's own projection. One can understand that the controller who chooses psychosis makes his choice for paranoid symptomatology where he suspects life, and where people and forces are conspiring to do things to him or to make him do things which he is not inclined to do. His delusions of reference, influence, and persecution provide reinforcement for his stance.

Psychotic, neurotic, or normal, the controller does not find the world a resort area in which he can relax. To the contrary, the world is a jungle, survival of the fittest is its law, and if it's a dog-eat-dog world, he must prepare himself to be the dog who does the eating. But he must keep one eye open while sleeping lest someone snatch his bone or attack him. Incidentally, the controller does have periods of insomnia (7) since conditions must be just right in order for him to sleep. "I just can't sleep except in my own bed," he sometimes tells us.

Since people are frequently unpredictable and unmanageable, the controller tends to shift his concerns to ideas and objects. We have already spoken of his tendency to accumulate ideas but he also accumulates possessions. He is frequently a collector, often a hoarder, and since he believes, as the comedians put it, "Rich or poor, what difference does it make as long as you have money?", he may decide to acquire, hoard, and not expend money. When the check comes to the restaurant table, he has an impediment in his reach.

Resistance to Being Controlled

In contrast to the person who actively controls is the individual who does not permit life to control him. He may be constantly late and make others wait for him. Swimming disconcerts him, and a trip to the dentist is life's most terrifying experience—next to flying. He is further recognizable through his three major fears, the three situations which would deprive him of control. First, he fears the loss of physical control—blindness, paralysis, etc. Second his fear is of loss of psychological control. He fears his "ego-alien impulses," "blowing his cool," or losing his mind. However, even if he could succeed in controlling mind and body, there is one element in life to which he must eventually relinquish control— the great controller, Death.

To avoid being controlled such people adopt several methods of operation. They circumnavigate the demands of others. Mothers lament about their children, "One word from me, and he does just as he pleases." Some controllers become overconscientious, a not uncommon phenomenon in controllers in general, and defeat others' control by observing their demands literally. To illustrate, a child comes home covered with mud, and his mother despairingly tells him to undress and to deposit all of his clothes in the washing machine. The child complies. Several minutes later hearing a thumping in the machine, she opens the lid and discovers the child's shoes swirling about amidst the clothes. When she asks the child why he placed his shoes in the machine, he retorts, "You said *all* my clothes."

Some, and this is notably true among adolescents, become "reverse puppets." When one pulls the right string of an ordinary puppet, his right leg raises up. When one pulls the right string of the "reverse puppet," his left leg elevates. The "reverse puppet" adolescent treats a demand from others, especially his parents, as a signal to do the opposite. He identifies himself as emancipated and independent, unaware that his freedom is illusory, that he is just as much a puppet as the more conventional puppet.

The more the controller attempts to avoid being controlled, the more he runs into it. One of my obsessive-compulsive patients, "deathly" afraid of death, reads the newspaper, turning each page gingerly and scanning it rapidly to assure himself that there was no mention of death on the following page. In this way he never missed an article which alluded to death. This relationship between avoiding being controlled and thus courting it was known at least as far back as King Solomon's time. A Talmudic story relates, "There were once two servants of Solomon, Elihoref and Ahyah, scribes of the King. One day Solomon observed that the Angel of Death was sad. 'Why are you sad?' he asked. 'Because,' he answered him, 'I have been ordered to take these two servants of yours who sit here.' Whereupon to save them from death, Solomon sent them to the district of Luz. When, however, they reached there, they died. The next day, Solomon observed that the Angel of Death was in cheerful spirits. 'Why,' he said to him, 'art thou cheerful?'' 'Because,' he replied, 'you sent them to the very place where I was to slay them!' "[1] A modern version of the story may be found in the frontispiece to John O'Hara's *Appointment in Samarra*.

The diagnostician will discover that women who resist being controlled hate wearing girdles. If they must wear them "to hold up their stockings," they still dislike the feeling of being controlled.

When the controller feels incapable, or as Adlerians would see it, he is unwilling to meet the life tasks, his fear of loss of control mounts. Then he may give way to a panic reaction or he may create hypochondriacal concerns in order to impress himself with the dangers of loss of control. He may develop phobic behavior, and a recent article by Leifer discusses the relationship of phobias to feelings of lack of mastery (12). Or he may create a sideshow—instead of controlling life, he diverts his attention to controlling himself. He deprives himself of his spontaneity because emotions can get out of control. He creates "ego-alien impulses" and then spends his time and energies controlling himself. Since these "ego-alien impulses"" are viewed as demonic, certainly he is not responsible for them. He has thoughts which must be controlled, and he creates elaborate rituals for controlling his behavior. Dreikurs[2] recounts the legend of the wizard who knew the entire art of black magic. His king, wishing to learn these secrets, summoned the wizard to his court, and offered him up to half of his kingdom if the wizard would induct him into the secrets of black magic. The wizard, wishing to earn the king's reward, exacted only one condition—"If you wish to learn black magic, you must never think about crocodiles." And so the king never learned because every time he told himself, "I must not think about crocodiles," he violated the wizard's prohibition.

To permit this fictitious battle with the "ego-alien impulses" the controller must create two antagonistic, competing systems roughly corresponding to a "good-me" and a "bad-me" and make of himself a battleground upon which the angels wrestle with the demons. In his verbal communications we hear him declaring, "I have to force myself" or "How can I make myself?", reflective of a "good-me" with the best of intentions and the "bad-me" which gives the "good-me" a hard time. However, the combatants must be endowed with equal strength. Otherwise one set of "forces" will prevail, and the battle for control will terminate. With the sideshow stopped, he would be compelled to address himself to the solution of the life tasks which he has been avoiding. One of my obsessive-compulsive patients who had not worked in years and who had retreated from social relations felt that Truman was good and Castro was bad. Without warning, the name "Castro" would intrude into his thinking, and he would counteract this intrusion by repetitively uttering, "Truman, Truman, Truman." When he then relaxed, he would, to his dismay, find his mind thinking, "Castro, Castro, Castro," and the process would continue. And thus we have the obsessive-compulsive locked in an unending heroic fight to the finish to determine who is stronger—me or me? One can appreciate how heroic when you consider that in contrast to other neuroses whose symptoms come and go, the obsessive-compulsive syndrome is a twenty-four hour a day neurosis.

In the psychotic categories the controller, as already noted, selects paranoid symptomatology and wrestles with his delusional demons. Among the psychophysiological reactions impotence and frigidity are common. The controller's impotence manifests itself in the effort to maintain an erection or in premature ejaculation. The controller's frigidity expresses itself in the ability to be aroused and the inability to achieve orgasm, since the latter is often perceived as a loss of control or a loss of consciousness or as being transported to ecstatic heights where control surrenders to passion. Most prevalent among the psychophysiologic reactions of the controller is colitis, partly because the bowel is a most appropriate organ for expressing in organ dialect the problems with control and partly because seeing the world as hostile territory and being hostile himself, as a colleague indelicately but graphically describes it, "He shits on the life which he feels shits on him." Other neuroses to which the controller is "vulnerable" are discussed in a previous paper (14).

Whether the controlling personality controls or resists being controlled, he sporadically must permit life to get out of control. He arranges the consequences in such a way as to confirm the dangers of loss of control and thus reinforces the conviction that one must always be in control.

Teleologically, what is the controller up to? The Babylonian Talmud, in discussing the various names of God, gives one of these names as "the all-capable, the all-wise, and the perfect." And this is the secret goal of the controller—to be omnipotent, omniscient, and perfect (2). Only then would he feel certain of having a place. The goal becomes transparent in the neurotic controller, the obsessive-compulsive, who usurps God's prerogatives over life and death in such compulsive thoughts as, "If I don't count to three, someone will die." Since he can never achieve this lofty goal, he is doomed to failure. He is "full of shit" but this is a metaphor for his self-image, not a cause of his behavior. The godlike aspirations have already been explained according to Adlerian theory as compensatory for the individual's inferiority feelings (2).

The Goals of the Controller

To leave it at this would not nearly do justice to insight into the person's goals. Since behavior occurs in a social context, let us examine the social functioning of the controller. At the same time that he exalts himself, he depreciates others and treats them badly. People are malevolent, enemies; only he is good. Yet if we look closely, we can observe that he uses his goodness to defeat. A parent nags his child all evening to do his homework but the child has other plans. When time for bed arrives and he is told to go to bed, his rejoinder is, "I've got to do my homework. Don't you want me to do my homework?" He is right; you are wrong. He has the best of intentions; you have the worst (Otherwise how could he be suspicious?). A patient in group therapy accused another of being "a phoney" whereupon the accused recalled a bit of "phoney" behavior of the first patient. Unruffled, the first patient retorted, "You're right but at least I'm an honest phoney. I *admit* it." You must do his bidding; he is exempt from doing yours. He is clean, and the remainder of the world is dirty (6). This contrast in cleanliness is most vividly exhibited in the neurotic controller, the compulsive with a washing compulsion, whose home reeks from the absence of any attempts at housekeeping (1). And in all of this movement we observe his lack of social interest. He lives only for the greater glory of God, and guess who God is!

What are some of the influences to which the controller is especially receptive in his formative years? Among the family influences, controlling parents influence children to be controlling, either in imitation of or in reaction to the parents. Similarly the parents' exercise of control in response to the child's efforts to control them eventuates in power contests where the child wins or the parents regret that they won a Pyrrhic victory. The child trains himself as a consequence in those forms of behavior which will permit him to control the situation or to avoid the control of others—temper tantrums, dawdling, stubbornness, stomach aches before school, crying and sensitivity and other forms of what Dreikurs includes under Goal II and Goal IV behavior (10). Dependency, when seen in Adlerian movement terms, may be defined as putting others into one's service and thus can be legitimately included in this category. While some personality theorists view the controlling individual as emerging from the pressures centering about toilet training, it seems more probable that parents who exert such control in toilet training also endeavor to control the child in other ways. More parents apparently fight over eating, and over a longer period of time, than they do over toilet training.

Social and cultural influences external to the family also make their contribution. Reward and punishment form the vehicles for distinguishing between prescribed and proscribed behavior. Despite the ineffectiveness of these methods in controlling behavior (11), educators declare their bankruptcy by utilizing them because they know no better methods for influencing behavior. Reward and punishment remain effective only so long as an authoritarian structure in interpersonal relationships is agreed upon and maintained. Since teachers often find it difficult to control children, the emphasis shifts to self control, and then it is no longer the teacher's responsibility. If the pupil does not conform to the teacher's wishes, he is merely given a check in "self control" on his report card. The communications media assault the eye and ear with advice on how to control the difficult to control—eating, smoking, weight, figure, and birth.

And psychology contributes its bit. To the extent that certain psychological systems portray man as driven, as irrational, as irresponsible, these systems must create certain psychological constructs to combat or neutralize the "base instincts." Every id must have a countervailing ego to oppose it and as the patient who is unwilling to accept responsibility for himself reminds us, "Intellectually I accept the interpretation but emotionally I don't feel it." A counterpart may be found in some religious instruction where the potentially evil substructure of man, his passions, must be controlled. And here we have an opportunity to see perhaps most clearly how the controller who attempts to avoid his responsibility for himself creates the necessary conditions. He perceives life as a drama in which God and the Devil are locked in unending struggle for his soul—with neither ever winning.

FOOTNOTES

1. This excerpt from the Talmud Succah, p. 53a, is the translation of Rabbi Irving Rosenbaum of Chicago.
2. Personal communication.

REFERENCES

1. Adler, A., *The Case of Mrs. A.* Chicago, Alfred Adler Inst., 1969.
2. Adler, A., "Compulsion Neurosis" (1931), in Ansbacher, H. L. and Rowena, eds, *Superiority and Social Interest.* Evanston, Ill., Northwestern Univ. Press, 1964.

3. Adler, A., "The Death Problem in Neurosis" (1936), in Ansbacher, H. L. and Rowena, eds., *Superiority and Social Interest*. Evanston, Ill., Northwestern Univ. Press, 1964.

4. Adler, A., "The Fundamental Views of Individual Psychology." *Int. J. Indiv. Psychol.*, 1(1), (1935), pp. 5-8.

5. Adler, A., *The Individual Psychology of Alfred Adler*. New York, Basic Books, 1956, pp. 273-276.

6. Adler, A., *Problems of Neurosis*. New York, Harper Torchbooks, 1964.

7. Adler, A., "Sleeplessness" (1929), in Ansbacher, H. L. and Rowena, eds., *Superiority and Social Interest*. Evanston, Ill., Northwestern Univ. Press, 1964.

8. Adler, A., "Two Grade School Girls," in Ansbacher, H. L. and Rowena, eds., *Superiority and Social Interest*. Evanston, Ill., Northwestern Univ. Press, 1964.

9. Adler, A., "A Typology of Meeting Life Problems" (1935), in Ansbacher, H. L. and Rowena, eds., *Superiority and Social Interest*. Evanston, Ill., Northwestern Univ. Press, 1964.

10. Dreikurs, R., *The Challenge of Parenthood*. New York, Duell, Sloan and Pearce, 1948.

11. Dreikurs, R., "The Cultural Implications of Reward and Punishment." *Int. J. Soc. Psychiat.*, 4(1958), pp. 171-178.

12. Leifer, R., "Avoidance and Mastery: An Interactional View of Phobias." *J. Indiv. Psychol.*, 22(1966), pp. 80-93.

13. Mosak, H. H., "The Getting Type: A Parsimonious Social Interpretation of the Oral Character." *J. Indiv. Psychol.*, 15(1959), pp 193-198.

14. Mosak, H. H., "The Interrelatedness of the Neuroses Through Central Themes." *J. Indiv. Psychol.*, 24(1968), pp. 67-70.

NEUROTIC VERSUS NORMAL REACTION CATEGORIES

Erwin O. Krausz

NEUROTIC	*NORMAL* (MATURE)
Extremism (Vacillation between Extremes)	Common Sense
Perfectionism	Realism
Literalism	Experimentalism
Dogmatism	Emotional Adaptability
Emotionalism	Discrimination between Values
Present-ism	Deferment of Emotional Reactions:
Impatience	Persistence
Intolerance	Self-control
Domineeringness	Synchronization
Disproportionalism	Foresight

Insight Psychology Based on Above Evaluations

The reaction categories listed above as neurotic prevent maturation and facilitate neurosis. Normality is the unimpaired ability to mature. (There is no saturation in maturation.) Neurosis or a neurotic attitude is the impaired ability to mature. Neurosis is sclerosis (hardening) of the mind; it is what impairs the process of maturation.

Psychotherapy is, therefore, the abbreviated procedure of maturation.

Extremism: Black/white; all/nothing; genius/mediocrity, etc.

Common Sense: The psychological definition of common sense is the sense of what I have in common with others. These are the things that make us feel humble, not the things of which we are proud. The intellectual definition of common sense is the sense of what I *should* have in common with others—meaning reason or prudence. Since I do not live alone, I must practice more and more reason (or prudence). Otherwise, I will never grow up or mature. I must try to probe the exact meaning that the other person has in mind instead of having to translate it into my own meaning.

Perfectionism means that, at any time and in any place, things must be 100% or just so. You can always recognize a perfectionist by the repeated use of the words, "I should" or "I should not." Perfectionism also involves the desire for complete or total admiration, which can never be had and, at the same time, tremendous fear of total criticism and blame. Again, where there is perfectionism there is also extremism. The perfectionist like the extremist operates in superlatives. Both are actually uncritical because they do not differentiate between what is important and what is unimportant. For the perfectionist, everything is equally important. Little mistakes are just as upsetting to him as big mistakes. Therefore, he cannot develop self-confidence, and he will always be tense.

Realism is the equivalent, on the non-neurotic side, of perfectionism, although the extremist will be very prone to suspect the realist of being an opportunist and of having no ideals. By using common sense I will be able to determine what there is that requires my total and perfect effort and attention at all times, and, on the other hand, when I can be relaxed. Instead of trying to waste my time doing the impossible, I will try to use my time to accomplish the possible. Hating, for instance is a waste of time. The realist will know, by practicing common sense, when to tense up and when to relax. Relaxation is the ability to have an easy conscience about unfinished business. Eliminate the word "always" and "never," and say "sometimes." Eliminate the words "should" and "should not." If I feel "I should," think "why should I?"

Literalism means taking an idea or a word at its face value, and taking things (words, etc.) literally. The identification with words or ideas is included; taking words for facts. It leads to word addiction, which in turn leads to disillusionment and frustrations.

Experimentalism: The opposite of literalism, on the normal side. Before I believe, I wonder. When I wonder, I investigate or find out or experiment, to get the facts or the proof. Experimentalism makes for scientific procedure. The literalist will expect things to be the way he thinks they are, as does the perfectionist. The experimentalist, not needing a guarantee for success, enjoys blundering. It would be nice if men could be as creative as nature is. (I must understand why I am doing what I am doing.)

Dogmatism: No doubt, or beyond any doubt; absolute conviction. The dogmatist is likely to be convinced that only his *feelings* are real. This is a very naive understanding of the purposefulness of feeling, and feelings become a supreme authority or guidance. A typical characteristic phrase of the dogmatist is "I cannot." The negativistic aspect of a dogmatic attitude clearly indicates that dogmatism is a defensive proposition. It fences other people or opinions off, a person's own opinions thereby remaining unchallenged or unchanged. Anybody with this attitude cannot conceive that one can more or less choose various ways of doing something.

Emotional Adaptability: The opposite of dogmatism. The neurotic, in his immaturity, will believe only what he feels. It is unthinkable to him that his feelings serve a purpose, that feelings are determined and influenced by the purpose and purposefulness of the individual in his social interrelations. The mature person will understand that emotions and feelings are flexible, because he will understand them as subservient to a purpose, in short, as means to an end. Mature persons will be guided by common sense, realism, and experimentalism, and their emotions will be equally influenced by the inevitable adjustment to the dictates of common sense, realism, and experimentalism.

Emotionalism: For most people, only what they feel is real to them, and this is mostly only what hurts them. This is probably because they remember their punishments. Emotionalism, however, means that in one's emotional life one fluctuates from one extreme to the other (extremism), a tendency intensified by the success or failure extremes, experienced in perfectionism and exclusively believed in by the literalism tendency, and by dogmatism. These fluctuations make one rely mainly upon one's emotions, as children and neurotics are inclined to do. This is not only unreliable and untenable but will understandably falsify the values which would lend some semblance of stability to the individual who is groping for security. It will falsify what is important into something unimportant, what is practical into something which is impractical. It might easily lend reality to something which is unreal or imaginary.

Discrimination Between Values: The opposite, on the mature side, is a *sense and discrimination of values,* arrived at by common sense, realism, experimentalism, and emotional adaptability. The individual whose sense of values will put first things first, will tackle the hardest things first. He will be more or less satisfied with what he has and appreciate it.

Present-ism: This word, not found in dictionaries, was coined by President Hutchins of the University of Chicago, and, according to his definition, means the cult of immediacy. I means "I want what I want when I want it," chiefly pleasures and fun, and it means I want to get rid of and be relieved of all that is unpleasant or annoying to me. Present-ists are followers of the pleasure-pain principle. Bearing our preceding points in mind, it may be understandable that the discrimination of present-ists is poorly developed, that pain will be rejected by them as a big pain, while pleasures will be only regarded as satisfactory when they immediately reach the state of total and top pleasures.

Impatience is connected with an anger reaction, also means getting things, or getting things done at one's own time. It also bespeaks an unwillingness to adjust to other people's pace or time.

Intolerance is closely related to impatience. It actually means killing off something that is in one's way, physically or emotionally. It is also closely linked with anger due to possible frustration from obstacles and other limitations.

Domineeringness, bossiness, tyranny, despotism, arrogant imperiousness, etc., are not characteristics or properties with which we are born. They are potentialities trained and developed for the purpose of immediate satisfaction and the attainment of what one wants or doesn't want now. It goes without saying that domineeringness embraces impatience and intolerance with its anger and frustration reactions, and that it will result in uncontrollable, extreme, and frightening emotional explosions which are still not more significant than the temper tantrums of a child, although their consequences might be more destructive. Destruction usually follows in the wake of explosions, emotional and otherwise.

Deferment of Emotional Reactions: On the more mature, normal or less neurotic side, the opposite of present-ism is deferment of emotional reactions. Between an emotion and its manifestation, a fraction of a fraction of interpolation of delayed expression is possible. Practice can make such delaying into a habit.

Sustained efforts are the equivalent for impatience. Sustained efforts are not a guarantee for success. One only buys oneself a chance for success by such sustained efforts. But on the other hand, a lack or absence of such efforts will become almost a guarantee for failures. Let us remember here that no rule is without exceptions: impatience and peak efforts, even if not sustained, may result in success experiences too, but such experiences most likely will not be convincing, satisfactory, or lasting.

Self-control is the antithesis of intolerance. The exercise of this attitude is only possible when we connect the five mature, normal, or nonneurotic characteristics of common sense, realism, experimentalism, emotional adaptability, and the discrimination of values with the practice of the deferment of emotional reactions. It would seem to go without saying that we are arriving at the picture of a so-called mature individual.

Synchronization: It would be easy to name as the antidote for domineeringness, the idea of cooperation. But I should like a less preachy term, one less fraught with seemingly moral or ethical connotations. I suggest the use of the more contemporary term, synchronization. This term lays less stress on prestige and status, and is therefore preferable. In a practical way, its accent is more on time and implicit acceleration or retardation when necessary, and eliminates any connotation of leadership and followership.

Disproportionalism: This term means an unreasonable willingness to pay a price or even a penalty for what we get when we want to get it now—that is, without any attention to the importance of proper timing. Disproportion is another word for lack of balance, a concept often applied to the neurotic. The imbalance that it describes is, however, definitely the imbalance of children with whom all these characteristics are legitimate. They, in themselves, are reason enough for immaturity but when this impairment continues into puberty, adolescence, and beyond that, we talk about the neurotic retention of factors which interfere with a more or less normal development towards maturation.

Maturation (Foresight): Maturation is a non-ending process. There is no saturation in maturation. Expecting complete maturation, instead of the continuing dynamism of maturing, would mean stagnation. There is a lot to be said about the various factors that could lead to this inner stagnation or sclerosis of the mind that is called a neurosis, but their enumeration and description belongs in a textbook of psychology or psycho-pathology and not in the framework of what is intended here—a guidance for an evaluational differentiation based on concepts strictly derived from psychologically systematized experiences.

Foresight: The contrast to disproportionalism. Foresight is a willed understanding of the effect of one's actions—physical, mental, or emotional—on oneself and one's future and on others and their future. Foresight involves goal setting and the goal. Flexibility, sense and discrimination of values, deferring emotional reactions, sustained efforts, self-control and synchronization are all determined, governed and increased by foresight. Together they can bring about the maintenance and increase of security at which one aims and/or, what matters so much more, the decrease of the fear of insecurity.

Maturity for some people may have the connotation of aging, of growing older. Quite the opposite, however, is true. The neurotic, with the characteristics of childhood not fully outgrown, tends to be self-centered and will find it hard to be a participating fellow-being. On the other hand, the mature or more or less normal individual will be confident and optimistic when pursuing extra-personal aims and contacts. His field of interests will be widened by his growing understanding. With Goethe he will learn, "He only is afraid of men who does not know them, and therefore when he avoids them will be bound to misunderstand them." While the neurotic with his egocentricity will not permit any criticism to shake the opinions in which he indulges, and therefore can always believe that he is right, the mature individual will welcome doubt and criticism as a preventative for stagnating smugness. This will help him to remain flexible and, since flexibility and awareness of the wealth of possible experiences is the most valuable property of youth, one can paradoxically say that the reward for maturing is continued and prolonged youthfulness.

REFERENCES

1. Krausz, E. O., "The Commonest Neurosis," in Adler, K. A. and Deutsch, Danica, eds., *Essays in Individual Psychology,* New York, Grove Press, 1959, pp. 108-118.

THE YOUNG HOOLIGAN

James Hemming

The young hooligan is not a new phenonemon. "They assaulted un-protected women; they drove their swords through the sides of sedan-chairs; they pulled men from coaches and slit their noses with razors, stabbed them with pen-knives, ripped the coaches to pieces, and, in some cases, killed." Thus writes Thomas Burke (7) in *The Streets of London,* telling about the behavior of wild young men in the eighteenth century. What makes young males—for it is predominantly young males—behave like this, destroying, it would seem, for the fun of it?

"You feel angry and want to smash something; then, when you start, you can't stop." Here we have a modern young hooligan talking about his experiences while being interviewed on television. Such a statement brings with it an implication both of compulsion and of a misdirection of human energy—a searching wildly and blindly to satisfy some need of personality that is being denied. What is this need?

It is today increasingly important that we should understand the na-ture of the young hooligan's unspoken, largely unconscious, need so that we may develop an effective social strategy against hooliganism. This we have to do as quickly as possible, because hooliganism is on the in-crease in technological societies. Furthermore, the power of the hooli-gan increases with the power made available by society. Modern hooli-gans can do immense damage as wreckers and killers—with firearms, with matches, with explosives, with cars. Hooliganism is today more than a social irritant; it is a problem that threatens to become over-whelming. This is the social situation. There is also the human need. The young hooligan is a lost, self-destroying personality who needs help.

It is the aim of this paper to suggest that an application of the in-sights of Alfred Adler to the problem of hooliganism would help us to attain better strategies than those commonly in use at present.

The Definition of Hooliganism

For a start we have to elucidate what we mean by hooliganism. Hooliganism could be described as a distortion of the natural energy of young males. Healthy young males are vigorous, competitive, status-hungry and need opportunities to let fly. Today we probably expect them to be too tame in their general behavior and should not confuse high spirits with hooliganism. Again, the Establishment in any country is always eager to condemn with the title of hooliganism any show of resistance to authority, or demonstration of resentment against social injustice. But resistance and demonstration can be social and courageous. Such action has to be clearly differentiated from hooliganism proper which is a random display of unnecessary violence. The battles in the streets of Paris, in May and June 1968, are not comparable with smashing a dance hall to pieces, beating up the member of a rival gang, or slashing the seats on a coach. The violence of social conflict is an issue warranting careful study, but it is not our concern here. Holliganism is *pointless* destructive violence.

The situation is complicated because hooligans are readily attracted by any demonstrations going on near at hand, and may be responsible for ugly incidents in social protests that would otherwise be free from them. Nevertheless, the type of person we are here concerned with exists quite independently of social protest. He subjectively needs to be violent. He admires violence. We have to ask why. And we have to search for effective methods of control.

Some Current Approaches

Social scientists, when faced with the behavior of anti-social young males, show a tendency to be lured into ineffective side-tracks. One is to enumerate all research that has been carried out on the young hooligan. This approach often concludes with the assumption that hooliganism is a mysterious phenomenon due to a complex of causes that will have to be sifted and elaborated for a long time before we can adopt any hopeful prophylactic strategy. *But we cannot wait for theoretical perfection before acting.*

Another not very useful approach is to write off men as violent by nature, in which case, presumably, the hooligans are the fully-released personalities and the rest of us are repressed into social conformity. Watching hooliganism break out in a football crowd hardly confirms that impression. The shouting, mauling mass behave more like automatons than like "full" human beings.

Yet another approach is to regard hooliganism as an act of resentment against a society which denies an individual the status he yearns for. This approach falls short in that it fails to explain why, in dynamic terms, the denial of status is such a painful experience.

Frustration theory suffers from the same weakness. It is true that violence is a common reaction to frustration. But frustration is a part of any life, a component of all experience. Why, then, does it unleash in some a wild explosive attack while in others it is accepted and lived through? Is it primarily because some have more self-control than others? That answer begs the question. Is it not, rather, because some kinds of frustration are unendurable to a *particular* emerging self? "Destructiveness," wrote Erich Fromm, "is the outcome of unlived life" (13).

We are in need today of a more comprehensive theory of hooliganism in young males to replace the piecemeal and conflicting theories at present in the field. Individual Psychology can provide that theory. Whatever remains to be discovered, and much does, the insights of Alfred Adler into antisocial behavior point the way for an effective prophylactic strategy. Let us then look, in briefest outline, at what Adler has to offer.

The Adlerian Approach

Adler described the basic striving of individuals as movement towards being. Every child, however genetically endowed, has to start from scratch, so movement towards being, or "becoming" (4)[1] is, to quote Adler, "from below to above" (6). It is a striving forward from a minus to a plus position, from inferiority to superiority, from helplessness in the life situation to dominance of the life situation—control. This is the unavoidable struggle of all individuals, whether they are potential geniuses or destined to a modest existence as very ordinary people.

In order to cope with this situation, every child unconsciously adopts a style of life—a set of evaluations, constructs, attitudes, and responses —which experience suggests to him is the effective strategy for successful living. The style of life may be a sound strategy which carries "becoming" and social involvement along together, or it may be an unsound strategy leading to posturing and pretenses which give a temporary feeling of significance without the reality of achievement and relationships. Every individual lives either by the assurance of genuine achievement and relationships, or by some compensatory masquerade, because no one can bear a sense of insignificance and worthlessness. The psychobiological movement is "from minus to plus"; to live in any other dynamic is totally thwarting. This is the reason why some people prefer to die rather than lose face.

If one cannot win a sense of self-esteem on "the useful side of life," there are only two major alternatives. Either one has to sink into the soft allure of fantasy, in order to achieve heroic stature in the private world of imagination, or one has to embark upon some compensatory tactics on the ostentatious, useless, side of life. All people at times use fantasy to bolster a damaged courage or self-esteem, and all people enjoy showing off their abilities. The crucial issue is not whether fictions and ostentations play a part in life but whether the individual, by and large, depends on real striving, contribution and relationships as the basis for his self-esteem, or depends, instead, on fantasy or egocentric, esteem-snatching techniques for keeping his courage up.

We need mention for our purposes here only one further aspect of Adler's system. Adler believed that individual emergence is inextricably bound up with social relatedness and vision. To strive for a personal "plus" without regard to others is not to enhance but to obstruct personal fulfilment, if only because it leads to psychic isolation. We grow into the best we may be by positive, cooperative interaction with others within a context of feeling "involved in mankind." Adler called this relationship between the individual and the whole human struggle "social interest" (1). He regarded it as the foundation of mental health.

It is the contention of this paper that the young hooligan, typically, is trapped in a cul-de-sac in his personal development. He has lost hope of attaining significance from the use of his own capacities. He lacks relationship to his society, and any actualization of his need and ability to contribute. His hooligan behavior is a compulsive attempt to fill the vacuum in his experience. Hence, the correct antidote to hooliganism is to prevent young people being trapped in this way, whenever this can be achieved. When it cannot, we should mount a powerful rescue operation in order to restore the shattered self-esteem of these young people, and help them to modify their erroneous life-styles so that they may attain to formative relationships—the means to continued "becoming" —with their fellows and with society.

We may derive from Adlerian theory that resentment, tension and a powerful motivation to compensate for inferiority, sometimes violently, will build up in any group of individuals subjected to a continuously undervalued status within society. True to expectations, we find that this is precisely what does happen in groups marked down socially, whether because they are not yet adult, because they are poor, because they are black, or for any other reason. Such a group will feel both alienated from the society which denies it opportunities for successful striving, and also antagonistic towards the negating social system. The members of such a group will each be under a compulsion to seek out some way of mitigating the imposed inferiority. Some, if courageous personalities, will strive through positive group action; others, lacking courage and relationship, will fall back on more egocentric compensations.

What is the evidence for this? As Professor C. H. Waddington once said, there is no need to prove it is raining if we are out in a storm. Once we accept that each personal history is a story of a unique striving towards self-actualization, and an increasing number of psychologists and psychiatrists find such a concept necessary to explain human behavior, then the negating forces in our society, and the consequent incentives to compensatory behavior, are obvious. Moreover, these influences are exacerbated by the hierarchical stratification of society itself. Whereas most technological societies open their doors to ability in such a way that each generation of children has some chance of sorting itself out in terms of personal capacity, it is also true that a fairly rigid stratification of ability and potential has established itself for most children within ten or twelve years of their birth. This is so because, by then, expectations about the children have been developed within the educational system. Teachers' expectations, we now know, tend to rub off onto the children who often behave as the adults around them expect them to behave (23). In addition, expectations in teachers' minds, once they are established, are often highly resistant to modification. Thus a child tends to get stuck with his reputation in a self-reinforcing cycle that only very good luck or very great effort can break.

Other things being equal, children who start from a well-established position in society have the bonus of a much more resilient springboard into life than those who are born into socially depressed circumstances. The latter often feel themselves to be written off as failures in terms of the values of the society that has fathered them and will be their environment for life. They feel doomed to permanent personal inferiority. Since no human being can tolerate such a crushing insignificance, young people, so rejected, either compensate by indifference to society, or else fight back in antisocial ostentation of one kind or another. So long as personal inferiority of this kind is created and reinforced by the society surrounding young people, including all too frequently the school community itself, so will the hooligan attitude be constantly regenerated in a proportion of young peope who unconsciously "choose" this means of compensation for an unendurable sense of inadequacy.

To be specific, let us consider the case of a boy—a boy from a poor home, and also a school failure—who was first in trouble with the police for trespassing in order to smash the windows of an empty house and, later, for being a member of a quartet of young toughs that seriously beat up a boy who, so far as one can make out, had done them no harm whatever, except that, in dress and bearing, he represented success in the society that had rejected them. Their unfortunate victim, it seemed, just happened to be at hand when the boy and his friends were in the mood for an ostentatious outburst that would both give a lift to their self-esteem and serve to revenge themselves on the society that failed them. The boy who carried out this outrage with his "supporters"—the right term, for these lads depend on one another to sustain the remnants of their courage and self-esteem—turned out to be a great admirer of everybody and everything that was tough. He was one of these low-attainers with whom the police and probation officers are very familiar wherever hooliganism is a problem, pseudo-toughs who are, at bottom, pathetically broken-down personalities—"formless," to use the descriptive term of a sixteen-year-old at a recent confrontation seminar between adults and young people.

It is not difficult to hypothesize the process that confirms such a boy in his useless, dependent, discouraged, ostentatious, violent style of life. Within a few years of starting school, he picks up, or has confirmed, the idea that he falls short of what is valued and admired. What the school would like him to succeed at defeats him; what he has to offer from his modest personal equipment is not appreciated. He is forced into a defensive position either as a loner, or, as in the case in question, as a member of a group of other low-attainers formed in order to salvage some vestiges of prestige over against a community that seems designed to rob them of any rewarding sense of significance. Self-confidence is constantly eroded rather than enhanced by his school experience until, one day, the boy finds he has something that will make people sit up and notice—his muscles. By violence he can gain a position of far greater significance than was available to him from any of the socially acceptable modes of self-expression previously offered. Thereupon violence grips and excites him; he worships the tough and the ruthless. What else, of equivalent moment, is available to him as a basis for his self-esteem? For years his daily experiences have been reinforcing a sense of inescapable inadequacy until he makes the discovery that he can after all make his mark—through violence. *Hooliganism, so interpreted, is primarily the explosive outcome of prestige hunger.*

But, it may be argued, if this is a correct diagnosis, why do not *all* status-denied boys become hooligans? This question, although frequently asked in social science circles, is illogical. It is really asking, "Why are not all human beings alike and why do they not all respond in the same way to similar circumstances?" The question neglects the uniqueness of each individual, the uniqueness of every individual's personal experience, the uniqueness of his evaluation of himself and others and, therefore, of the strategy he adopts to deal with life. A boy of poor ability from a bad home, who, nevertheless, has warm support from an older sister and encouragement at school for what he can do, is in a very different situation from a boy of poor ability, from a bad home, who has no supplementary support and encouragement.

What can be helpful here is the insistence of Individual Psychology that the secret of behavior lies in the uniqueness of each personal life. If a child shows evidence of an antisocial style of life we have to ask, *for this particular child,* "What are the sources of this child's discouragement?" "What is the compensation to which he is turning to bolster his self-esteem?" "How can we restore his courage in himself and win him over to a positive orientation to life?" The answers to these questions mark the lines along which a solution to a young hooligan's problems —and, through his, society's also—are to be found.

The Hooligan Syndrome

Not all hooligans are dull. Nevertheless, low attainment, social alienation and hooligan behavior are so frequently found together that we have to regard this syndrome very carefully if the ranks of young hooligans are not to be constantly recruited from its regeneration. Indeed, if this source of recruitment alone could be stemmed, the whole position concerning hooliganism and delinquency could be transformed.

The simplicity of the social truth is sometimes blurred by references to delinquent sub-cultures in which violence and opposition to the law are standard behavior patterns. Hooliganism is then presented as normal for the young people of such sub-cultures. This is true enough, but it merely projects the real problem one stage further back. A sub-culture is simply *another kind of status system* which the rejected of a society build up, *and need to build up,* in order to provide themselves with a sense of value. Status is built-in prestige. Everybody wants to be somebody. A society that makes a nobody of you has to be replaced either by a loner's private world or by a sub-culture system within which striving for prestige *is* a possibility. A sub-culture is simply a system of social relationships and attitudes in which the yardsticks of recognition, prestige, and human dignity are different from those of the cultural mainstream. In this regard it is important to notice that all youth is forced to react as an inferior subculture, to the extent that it is treated as such by the adults in the society.

At this point it is appropriate to take a brief look at the situation of girls. As has already been said, hooliganism is mainly a masculine phenomenon. Although cases of violent young women are being reported more frequently than formerly, these are still comparatively rare. The reason is not only that young females seem to be naturally less violent than young males, but also that the young woman has an alternative source of recognition and prestige. Whereas the low-attainer among young males discovers physical strength during adolescence, and may use it to shore up a failing self-esteem, the girl of poor attainment discovers sex and may use it to a similar end. Hence, the typical delinquency of girls is sexual delinquency.

An appalling error of our society is that we have well-developed systems of rejection and inferiority built into our educational and economic systems. This makes hooliganism and delinquency endemic in our kind of society. The more frantic the efforts to alleviate them, the more they grow, because those involved in prophylaxis are loath to accept the basic simplicity of their problem, that man is a striving, status-seeking creature and, if you make nonsense of his striving and deny him adequate significance as a person in society, you will build up a mounting pressure of anti-social status-seeking.

This is all so obvious that it is incredible how little attention, apart from some lip-service, is paid to the essential social dynamics of hooliganism and delinquency. Indeed, we must at this stage attempt a guess at why the social scientists and administrators are so resistant to the obvious. Presumably it arises from two sources. One is the confusion sown by the long dominance of the Freudian view of human motivation. This made too much of the sex drive in man, and too little of the status drive, while almost entirely ignoring the drive to self-actualization which, through the inferiority-superiority dynamic explained by Adler, is intimately associated with the attainment of a social status sufficient to satisfy the individual in question.

The other resistance to looking an esteem-loaded dynamic squarely in the face arises, we may infer, from the fact that all those in authority over the young are themselves entangled in status striving, and are disturbed by seeing their own anxieties reflected in the behavior of the young hooligans. Rob a teacher or a judge of a bit of status he feels he is entitled to and resentment, if not anger, quickly mounts. Until we admit this in ourselves and one another, we shall never understand the antisocial fury of the hooligan, who, often enough, is so bereft of status that he hasn't any capital of confidence to build on. He is bankrupt for prestige, drowning in a sea of inferiority feelings. A teenager who knifed and killed another youth in the streets of London was asked by the judge why he acted as he did. The reply was, "He turned round and looked at me when we was in the pictures." If one is destitute of any kind of self-etseem, then the smallest insult can become an unendurable outrage.

Strategies for Eradicating Hooliganism

What of the home? Inadequate family care and relationships can readily cripple a child's self-esteem, and create a false life style which may lead to destructive compensatory behavior later on. We have to help our defeated homes all we can, improve the standards of housing and nutrition and child care all we can. Such things are humanly desirable and will pay good social dividends, *but only so long as we take self-development, status and significance fully into account in the overall life that we provide for our children.* Important as the home is, it has become too much of a scapegoat for the failure of our society to civilize its members.

It is notable that the establishment of the welfare state in Britain has *not* reduced youthful hooliganism; rather the reverse. And for an obvious reason. Well-fed young people who are denied adequate self-esteem, social significance and status are more likely to lash out than half-starved ones. If we are to get anywhere with the problem of the young hooligan, we have to pay an equal attention, at home *and* at school, to providing a *total* environment in which the particular child's self-confidence and self-esteem are continuously sustained by adequate love, encouragement, challenge and stimulation. The *worse* the home in these terms, the *better* the school needs to be. When society heaps inadequate schools on top of the experience of inadequate homes, hooliganism and delinquency become inevitable. Each generation regenerates the problem. Indeed it does rather more than that because rejected and despairing people are liable to have large families, since they have very little outlet for prestige except through procreation. Recently, in an English court, an exasperated magistrate, faced once again by the same dishonest, unreliable, work-shy individual, asked, "Have you done *anything* of which you can feel proud?" The man replied, "I have seven children."

The problem of overcrowding accentuates the need for an intensive positive strategy towards hooliganism. A wealth of evidence has shown that social controls weaken when a species becomes overcrowded. Primates that live equably with one another in open terrain may become nervy and vicious when overcrowded in captivity. An individual needs space enough for his uniqueness to establish itself. Identity cannot emerge in a mass. Once again it is a situation of piling Ossa on Pelion. Combine low attainment, poor schools, and overcrowding and you reach a certain recipe for hooliganism and its close relatives, delinquency and crime.

A glance at societies in rapid transitions, as in Africa, illustrates where we are failing in our society to sustain young males in their personal development. From the Adlerian viewpoint, unspoiled village life among many tribes of Africa is ideally suited to build, at the same time, self-esteem, status and social interest. Each age-group in rural African society has its well defined responsibilities, and also a range of age-group activities that permit individuals at every stage of growth to sort out, naturally and gradually, their capacities vis-à-vis one another. Nobody is left out; everybody has a place, a part, a value. Often the less fortunate are given special consideration. For example, among the Kikuyu of East Africa, it is considered very bad manners for the pretty girls and handsome boys to monopolize one another during the pre-marital years. The more favored are expected sometimes to share their special graces with the less favored, so that everybody gets a look in (18).

At some time during the teens, or early twenties, comes initiation. This provides both comprehensive instruction in what responsible adulthood entails, and the assurance of recognition and status through tests of one kind or another which, once surmounted—and the pass rate approaches 100%—accord the full prestige of adulthood. Thus, every member of the tribe, regardless of a wide range of individual capacity, feels valued and accepted as an adult tribesman or tribeswoman.

The point to be noted is that in an African village anti-social behavior of any kind is very rare. However, once the prestige pattern is broken by migration to the towns, the whole gamut of anti-social behavior quickly appears. Professor Philip Mayer (20) of Durham University, England, and his wife, have recently completed a fascinating comparison of sex and violence among adolescents in the Xhosa village communities of South Africa and among the urbanized Xhosa. In the village communities sex and violence are contained and *used* to develop responsibility and social feeling among the young people; in the urbanized groups, both tend to run riot. A potent factor in this is that, in the urban setting, individuals are liable to lose their sense of value *in relationships with others* and seek alternative egocentric or gang-centered self-esteem. The destructive behavior of a hooligan minority of young Africans, to be observed in some African townships, is a replication of what happens among similar groups in London, New York or Glasgow, and for the same reasons—low status, lost individual value, a paucity or absence of social understanding and involvement.

Comparisons of school with school in western society, now beginning to be done effectively, bring out the same point. Two schools of similar type, in similar areas, may have very different records of hooliganism and delinquency. "Last year delinquency" is a well-known phenomenon in England among the group of boys who leave at fifteen[2]. Very frequently, the difficult boys, as we would expect, are the low-attainers One school on the fringe of London had a particularly good record in holding the last-year boys. The headmaster put this down to two innovations. For one, every boy was asked to suggest what he felt would be of most value for him to study during his last year at school. This gave the boy the dignity of choice and the relationship of self-involvement. Secondly, every senior boy had the option of becoming a "citizen of the school," which meant that he accepted the responsibility for his own behavior instead of being bound by the school rules—*a source of status and self-esteem available to every senior boy.*

The proposition I wish to reinforce by these references is that there are dynamic influences operating towards generating compensatory violence in the young men of our kind of society, and that we shall make inroads on the problem of the young hooligan only when we establish our prophylactic strategy in terms of them. We are concerned to provide for all children an overall experience, regarding home and school as complementary influences, which will secure for every boy the relationships, source of personal value, and achievements that will rescue him from the need to find his significance by antisocial ostentation and will, rather, draw him into an ever-more-involved participation in the life of his community and his society, not as a conformist only, although social life always involves an area of conformity, but as a self-confident, self-actualizing, creative personality.

It should be noted that, in order to achieve this outcome, several components of a formative syndrome must be present together during the years of growth. They may be summarized as follows:
1. Relationships of love and encouragement that reach out towards

the child and draw him into a happy, secure association with others. Every school should offer such relationships to all its members but, when the home is deficient in this regard, the school *must* be especially warm, especially caring, especially encouraging, if the child is ultimately to come out on "the useful side of life."

2. The experience of the child in so far as we can control it, and we can control much of school experience, should consistently build up the self-esteem and self-confidence of the child, through the provision of incentives and opportunities to succeed in ways that will bring satisfaction to the child.

3. The school must represent a set of values in which all can share on equal terms as human beings, *not* a set of values which automatically stratifies the children into the "cans" and the "can'ts." The staff need to work out and agree together what these values are. Three values to start with are cooperation, contribution, and quality of work *at the level of ability.* Human beings are naturally cooperative, love to contribute in a way that is appreciated, and are far happier doing their best than being slipshod. If these behaviors do not flower naturally in a school, there is something wrong with the aims, or incentives, or social structure of the school.

4. The satisfaction/frustration ratio should be examined for every child who is showing signs of apathy or withdrawal or revolt. The crucial formula is:

$$\frac{\text{Satisfaction}}{\text{Frustration}} = \text{Involvement}$$

For any human being an experience of any kind that brings consistently low satisfaction and consistently high frustration will soon be rejected as "not for me." Every psychologist is familiar with cases of truants, anti-social nuisances, and potential drop-outs for whom the school is offering no incentive likely to involve them in its life.

5. Every school needs to establish within its own community not only a counsellor or psychologist, or both, but a network of care which includes every member of the staff, so that social isolation, destructive behavior, and other signs of personal failure and stress are quickly spotted and given help. If we want young people to move towards *our* society, we must demonstrate beyond all doubt in our schools that we are quick to understand and move towards *their* difficulties in their struggles to "find" themselves and grow up.

6. Social concern for the wider community requires an evocative content of knowledge and understanding about society, human striving, and the modern world. Social studies are still too often limited to information whereas the development of "social interest" requires that the feelings and imagination of the pupil shall also be reached. Too many children are today leaving school feeling lost, and lacking

any sense of human dignity through a consciousness of involvement, as people, in the struggles of mankind.

Other headings could be added, but if these six components of a personally formative school experience are present, then we have created the basic conditions for growth towards personal and social maturity.

Contemporary man can produce the skill and the money to land on the moon; it is certainly not beyond his powers to remodel the environment of children in order to replace a high risk of desocialization with a good chance of wholeness in personal development and social relatedness. *Enough* of the relevant factors *are* known to make this possible. And the cost? The costs of containing the consequence of alienation and truncated personal development are already astronomical—the size of the police force, the costs of endless court cases, the prisons, the approved schools, the borstals, the mental hospitals. In the end, an assiduously applied prophylactic strategy would be cheaper than the largely wasted costs of attempted cure. Basically, hooliganism is as preventable as rickets; it is a matter of providing the nourishment a growing personality needs.

FOOTNOTES

not a 'being' but a 'becoming'." (*The Problem Child*. New York: Capricorn Books.)
2. The age of leaving school in England has now been raised to sixteen.

REFERENCES

1. Achebe, C., *Things Fall Apart*. London, Heinemann, 1958.
2. Adler A., *Social Interest: A Challenge to Mankind*. London, Faber & Faber, 1938.
3. Adler A., *What Life Should Mean to You*. London, Allen & Unwin, 1932.
4. Allport, *Becoming*. New Haven, Conn., Yale Univ. Press, 1955.
5. Ansbacher, H. L. and Rowena, eds., *The Individual Psychology of Alfred Adler*. London, Allen & Unwin, 1958.
6. Ansbacher, H. L. and Rowena, eds., *Superiority and Social Interest*. London, Routledge, & Kegan Paul, 1965.
7. Burke, T., *The Streets of London*. London, Batsford, 1940.
8. Cowie, J., Cowie, V., and Slater, E., *Delinquency in Girls*. London, Heinemann, 1968.
9. De Vore, I., ed., *Primate Behavior*. New York, Holt, Rinehart & Winston, 1965.
10. Douglas, J. W. D., *The Home and the School*. London, MacGibbon & Kee, 1964.
11. Dreikurs, R., *The Challenge of Parenthood*. New York, Duell, Sloan & Pearce, 1948.
12. Durkheim, E., *Suicide*. London, Routledge & Kegan Paul, 1952.

13. Fromm, E., *Man for Himself.* London, Routledge & Kegan Paul, 1949.
14. Gottlieb, D. and Reeves, J., *Adolescent Behaviour in Urban Areas.* London, Collier-Macmillan, 1963.
15. Hargreaves, D., *Social Relations in a Secondary School.* London, Routledge & Kegan Paul, 1967.
16. Hemming, J. *Individual Morality.* London, Nelson, 1969.
17. Kelly, G. A., *The Psychology of Personal Constructs.* New York, Norton, 1955.
18. Kenyatta, J., *Facing Mount Kenya.* London, Secken & Warburg, 1938.
19. Lorenz, K., *On Aggression.* London, Methuen, 1966.
20. Mayer, P., *A.S.A. Monograph No. 8. Socialization: The Approach from Social Anthropology.* London, Tavistock Publications, 1970.
21. Morse, Mary, *The Unattached.* London, Penquin, 1965.
22. Rogers, C. R., *On Becoming a Person.* London, Constable, 1961.
23. Rosenthal, R., "Self-Fulfilling Prophecy." *Psychol. Today,* 2(4), (1968), pp. 44-51.
24. Storr, A., *Human Aggression.* London, Penguin, 1968.
25. Wilmott, P., *Adolescent Boys in East London.* London, Routledge & Kegan Paul, 1966.
26. Yablonsky, L., *The Violent Gang.* New York, Macmillan, 1962.

THE PSYCHOLOGY OF ADDICTION

Donald N. Lombardi

Drug addiction has become a major national health and social problem. A unitary concept of motivation can be used to explain the reasons for drug use of one kind or another. This follows the traditions of Adler's striving for superiority, White's fundamental urge toward competence, Allport's becoming, Maslow's self-actualization, Roger's drive for growth, and Combs and Snygg's need for adequacy. The author views the unitary concept of motivation in terms of adequacy and security. All varieties of and approaches to motivation are seen as reducible to this basic need; it is the common denominator factor of diverse motivational terms.

A unitary concept of psychopathology parallels the motivational aspect as it pertains to drug addiction. It implies a unified concept of mental disorders in which the various psychopathologies are seen as more alike than different—all efforts to find adequacy and security. The unitary concept of psychopathology follows the general tradition of Adler, Rogers, Menninger, Angyal, Szasz and Glasser.

An Arabic tale helps make the point that all drug users want to go to the same place, but have different ways of getting there. "The alcoholic, the opium addict and the user of hashish arrived at the city after nightfall when the gates had been closed. The alcoholic shouted, 'Let us bang on the gates until someone is aroused.' The opium addict murmured, 'Perhaps we should all lie down and sleep quietly until morning.' The hashish user whispered his alternate suggestion, 'Let us slip through the keyhole.'"

A great variety of narcotics and other drugs are available to the drug user. They include heroin, codeine, cocaine, barbiturates, amphetamines, tranquilizers, marijuana and other hallucinogenic drugs such as glue and LSD. Some of the drugs are stimulants ("uppers") and others depressants ("downers") to the central nervous system. Whether the drug makes the drug user go fast or go slow, or whether both are used at the same time as some persons do, the net result or effect is the same.

71

There is a change of body chemistry, an alteration of consciousness and self-concept, so that he feels less anxious and more secure and adequate.

While alcoholism is principally a problem for the older person, drug addiction frequently involves younger persons. Drug addiction is one of the ways in which juveniles can strive for maturity and masculinity (8). From a developmental point of view, Winick (11) offers the "maturing out process" to account for the declining numbers of drug addicts with age. During the adolescent period, personal, social, vocational, and sexual adjustments are of great concern to the growing youngster. But with passing years these concerns lose their sense of urgency and partial, although unsatisfactory adjustments are made to them.

In an effort to study the life style of the drug addict, the early memories of addicts and matched control subjects were examined (6). A comprehensive analysis of the results revealed the addict as a leaning-dependent type who lacks direction and goals in life. His social interest is undeveloped and he finds the world a hostile and dangerous place. The addict is further described as finding it "difficult to compete and excel in life. It is hard for him to exist. He is impulsive and is racked with anxieties and tensions" (9, p. 28). The hallmark characteristics of his personality are identified as immaturity and childishness. This is one of the reasons why the therapy and rehabilitation of the drug addict have proved so difficult. If one's basic personality is immature and childish, sometimes even infantile, how can one be changed into an adult overnight? A way to speed up the maturation process has not yet been found. Little difficulty is experienced in working with the addict in breaking physical dependence or detoxification. This is relatively easy. The big problem is his psychological dependence, his frame of mind which requires a chemical in the form of a pill, capsule, bottle, or needle for his everyday adjustments. The most successful efforts in treating the addictive personality have followed the traditions of Alcoholics Anonymous, Daytop, and reality therapy.

The Ansbachers report that the addict is a person confronted with a problem which seems insoluble. A veiled or disguised attack on others is often present. Very frequently the beginning of addiction shows as an acute feeling of inferiority marked by shyness, a liking for isolation, oversensitivity, impatience, irritability, and by neurotic symptoms like anxiety, depression and sexual insufficiency. The craving or addiction may addict, Laskowitz (4) says that frequently the addict has feelings of omnipotence. Though the addict fully acknowledges that no one can take drugs without becoming an addict, he feels confident that he is different. He often boasts unembarrassedly of his ability to get away with criminal activity. Laskowitz further believes that the drug elevates the threshold for perception of threatening stimuli and thereby safeguards against anticipatory feelings of inadequacy. He characterizes the addict as experiencing inadequacy in meeting the external demands of the life tasks, a feeling which leads to the reinforcement and intensification of feelings of inadequacy. The addict lacks courage and desires to be shielded from dangers; he interprets "growing up" as meaning freedom from control. Laskowitz further sees the addict as impulsive, unable to defer gratification and keeping at a distance socially. He is pampered and wants to be pampered.

One summarizing statement about the addict is that he is not prepared to live life as an adult in a socially responsible way. This lack of preparation for adult living can result from being either overprotected or neglected and rejected. This may be illustrated by an analogy. Two mothers are trying to teach their sons how to swim. The first mother brings her son to the pool daily. She is always in the water with him and constantly holding and assisting him. He never practices swimming without assistance from her, and thus never has a chance to really acquire the skill or to correct mistakes. The second mother instructs her son verbally, tells him to watch others swimming, but never allows him to go into the water. Both of these persons will have difficulty in learning to swim, but for very different reasons. The same is true with regard to preparation for life and the use of drugs to solve this problem.

Gilbert and Lombardi (3) compared the personality characteristics of 45 young male narcotic addicts and 45 non-addicted males of similar socio-economic level. Although some maladjustment exists in both groups, the results suggested deep-seated and widespread pathology among the addicts. Outstanding were the addicts' psychopathic traits, their depressions, tensions, insecurity, and feelings of inadequacy, and their difficulties in forming warm and lasting interpersonal relationships. Most addicts seem to be suffering from a basic character disorder although many also have associated psychoneurotic or psychotic traits. The authors also found that the addicts differed significantly from the controls in social desirability, that is to say, the addicts were more willing to admit to socially undesirable traits within themselves.

Lombardi and Di Peri (7) have noted a striking analogy between a person's relationship to heroin and other narcotic drugs on the one hand, and a person's relationship to God and religion on the other. For example, God is the center of one's life for the truly religious person, and for the drug addict narcotics are the center of his life. Another similarity is a feeling of belonging. "In both religious practice and drug use there is, by virtue of one's membership and participation, a sense of security and adequacy." Additional similarities are noted and the therapeutic implication considered by the authors. Lombardi (5) also shows how the special language of the addict can be interpreted to better understand the personality of the addict and the psychology of drug use. For example, "the favorite descriptive term for one under the influence of drugs (and alcohol) is being *high*. The apparent implication is that one is low and needs a lift." Another illustration is that among "his drug peers the addict is known as a *junky*. This is because he uses *junk*, the name for heroin and other drugs. Junk is also referred to as *stuff*, *crap*, and *garbage*. The basic idea here is that the drug addict or junky is no good because he uses junk and crap. He is a *dope* addict who uses dope to stupefy himself. Thus one begins to see the addict as a person who has a very poor self concept and image and equally low self esteem. This picture is further reinforced by the terms *fix* and *spike*. The former term refers to an injection of heroin or a dose of dugs. The latter term, 'spike,' describes the hypodermic needle or 'works' required for the injection. Now the implication is of a person who is in such a bad state of repair that he needs to be fixed. A spike, like a nail, must be used to hold the pieces together." The picture that emerges from such an analysis is quite compatible with the professional consensus of him as a deviant person. Lombardi suggests that knowing the vernacular of a particular nosological group, which is really a form of expressive behavior, can greatly help in understanding the symptomatology, dynamics, and etiology of any type of psychopathology.

REFERENCES

1. Ansbacher, H. L. and Rowena, eds., *The Individual Psychology of Alfred Adler*. New York, Harper Torchbooks, 1956.
2. Caboir, N., Kutzberg, R. and Lipton, D., "The Development and Validation of a Heroin Addiction Scale with the MMPI." *Int. J. Addic.* 2(1967), pp. 129-137.
3. Gilbert, Jeanne and Lombardi, D. N., "Personality Characteristics of Young Male Narcotic Addicts." *J. Consul. Psych.* 31(5), (1967), pp. 536-538.
4. Laskowitz, D., "The Adolescent Drug Addict: An Adlerian View." *Journal of Indiv. Psychol.*, 17(1961), pp. 68-79.
5. Lombardi, D. N., "The Special Language of the Addict." *Pastoral Psychol.*, 20(1969), pp. 51-52.
6. Lombardi, D. N. and Angers, W. P., "First Memories of Drug Addicts." *Indiv. Psychol.*, 5(1), (1967), pp. 7-13.
7. Lombardi, D. N. and Di Peri, J. B., "Heroin and God." *The Catholic Psych. Rec.*, 3(1), (Spring, 1965), pp. 35-38.
8. Lombardi, D. N. and Ferindin, W., "Masculinity Strivings in Juvenile Offenders." Unpublished paper, Newark, New Jersey: Essex County Youth House, 1967.
9. Lombardi, D. N. and Isele, F. W., "The Young Drug Addict." *NJEA Rev.*, Feb., 1967, pp. 28-29.

10. Lombardi, D. N., O'Brien, B. J., and Isele, F. W., "Differential Responses of Addicts and Non-addicts on the MMPI." *J. Proj. Tech. and Pers. Assessmt.*, 32(1968), pp. 479-482.
11. Winick, C., "The Life Cycle of the Narcotic Addict and of Addiction." *U.N. Bull. on Narcotics*, Vol. XVI(1), (Jan.-March 1964), pp. 1-11.

HOW TO MAKE THE MOST
OF THE MIDDLE YEARS

Danica Deutsch

Of life's various stages, none starts suddenly. Adolescence, adulthood, middle age, old age and senescence are all prepared for by previous developments, starting as early as infancy in accordance with the individual's life style. Each stage finds its orientation to life documented in the earliest childhood recollections.

Some women are able to improve their faulty childhood attitudes by learning from experience. They are the lucky ones, who re-form and improve their personalities throughout life.

Others, whose life styles prevent them from changing spontaneously, seem condemned to repeat their childhood maladaptations over and over again, even into old age. For example, the individual who invariably "knew in advance" that she would fail or be disappointed or rejected, finds that life willingly and tirelessly confirms her negative expectations (3). This is especially true for women who feel defeated by limitations imposed upon their role by society's prejudices (1).

For such persons, the middle years may be a time of crisis, They realize that youth is slipping away, and that whatever daydreams they may have indulged in about a miracle that would change their luck will probably never happen.

For these people, the middle years may provide a unique opportunity to review their past and to define more clearly their precise areas of dissatisfaction. They may finally be persuaded to see the advantage of calling a halt to self-defeating behavior patterns, and to strike out in new directions towards more gratifying goals.

The woman in her middle years is still young and energetic enough to undertake new studies, develop additional skills, and embark on undertakings that challenge her to expand her personality as well as enrich her relationships with others. What she needs most is a hopeful outlook and encouragement from people she respects, to motivate her to transform negative attitudes into constructive activities.

In a workshop, the leader can help her discover that her faulty adaptation to her environment is often based not on reality but on a misconception of life formed in early childhood. The leader can stimulate her to reorganize her expectations of herself and others more realistically, so that she may anticipate possibilities of success in areas where she has genuine abilities. She can learn that it is not essential to her self-esteem and happiness to become an extraordinary achiever, but that she can gain deep satisfaction and self-respect from small gains, which she may use as stepping stones to continual self-development and accomplishments.

Adlerian theory provides several tools for helping the woman in this endeavor.

1. She may be aided to discover her faulty life style through her earliest recollections and dreams.
2. She may be made aware that she is not just a helpless pawn of circumstances, either familial or social, but that she is endowed with a "creative power" to produce her successes or failures.
3. She may learn that she need not be totally handicapped by feelings of inferiority; rather, that she can take realistic, socially useful steps to compensate for any actual inadequacies.
4. She may be stimulated to develop her inborn potential for social interest and cooperation with others as a means of overcoming feelings of loneliness, isolation, convictions of helplessness and fears of the future.

In a workshop, this is a team effort, to which all the participants as well as the leader make major contributions to the better self-understanding of the individual member. Sharing reactions with other members of the group leads to the comforting insight that what was considered to be a personal predicament is in reality a universal problem that challenges every woman in the middle years.

The Workshop and Its Rationale

With this hypothesis in mind, the author initiated a fifteen-week workshop for women in their middle years, at the Alfred Adler Mental Hygiene Clinic.

The group was made up of eight women ranging in age from the late forties to over sixty-five and included a commercial artist, an occupational therapist, a teacher-counselor, a guidance counselor, a dancer, a teacher-writer, a home teacher, and a writer. Two of the women were married, two widowed, two divorced, and two were single. Three had children.

Only half the members of the group could attend the workshop regularly because of other commitments. It was understood that the participants would have the prerogative of attending to more urgent matters whenever necessary, as these sessions were designed not to make life more difficult for them, but the reverse.

The middle years are a period of critical changes in the patterns of living of three generations: grandparents, the middle-agers themselves, and their adolescent children.

Grandparents, finding their energies dwindling, face the prospect of becoming increasingly dependent upon their children. They may have lost a mate, and the question of moving in with a son's or daughter's family arises. The uncertain future makes these older people more tense and demanding.

Changing mores produced by the stepped-up tempo of contemporary life and overcrowded living accommodations put an extra burden on the older generation. They must give up expectations of being cared for by their children in the same way that *they* took care of *their* parents in their later years; i.e. of moving into the son's or daughter's home and being looked after personally as long as they live. Because of this tradition, many older people today regard it as a stigma to be placed in a home for the aged. They interpret it as abandonment and rejection, and resist it strenuously.

The middle-ager is faced with the dilemma of how to fulfill her obligations as a dutiful offspring and at the same time to satisfy her own needs as an individual and respect the needs of her marital partner and her children for a comfortable home environment with ample opportunities for developing their own potentials. She is torn by the conflict created by the older generation's insistent demands for more attention, and by her guilt feelings for not being able to satisfy these demands in her parents' time of stress.

In the meanwhile, her teenage children are trying to break away from her and all authority, often becoming rebellious and even antisocial in their attempts to do so. So the middle-ager is truly in the middle. She bears the brunt, not only of her own personal crisis, but also of the emotional turmoil plaguing all the members of both the older and younger generations in her family.

Yet this period of crises on multiple levels is a time when the middle-aged woman in particular has her greatest opportunity to exercise a benevolent and healing influence on the development of the oldest as well as the youngest generation. She can regard her dilemma as a challenge to find ways of directing both generations along constructive, rather than self-destructive, paths.

To succeed in such an effort, she must be persuaded to see herself as a *creator* of circumstances rather than as a victim of her family's or society's prejudices against women. Once she develops a profound belief in the possibility of many years of personal satisfaction ahead, she will be inspired to give herself to new plans and activities with enthusiasm and devotion.

"Caught in the Middle"

One member of the workshop was in conflict with her aging mother, who constantly complained about her grandson's indifference. The youngster objected to visiting his grandmother in the old-age home because he "didn't like old people."

After much discussion in the group, it was agreed by all that she must have the courage to explain to her mother the "generation gap" and the rebellion of today's youth against the demands of the older generation. Furthermore, she must learn to listen to her mother's expressions of discontent without feeling personally guilty. Such an attitude would help her to avoid defensive behavior with either her mother or her son.

The next time she visited her mother, she was greeted with the usual outbreak of hurt and resentment: "Nobody cares for me . . . why do I have to live so long? . . . is this the only way you can raise your children? . . . if they don't respect me they won't respect you when you get older," etc.

This time, however, she did not respond with her customary appeasement or impatience. Instead, she patiently explained the facts of "the generation gap," stressing that this was not a personal rejection of her mother but simply a trend of our era. She pointed out that she herself had to accept her son's indifference or disregard it, even at her age.

To her astonishment, her mother stopped crying, and she left the older woman in a much better frame of mind, at least for the time being!

The Father's Victim

Bea, a dancer, lost her father between two sessions of the workshop. In telling the group about it, she revealed her past rebellious attitudes towards both parents. This opened up a discussion of the need to resolves one's problems with parents while they are still alive in order to prevent feelings of guilt later. The majority of the group, not having made peace with parents still living, found in these discussions a common ground which helped them to identify with each other. This also contributed to the cohesion of the group.

One member brought up her conflict with her father, who contributed to her financial support, then tried to interfere in her personal life. It was pointed out to her that her father's style of life was obviously to give financial help for the purpose of keeping his children dependent. Such a behavior pattern cannot be changed by fighting, or even by discussion. It must be recognized and accepted.

Therefore, she could make one of two choices: either to refuse her father's support, which might hurt him even more; or to accept it, knowing that he would continue to interfere with her plans. But she still had the option of making her own decisions. By understanding his motivation, she could free herself from reacting with temper or resentment, thus avoiding guilt feelings for her "disrespectful" attitude.

A Dependency-Independence Conflict

Ann, who is an occupational therapist, reported the following earliest recollections: lying in a crib in the sunshine, with a pleasantly warm feeling, mother sitting beside her; being wheeled in a stroller by her mother and enjoying this experience.

Both recollections indicate her enjoyment of the "twosome" relationship with her mother. They also reveal her pleasure in passivity and dependence upon her mother for making her feel good, plus her preference for an exclusive relationship.

Interestingly, she had compensated physically for these dependency strivings, first by developing skill in sports (she was a fine skier) and then by entering a profession where she functioned as an authority and helper.

But interpretation of her earliest recollections made her aware that she was still not *emotionally* emancipated from her mother. This gave her insight into the conflict within her own personality: on the one hand to be independent, on the other hand to be close to her parent.

At the time of the workshop, her mother had become widowed and desired to move in with her. Discussion of the "family life style" (2) helped her gain additional insight into the nature of her conflict. She told the group how she had suddenly recognized her mother's personal as well as family life style, which had always bothered her, but which she had never before been able to define exactly. Now, she told the group, she could see that her mother (following her own family tradition) put on a show of being a very generous public benefactor by involving herself in charitable organizations, while at home she was niggardly, made exorbitant demands upon her husband for financial success, and upon the rest of the family for total attention, enslaving them to her whims and desires.

This insight helped her to protect herself from her mother's constant and excessive demands, without blaming herself for being undutiful or selfish when she could not meet them. She was now able to decline her mother's suggestion to move in with her. Instead, she helped her mother to make arrangements to live by herself. In this way she achieved a realistic balance between fulfilling some of her traditionally-expected filial duties, her need to be close to her mother, and her equally strong need to be independent in her professional as well as private life.

The Woman Who Didn't Dare

The question of satisfaction with one's work came up frequently. Fear of losing one's job or not being able to apply for a new position loomed large in the minds of most of the participants.

Sue, the oldest, a dietition over sixty-five, found that her job had become too taxing. She expressed great fear of never being able to get another like it because she lacked the necessary academic degree. Browbeaten by fate many times in the past, she could not believe in the possibility of "good luck" for herself. She was capable of fighting for benefits for her subordinates, but she didn't dare speak up in her own behalf.

A suggestion that she might look for better employment threw her into a state of severe anxiety and depression. She was encouraged to see a psychiatrist for medication, which she did, and became much calmer. Thereafter, she began actively to support the other members in their specific endeavors. They, in turn, kept pointing out to her that the reason for her long tenure in her present job must be due to her intelligence and efficiency—qualities which would make her equally desirable for other employment. On this basis, they urged her to risk a showdown with her employers.

Lo and behold, one day she announced to the group the happy results of her demands for better hours and a reduced work load. Soon afterwards, she felt she no longer needed the group's support and celebrated her "graduation" by bringing in a big, delicious, home-made cake.

"I'll Stick With What I've Got!"

Ruth, the commercial artist, offered this earliest recollection: She was playing cards in a neighbor's house. She recalls that "somehow" she wound up at home with the cards in her pocket. She was afraid to tell her mother that she had them, and not knowing what else to do, she flushed them down the toilet.

This indicates the life style of a person with a highly developed sense of right and wrong, though not always the ability to implement these values because of the fear of consequences. This aspect of her personality was reflected in her situation with her current male friend, whose negative qualities she repeatedly stressed. He was the divorced husband of her best friend, whom she had not told about the relationship.

At first, Ruth, who was of European background, was quite timid and reticent. With the group's encouragement, she began to talk about her relationship to this man. The fact emerged that he was quite irresponsible, but despite her dissatisfaction, she clung to him. The group pointed out that she was probably afraid she would be unable to find another male companion. To combat such fears, they continually stressed her attractive appearance and interesting personality, and they expressed their conviction that she could, with some effort, find a more suitable friend.

After the summer, to the amazement of all, Ruth reported that she had placed an ad in a newspaper for "weekend company" from which she had received quite a few favorable responses. She had already seen and rejected some of the "applicants" and was following up others.

Now she turned her attention to her work. She discussed the disappointing results of several interviews for a better position. Finally, she decided that the best solution would be to return to school for a degree. At present she is studying American History to fulfill requirements for college acceptance.

"I Hate Indian Givers!"

Jane, a fifty-one-year-old writer, related the following early recollection:

At the age of three, she was with her parents and an uncle's family in the park. With them was her six-months-older cousin, who was always lauded as a model child for sharing what she had with the rest of her family, in contrast to Jane who had already been labeled a selfish "rotten kid." Jane's father bought her a box of Crackerjack. Then he asked her for some, which she gave him. He asked for more, which she also gave him. But when he asked a third time, she threw the box at him in a fit of temper, crying: "Here, take the whole box!"

This recollection indicates a style of life which interprets all requests as "taking back what one has been given." In the discussion, she recognized that she tended, for instance, to break up business relationships at the first suspecion of being exploited. She later reported that this discussion had helped her to overcome much of her resentment towards her present employer, who she felt was "taking back" many of the benefits he conferred upon her by making frequent and (to her way of thinking) undue demands for her services.

The Overambitious Mother

Bess, a guidance counselor, was deeply involved with her fourteen-year-old son's future. She desired him to excel, not on one level like other adolescents, but as a top amateur swimming star, while simultaneously achieving the highest grades in his academic subjects.

Her determination to get what she wanted is revealed in this earliest recollection:

She was in the crib at the age of one and a half years. She opened the gate to get out. Her grandmother came in, saying, "Don't do that!" and locked the crib. Bess climbed *over* the gate and got out.

But Bess did not see her relationship with her son as one in which she was determined to get her own way. On the contrary, whenever she talked about him, her eyes filled with tears as she protested: "It's not for me . . . I just want *him* to be happy!"

The group explored her motives and, despite her denials, helped her to see how she was pressuring her son. When the boy's failing marks in school brought matters to a crisis, she was persuaded to give him a real opportunity to choose his own direction for the future. Her sincerity was rewarded by his decision to give up his endeavors to become an athletic star, and to concentrate on his studies.

The group also brought to her attention that she never mentioned the role of her husband in relation to her son. They wondered if the father shared her wishes, or was this another proof of her domineering attitude? She then revealed that her husband had completely cooperated with her as long as the son pursued both goals, but that intrinsically he was in favor of the boy's giving his academic studies preference.

She added that a by-product of the son's decision was the alleviation of some underlying tensions in the marriage, which she had previously ignored.

Further discussion disclosed that Bess was finally becoming aware of the extent to which her personal ambitions had been tied up in her son's activities. Despite her disappointment at the way things turned out, she was able to accept his decision. One reason for this was that she was finding a great deal of satisfaction in her ability to free him from her demands, as well as in the concomitant sense of freedom it gave her to pursue gratifying *personal* goals (in accordance with her earliest recollection).

Conclusions

A workshop for the middle years has several unique advantages:

1. The time-limited approach to the individual's problems (fifteen weeks) often impels her to make immediate concrete improvements in her way of life, rather than defer them for months, even years (4).
2. It is of modest expense compared to individual therapy and can be useful to people with limited budgets.
3. Although it is not termed "therapy," the workshop has definite therapeutic results for most of the participants who stay to the end, and it encourages some of them to seek further help.
4. It attracts and benefits some individuals who avoid individual therapy because of the stigma sometimes attached to it.

Another value inherent in the workshop experience is that, though it is of limited duration, members quickly begin to "take the group home with them." This helps to counteract their former feelings of isolation, which are so conducive to secretive and negative behavior. Knowing of the group's interest in them, they use it in their imagination as a "forum" for arguments and counter-arguments in arriving at decisions between the sessions. As a result, their choices now tend to be less self-defeating.

It is interesting to note that sexual problems were dealt with only occasionally. Professional problems and conflicts with parents or children were more pressing. (In one session, when discussion centered around the commercial artist's relationship with her unsatisfactory friend, some of the members in the group said they would rather forego sexual relations altogether if the partner's standards were far below their own.) But it is obvious that in other workshops, or even in the same workshop at a different period in the participants' lives, sexuality, dreams and other aspects pertaining to the role of being a woman as seen by Adler, might become the main focus of attention.

After the summer, some workshop members returned to the therapist-leader for individual sessions, in which they discussed the impact of the workshop on their lives. Many interesting changes were under way, and suggestions for further improvement were given when requested.

Perhaps their general feeling about the effectiveness of the workshop as a turning-point in their lives is best expressed in the following dream, which was reported in the last session of the workshop.

The member dreamed she was sitting at a long table at a dinner honoring the workshop leader. Everyone commented on the leader's youthfulness. "What's her secret?" they kept asking each other. Each participant told what she thought was the secret. The dreamer was sitting directly across the table from the leader, who finally stood up and announced: "Everyone is guessing at my secret, but no one has given the right answer." The dreamer looked at the leader expectantly, certain she would say: "The secret is social interest and cooperation." Instead, to her amazement, right before her eyes, the leader turned into a sparkling eighteen-year-old girl, who has all of life ahead of her.

The member interpreted this dream as a reflection of the impact made upon her own and the group's development by a leader whose life she saw as a constant call to other women for continuous personal growth in spite of the limitations imposed by society.

REFERENCES

1. Adler, A., *What Life Should Mean to You* (1931). New York, Capricorn Books, 1958.
2. Deutsch, Danica., "Family Therapy and Family Life Style." *J. Indiv. Psychol.*, 23(1967), pp. 217-223.
3. Merton, R. K., "The Self-fulfilling Prophecy." *Antioch Rev.*, 8(1958), pp. 193-210.
4. Shlien, J. M., Mosak, H. H., and Dreikurs, R., "Effect of Time Limits: A Comparison of Two Psychotherapies." *J. Counsel. Psychol.*, 9(1962), pp. 31-34.

A DREAM'S HELP TOWARD HEALING

Joseph Meiers

The case of Marina V., a 36-year old white American woman, a Registered Nurse, unmarried, with what seemed to her then a most unsatisfactory erotic life, is reported for several reasons:

First, because during the latter course of her therapy, but particularly in the ensuing approximately ten years, there has occurred a remarkable change in her life style, at least in those facets which had been obstructing her professional success and her "happiness," up to 1958. This change has become observable because during those last ten years and across the breadth of the United States she has kept in occasional contact with me, thus enabling me to follow up her progress.

Second, because it seemed remarkable to me, examining the case both toward the end of the treatment and again after ten years, that there is a basis for assuming that this change in life style (2, pp. 172, 358) may be a consolidated one.

Third, this case history presents an instance of the perhaps not so rare cases where the important device of the Early Recollections was not really applicable (or, at least not applied)[1]—a device which otherwise is one of the remarkable diagnostic "short-cuts" systematized by Alfred Adler (2, pp. 152-153) and which has proved valuable in providing hints to the therapist to clarify the patient's life style and also permitting a check on the change of life style during and after successful therapy (3, 6, 8, 9, 13).

Fourth, the account of this case seems to me not without some special psychiatric interest in two aspects. In the first place, it was both necessary and possible to help the patient to maintain her job, in spite of her rather severe suffering from occasional outbreaks of "unbearable" friction in hospital and also in home nursing (to which she would, particularly in the early stages of treatment, give stark expression in loud, shrill crying)—without having to expose her to the risks of hospitalization (7, 11). In the second place, until shortly after the first third of treatment, psychotherapy was supplemented by relatively mild medication with tranquilizers.

Finally, fifth, as expressed in the title of this report, one of the note-worthy features of the case was the role which one dream, or rather her association to it played in her therapy. It not only confirmed the life style diagnosis made earlier by this therapist but—more important—this dream association, by strongly impressing the patient, significantly contributed to her propelling herself toward greater and more acceler-ated improvement.

The Case History

The initial interview took place at the Alfred Adler Mental Hygiene Clinic in New York City in September 1957. The interviewer, a social worker recorded:

Miss M. V. stated that for approximately the last two years she has been feeling very depressed. At one time she had thought of suicide "in a way," but since that time had thought very little about it.

Miss V. stated that her "primary recollection" was the miserable way in which her parents got along. Her father was described as being, on the surface, a very quiet and sweet person but underneath a "cheat." Her mother was described as a "vicious neurotic." Still, as a girl she idolized her mother.

Miss V"s father was a farmer; he insisted that his children begin work on the farm at the earliest age possible. Miss V. could recall doing farm chores from about the age of five or six on. She could not recall ever playing with other children because of the insistence on and need for work on the farm.

Miss V. was next to the youngest of five sisters, the next to the young-est out of eleven children altogether.

She claimed that her parents "never exchanged a kind word in a period of thirty years." Miss V.'s parents obtained a divorce when she was about fifteen; she remained with her father until his remarriage. At that point, Miss V. felt that "the home had collapsed," and so she left. She never felt "socially accepted" in school because of her poor clothing and lack of time to be with the other children. She also got "the feeling from her own family that she was not a bright child." After leaving her family home about age sixteen, Miss V. became a domestic for some eight years. She thought it was a period in her life again "with no fun and all work." She noted that during this period of time she was paid a salary of three dollars a week. Subsequent to this employment, she entered the U. S. Navy (in about 1944) as a volunteer. Subsequently, through the service there, she was able to obtain two years of college education and finished nursing school in 1951 (at the age of thirty). Since then, she has always had nursing jobs. It was noted that Miss V., not knowing "what to do with her spare time," has always sought additional employment (night nursing, etc.)

At the present time, Miss V. is engaged in private nursing duty. This job she has had for eight months, with one particular patient whom she described as being "very senile." She thought he was constantly trying to involve her in his own household affairs. She noted that, in addition to nursing duties, she had to plan for shopping and meals. She felt that she could not break away from this relationship. She noted that she was "practically married" to this job, and in the last eight months had had no time off, working seven days a week. Her increasing resentment came up on occasion when she expressed herself as "feeling that she could scream at times." She has practically no social life, having had three days off in a period of seven months.

Miss V. has had some boyfriends in her life, but she did not seem to be too interested. She indicated that the boyfriends she had met had encountered some objections on her part, on one ground or another.

Miss V. didn't know what she might expect to find at the Clinic. She was just aware of being unhappy, and in a vague sense, of needing some help.

Intentionally, the preceding text of the interview is reproduced here verbatim and almost in full. The general history is recorded, including the "presenting complaints," the work, the family and sex situation. Also—as in, probably, any Individual Psychology clinic anywhere—it is the practice to ask the therapy-seeker about his positions among the siblings (Family Constellation) and his Early Recollections. The interview shows that this patient, M. V., felt unable to reply to the question, "What can you recall as the earliest happening, or scene, in your childhood?" other than to launch into a general description, a global evaluation, of her sad and oppressive childhood years. Because of various circumstances, among them her unusually tight nursing schedule in the private home, nine weeks elapsed before she began therapy.

Initial Psychiatric Evaluation

Therapy was preceded by the psychiatric evaluation, including diagnosis-therapy recommendations. In her case, as one of the supervising psychiatrists, I functioned as evaluator (5). The initial diagnostic impression was: Psychoneurosis, moderately severe, of long standing (recently exacerbating), with mild-to-moderate depression in a 36-year-old unmarried woman, of Protestant upbringing in low-income farm family; without earlier work disability: presently, since 1951, Registered Nurse. The depressive features came to the fore mainly as glumness, the relatively mild verbalization of desperation, and in an outspoken "gloomy" view of her future; there were also complaints of sleep difficulties. There was, however, no retardation of behavior.

It is noteworthy, too, that in this psychiatric interview she repeated almost exactly her earlier reaction when asked to relate any particular scene remembered from her early childhood. "Suggestive" hints by the interrogator were avoided in order to leave this procedure as uncontaminated as possible.[2] At this repeated inquiry, Marina V. again stated that she could not remember any specific incident just as she had been unable to do, she stated strongly, when asked about it "only several weeks ago." She then, with understandable near-annoyance, started to reproduce the over-all description of her bleak and oppressed childhood which she seemed to remember from her fourth year on, giving, on the whole, almost the same generalities as in the initial interview.

Family history: on question, no neurotic or "nervous" illness in the family except the "hateful" relationship of parents toward each other. Family constellation: tenth of eleven siblings, the next-before-the-youngest of five girls; two years the elder of the baby sister. The problem of the "absolute" birth order appeared in this case, as seen later on, not of equal significance to her "relative" position in regard to her next-younger sister. The therapeutic recommendation was: "Individual therapy (with medication as necessary) possibly to be combined later with group therapy" (16).

Early Course of Treatment

The following features were seen as most prominent in the early course of the therapy:

First, her goal-mindedness (2, p. 103). M. V. was not floundering, not unaware of "what to do", as one finds with increased frequency among depressed patients of the younger generation. Rather, she had the outspoken goal of improving herself, primarily in her professional situation, closely tied to her still precarious economic condition. She clearly viewed her continuing "aggravations" and depressive mood as being distinct obstacles to any strongly intended improvement.

Second, she was aware, though perhaps more vaguely, of the goal of achieving a more successful "love life" than she had previously. As an unavoidable premise for any progress toward either of these goals, the therapist envisaged that the patient would become aware that it was the obstacles she had been building up in herself, almost unconsciously, that prevented her from approaching these desired goals. In other words, this patient would have to come to recognize, no matter how gradually, what is called in Individual Psychology her "faulty life style." Judging from her "cool-sounding" statement, at the end of her initial interview: ". . . . the boy friends she had met had encountered some objections on her part, on one ground or another," it appeared that the second area, her erotic life, including her sex life, would present the greatest difficulties toward self-insight into her life style.

Psychotropic medication, whose use is still considered, by some, as controversial in psychotherapy, played only a limited role in treatment (1).

Dreaming in the Patient's Past

Since the start of therapy, it was intimated to her that it would be "quite useful for the cooperative enterprise of therapy" (14) to tell the therapist her dreams. Without voicing objections in principle, she stated during the first four or five weeks that, regrettably, she did not have or did not recall any dreams. Besides she had "never been much of a dreamer, except, perhaps, as a child." Asked then, about dreams in childhood, she could not recall any particular dreams. On further inquiry, she could not remember having had any dreams in which she felt frightened or chased. Also, she denied any memory of a dream "repeating itself many times" (10).

In stating that she hardly ever dreamed and clearly implying that she did not or "could not expect" to have dreams now in psychotherapy more than she did before, Marina V. showed her characteristic quality of "self consistency" (amounting in her to rigidity)—what many, perhaps most, people express by saying, "You know how I am," or, "That's the way I've always been."

Inducing Attention to Dreams

I may mention here the assembly of small "devices" which I employ to induce in a patient the process which I call "the occupation with dreams," which includes not only the dream but the association to it as well. It is true that in the majority of psychotherapies, in mine as well as in other therapists' experience, the patient starts reporting dreams. However, I do not doubt that, on the other hand, there remains a large number of patients who seem to exhibit resistance against remembering dreams, or inability to remember them[3].

It is for these reasons that I have applied the following "devices": (1) giving explanations or supplying examples of how other patients benefitted from recalling and telling their dreams; (2) when questioned by the patient, especially if he is more theoretically minded, showing him, as it were, abstractly why dreams and their discussion would further the therapy. Finally, (3) particularly within the last ten years or so, I have even used the results of the newer dream physiology on occasion, to show that with very few exceptions, i.e. only under abnormal conditions, all persons from childhood on dream about five times every night (rapid eye movement sleep periods).

Thus it is now only the problem of whether the dreamer recalls his dream upon awakening. This again seems to depend mostly upon whether the dreamer feels that the "picture," or "story" presented by him in his dream appears to have some bearing on his "self"; or, at least, that the dream (non-recalled in detail) put him in a particular mood.

Finally, in a few cases of "not remembering dreams" I have found it expeditious to recommend to those eager to cooperate with the therapist (while believing themselves unable to dream or to recall dreams) a small choice of non-technical but reliable paperbacks (4). I have found these devices to be effective in varying degrees. Thus, recalling one's dream is, surely, not a matter of logical conviction on the part of the patient; it is rather "induced" by creating in him a mood, an atmosphere of interest in cooperating with the dream-interested therapist.

Dreams Occurring in the Therapy of Marina V.

When she had started to develop a fairly good rapport, M. V. recounted a few dreams. Most of these reflected, without obscure symbolisms, difficulties in her day-to-day professional life, inter-personal hardships which badly taxed her feelings. Almost no dreams connected with surviving persons of her family, i.e., her siblings, were recorded; those recounted required almost no interpretation.

Work and Love Life

The wounding friction with her senile patient continued. The friction with his wife was even greater, since the latter was openly jealous of and antagonistic toward the much younger woman. Still, she did not dare to lose the excellent and hard-to-replace nurse. One may ask why Marina did not change her job, or at least, contemplate such a move. To some extent, it was the much better pay, plus free board, offered by the old couple. This offered her the only hope to save enough to move from her miserably small one-room place in New York City, and eventually to return to her native West.

On the other hand, to return to a hospital as a "specialing" nurse, where she had been known and generally well appreciated, would have been unrealistic because of her former frictions (never forgotten by her) with many floor nurses. Characteristically, such frictions occurred not because of any deficiencies in nursing duties. Rather, she disdained, as it were, working with nurses who earned the same as she, because she considered herself as having a much higher professional education. (Her education level was, probably, higher). Such "injustice" was "infuriating" to her.

Meanwhile, her uneasiness, even suffering, in the erotic field continued. She would hear rather irregularly from her boyfriend who resided several hundred miles from New York. He visited her even more rarely. She did not accept this easily, but she did not want to break this relationship, brittle as it was, though she seemed to be aware that prospects for durability had not improved after more than a year and a half. They had been having intercourse at those infrequent meetings. She reported that he clearly expressed dissatisfaction with her irritability and ill humor. Working through these "depressing facts," both of her work life and of her erotic life, the therapist tried to show her her own attitudes and her behavior toward others—namely, "blaming herself but blaming almost all others more," an expression of her life style of bitter rivalry. She hardly defended herself against the unflattering part of what was being shown her. She did not refute it as "not being her case" but neither did she seem to accept this picture being delineated to her of a "faulty" lifestyle. She was too intelligent to try to deny it outright[4]; but it did not "sink in."

Thus, for over two months, there was barely any forward movement in treatment, except that the external situation, i.e., her job, had become less irritating to her.

A Dream and Its Unexpected Effect

After two months, she told in a somewhat subdued, almost sad voice, the following dream: "The dream was rather 'foggy'; something about a party, a narrow street between tall houses." In the dream, she knew she was losing her boy friend and searched for him, bewildered . . .

The therapist adhered to his rule not to offer an interpretation nor even to try to help the dreamer's attempt at self-interpretation of a dream before the dreamer has been offered the opportunity to give an association. In my practice and on the basis of my experience, such opportunity is given, advisedly, not by asking for "interpretation" nor for "associations" nor even asking: "What do you think about your dream?" The query is limited strictly—in a typical case—to "Anything come to your mind . . .?"

To this brief query, Marina said: "When I was very small, just about two years old, I tried to strangle with my own hands my infant baby sister. My mother came upon me, pulled me away . . . I myself do not, really, remember having done that. But it must be true, must it not? My mother and the older children later told me more than once about it." When later talking to me, she added, "They would not ever have teased me with a false story about such an awful thing . . ."

At that juncture, the therapist decided to refrain from exploring with her why she had not told earlier about such happening, nor in what way she thought she had "connected" that sudden remembrance with that particular "foggy" dream (losing her boyfriend). It was clearly observable that M.V. was deeply impressed, even overwhelmed by what she had brought up. She wept, briefly and quietly. She was, no doubt, in a kind of psychological shock. This circumstance induced me to abstain, for the moment, from any immediate exploration. Also, I did not see any urgent necessity to press this patient, who was still in a depression, for clarification, certainly not from a therapeutic viewpoint. However, I would agree that from a scientific-theoretical standpoint, there would be, perhaps, considerable interest in unraveling the skeins connecting the dream with the surely unexpected association.

No immediately observable improvement ensued after this "shock," nor could I say that I would have expected such immediately. What did become noticeable was a somewhat greater readiness to delve deeper into a comparison between, on one hand, her style of life of severe rivalry and of "looking down" on others (as it had been presented to her by the therapist and which she could not refute entirely, as containing at least a "possibility of truth") and, on the other hand that stark, new, shock-like impression left in her by the recent and sudden surfacing in her mind of the "memory" of the old misdeed which, according to her, she had not done knowingly (17).

That this memory arose in her, unundertandably to herself, tied to the saddening dream of "lost love" made that shock-like impression no less strong, perhaps more so. Within a few weeks after this dream-plus-association episode, she started to clearly evince in many of her utterances a better comprehension than before of her prevailing "rivaling" life style, as it had been presented to her and observed by her, though not sharply, in her psychotherapy.

From the Adlerian viewpoint, it appears quite understandable that the "losing the boyfriend" dream can be considered as a kind of self-training for enduring such loss. How would this lead us to understand the "bridge," the association to the "crime" remembrance? On the basis of this one model, such clarification appears to me unfeasible. Perhaps accumulating more cases of such "implausible" associations may lead to better understandings.

On-Going Changes

It must not be assumed that from then on there was "plain sailing." Only quite slowly did the initial symptoms of irritability, tension and depressive hypersensitivity to the behavior of others recede. However, as noted before, she must have started to feel better, since in early April, for instance, she said that she was "forgetting to take the tranquilizers."

Such improvement of feelings occurred in spite of external events which were to buffet her sharply. Thus, for example, in early April her boyfriend wrote her, among other news, that he wished she "could have another (i.e. a more fitting) boyfriend"—thus virtually presaging a further loosening of their relation. Also, the stress of her living quarters as well as the winding-up of her nursing of the "senile" man were experienced by her as harassing. Still, she was now able to start to cope with them. Earlier she had felt unable even to contemplate a change of job. Now, looking for new work, she, a nurse with "high reputation for working with difficult cases," was offered a job with a middle aged person with an injury to his nervous system, the prognosis being doubtful, even as to length of survival. She started immediately, first in the hospital, later in his home. Not only the patient but also his wife appreciated her skill and dedication very much, so that when he had to be transferred to the West of this country, this rather wealthy family prevailed upon her to stay with them. This unexpected opportunity transcended her highest hopes; she had felt virtually "stranded" during all of her more than four years in New York. There was still great external stress evolving about settling her rent-lease obligations. But the buoyant expectation of returning to her "homeland" and even better earnings there erased her depression almost entirely.

In mid-May 1958, her psychotherapy here ended. The following "final diagnosis" was recorded in the files of the Clinic: "mixed neurosis, moderately severe (with severe irritability and with compulsive and depressive features), in an aggressive-dependent personality. Note: Additional drug therapy.—Duration: ca. five and a half months. Result: satisfactory (restoration to full working level)." The therapist then added, as prognosis: "favorable but still guarded." Of such caution I do not feel ashamed, though the record of the ten and a half years since then has not justified the over-cautiousness of 1958.

Healthier Life Style Consolidating?

What has impressed me most is that from the earliest age of the patient explorable to us, namely from her own story, we can differentiate two strands. One we may call the "useful"—as Alfred Adler named that quality—which included her goal-mindedness, her steady work habits, and most important, her social interest (Gemeinschaftsgefühl) (12) so clearly expressing itself in her strong dedication to all her patients.

The other strand, fully intertwined with the healthy ("useful") one in her life style, is the "faulty" one about which most of the previous part of this report has centered. In the ten years since completing treatment, Marina V. has remained in communication with me. She addressed five long letters to me during 1958 and 1959; and, in response to a brief inquiry by me, also a six-page letter in early 1969, while I wrote much more rarely and in rather brief missives. In the years from 1960 to 1964, there were Christmas-New Year's messages, with brief reports about her life. The long "reporting" letter of 1969 culminates in two main facts: (1) She had been working throughout all the years since 1958, acquiring in the meantime a larger house, with a "shack," situated together, and lovingly cultivating a garden. She had worked, in 1959 for one year as an industrial nurse. She returned to the same factory, as head nurse, after nine years. In between, she had founded her own agency, "a small one, for visiting nurses." Then, in 1967, she managed a home health agency, which proved, however, unprofitable. This was the cause for her returning to the good job in the industrial plant. (2) She has had a new boyfriend for the last eight years. "He has not married me, is a born bachelor; but he loves me and does a lot for me."

It seems to this writer that from the above we can draw the conclusion that this patient's healthier life style has been consolidating in the ten years after treatment. Regrettably, a new attempt was not made to elicit from her an "Early Recollection" inasmuch as it appeared unsuitable to this therapist to put such "inquiry" to the former patient in a letter, which question would, then, have to be answered by her, again by letter.

FOOTNOTES

1. One suggestion which derives from the presented case study is that a systematic investigation of cases where early recollections could not be obtained from patients would be quite desirable to yield more information about unexplored facets of this gem of the Adlerian diagnostic armamentarium.
2. Many Adlerians do not adhere to this practice. Some will, for example, attempt to secure the recollection of the first day of school—Ed.

3. There does not exist yet, to my knowledge, a statistical study of the differences between ready recallers and non-recallers of dreams.

4. The level of the patient's intelligence could be inferred with sufficient reliability, since no intelligence test was administered, from the fact that several years before therapy, she participated in a socio-psychological project directed by a professional psychologist.

REFERENCES

1. Adler, Alexandra, "Modern Drug Treatment and Psychotherapy." *J. Indiv. Psychol.*, 13(1957), pp. 146-149.

2. Ansbacher, H. and Rowena, R., *The Individual Psychology of Alfred Adler.* New York, Harper & Row, 1956.

3. Beecher, Marguerite, "Two Hundred Cases in Retrospect." *Amer. J. Indiv. Psychol.*, 11(1954), pp. 9-22.

4. Diamond, E., *The Science of Dreams.* New York, Doubleday, 1962.

5. Dreikurs, R., "The Psychological Interview in Medicine," *Amer. J. Indiv. Psychol.*, 10(1952), pp. 109-110.

6. Friedman, Alice, "Early Childhood Memories of Mental Patients." K. A. Adler and Danica Deutsch, eds., *Essays in Individual Psychology*, New York, Grove Press, 1959, pp. 200-296.

7. Hartlage, L. and Hale, P., "Self Concept Decline from Psychiatric Hospitalization." *J. Indiv. Psychol.*, 24(1968), pp. 74-76.

8. Hedvig, Eleanor, "Stability of Early Recollections and Thematic Apperception Stories." *J. Indiv. Psychol.*, 19(1963), pp. 49-54.

9. Kadis, Asya, "Early Childhood Recollections as Aids in Group Therapy." *J. Indiv. Psychol.*, 13(1957), pp. 183-187.

10. Kimmins, C., *Children's Dreams.* London, Allen & Unwin, 1937.

11. Levinson, D. and Gallagher, E., *Patienthood in the Mental Hospital.* Boston, Houghton Mifflin, 1964.

12. Montague, A., "Alfred Adler: The Challenge of Social Interest." (Memorial address on Adler's 100th birthday.) To appear.

13. Mosak, H. H., "Predicting the Relationship to the Therapist from Early Recollections." *J. Indiv. Psychol.*, 21(1965), pp. 77-81.

14. Munroe, Ruth, "Other Psychoanalytic Approaches (Adler, Jung, Rank)." In S. Arieti, ed., *American Handbook of Psychiatry, vol. II.* New York, Basic Books, 1959, pp. 1453-1456.

15. Neufeld, I., "Review of W. Toman, Family Constellation." New York, (1961), *Indiv. Psychologist,* 1(1963), pp. 17-18.

16. Papanek, Helene, "Combined Group and Individual Therapy in the Light of Adlerian Psychology." *Int. J. Grp. Psychother.*, 6(1956), pp. 136-137.

17. Schachtel, E. G., "On Memory and Childhood Amnesia," *Psychiatry*, 10(1947), pp. 1-26.

SOCIOMETRY OF THE FAMILY

Adaline Starr

The Family

The family has long been recognized as the molder of character. The "why and wherefore" has been occupying men's minds since the beginning of time. More particularly, today, students are concerned with the dynamics of the family group, which is viewed as a household of people intimately related as parents and children, perhaps grandparents, and the sum total of the relationships existing within it. "The members of such groups have a common past, expect a common future and share a life together" (6, p. 78). Yet each interprets differently this close association. Over fifty years ago Adler concluded that each child in the family, out of his own inner capacities and his appraisal of the outer environment, experiences a different situation. He joined these attitudes into a characteristic pattern of behavior that he called the life style, a line of development from early childhood to the adult, in one continuous pattern. Character traits and qualities, then, became the result of relationships, a family transaction.

The Individual Within the Family

When Adler rejected Freud's idea of the psychosexual development of man, and thought rather "a child's love life is directed toward people, not his own body" (3) it opened the door to the importance of the cultural and economic surroundings of the world the child lives in. Man is, then, a social being, concerned with and striving to correct the difficulties of his life situation. His desire to belong to the group, to have friends and to feel that others are responding to him seems to be a reaction existing in all societies.

People who live together respond to one another with some sign of an interchange of feelings, either outwardly shown or inwardly felt. This is expressed in a positive, negative or indifferent way. This feeling or decision about people is what sociometry measures and the sociogram charts. The interchange of these feelings toward every other member, not only of his family, but of his acquaintanceship, in sociometric terms, is his social atom. It describes the smallest unit of interaction (7). This pattern of attraction and rejection crystallizes the social structure of the family into patterns which draw a line of mutual acceptance between pairs, or a line of acceptance between three people to form a triangle, or it can form itself into a chain of relationship. The rejections are readily seen, by using a broken line to show the break in relationship. This emotional feeling each has for other family members *(tele)* has the meaning of distance, or far, not as the Adlerians use the term "teleological" to mean end or purpose.

"Children have acute perceptions of the people who love them or who are threatening to them. A child between 24 and 30 months has definite likes and dislikes for the people around him and makes accurate decisions when he moves toward a person or withdraws from him. Attraction and rejection of his mother is evident very early and children do not err in their assessment. This, too, is *tele*" (6). Adler describes this attitude as taking place at birth and calls it "social interest;" "from the moment of birth, a baby seeks to connect himself to his mother. This is the purpose of his movements. . . . It is in this situation that the ability to cooperate first develops. . . . On every occasion she (the mother) is providing an opportunity for the child to like her or dislike her, to cooperate or reject cooperation. We mean nothing else by a mother's skill than her ability to win the child to cooperate with herself" (3, p. 121). A happy interaction between mother and child depends on her skill and her acceptance of the mother role in answering the biologic needs of the infant.

Structure of the Family Group

A basic concept in Adlerian therapy is the family constellation—the child's situation in his family during his early years and the pattern of interaction (1, 2, 3). An essential procedure in psychodrama, a therapeutic enactment of relationships, is sociometry. A sociometric test, either verbal or written, precedes psychodrama, thus informing the director of the distribution of choices and rejections in the family, and this steers the course of the therapy to follow. The element common to both systems is the significance of the interfamilial relationship. The sociometric score depicts the current status of each—the response the child has made to his particular situation. The family constellation indicates this too, and Adler developed a theory of how this happens. Many questions are raised as one looks at a sociogram with the goal of assessing and differentiating the wide range of attitudes with which a child may appraise his milieu. Adler's theories on the effect of birth order, sibling rivalry, and the relationship of the parents casts light upon the sociometric findings. The sociogram becomes an action diagram when we see the positive and negative choices as behavioral responses.

Social Atom and the Types of Relationship

The mother is the natural auxiliary ego with a twofold function—to give the child an experience of love and to guide the child into having feeling for others. When the mother is a spoiled child herself, angry that her husband does not provide the kind of pampering that she hopes for, the child may feel rejected and turn to the father. In some instances the father responds to the child and they form an alliance against the mother.

The father, too, may show his family the way to be cooperative and to have social feeling. "It is very valuable in the development of children that they should learn that the family is a unit of a larger society and that outside the family there also exist trustworthy human beings and fellow men." (A father is able to do this for his family when he manages to solve the problems of working, loving and friendship)—"His influence is so important that many children look on him, throughout their lives, either as their ideal or their greatest enemy" (3, p. 135).

The relationship of the mother and father is like an umbrella over the family. If they are unhappy with each other, it is unfortunate for the children. If they are cooperative and respectful of each other, the children are likely not to be as competitive with each other. In fact, the parents offer a complex area of relationship that often it is necessary in psychodrama to work with them separately from the children, or even from each other, using an auxiliary ego for the role of the spouse. This is indicated when the relationship is very agitated. The concept of family interaction is not eliminated but delayed, as a preparation for the full family participation.

Each child differs from the other because of the birth order. Each is in a different relationship to the parents and to each other, and so interprets the experiences of the group situation in light of this position and his physical endowment.

Three birth positions are uniquely placed in an atmosphere of excessive warmth: the oldest, the youngest, and the only child. It is easy to see how this is a favorable climate for a child's being overly dependent. The oldest may yearn for the good old days of being the only one; the only child is often cared for too intensely. The youngest is in the situation of the only child, i.e., he is never dethroned, with the added challenge of the siblings who are ahead of him. In contrast, the middle child, if discouraged by the first-born, feels that he hasn't the power of the older, nor the charm of the baby and so may feel "it's an unfair world." If, though, he is not overwhelmed by the pacemaker, he may be quite aggressive and rebellious and put the older child down.

Every child must find his place within the family. One child may learn that being demanding assures him a place; another may see the value of compliance, or of being the clown. As his style of life is established, he integrates each new experience into his perception. He becomes the actor and the playwright-producer, as he organizes himself according to his views of things, some of which are fallacious. Fortunately such basic assumptions are readily recognized in children. Children show their attitudes openly, and these can be understood. Dreikurs, in discussing the goals of disturbing children, names them as attention, power, revenge, and the demonstration of inadequacy (5).

Each family becomes an interacting unit with the culture and incorporates a value system that influences each member of the household. The formation of relationships is expressed positively as cooperation or negatively as hostility. It is a two-way process. As they emerge from the family transactions, character traits, temperament and skills show definite differences which reflect the competition between the siblings. The competitive relationship between the first and second child in the order of birth is the strongest. This pair appears as a mutually rejecting one. As a rule, then, the sociogram reveals a family of two children, each rejecting the other; it indicates an active fighting stance toward each other. In a family of two siblings, competitiveness between the two may be shown as positive tele in one direction and rejecting in the other. This may signal the presence of a discouraged child. If there is a mutual pair positive (i.e., there is no open rivalry), the two are declaring that they accept the sybiotic relationship, perhaps one of the strong caring for the weak.

In a family of three siblings, the mutual pair will show an alliance with each other and a negative choice, usually directed toward the mother's favorite. Where all the choices are seen as positive, the parents may be relating very well to each other or the child is concealing his feelings toward the family. The larger the number of siblings in a family, the less intense the rivalry becomes, as the reciprocated choices are duplicated.

A sociometrist expects desirable changes to occur when the child's environment is sympathetic and congenial. We see, then, that the preferences may be understood as expressing what, why and whom the child is choosing and the therapeutic significance of this. It is beneficial to use the information of the sociogram to restructure the group along more harmonious lines. The psychodramatist can encourage the children to meet as a family, to regard all problems as group problems, and to seek solutions through the democratic process. If one child is allowed to choose the task and with whom the task is to be performed, the compatibility of one child with another is more or less achieved. By asking the individuals within the family to select the duties (including alternate tasks) they are willing to perform, in the order of choice, the experience of participating in decisions relating to their life situation is offered; decisions imposed not by the parents, but self-selected. This is a sociometric therapeutic intervention.

Another instrument for helping the disturbed relationships in the family, psychodrama, emerges out of the group. The acting out of situations by family members has the effect of catharsis, as well as improving the perceptive skills by role interaction. "Drama is an artistic form of empathy and identification" (2, p. 61).

The dramatization of the interpersonal relationships provides the psychodramatist with the opportunity to see at first hand the presenting problem and to start facilitating change. This form of family psychodrama in which common problems are dramatized and shared, focuses on actual situations (although fantasy situations are sometimes dramatized) and suggests practical solutions. The psychodramatist attempts to recreate the experience of the child playing his own role in interaction with the members of the family portaying themselves or with other individuals who were concerned with the particular experience.

The members of the family sit in a circle as the psychodramatist explains the purpose of the meetings, that the group is not a court trying to find a guilty person on whom to lay the blame, but rather a family trying to understand one another better. "Let's begin by each one saying who in this family bothers or upsets you, and what it is he does. If anyone considers a comment made by another as inaccurate or unfair, simply announce, 'I object'. You will then be given an opportunity to explain to what you are objecting." This initial session explores the interaction of the family members as the parents and siblings act out real or fantasy situations. These scenes reveal how the child-with-the-problem manages sibling rivalry or competition in his feelings toward the group, how he reacts to punishment, praise, and criticism. The role of the mother is the focal point of the first session. Is she punitive, overprotective or overly strict? This interaction of mother and child can be seen in the child's behavior as he responds as a tyrant, as withdrawn, as excessively polite, as sensitive to criticism or as overactive. All are answers to the situation.

Experiences acted out are not only those affecting the family relationship but those affecting the outside members of the child's world as well. A member of the family may play the role of another member, friend, teacher, or the child himself. However, while the other relationships are examined, the focus of the conflict and disturbed behavior is to be found in the family maladjustments. In occasion we have introduced a member of the outside group into the psychodrama although this procedure is ordinarily unnecessary. This is less true when the patient is an adolescent when family ties weaken and outside ties become stronger.

Psychodrama of a Child

Stan, a nine-year-old boy, quiet, withdrawn and friendless, was failing in his studies and making a poor social adjustment. He had been placed in group therapy with children his age without its being beneficial. We then invited his mother and younger brother to participate with Stan in the first session. Stan's participation in this group was in marked contrast to that in the other group. He was transformed from a bland, withdrawn, disinterested boy to one who spoke out in violent disagreement with his mother, beat up his younger brother, and denied that he stayed up until midnight to watch television. With his peers he seemed dull-witted and babyish. In his family group he was a forceful tyrant. Since Stan was unwilling to enter into the acting out of his behavior, the mirror was employed. Stan watched as his mother played him; the brother played himself, and the director assumed the role of the mother. Stan's resistance slowly dissolved as he observed his mother acting the part of a nine-year-old boy. The mother (director) was releasing hostility aimed at Stan and at the same time witnessing her destructive preference for the younger boy. One facet of the sibling rivalry was thus felt rather than explained, i.e., that some mothers encourage fighting by taking sides in a rivaly situation.

During the discussion which followed, Stan continued to deny that the role as played by his mother accurately reflected his behavior. Yet he became less defensive and was willing to act a less threatening role, that of fulfilling future ambitions. He chose the "tycoon of industry" role. The mother, brother, and director became actors and supported his demanding attitude. Until this point the mother was completely discouraged by the son who would not learn to read or to study. Now she was delighted with the skill with which he negotiated the scene. It gave her a picture of a bright future and permitted her to respond in a warm and friendly fashion toward the future "tycoon of industry." After a few sessions there was marked improvement in Stan's willingness to be tutored. As the mother's nagging and overprotective attitude toward the children stopped, Stan's feelings toward his mother and brother also changed. The role of baby, of being quiet and timid with outsiders, was dropped.

The mirror technique, in which a member reflects the child's behavior so that he can watch it, was used to deal with Stan's resistance. When a mother is openly angry at a child, the child may refuse to act with her. This response gives us an insight into the nature of the relationship. In some instances where the material may be too threatening, as we found it here ("The person I most depend on is angry with me. I prefer to think I do the right thing. It's mother who is unfair.") a character can be used who acts in the same way as the patient. Sometimes this is necessary when the child objects emphatically to the mirroring of his behavior. Then the director attempts to establish a relationship with the child by inviting him to direct the session.

Psychodrama with an Adolescent and His Family

The next psychodrama is of interest because it brings into focus several aspects of psychodrama with an adolescent.

This is the psychodrama of a high school dropout. Barry, age fifteen, was doing very badly in high school, although he was of normal intelligence. He was the youngest in a family of two. His mother and father were both high school graduates who placed great emphasis on material success. The mother was a fastidious dresser and hostess, the father, a captivating salesman. The father had some difficulty in meeting his wife's expectations and began drinking heavily. They were called to school and Barry's behavior was made known to them, particularly that he was truant and refused to attend any class he wasn't interested in.

The battle between the school authorities and Barry took the form of "as long as you won't do what I want, I won't do what you want." Barry wanted to be on the school newspaper; the school authorities said, "You can be on the school paper as soon as you make a 'B' average." Barry found a friend with the same attitude toward the school, and they spent most of their time reading comic books on trains and in going to downtown movies. This stubbornness, it was explained to his parents, required psychiatric attention. Barry managed to defeat the psychiatrist, who sent him into a psychodramatic group of his peers to motivate him. The peer group, too, was unable to arouse Barry from his fixed position of "they don't have anything I want. I want to write for the newspaper, or be a bum." He left the group, and a year later his mother called to say that he and his friend had been expelled. It was then suggested that she call together all the people intimately related to Barry—sister and brother-in-law, aunts and uncles, three husbands and wives who were as substitute aunts and uncles, very close friends of the parents, and the boyfriend, who also had been expelled, with his mother and father, to have a session in the home.

Barry was the only one, besides the director, who had any experience in psychodrama, a condition which pleased him no end. It was explained to the group that they were going to experiment with a new, perhaps a different approach, to help Barry arrive at a decision, since he was at a critical moment in his life. They were not there to tell Barry and his friend what to do, but to help them explore the avenues open to them. This was, in a sense, a movement into the future, but in order that all of them could catch up with the events of the past, they would begin with the parents being called to school. The director of this session said, "it is important for me to know you and you to know me, for us to establish a working relationship that will result in an effective solution for Barry. Let me tell you a little about psychodrama. It is a learning method to explore areas without paying too high a price in Barry's real living. Experiments in learning seem to indicate that a person can practice at living and learn to be free enough to act, to move. Everyone of us here realizes the value of a continuing education, and we try, in a variety of ways, to influence those near and cherished by us, to further their education, as a preparation for life. We know this, Barry knows this, and so does his friend, but something blocks them. Our plan for this evening is to help Barry become free to move in any direction, to see alternate routes. Barry knows all of you here; he is, perhaps, the only one who does. Let's begin by introducing ourselves, and if there are any more questions, they can come up as a way of getting to know each other."

The director was warming up the group to the experience of solving a problem in an unaccustomed manner. It would have been presumptuous to move to the enactment of the problem without preparing the audience.

During this session, a sociometric analysis of the group was made, which disclosed that Barry's figures of influence, people with whom he had already established a good relationship, were his mother and brother-in-law. The brother-in-law had been honorably discharged from military service as an officer. He was the only college graduate in the group. The mother related in an intense and positive way to her friends, three men and their wives, who had been meeting socially for over twenty years. Barry's father was not as financially successful as the other men in this social group and played the role of the beloved clown. Barry and his father were both viewed as "odd." The father's drinking was unusual behavior among Jews. Barry's non-acceptance by his peers and his expulsion from school supported the general view that he was a problem child. It was probably his apathy, his lack of aggressiveness, and his social isolation which bewildered them. The goal was to help Barry out of his apathy, out of his indifference, and into a course that would make him more productive. A further goal was to help the group to be more understanding of the ways in which they could support the parents. A summary of the steps taken follows:

1. The first step was exploring the attitudes of the group.

2. This was followed by an enactment of situations. The first scene presented the problem of Barry and his friend being expelled from school.

3. The reaction of the parents, including the boys' confronting them with this development, was explored along with an exploration of the parents' resources for managing problems. The mother of Barry turned first to the husband who was cynical about the school and said, "They're a bunch of dumb clucks, and they finally caught on to Barry." She then turned to her best friend, Shirley, and exclaimed, "Oh, that's awful! He shouldn't do that. What does he want? Go to the Army?" Shirley replied, "Thank goodness, he needs your signature. He's too young to enlist without it." Barry's mother, who suffered from high blood pressure, was desperate when she had telephoned me and the enactment of this scene revealed her desperation as well as Barry's.

4. The director, before moving into the next situation, summarized by explaining that we had seen a sample of the feelings and reactions

set into motion by Barry's failure to meet the school's requirements. "Let's see from Barry and his friend now what happened to them, what is their reaction to the school's decision." They acted jubilant; this was just what they wanted. "No more school. Let's join the Army." "We'll have to get permission from the folks." "I don't think we'll have any trouble doing that."

5. The director stopped the action and asked them if this was really what they wanted. They assured the group that it was. The scene was then set for a recruiting station, with the brother-in-law using his prior Army experience to give an authentic picture. The brother-in-law was requested by the director not to color or flavor the role of recruiter with his own biases. The boys were accepted by the military pending the signature of the parents. "If you get your parent's permission, you're in."

6. A scene was devoted to the realistic interview between a young recruit and a recruiting officer. This was followed by a discussion in which the other men talked about their own military experiences.

7. The director, sensing the negative feeling developing in Barry and his friend toward the group of adults trying to scare their young and save them from the dangers of life, found it necessary to remind the group that our position was to help the boys to be free to move in any direction they want. "If they want to join up, let them. But what other ways, Barry, do you see open to you?" He responded, "Get a job." His mother countered, "Go back to school. Get reinstated." Barry and his friend replied, "Never!" The director then negotiated a contract. The boys were to be free to go back to school, get a job or to join the military. The parents would not withhold the signature if the boys decided on the latter course of action. On the other hand, the parents would not financially support leisure, the doing of nothing. The boys either had to decide on work, school, or the Army.

8. Questions and answers followed. The director admonished the adults not to interfere by warning of future dangers, to avoid directly or indirectly trying to influence them, to permit them to arrive at their own decision.

The results of this session were dramatic. A week later the mother telephoned to report that Barry had obtained a job in a warehouse. Unhappy with it, and seeking a more comfortable way out, he had asked if there were a private school he could attend. It was late in the season, but one was found. He was assigned, not only to journalism, but to the radio station of the school. He found his place, graduated from high school and later from college. He served his military time as a photographer, and is presently earning his living in journalism. He knew what he wanted and got it.

The group of his parents and their friends were so impressed by the evening of psychodrama that they gave up their weekly card game and met regularly as a couple's group to work out problems in relating to each other and to their children.

In reviewing this experience, the significant aspect may be that a group of people responded to a crucial moment, expressing concern and sharing their life experiences without pushing a troubled person into a costly act. Barry, a pampered boy, until then had been acting out his life scheme with the false notion that one should only do what one likes to do. It was not necessary to change this whole concept, but only to put it on the constructive side, to discover his major condition for functioning (journalism) and help him discover a useful way to achieve it.

Psychodrama with an entire family helps them reach a consensus of feeling and action. In order to illustrate the predicament, it is reconstructed; in order to change, the whole group needs an interactional experience. This family interaction teaches them a different approach to solving problems, encouraging the family to give up ineffective techniques for better ones. The strategy is to allow the adolescent to have more growing room, to have an area in which he can operate without putting pressure or force on him. This leaves him free to act within the limits of reality. With reference to Barry, the parents' decision is a declaration of "This is what you can expect of me. I agree to this and this, but not this." Barry had the choice of action, free to do whatever he wanted, except that he must meet the reality of the military, the warehouse and his parents. The parents, too, must meet the counter-spontaneity of their son. They could assume an authoritarian attitude and decide what's best for him and lose the son. Authoritarian behavior on the part of parents has lost its previous effectiveness. In this demonstration, we have an illustration of training parents to effectively deal with adolescents.

Summary

Sociometry is an instrument for investigating the social structure of a group. While paper and pencil diagram was not made in either session described, the relationships in the group were observed and understood in the light of sociometric insight, that an individual suffers from a low sociometric score. In both examples, the patient was the least chosen person in both his family and peer group. The sociometric therapy in the case of the nine-year-old was in restructuring the relationships around the patient; in the case of the adolescent, we did reassignment therapy, i.e., to find a group in which his group position is altered. The method in both cases was an action technique—psychodrama.

The family constellation was an important frame of reference to unravel the disturbed relationships. The commonsense and practical solutions which are characteristic to an Adlerian therapy were used in dealing with current experiences and the logic of the "moment." This approach, in both examples, made a strong impression on the families and helped solve their current dilemmas.

REFERENCES

1. Adler, A., *Social interest: A Challenge to Mankind* (1930). New York, Harper Torchbooks, 1964.

2. Adler, A., *Understanding Human Nature* (1927). Greenwich, Conn., Premier Books, 1954.

3. Adler, A., *What Life Should Mean to You* (1931). New York, Capricorn Books, 1958.

4. Ansbacher, H. L. and Rowena, eds., *The Individual Psychology of Alfred Adler* (1956). New York, Harper Torchbooks, 1964.

5. Dreikurs, R., *Psychology in the Classroom* (1957). New York, Harper & Row, 1968.

6. Moreno, J. L., ed., *International Handbook of Group Psychotherapy*. New York, Philosophical Library, 1966.

7. Moreno, J. L., *Psychodrama*. 3rd ed. Beacon, N. Y., Beacon House, 1964.

8. Starr, Adaline, "Psychodrama with a Child's Social Atom." *Group Psychother.*, 5(1953), pp. 22-228.

9. Starr, Adaline, "Psychodrama with a Family." *Group Psychother.*, 12(1959), pp. 27-31.

THE CARTOON AS THERAPEUTIC CATALYST

Asya L. Kadis and Charles Winick

Alfred Adler was a man of few words, but how he made them count! He could characterize a complex human situation with a pithy comment which communicated his point without inundating the patient with excess verbiage. He emphasized the importance of early childhood recollections and images, in understanding the patient's total personality and life style.

Adler had an extraordinary talent for graphically confronting a patient with his life style, in phrases or sentences which became unforgettable. During the senior author's last meeting in Vienna with Adler, she complained about the troubled world political situation at the time. He asked, "What do you do when the weather is rainy and stormy? Do you sit at home not caring to go out?" "Of course not," she replied, "I put on a raincoat, galoshes, take an umbrella and go out to do what I have to do." Adler's talent for presenting the patient with an unforgettable image of himself is comparable to a cartoon that confronts the patient with a significant aspect of his life-style.

This is a report on the circumstances in which sharply drawn, insightful cartoons can represent excellent diagnostic and therapeutic tools which are particularly applicable in eliciting the kind of meaningful early material which was stressed by Adler. Such cartoons may be worth a thousand words in provoking a much-desired shock of recognition in the patient.

Man's conflicts have been depicted graphically for thousands of years but the modern cartoon has added a new dimension. The cartoon is a stylized drawing, often of people in a social situation, which exaggerates their foibles. It can have a tremendous effect on the viewer without his having to make the kind of commitment of attention required by reading. The cartoon's impact depends on how trenchant is its message (usually conveyed with few if any words) and the extent to which it parallels and reflects the viewer's own life situation. If he responds immediately with an "aha" reaction, the shock of recognition might evoke pain and/or make him smile. The cartoonist is a latter-day representation of the wish expressed in Robert Burns' famous words:

> "Oh wad some power the giftie gie us
> To see oursels as others see us!
> It wad frae monie a blunder free us,
> And foolish notion."

In a number of western countries, there has been a strong interest in cartoons since the end of World War II. The polyvalence of values of the last thirty years has sensitized many people to symbolic meanings and the significance of gestural and other nonverbal vocabularies of emotion. The cartoon is a communication which reflects our set toward perception of nonverbal meanings.

Europe has long had a tradition of magazines which featured cartoons concerned with incisive comment on human relations (*Bizarre* and *Le Canard Enchaine* in France, *Punch* in England, *Simplicissimus* in Germany, *Candido* and *Travaso* in Italy, and *Krokodil* in the Soviet Union).

For decades, political cartoonists have enjoyed considerable eminence in the United States. Cartoonists who have begun as local newspaper editorial page features (e.g., Mauldin of the *Chicago Sun Times,* Herblock of the *Washington Post,* Conrad of the *Los Angeles Times,* and Oliphant of the *Denver Post*) have become national figures. Caricaturists Ronald Searle's Dickensian and witty comments and Gerald Scarfe's disemboweling caricatures of various kinds of human foibles have been widely reprinted in America since their original appearance in England. For decades, Al Hirschfeld's consistently brilliant cartoons of celebrities and, more recently, David Levine's funny and savage portraits of politicians have added new dimensions to caricature.

Psychoanalytic ideas have been very important to the work of cartoonist Jules Feiffer, who has been widely syndicated since he began appearing in 1956 in *The Village Voice.* The kind of private anguish expressed in Feiffer's cartoons appears to have found considerable resonance among many young people.

In this country, *The New Yorker* has long carried cartoons which make incisive observations on social life and contemperary problems. *The New Yorker* pioneered in cartoons which were based on some aspects of psychoanalytic doctrine. Cobean's cartoons in the magazine, during the 1950's, used a balloon above a character's head in order to communicate what he was experiencing, on a depth level.

During the last few decades, a number of cartoonists have become known for their wit and sensitivity to recurrent problems of human relations and have developed reputations akin to those of best selling authors. They are readily identified by their last names alone. "Did you see the cartoon by . . . ?" has become a common way of communicating sophistication and expressing a feeling of being contemporary and "in."

The art of the cartoonist seems to flourish in difficult times, of which we certainly have had our quota in recent years. The cartoon can offer us a summary of a situation in a dazzlingly apt graphic image which fixes a personality or relationship or institution. Originally a delight of big city intelligentsia, the cartoon has become more widely accepted in the arena of general public discussion.

The success of the cartoon in psychotherapy is not necessarily linked with any particular phase of treatment but rather to its presentation to a patient whose continuing verbosity is self-defeating. The cartoon may be helpful if it illuminates a core problem or an issue of life style. Patients who are eidetic, use visual imagery more than that of the other senses, or enjoy the plastic arts, are especially likely to be candidates for the use of a cartoon. In some ways, the cartoon in psychotherapy has functions similar to those of music: for a certain kind of patient, it seems able to reach through defenses and provide a vocabulary of emotion which is more accessible than words (1). In general, the more sophisticated the patient, the better he responds to a cartoon. Especially in a large city, patients who have "been around" and had considerable therapy are likely to be able to talk about and around their difficulties without any necessary insight and/or improvement in their life situation. Some of these patients may be able to respond to cartoons in a therapeutic situation.

Choice of Cartoons

The cartoons used as adjuvants to psychotherapy have been prepared by their creators for their own purposes and goals, in terms of self expression and their desire to communicate an insight into the human condition. We have found cartoons by William Steig and Abner Dean to be especially valuable in working with patients. Neither cartoonist could have known that his work would have a later use in psychotherapy. Dean's work has appeared in many publications and Steig has been contributing cartoons regularly to *The New Yorker* since 1930. These two artists have created, in their cartoons, some of the most hauntingly evocative and memorable visual characterizations of the recurrent problems and interpersonal relations of our time. They are genuine artists rather than visual journalists.

These two artists can convey universal problems with perception, humor, and often pathos. Frequently, no caption is necessary to get the full impact of their work. One reason for the extreme usefulness of cartoons by Steig and Dean is that the artists are extremely sensitive to psychotherapeutic and psychodynamic concepts. Steig has observed that " . . . people are basically good and beautiful, and neurosis is the biggest obstacle to peace and happiness. In my symbolical drawings I try to make neurotic behavior more manifest . . ." (2, p. 7). Steig is a very sensitive and astute observer of human beings who has an extraordinary awareness of body imagery. Machover has observed that the artist's " . . . suffering and deep analysis of himself makes it possible for him to expose to conscious view archaic, irrational, and regressive processes, usually submerged, avoided, or denied consciousness by most of us . . . Yet when we look at his drawings, we have a vague sense that although he is talking with his guts, he is really talking about ours, as well" (3).

Dean is a very keen student of interpersonal relations in our time, as well as a brilliant humorist. Because Dean's characters are naked, the element of defenselessness is particularly significant among his themes. He is especially sensitive to dimensions of values, conscience, motivations, morals, drives—in short, the bases of humanity.

Techniques of Presentation

The cartoon should be used very cautiously and only presented to a patient when he appears to be ready to consider the possibility that a problem which he has is central to the cartoon. Both artists have had their work collected in books, so that the mechanics of presenting a specific cartoon to a patient can be easily handled.

There are various ways in which a cartoon may be shown to a patient. One way is for the therapist to open the book to the appropriate page, cover up the caption, present the cartoon, and say, "I have a feeling that this is what you are talking about" or, "Does this call anything to mind for you?" He may say "This makes me think of you," "This may interest you," or similar phrases. One simple approach is to open the book to the proper page and ask, "Would you look at this cartoon?"

The patient may laugh at the cartoon or become intensively interested in it or say something like "I know what he means." Or, he may appear pensive and not respond immediately. If the patient hesitates or otherwise expresses reluctance, and says, "I don't see how it relates to me," the therapist might say, "O.K., maybe we will come back to it some time." The cartoon is a form of non-verbal interpretation and a technique for penetrating resistance. A patient whose resistance is intense and who has difficulty in responding should, of course, not be pushed to do so. The therapist ought never to make an issue of a patient's non-response to a cartoon. A disturbed reaction may be reflected in a long silence, like the red shock in response to the Rorschach.

Some Examples

Patients undergoing prolonged individual therapy at times seem to become almost immunized to words—their own and others. Every psychotherapist has heard a patient say, "Why didn't you ever tell me that?" or "Isn't it a little late to bring *that* up?" in reference to something mentioned several times in his hearing. This "deaf ear syndrome" is exemplified in an interchange between a mother and her teenage son. She impatiently said, "Whatever I tell you simply goes in one ear and out the other." He said wearily, "No, Mom, it doesn't even go in!"

A patient may fail to listen or retain verbal communications for self-insulation against increased anxiety. "Reaching" people who are at the point of absolute saturation with words presents a real problem. Yet an appropriate cartoon at the right time may trigger a shock of recognition that leads to therapeutic progress. The excessive verbalizing of our sophisticated society pervades the therapist-patient relationship and many other situations. Some patients talk, talk, talk to avoid being drowned in the therapist's sea of words, as well as to avoid insight.

Estelle, a most attractive and intelligent young woman, sought help because she had the normal desire for male companionship but experienced several unpleasant somatic reactions at the mere thought of keeping a date with a man. Gastric difficulties, sweating, flushing, and similar reactions invariably caused her to break the engagement at the last moment. After she had discussed the most recent such episode the therapist showed her a Dean cartoon of a very tall man walking on stilts, with a light bulb attached to his behind (4). A woman standing below the figure looks up at him in awe. Estelle blushed furiously, seemed to shrink, and then said bitterly: "You're right. There's little old helpless no-good me, admiring the man on a pedestal." She reflected that her mother and grandmother had both favored her younger brother, giving him a great deal of attention and admiring all his accomplishments. She felt inferior to him; unable to cope with the overpowering admiration he received, she adopted the same attitude as her mother and grandmother.

At the next session, she said, "What a dope I've been to let this *idée fixe* mess up my life. What makes me act as if all men are godlike when I *know* plenty of them are nobodies? I'm just as silly as that girl in the cartoon to go into a decline when I have a date. It's demeaning and I'm sick of it."

The last time the therapist saw her, about a month later, she related that she had had three dates, and had not experienced flushing, sweating, or diarrhea. Although a little nervous at first, she kept reminding herself that men are only *people*—some special, some not. She didn't feel either unworthy of their friendship or scared to death. Her next communication to the therapist, six months later, was a one-line note saying, "Men do *not* have light bulbs on their behinds!"

Jim, a brilliant man, had a job in no way commensurate with his intelligence and abilities, and considered himself a third-rater in all respects. The therapist had not succeeded in bringing home to him the need to change the poor image he had created for himself. A college drop-out, he continuously pointed out that although he had never made the grade, his brother was a doctor, someone to be proud of. After a year in individual treatment, he still referred to himself as the "dumb" one in the family, the "under-achiever"—a failure in business and in social life, in contrast to his successful doctor-brother. One day the therapist showed him the Steig cartoon of a sad, beaten-looking little boy straining to hold down one end of a seesaw, while a smiling, triumphant boy, with arms folded, is basking in the sunshine on the elevated end of the seesaw (5). Jim studied it. When asked if he was reminded of any situation in his own life, he said "No." When the therapist showed him the cartoon again during his next session, he examined it more closely, still without comment. The therapist said: "It looks as if the child on the ground needs to hold himself down, so he can keep his friend propped up in the sunshine." Jim seem startled, took another

look and said, "He *is* holding the seesaw down; I wondered why the balance was off when the two kids were about the same size. It ought to go up and down. I guess you have a point. I have to hold myself down so my brother can shine in solitary splendor. Mother always considered him the gifted one and I didn't want to disappoint her by spoiling his image."

The therapist suggested that Jim join a group where he could work out the symbiotic relationship with his mother, aided by the prototype family figures of the group. Jim discussed the cartoon in the group. One of the members, sensing Jim's need to run himself down in order to enshrine someone else, said: "You know what, Jim? We won't let you do that any more. Let your brother fall down from the clouds and take a good bump on the ass. It's *your* turn to go up on the seesaw."

With increasing understanding of his destructive self-concept, Jim slowly began to correct the distorted image he held of the "successful" brother, and in time admitted that his own intellectual potential might be as good or even better. With support and encouragement from the group, he returned to college to complete his B.A. and studied for a

112

graduate degree. He now has a very responsible and satisfying position, is married, and has a child. There can be no doubt that the seesaw cartoon provided a valuable breakthrough for this man.

When Val, another patient in the group, saw the same Steig cartoon, which was passed around the circle with each person commenting, he said: "That's me, the bottom dog. What do I have to smile about? I float around all day on a barge in a sea of shit." Val was a masochistic, nihilistic person whose dreams reflected his engrossment in self-humiliation. Val asked to see the cartoon again and studied it. A member of the group asked Val, "Why is there no sunshine in your life? Because you're like the fellow in the cartoon, you won't go after it. You can't see yourself pushing up and getting out of that sea of shit. You're like the character in the play, *He Who Gets Slapped,* only you run after the slap." This session represented the beginning of a major turning point in Val's treatment, although it was some weeks before he began to make therapeutic movement.

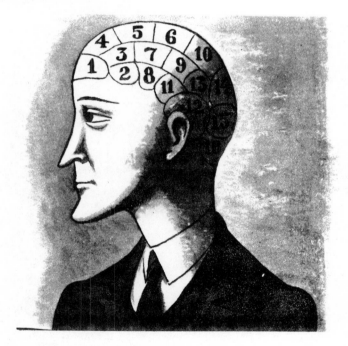

Warren, an obsessive-compulsive patient, had been in individual therapy for two years. He would relate countless details of his daily life without revealing any significant thoughts or feelings. One day the therapist decided to show him the Steig drawing af a man's skull, with each section neatly partitioned and numbered (5). He studied it and then said, "Sure I file everything; what else can I do with it? True, it's mostly junk. What I need is a better filing system up there." Then he launched into another blow-by-blow account of his day: "I went to the library and changed two books, one had eight cents due. That was *The Revolution in Politics* I think, then I went to Nedick's and had an American cheese on rye, two brownies and coffee with cream, then I took a bus to the barber shop." The therapist interrupted him. "Is that from the Section 5 file? Let's skip Section 6 today." Warren became angry, but he subsequently was far less likely to give meandering accounts of his activities. The cartoon was able to effect a loosening of his rigid patterns, although verbal interventions by the therapist had been unable to do so.

One cartoon which has proved to be valuable not only with obsessions but even with some patients who are near-paranoid is Dean's "The Obession" (4). It shows a man running down a road which is lined by many female breasts. Sam had been in treatment for some months when the therapist showed him "The Obsession." Sam looked intently at it and muttered, "He's running away from all those breasts. No, those aren't breasts, they're woods. The man is making them into breasts."

He closed the book and looked into space. "Maybe I am running away from things too. You know I was a runaway kid, always afraid of the teacher, my folks, everybody." The cartoon seemed to penetrate his system of defenses and provide a point of departure for a serious confrontation with his central problem.

Use in a Group

Sometimes a cartoon may be presented to a patient in a group by the therapist. Although it is shown to a specific patient because the therapist feels it can be helpful to him, the other group members might also benefit.

Indecision

Irving, after some time in group psychotherapy, was still unable to make any decisions affecting himself, although he freely gave sound advice to others. Fearful of making wrong decisions about himself, he made none whatever; he was the victim of his wavering impulses. One day the therapist showed him the Dean cartoon of a man firmly grasping a tree trunk with his arms and legs, while a girl's pretty leg is disappearing around a nearby tree (4). After Irving finished with the cartoon, it was circulated throughout the group. "He certainly fixed things up fine," one male group member commented, "by the time he gets untangled the girl will be in the next county." A woman turned to Irving and said, "If *you* wouldn't immobilize yourself, *you* could get somewhere. You've got the brains and ability but you can't make up your mind." Another woman said, "Maybe Irving thinks the *status quo*, no matter how lousy, is safer than the unknown." The group continued to discuss

115

his continuing need to adopt the pattern of indecision—as a possible means of avoiding hurts or errors. Finally Irving said, "I'm like that fellow; I create my own obstacles. If I'm going to get a girl or anything at all, I'll have to let go of the tree first." This session marked a turning point in Irving's therapeutic progress, which accelerated rapidly.

Sometimes it is possible to introduce a cartoon into a group where a particular kind of mood has developed. In one group, the therapist passed around the Steig cartoon of the man raised on a seesaw, asking, "How do you feel about this?" One patient said, "Gee, maybe the therapist doesn't want to sit up there—we keep her up." Another patient began to laugh, "She showed us the cartoon—sure, we're keeping her up in the air." Group discussion centered on the extent to which members saw the therapist as an idealized, omnipotent parent. The rest of the very productive session was devoted to exploration of how the patients, in situations outside the group, so often tended to downgrade their own abilities.

In another group which had a somewhat similar mood, the therapist introduced the Dean cartoon of a man on stilts. It led to an active exploration of the nature of passive dependency and how it related to hostility. The patients moved from a discussion of their admiration of the therapist to expressions of animosity and the interrelations between such seemingly antipodal felings were very productively probed during the next few meetings.

Parent and Child

Steig is exceptionally attuned to the nuances of parent-child conflict. He has explained his interest in children: "Since they (children) are still so full of life, the conflict between life and social insanity is more dramatic to them" (2, p. viii).

In his volume on *Agony In The Kindergarten*, Steig has three cartoons which depict the helplessness of the child who is consumed by an overprotective parent. When one of these cartoons is shown to an overwhelming, controlling parent with the question, "How do you feel about this child?" there is usually a long silence. And then a glimpse of recognition of the destructive elements of the parental role may be manifested. One mother, shown the cartoon "Don't," asked, "Do you really think that my disciplining of Johnny can make him a passive male, which I *hate?*"

Ruth, a tall and heavy mother who had a low alto voice, and shouted while talking, complained that her son Jackie never listened, no matter how often she called him from the playground to go home. Shown "Willie!", she exclaimed, "Do you really think that he sees me that way . . . ?" (Yelling, still yelling.) "That would be *terrible!* But I can't help it. My voice is so loud." The therapist in this case did not say anything.

Ruth wept bitterly, telling about her sadness after losing her mother at an early age. She had long had the feeling that if her mother had lived longer, her own life would have been different. She said, "I gave up my executive job just to stay home to take care of my Jackie." At this point the therapist showed her another Steig cartoon ("Mother loved me, but she died") (5). The mother exclaimed, "That's exactly what I didn't want to become. I wanted to be self-sufficient, without self-pity . . . and now I am confused." At which the therapist remarked, "Perhaps there is still another way for a good parent." This encounter was the beginning of forward therapeutic movement for Ruth.

Family Therapy

In many circumstances, therapy of the whole family is the best way of treating a pathological situation and it may be possible to use appropriate cartoons in doing so. A pediatrician had referred to the therapist a couple which was having great difficulties with their four children, who were 14, 11, 9, and 6. The father called and asked if the whole family might come: "It's Sodom and Gomorrah at our house with those kids—I'd like to bring them."

After an hour of the initial consultation, the therapist opened a volume of Abner Dean cartoons to "Family Conference". The therapist said, "You've a good sized family and really have fun together. Here's something that might interest you," and handed the book to Joan, the 14-year oldest daughter. Joan looked at it and slammed the book shut: "We didn't come here to see pictures—don't think my mother and father are such fools." The cartoon presents twelve members of a family in a complex but close series of interrelationships, including sitting and standing on one another, arms linked, leaning over others, etc.

The parents told the daughter, "Wait, we want to see the picture." They looked over it and at each other, silently. Finally the wife said slowly, "We wanted to be pals with our children, not authorities the way our parents had been. But we have become too close—we have really wronged our youngsters." Other members of the family responded to the cartoon and the next four sessions were devoted to exploration of

the unhealthy aspects of the family's intense closeness. The last two sessions proved enlightening to Joan, who began to gain some insight into how she had manipulated her parents and siblings. By the fifth session, which was the last, both parents and children had decided to manage their relationships differently.

Man and Woman

Married couples in therapy have been helped by the use of cartoons. Not uncommon is the case of the man and wife who come for therapy but are maintaining an elaborate system of self deception. They believe that by being civil and never quarreling in front of their children, they are not communicating their problems to them. For such couples, the Steig cartoon, "Quiet Evening At Home," could be very valuable (5). It shows a man and woman sitting quietly in separate chairs and not looking at or not talking to each other. Each, however, is holding up a grimacing puppet which is facing a scowling puppet held by the spouse.

The therapist showed this cartoon to one such couple, which was shocked by it. The husband said, "That's us. We want the kids to think we're happy, so we don't yell. We don't want them to know how angry and separate we really are. That picture is us." The husband and wife were able to ventilate the murderous rage which they were feeling toward each other and to explore its occasions and consequences in the therapeutic situation. The cartoon had produced an immediate confrontation with a central problem of the marriage.

Another such outwardly harmonious couple was shown the Steig cartoon "Family," in which both parents are tied together with the child roped between and to them (5). After seeing the cartoon, these parents were made jarringly aware that their symbiotic relationship was not of much help to either themselves or to the child. The mother responded to "Family" by asking, " Do you mean that we are not staying together for Tommy's sake, but are using him to stay together?" The therapist had been unable to bring the couple to this insight by words but the cartoons were able to provide a confrontation with themselves, their lives and their own styles.

Another couple in therapy, after a few sessions, seemingly not being able to accept their own roles in their weblike or intertwined relationship, was shown a Steig cartoon of a man and woman caught and enmeshed in a hopeless snarl of twine, inescapably caught and further entrapped with each movement toward escape (5). Being confronted by this cartoon, the man exclaimed, "You are absolutely right. Any discussion that we start keeps us up all night, deeper and deeper, and seemingly farther and farther apart. Sometimes it keeps us up till five o'clock in the morning. What do you expect me to do? How can I stop it? She doesn't stop."

The wife said, "It is true, but you must do something to keep me going."

Her husband replied, "I know now. I have to keep some scissors under my pillow so I can cut the net. Maybe this will free us from each other."

She added, "Maybe we will then be able to communicate with each other, instead of tearing at each other."

The wife shuddered and asked, "How can we cut it?" Her husband looked at the cartoon, and said, "I don't want to be in a net." The cartoon enabled them to plunge into a meaningful discussion of their extremely difficult problem together.

Delayed Responses

Some patients may not respond directly to a cartoon because they are not yet ready to assimilate its insights. An instance of such a response was provided by Tom, a very sophisicated patient who had been seen three times a week for five months, but who had to leave the United States on business for a month. About two weeks before, he had been shown the "seesaw" cartoon but did not have any response to it. When he returned from abroad and walked into the therapist's office, he asked, "Where is that book you showed me—do you mind if I look at it again? I want to see it once more—it is blurred in my mind." He looked at the cartoon for a few minutes and then said, "That's very strange, I had thought the man on top of the seesaw was a woman."

Tom's mother had been his ideal. He continued, "Do you know what else I didn't see? I didn't see that his head was down." In the session during which this occurred, he continued to discuss what was clearly his core problem. So long as his mother was his ideal, he saw her on the top end of the seesaw. As he developed a more realistic perception of her, he was in a better position to equalize the balance of the two ends of the seesaw. In his life situation, Tom found he was able, for the first time, to disagree with female colleagues. Tom was able to make the interpretation of his problem by himself because he was evidently ready to do so, after returning from his trip. He is typical of the experienced and over-verbal patients who might be helped, via cartoons, by confrontation with a wordless image.

Another delayed response occurred in the case of a couple which had been shown the Steig cartoon of a couple in a mesh, about a month before they left on vacation. They did not respond to it at the time and the therapist did not pursue the matter. When they returned from vacation, the husband began discussing the cartoon, as if he had seen it just yesterday. "You remember that cartoon you showed us? That really represented our situation. We fought almost every day we were away. I can't help but think that my wife and I really need this wearing on each other. If I wanted to cut the net we are in, I wonder if my wife wouldn't make sure to dull the knife. We may both need it but I can't stand it."

Seeing the cartoon and thinking about it over a period of several weeks had finally made the couple dramatically aware of their negative mutual dependency and sado-masochistic bond. They both wanted to work on and try to save their marriage. The cartoon had a catalytic effect on the couple, although considerable verbal sophistication had gone into their previously unsuccessful attempts to come out of the shell of their neurosis.

Children

The cartoon confrontation technique has proved to be effective with children who might have difficulty in comprehending a verbal interpretation. In a school where the therapist was a consultant, the kindergarten teacher complained that five-year old Donald talked incessantly throughout the afternoon rest period. While the other children tried to doze on their pallets, Donald talked to anyone within earshot. The teacher had remonstrated with him, to no avail.

The therapist showed him the Steig cartoon "Nap Time," which shows three young children resting or sleeping peacefully in the foreground while one youngster is excitedly talking to another in the background (2, p. 98). His companion is holding his thumb in his ears.

The therapist observed, "It's OK if you don't want to sleep but look at what you're doing to the others." Donald tearfully complained, "But it's so hard to be quiet!"

Donald looked again at the cartoon and said, "Oh, look at the boy holding his toy. I'll ask the teacher if I can bring a toy from my house and I'll talk quietly to my toy." He did bring a toy, talked to it for a few days, and then dozed off with the other children, holding the toy in his hand. This was a therapeutic use of the cartoon although Donald was not in therapy.

Patient Picking Up Cartoon

On only one occasion has a patient picked up a book of cartoons and responded to one. While sitting in the waiting room, Roger, a 32-year old man who was very depressed, picked up a book of Abner Dean cartoons. He was, like many other depressives, unable to be by himself without "doing" something, and the book happened to be nearby.

He turned to a cartoon of a man who has shrunk, a man who has placed himself into an opening in a wall (4). A dog is walking by and doesn't look at the man.

Discussing the experience in his group, Roger became pale as he commented, "Even the dog doesn't look at him. If I could do so, I would crawl into the wall." As he elaborated his responses, he began to become aware of the reasons for his profound identification with the car-

Martyr Complex

toon. Roger had been a patient for some months but had not previously been able to face his depression and suicidal tendencies. Roger would sit against the wall in his therapy group, almost outside the room. He thought that the dog was urinating on the man's leg: "I'm lucky I'm not really that man, or I'd get wet."

Roger was suspicious of people and felt that nobody invited him anywhere. He projected his rejection of others onto them, while making himself as inconspicuous and unattractive as possible. Over a period of two months, his appearance improved, his clothes became more presentable, and he spoke more frequently in the group. One day, he got up from his place in the far corner of the room and carried his chair to the center of the room. The group members were delighted and one said, "We like you to sit in the center of the group. You make it easier for us to talk to you." This move to the center represented a colossal effort on Roger's part and was a symbolic expression of the improvement in his condition. The chance encounter with the cartoon made this possible.

Future Uses of Cartoons

There is every reason to expect that the cartoon will continue to be a modality which can offer a great deal of opportunity for therapeutic movement for some patients. Its use provides an opportunity for bringing into the therapeutic situation the dimension of nonverbal communication and of a confrontation with the patient's recurrent and core problem.

In every case discussed above, the cartoon was introduced when it seemed to be an organic outgrowth of the therapeutic situation. The patients represented a wide variety of personality and diagnostic types. Age and sex did not appear to be significantly related to the ability to react with insight to cartoons.

As psychodynamic insights become even more accepted by cartoonists of the future, we may expect that the next generation of artists will be integrating psychological concerns into their work at least as explicitly as Abner Dean and William Steig. The availability of such materials may lead to more precise use of cartoons in psychotherapy. The possible depth of patients' reactions suggests the desirability of using this potentiating tool with care and advance planning.

REFERENCES
1. Winick, Charles, and Herbert Holt, "Use of Music in Groups." *Group Psychotherapy,* 13(-960), pp. 76-86.
2. Steig, William, *Dreams of Glory.* New York, Knopf, 1953.
3. Machover, Karen, "The Body Image in Art Communication As Seen in William Steig's Drawings." *Journal of Projective Techniques,* 19(1955), pp. 453-460.
4. Dean, Abner, *It's a Long Way to Heaven,* New York, Farrar, 1945; *Come As You Are,* New York, Simon and Schuster, 1952; *Cave Drawings for the Future,* New York, Dial, 1954.
5. Steig, William, *The Lonely Ones* (1942), *All Embarrassed* (1944), *Small Fry,* (1944), *Persistent Faces* (1945), *Till Death Do Us Part,* (1947), and *Agony in the Kindergarten,* (1951), all of which are included in *The Steig Album,* New York, Duell, Sloan, and Pearce, 1953.

FICTION AND RELATED MEDIA AS ACCELERATORS OF THERAPY

Sophie Lazarsfeld

This paper deals with the application of Adlerian concepts to a field within psychotherapy which was one of his favorites. The technique was almost forgotten after Adler's death. This paper will show the usefulness of including various fictional material as a serviceable tool for psychological treatment, proven to be successful in many cases.

Chronological Development

Originally, Adler started to apply his own psychology to the analysis of classical literary works in order to deepen his understanding of such literature (1, 2, 3, 4). Then he went one step further. Just as literary works could be better understood by applying psychology, so might psychotherapy gain valuable support by using fictional material as one more new technique.

To analyze fictional characters and events was no great novelty; others had done it before, as exemplified by Freud's analysis of *Oedipus Rex*, Frederick Wertham's book based on belles-lettres (5), and the forum for bibliotherapy which Gutheil introduced in his *Journal for the Advancement of Psychotherapy* in January, 1949.

There are well-known examples of the influence of books on individuals as well as on masses. A classic case where individuals are lead into action by reading is immortalized in Dante's *Inferno*. Francesca and Pablo are reading the love story of Lancelot and Guenevere. Suddenly Pable stops reading, kisses Francesca, and . . . *"Quel giorno piu non ne legeme avanti"* (that day we read no further). They probably would have started action sooner or later without the reading, but it certainly triggered it off at that moment.

For the influence of fictional material on mass movement, we know about the effect of *Uncle Tom's Cabin* on slavery, Dickens' works on the abuse of children, Beaumarchais's *The Marriage of Figaro,* which helped create the atmosphere that shook down the "ancient regime," and the most famous, Goethe's *Werther,* which led to an epidemic of suicides among young men—which was not the purpose of the book. Goethe wrote it to overcome his own unhappy love, and being a poet he let his fictional hero do the shooting instead of shooting himself. When the growing number of suicides became known to him, he wrote into the next edition, "Do sympathize with me but do not imitate me."

The value of fictional material was also brought to our attention by some of the people who came for psychological treatment. They would often ask us to read certain books because there we would find "exactly" their problems. Seldom could we find "exactly" their problems in the pages to which the people referred us, but it always aided our understanding of their problems because we found their image of themselves and what they considered to be their problems. Fiction is not only useful for diagnosis but it also helps people express themselves better than they can through verbalization. All this was known before, but the contribution made to this field by the Adlerian school is to have built it up to such a point that it can be systematically taught, learned, and used within goal-oriented therapy.

Collecting Projective Evidence

Up to this point we had gathered some historically well-known facts and some professional experience of our own. But the latter had occurred only spontaneously and occasionally. The next step was to collect our material more systematically. We wanted to know whether or not within a deliberately staged situation the introduction of literary or fictional material would bring a reaction and what kind.

Since we had no funds with which to do a full-scale study, we enlisted the gracious cooperation of colleagues and personal friends. We certainly could not use patients as guinea pigs.

The first experiement I conducted was to ask a group of people—colleagues as well as non-psychologists—which fairy tale had remained most vividly with them, regardless of whether they had read it themselves or had had it told or read to them. In order to give them no time to think or to select, I brought this request to them at the end of one of our usual meetings. This forced them to answer immediately and spontaneously.

As it happened, three out of four in the audience—myself included—best remembered the same fairy tale, which was also their favorite, "The Little Mermaid," by Andersen. The tale is full of events: There are love and disappointment, hope and pain, expectation and loss, and supreme sacrifice in the name of love. Everyone taking part in the experiment was asked to tell what had impressed him most. It was highly interesting to observe that in doing this each participant revealed a pronounced character trait. A jealous woman recalled that the prince had forsaken the mermaid to marry another woman; a malicious man remembered the pain the little mermaid had to endure with every step she took when, in her great yearning to become a human being and win the prince she loved, she had to relinquish her shiny tail for feet. A musician recalled her beautiful voice and the songs she had sung before she had sacrificed her tongue to the sea-witch in return for the potion that was to transform her into a human being. A man whose evaluation of life was based exclusively on professional achievement and a withdrawal from all emotion, did not recall the love theme at all. For him there had been no prince in the story. Each memory corresponded with the life style of the adult who had told it.

Next I asked the group to tell the ending of the tale, again not giving them time to recollect consciously. Each participant gave the tale a different ending, but none recalled the real final scene of the tale. That the difference in endings corresponded with the difference in personality and character of the individuals in the group is clear enough.

But why could nobody—not one person—remember the real ending? After the meeting we checked the book and found that *after the ending proper,* there had been added a piece of imagery which was meant to induce children to "behave well" for the sake of the little mermaid. She had failed to become human, but neither could she return to her natural element, the water. Before being allowed to return home, she had to float in the clouds for three hundred years. But every time she flies past a window and can see a child "behaving well" one year is deducted from her purgatory. Now what child, and even what adult would like to be called upon to "behave"? Therefore the end of the tale was conveniently shifted into oblivion by all of us.

Another test consisted of asking several people to read the same book (7) and then report what had impressed them most. It was a book about a man's four love affairs at different ages during a long lifespan. Without exception everyone found that story the most exciting which corresponded with his own age. After having collected some more deliberately provoked responses, I allowed myself to apply it within therapy.

Favored Fiction

The first case in which I used the fiction approach was that of a woman who wanted to save her deteriorating marriage. She complained that her husband was inconsiderate and often even cruel to her. She would have liked to end the marriage but they were Catholics. The help she expected from me showed a complete misconception of psychotherapy. She asked me to invite him for a meeting and then to teach him to treat her in a better way.

According to her version the fault of the declining marriage was all his. She, to her best knowledge, had done nothing to impair the marital relationship. Experience in psychotherapy had already taught me that persons who catalogue the faults of their partner but none of their own usually have contributed to at least half of the problem. And the more the woman went on to paint her husband in darkest colors, the more grew my conviction that she had contributed substantially to her marital troubles and needed therapy herself. I suggested more sessions in order to discuss her problems, and after several sessions, therapy could be started in the real sense; however, I found her unreceptive and impregnably enclosed in her own set of ideas. Finally I resorted to the "Fiction Test" and asked her for books that had especially impressed her. Instantly she named three books, the contents of which differed widely. But there was a similarity in all three books, concealed but significant—the heroines, upon analysis, were the same. Each got everything she wanted from the hero without herself contributing anything. It was like a formula—men must give; the role of woman is to receive. Furthermore, all three authors had painted this arrangement in the agreeable colors of normal, moral status. Subsequent sessions verified my belief that this was her attention to it. She said that she never had been conscious that this was her attitude, that it was unusual, or that it should be questioned. When the inequity of such love-relationships was brought to her awareness, she understood that her problems originated in her irrational expectations, and the marriage started to improve.

A Fairy Tale

The second case is that of a young woman who was, of the three children in her family, so much the favorite of her mother that a neurotic bond was established between them—a neurosis that continued to wreak damage long after the woman had died. The woman was married and in a favorable financial and social position, but her complaint was that she could not enjoy life and was more often than not in a depressed mood. In addition, she was suffering from recurrent migraine headaches, against which all medication had proved useless.

With treatment she understood the nature of her problem, but only intellectually—there was no emotional response. Therefore, while she made a conscious effort to change her attitude it did not prevent her from continually relapsing into her old pattern of unhappiness. Her dreams indicated that she was struggling with her problem, and I thought that fiction might accelerate the process. Thus, without apparent connection with what we had been discussing previously, I casually asked her if she remembered one particular fairy tale, which I know was popular among European children.

The tale tells about a princess who once had been very happy, but later became subject to destitution and great suffering. My client could not remember the tale immediately, but when I reminded her of the princess' former great happiness and later sorrow, she suddenly quoted from the tale the very line I had hoped she might recall. *"Wenn das Eure*

Frau Mutter wuesst, das Herze wuerd ihr brechen" "(If your mother could see this, it would break her heart)."[1] She articulated the quotation under great emotional stress, and spontaneously pointed out the similarity between herself and the princess. It was the first breakthrough, the first deep insight into the source of her unhappy style of life. From then on therapy proceeded much better, and the migraine attacks vanished permanently. I can offer no explanation for the disappearance of the attacks other than the general belief that psychological factors always seem integral in cases of severe migraine.

I present these two cases because they depict the very beginnings of this technique. Up to this point I had used books and recollections of childhood stories—the same means which had proven serviceable in the experimental phase.

In retrospect these cases and their solutions look very simple, and in a way they were, compared with much more complicated ones to come. Therefore techniques had to be expanded as well, and at the end of the paper such a case will be discussed. In the meantime I had realized that a greater variety of fictional material was needed than just novels or fairy tales. It was fascinating to learn from subsequent patients of other types of fictional material which had not come up before.

A Folksong

One such example is the case of a young man who during treatment mentioned that he was obsessed with a folksong—so much so that he had to hum or whistle it constantly. He could not recall the words, therefore the melody haunted him all the more. Perhaps the obsession would stop if he could find the words. I asked him to whistle the song, and by chance I knew it. Immediately two lines of the text sprung up in my memory. In these two lines the lover demands that the girl love him as much as he loves her, meaning that he loves her deeply and she takes love in a lighter way. Because the young man had known the text before, had forgotten it, and was so ardently seeking it, the song must have had some special meaning for him. This led me to the assumption that the love affair in the song might have some similarity to a love affair of his own. He had told me before about some of his relationships with women but had given them no importance. Such an attitude is often indicative of a fear of becoming too deeply involved.

At this point I did not consider him ready to be confronted with something he had to work out for himself. Because of this I told him neither the words nor what the song had told me. I did not even mention that I knew the song at all. I am sure that the problem would have become apparent sooner or later during our work, but I am equally sure that this little event was instrumental in accelerating the process on the basis of the insight that I gained into his problem.

The experience went even further. Why did I immediately recall these two lines? Having considered the question, I realized that the young man must have given me some indication of his attitudes towards love. There must have been some signals before. Had I not recognized them, or had I not understood them? I tried to recall as best I could the material that had been manifested in former sessions and the conclusions that I had drawn from them. My impression of his style of life had been that he was quite accustomed to having his own way in most matters. I must have known in the back of my mind that the same pattern would be manifested in his love relations. Those two lines had sprung up in my memory to make me understand the problem more clearly.

After a few more sessions, I felt it to be the right time to mention the lines of the song. I very casually said that I knew the song that haunted him (he had mentioned it several times) and that I could tell him some of the text. He was eager to hear it, and when I cited the two lines, he emotionally cried out, "That's it, that's it!"

This event happened at the end of this session. During the next one, he seemed more relaxed than ever before. He began the session by telling me that what had happened in the previous session had helped him realize that it was not the song, but his own love situation which was similar to the song that had haunted him. He, who had always believed that man-woman relationships—including his own—were not important, could not admit to himself that this one had become very important to him. It was the love affair which haunted him, a clear case of shifting a problem that is too painful to admit to oneself to an acceptable one. From then on, he was able to discuss freely his present love affair, and he came to understand his own contribution to the difficulties, generated by his need to have his own way.

Demanding one's own conditions is a well-known symptom of doubting one's own ability to cope with other conditions. After the "song" session, as he called it, and his ensuing insight into his problem, he gained the courage to become involved in a love-relationship, even though it was not subject to his own conditions.

The Responses of Perfectionists

The three cases presented thus far, although different in situation and specific problem, have one common denominator. All these people felt deprived of what they believed to be rightly theirs. We shall now view the type of person who has the opposite problem. He is obsessed with the need to do in all situations what is absolutely right. His lack of self-confidence drives him to compensate by not daring to be less than perfect in everything.

It is one thing to develop and perfect whatever has been given by nature; this is a necessary and healthy attitude. But it is quite different with the perfectionist as a neurotic type. He is not satisfied with improving his qualities or capacities; his goal is to become *perfect himself.* Among these types of perfectionists, two are especially harmful.

One is the "ethical" perfectionist, who lives exclusively according to the highest moral principles, and by doing so sometimes ruins his life and the lives of those with whom he interacts.

The heroine of Marcia Davenport's novel, *The Valley of Decision* (6), is such an ethical perfectionist. My perfectionistic patients admired her so highly that some even wanted to follow her example. To accomplish this, they asked me to read and discuss the book with them. During the discussions, however, some of them realized that this "noble" woman— by insisting on uncompromising loyalty to the highest ideals—piled countless misfortunes upon those around her, including those she loved most. She is convinced that she does this to benefit the others and at the expense of sacrificing herself. For example, she forces the man she loves and who loves her and wants to marry her into a marriage with a woman he does not love. Later she drives this unloved wife to suicide and creates many other similar misfortunes—all on the basis of her high and inflexible moral standards. When we analyzed the book, psychologically examining the heroine's motivations, my perfectionists began to realize that these motives were far less altruistic than the heroine believed and that they were used for her own ethical glorification. One of my perfectionists went so far as to suggest that the book would better be called "The Valley of *Wrong* Decision." Another asked me if the author —who is known as one of merit—had really believed in the perfection of her heroine or if the book had been written "tongue in cheek" to depict in an exaggerated way the danger of *perfectionism.* Whatever the author's intention, the book helped some people realize that they might have developed a similar pattern, and that they might be able to change their style of life—an accomplishment some of them achieved.

There is another type of perfectionist who, by continuously searching for the perfect decision, becomes emotionally paralyzed to such an extent that he cannot make any decision, no matter how important.

To this type of person, making a mistake means defeat, which must be avoided at any cost, usually to the detriment of others. Being without foibles is not in the realm of human capacity. The illusion of perfection can only be retained by fictitious means. One of them is the inability to make any decision and thereby being saved from making a wrong one. These people need the courage of imperfection.

In her book, *The Whole Heart* (8), Helen Howe presents the hero as the perfect example of this type of perfectionist. By never making a decision, he creates numerous calamities for himself and those surrounding him. He marries four times, and all four marriages fail. After so many failures he consults a psychiatrist who advises that he acquire "the courage of imperfection." In the book, this phrase, printed in italics, is the starting point for improvement. At the time the book was published, some of my perfectionists had already perceived that their problems grew from their "all or nothing" attitude, but the dynamics of emotional understanding were missing. I advised them to read this book without telling them why. Some could not see any connection between the events of the book and their own problems, but for others the parallel struck like lightning when they came across the above-mentioned quotation. Some even went so far as to reproach me for never having given them a formula as helpful as this one.

I certainly had used this "formula," as they called it, because it was more than familiar to me. It happens that I had coined the words as the title of my first publication many years before (9).

This example leads straight to the core of the subject of this paper: why did the same words, coming from the therapist, not sink in and not provoke emotional response, whereas they made a great emotional impression when coming from fiction. This question will be discussed within the framework of the summary.

Fiction and a Painting

The next example shows how fiction and a painting interacted helpfully. It happened quite unexpectedly and without any intentional intervention on my part. It is the case of a young woman who was bothered with two problems; one that was very important to her, the other she considered unimportant but embarrassing. This latter problem consisted in the fact that one particular word always escaped her memory when she needed it. She neither could recall it nor could she replace it with an adequate substitute. When I asked her for the word, she again could not remember it. Any experienced therapist would recognize that this symptom was not as unimportant as she believed, but that the word must have had a special meaning for her.

Her "major" problem played a disturbing part in her marital life. Every time her husband's hand approached the hem of her clothes, it frightened her and she recoiled physically. Although she had previously undergone a long analysis which had helped her considerably, these two symptoms remained. A friend had told her about the fiction technique, and it appealed to her because she was well-read and interested in fiction. Thus, she had decided to try once more.

From the first session on, she spontaneously recollected and related books from her childhood as well as some that had impressed her as an adult. Her favorites were fictionalized biographies, especially those of women. We spent several sessions discussing this material, including the possibility of latent lesbianism because of her preference for female biographies, but nothing resulted. Early childhood recollections of exposure to the frightening approach of a male hand to her skirts (which often happens to female children) had already been examined during her former analysis, but we nevertheless went through them again—

and once more nothing helpful came up.

During previous biography sessions she had mentioned that her favorite heroine was Mme. de Recamier. I asked her for details of the book. This she could not relate offhand, but she immediately started to describe a famous painting in which her heroine is presented reclining on a small sofa of the kind that is called a *canapé*. At this point in her description she stopped, felt embarrassed, and said, "reclining on a carpet." She immediately realized that this was nonsense; she knew this was the "ominous" word that she could not recall and had substituted for it an inadequate expression.

After this experience I asked her for more situations in which the same problem had occurred. One situation arose when she wanted to use the word "canopy" for a baldachin and uttered the word "davenport," which she knew very well did not mean a baldachin but a kind of sofa. A similar situation arose when she had wanted to order food for a party she intended to give. She had had to tell the caterer that she wanted little pieces of trimmed bread because she could not recall the word canapé.

By that time I had no doubt that the ominous word was "canapé" no matter to what the term referred: *canapé*-sofa, canopy-baldachin, *canapé*-bread. But why did this one word have such an effect on her?

I returned to the painting and asked her to tell me what she saw in it, as one does with the TAT, but nothing helpful emerged. At this point it was clear that the story behind the word must have been very painful and probably shameful. I tried a shot in the dark and asked her to read a then very popular book—one I usually do not recommend; but I chose it because her behavior while working on the "unimportant" problem of the forgotten word led me to believe that the problem might lie in the area of sex, with which this book deals.

In the book a girl is sexually abused by her stepfather at the age of puberty; and that was precisely what had happened to this woman at the age of thirteen—on a canapé. She had purposely never told this to her former analyst, nor had she mentioned it to me. But when she read the description in the book, the old horror of her experience became so vivid that it broke the barriers of silence. This she told me after having read the book.

After that session she was never again troubled by the ominous word. To overcome the sexual problem in her marital relations required much more time, but the problem decreased steadily.

It is interesting to note that the seemingly "unimportant" problem held the key and opened the door to the very important and larger one. It may also be of interest that in this case a non-verbal element, the painting, interacted effectively with the fiction technique.

Summary

I shall now return to the question of why a reference to fictional material can accelerate the process of gaining a deeper insight in certain cases where the usual methods have not succeeded.

In such cases the suspicion sometimes lingers in the mind of the patient that the analyst is trying to "sell" him a preconceived idea of the problem. This suspicion often provokes resistance, thus blocking the emotional response and impeding the work of the analyst. In contrast, the author of a book does not know the reader at all, hence his interpretations, being neutral, are more easily accepted by the reader as unintentional and therefore trustworthy. This may aid in decreasing the resistance. For some patients this neutrality and the knowledge that there are others with similar problems helps also.

Often a patient will suspect that the therapist wants to model him in his own image. The patient's reaction to fictional material can be helpful in revealing this distrust to the analyst. There are two advantages here. As mentioned above, the therapist's understanding of his patient's attitude towards him is extended, and sometimes it increases the therapist's own self-understanding by spotlighting some dark, critical area of his own. He may wonder if there might not really be a dormant tendency within himself to take himself as the best model for "remaking" the patient, and that the patient might feel it. If such suspicions are present in the patient's mind, they will manifest themselves sooner or later and must be analyzed, but fictional material can accelerate the process.

Another advantage of the fiction technique is that fictional material can stimulate the imagination of a patient. In front of the therapist the patient is often a passive object receiving a greater understanding of himself. But when there is resistance on the part of the patient, it is easier for him to identify with the characters in a book, to visualize them and make his own discoveries. He is active because he is using his own imagination and creativity, which gives him a feeling of satisfaction and renewed confidence. His resistance diminishes and therapy can continue.

The technique has its limitations, however. These lie mainly in the personalities of the therapist and the patient. Concerning the patient, there are undoubtedly a great variety of responses to the technique. Some regard it with skepticism and some reject it completely, for reasons corresponding to their individual personalities and life styles. Some accept it intellectually but do not respond emotionally. Concerning the therapist there is one very important limitation to consider, he must be sensitive to the material he uses and it must have meaning for him. His entire success hinges on this. Whether it be *belles-lettres,* cartoons, comic strips, television or whatever he prefers makes no difference. What matters is that the material be meaningful to him.

This paper does not intend to suggest that this technique could do more or better than any other. Yet when skillfully applied, it can enrich the wide range of therapeutic methods.

FOOTNOTE

1. "Fallada and the Goose Shepherdess" (Grimm's Fairy Tales) Fallada is a talking horse who speaks these words.

REFERENCES

1. Adler, A., "Dostoievsky," in *The Practice and Theory of Individual Psychology* (1927). Paterson, N. J., Littlefield, Adams, 1963.
2. Adler, A., "The Fundamental Views of Individual Psychology." *Int. J. Indiv. Psychol.,* 1(1), (1935), pp. 5-8.
3. Adler, A., "The Prevention of Delinquency." *Int. J. Indiv. Psychol.,* 1(3), (1935), pp. 3-13.
4. Adler, A., "Verdrangung und 'Mannlicher Protest': ihre Rolle und Bedeutung fur die neurotische Dynamik," in A. Adler and C. Furtmuller, eds., *Heilen und Bilden: Arztlich-padagogische Arbeiten des Vereins fur Individualpsychologie.* Munich, Reinhardt, 1914, pp. 103-114.
5. Aswell, Mary Louise W., *World Within.* With an introduction and analyses by F. Wertham. New York, Whittlesey House, 1947.
6. Davenport, Marcia, *The Valley of Decision.* New York, Scribner's, 1942.
7. Galsworthy, John, *The Dark Flower.* New York, Scribner's, 1935.
8. Howe, Helen, *The Whole Heart.* New York, Simon & Schuster, c.1943.
9. Lazarsfeld, Sofie, "The Courage for Imperfection." *J. Indiv. Psychol.,* 22(1966), pp. 163-165.

GUIDING FICTION AND MENTAL HYGIENE

Paul Brodsky

Larger Than . . . [1]

Larger than I is You,
larger than You is We,
larger than We is They:

family, friends,
mankind and earth,
humanity, universe.

It all depends now whether
we're just holding out
    our hands
or are lending them
to make it love.

Mental Health

To experience oneself as part of an extrapersonal whole is a prerequisite for mental health. Since the society of man is one aspect of that extrapersonal whole, mental health can be defined by the extent to which an individual accepts his social integration (9). Mental health is thus a function of his social integration. In order to attain reality-awareness it is necessary to establish a distance between one's self and the surroundings, that is to say, to establish one's identification. "Analogous to 'Give me where I stand,' the opening words of Archimedes' 'Give me a fixed point and I shall move the earth,' the child seeks to gain a standpoint from which to appraise the distances to life's problems" (2, p. 98).

135

Attaining self-awareness is a gradual process. It is essential to realize that there are various levels of mental health parallel to the individual development from infancy through adulthood. Thus, a lack in self-awareness is normal for the newborn, while such a lack in childhood or adolescence would be an indicator of some personality disorder such as childhood autism or schizophrenia.

Childhood curiosity and inquisitiveness provide the stimulus for seeking that distance through identification, while the human mind's potential to think abstractly, to anticipate, is the tool for establishing the relationship between the "I" and the environment. In taking cognizance of the response of the environment to his movements, the growing child accumulates a storehouse of experiences which will help him to evaluate the meaning, purpose, the function of the elements composing the environment.

The neonate finds himself in the center of his environment, the family. He has very little to contribute, being almost totally dependent upon his environment for attention and nurture. As he grows older, that relationship becomes more of a two-way street. The reciprocity in that relationship makes itself felt in a wider range of give and take with other elements in his environment. By the time the child has reached school age, he can perceive himself as a factor in the field of interaction of someone or something else, perhaps his mother or his pet or the school routine.

Growth in the perception of self as part of an extrapersonal whole (1) reveals itself in a gradual decrease of the childhood self-centeredness. It will be reflected in the child's feeling of insecurity as he faces the intricacies of adult life and senses the loosening of the ties of dependency that connect him with his familiar environment (4). In an attempt to compensate for his feeling of insecurity he will find a prototype or a set of traits to emulate—a television hero or an athlete, a sinister scientist in the movies or an astronaut. He can find it in the way an actress carries herself or in the manliness of some actor's sideburns and leather jacket, in father's position within the family or in any person who impresses him strongly through his achievement. Slipping into the personality of his idol, hanging his traits around his shoulders, the child attempts to be "like," to be big and in his way find a place. In this process the child responds to the way people conduct themselves, to situations and incidents, to happenings as he observes them and relates them to his own concept of security and his personal goal. He establishes his manner of approaching that goal, which becomes his style of life.

In the setting of his goal and style of life one can see the operation of the child's creative power as he abstracts from his experiences his concept of the "I" and surroundings, his guiding fiction. The guiding fiction is originally the means or device by which the child seeks to free himself from his inferiority feelings, to give him greater security.

The Guiding Fiction

Abstracting, choosing, selecting, and evaluating are manifestations of man's decision-making capacity. However, the stimuli reaching the individual will not be evaluated with equal accuracy as to their relatedness to the anticipated goal of security at each age level and under all circumstances. The neonate, for instance, will translate a stimulus aroused by a basic need such as hunger into a movement towards its satisfaction. Because of his lack in self-awareness he will associate comfort with the vehicle, the mother, rather than the means, the milk. Gradually this will change into the experience of being able to provide comfort by getting the milk-providing bottle himself, that is to say, it will change into the experience of "I-can-do-it-myself." His abstraction, "I have to call for mother," changes to "I go for something to eat." In fact, what was formerly a source of discomfort, hunger, will become something enjoyable in anticipating the choice of something to eat according to likes and preferences. By that time food will have become a means for maintaining reciprocity in his relations with the surroundings, as the self-related basic needs are replaced in dominance by the socio-related higher needs such as the need to belong, for being taken seriously, of giving love (5).

That change will be accompanied by a growth in comprehension, in the ability to draw conclusions and to transfer experiences from one situation to another, in other words conceptualization, which will facilitate decision-making. The satisfaction of the higher needs will prove of equal consequence in that process as the satisfaction of the basic needs. The need for feeling secure, as one of the higher needs, is met by the child striving for familiarity, i.e., the motivation for him to reach out into his environment by grasping, mouthing, holding, by hiding and moving behind, above, beneath, by peeking, listening, observing and watching. This way he learns, discovers, applies, and creates as he observes the responses of the environment. His actions evoke a feedback in the form of consequences. On the basis of these responses he forms his self-concept, the distance between himself and the world around him; he establishes the concept of his I-in-the-world. As this feedback serves him in wending his way through life, it helps him form his guiding fiction.

In a dialectic way the feedback becomes a stimulus itself. As counter-fiction it may reinforce a concept upon which a decision has been based or lead to a revision resulting in a different decision. That interplay is of the greatest importance from an educational point of view as it offers the possibility for guiding the child by ways of consequences (7). "It would be extremely hazardous to expose a child who is equipped only with conditioned reflexes or with innate abilities to the test of a world which is continuously raising new problems. The solution of the greatest problem would always be up to the never-resting creative mind" (2, p. 174).

The framework within which the creative power functions is the sequence: stimulus-evaluation-decision-action. In that sequence the stimulus can be anything that reaches the mind through the sensory organs; it can be anything occurring within or without the individual. A stimulus cannot be ignored; it must be attended to and evaluated. There must be some response. With the evaluation, the recognition of the happening, a corresponding emotion is aroused (6). The decision will result in the individual's acting actively or passively, depending in each instance upon the anticipation of an effect. If the effect coincides with the anticipation, satisfaction will be experienced; otherwise dissatisfaction ranging from a simple "oh, shucks!" to severe frustration will occur. It is worth noticing that emotions are aroused at Link 2 and 4 of the sequence. They follow the evaluation of the stimulus at Link 2 and the evaluation of the effect of action at Link 4. Since evaluation is subject to training and learning, Link 2 and Link 4 offer the opportunity for learning, teaching, guiding, and therapy. It additionally affords the opportunity for prophylaxis.

In arranging the sequence vertically some of the pertinent aspects which influence each link can be indicated:

State and condition of the brain, the sensory organs, and the perceptors.   1. Stimulus

Source and intensity of the stimulus.

On a thalamic level: mainly pleasant-unpleasant.   2. Evaluation and emotions

On the cortical level: familiar or unfamiliar, thus promising security or not.

Attained level of self-identification.

Acquired information.

The personal goal and expectations, i.e., whether the goal is realizable.   3. Decision

Physical and mental maturity.   4. Action

Style of life.

Personal goal of security.

In view of the many factors influencing the formation of the guiding fiction, all disciplines dealing with human behavior need to take cognizance of them. This would be of particular importance as the "distance" between the "I" and the environment reflects the interplay between these two factors as guiding fiction and counterfiction. In other words that interplay reflects the continuous process of the individual responding to his personal concept of reality.

The guiding fiction provides the answer to the question of the predominance in personality formation of heredity or environment. It establishes their integration by the goal-directedness of the "I." The inner environment serves the individual in establishing his relations to the external environment represented in the tasks of life, and through the outer environment he forms his identification as part of the whole. The skill in handling himself in that reciprocity of relations will depend on the development of his potential. To what extent the child's environment will offer or deny him the opportunities for that development may prove decisive for the mental health of the individual.

Mental Hygiene

Mental hygiene refers to the provision of an atmosphere within which the child may grow and realize his potential without any of the day-to-day educational situations becoming trigger mechanisms for possible emotional disturbance. As with all prophylaxis it concerns itself with the "well" child rather than the already emotionally vulnerable one. It incorporates the home and school environment, both of which have the greatest stimulus-potential both as to the number and variety of the experiences offered and the influences exerted. The main task of education, formal or informal, is to find possible errors in the child's abstractions and then to assist him in correcting them.

I should at this point differentiate between primary and secondary prevention. The former is directed toward handling of normal educational situations skillfully in order to arrive at acceptable solutions; the latter concerns itself with dealing with situations already threatening to deteriorate. Consequently, primary prevention concerns itself with families during the child's formative years while secondary prevention most often will deal with pre-adolescents and adolescents. Since both the home and the school must be responsive to enormous changes created by the advances in science and technology, it is imperative that the findings of modern pedagogy and psychology be made available to these educational units to enable them to cope more effectively with the demands of modern society.

Thus, the main goal of a preventive approach to problems of mental health is to assist parents and teachers in adjusting themselves and their educational concepts to the general evolution of society. Admitting their educational limitations without fearing loss of face or self-respect will encourage them to learn more about the rearing of children. How much more relaxed the child-parent-teacher atmosphere will become when each can step down from his self-erected pedestal of perfection, of omniscience, to which each has committed himself.[2]

A mental hygiene movement must devote itself to early detection of conditions which may lead to emotional disturbances. While based upon the assumption that most parents do love their children, it must be centered on the improvement of skill and know-how as supplements to love and dedication (3, 8). In this way the parent's self-esteem will be safeguarded and their cooperation will be easier to obtain. It is not their goals but their techniques that we first focus upon.

The way parents and teachers usually respond to a child's behavior is by reacting to his actions rather than to his motivations.[3] They will find themselves caught in a vicious cycle which prevents the child from eliminating or altering a behavior pattern which appears to him to bring about what he was aiming at in the first place. Yet, since a child's misbehavior reflects his interpretation, it requires understanding of his misinterpretations if we are to understand his behavior. One should keep in mind, however, that these misinterpretations may also be those of the people close to the child.

Close cooperation of home and school is an essential factor for a preventive approach. The combination of parental familiarity with the child and the observation at school by trained personnel should prove to be ideal for early detection of difficulties and for the initiation of remedial or preventive steps. If mental hygiene facilities were provided by the school, it would avert the possibility of the child becoming stigmatized as in the case of private or agency consultation. Parents would be encouraged to utilize these facilities which would be similar to other remedial services, such as remedial reading, which are offered as school services. Families with acute or more serious problems would be referred to other than school sources for help. Since this service could be offered to the "well" child and his family, school personnel could be trained to engage in such counseling.

It is important to bear in mind that prevention is not limited to a particular child. It is thought of as a general assistance approach to parents and teachers in adjusting to the educational demands of a changing society. Parents and teachers should be encouraged to demand of their schools that they provide these services. A teacher's warning that "Susan is a lovely child, but she does not work up to capacity" is meaningless since it leaves the parent without any idea of how to go about bringing Susan up to her capacity. A school mental hygiene program could help supply the answer.

FOOTNOTES

1. From "Come To Think of It," a collection of poems by the author.
2. See Wade, "Teachers Are People, Too." This volume.
3. See Weill, "Reminiscences of a Child Psychologist." This volume.

REFERENCES

1. Adler, A., Social Interest: *A Challenge to Mankind* (1930). New York, Harper Torchbooks, 1964.
2. Ansbacher, H. L. and Rowena, eds., *The Individual Psychology of Alfred Adler* (1956). New York, Harper Torchbooks, 1964.
3. Beecher, W. and Marguerite, *Parents on the Run* (1955). New York, Agora Books, 1966.

4. Brodsky, P., "Dependency-Interdependence." *Indiv. Psychologist,* 1(2), (1963), pp. 13-17.

5. Brodsky, P., "Problems of Adolescence: An Adlerian View." *Adolescence,* 3(1968), pp. 9-22.

6. Dreikurs, R., "The Function of Emotions." *Christian Regstr.,* 130(3), (1951), pp. 11-14, 24. Also in *Psychodynamics, Psychotherapy and Counseling.* Chicago: Alfred Adler Inst., 1967, pp. 205-218.

7. Dreikurs, R. and Grey L., *Logical Consequences: A New Approach to Discipline.* New York, Meredith Press, 1968.

8. Dreikurs, R. and Soltz, Vicki, *Children: The Challenge.* New York, Duell, Sloan and Pearce, 1968.

9. Shoben, E. H., Jr., "Toward a Concept of Normal Personality." *Amer. Psychologist,* 12(1957), pp. 183-189.

HUMAN VALUES
IN PSYCHOTHERAPY

Alexandra Adler

To what extent can the psychotherapist influence the basic values of those who seek his help? Should he influence them by imposing his own upon them? Can patients be helped more by trying to change their attitude toward general human values, rather than by working on their own specific difficulties? In the following we want to consider what impact a change in the patient's attitude toward what is "good" and what is "not good," to put it simply, has upon his mental difficulties.

In recent decades a marked change has appeared in the approach of many therapists to the psychologic problems of their patients. Some schools of psychotherapy, however, particularly the psychoanalytic, still consider the patient a product of his drives and instincts. These causalistically oriented systems logically postulate that only by unearthing the deepest roots of a personality, through the laborious process of free association, can any change be achieved. The patient's mistaken development is traced back to traumas in infancy or early childhood. How such procedures can possibly change a structure developed by an infant seems incomprehensible to many. Furthermore, to use a picture from nature: if a plant is failing, we do not uproot it to discover the cause, although we know that the roots are very important to the life of the plant. Instead, we fertilize it, vary the amount of water given it, and clean the leaves so it can breathe better. In a similar way, we have learned to deal with the psychologic difficulties of human beings in the light of their present environment.

According to widely accepted standards today, an individual will be judged by his attitude towards his fellow beings, by what Alfred Adler refers to as Gemeinschaftsgefühl or "social interest" (5). As a consequence. values and conflicts of values only become meaningful as they relate the individual to other human beings and to society as a whole. Experience has taught us this through the ages, and we find it eternalized in our most prized literary and religious documents, such as the Bible, in which we find the injunction—"Thou shall love thy neighbor as thyself." History is witness to the fact, however, that the general level of social interest has often been low, and the struggle for power, both nationally and internationally, is in the ascendancy in the world. Here one cannot help being reminded of Freud's comment, "Why should I love my neighbor . . . he has more claim to my hostility and hatred . . ." Adler characterized this statement as the cry of a pampered child who cannot give up his self-centeredness for fear of losing his privileged standing.

It is desirable to encourage the patient to adopt positive human values, but this he often finds difficult because of real or imagined disappointments and frustrations in the past.

An example of a human value which not only psychiatric patients but a large part of humanity have difficulty in living up to is that of refraining from resorting to violence in settling conflicts, be they personal or international. In its most virulent form, violence breaks out when nations attempt to solve their problems by throwing hardware at each other, by invading and disturbing another country, for ideological or other reasons. In the present state of society, however, as well as of our understanding of human nature, violence cannot always be avoided, unfortunately. Exception will obviously have to be made in those instances where violent action is required for self-defense, or in which a madman or a tyrant gains control over a whole nation, with all the tragic consequences recently witnessed in Germany and Russia.

In deploring the dearth of positive, moral values in present-day society, we should not forget the growing attitude of non-participation, or at least passive participation, which is developing in many of us, the tendency to let the world go by, while we follow it, from a safe distance, on the television screen in our living-rooms, or through other communication media.

Today's mental health therapists have taken over some of the functions formerly served by the priest, the minister, and the rabbi. These spiritual leaders understood, although perhaps less clearly than the modern psychotherapists, the role played by ideals and positive values in the formation of the personality, and that these are as susceptible to illness as the human body.

Insight alone, however, can not provide an adequate method of treatment. Today, more and more attention is directed toward helping the patient to overcome his self-centeredness and to face reality. In this way the goal of psychotherapy is becoming forward-oriented, making the patient strive for greater perfection in tune with the demands of the environment. Social interest represents an innate human potentiality in the newborn child which, however, must be developed and perfected by adequate upbringing; if not, it may be delayed in its development, or thwarted altogether (5).

Let us now turn our attention to some of the various categories of mental difficulties which psychotherapy treats, and examine the influence that ideals and values have on their causation, on their perpetuation or eventual resolution, or at least on their amelioration.

We may begin with the criminal, who constitutes one of the largest groups of personality deviants in society. Adler (7) describes the early life pattern of the criminal as that of a child who meets the demands of society with a "no." Evidently feeling that his only hope of success lies in fighting his environment, the criminal behaves as though he were surrounded by enemies. He rejects human experience, which teaches that human beings must learn to live together and help each other in order to survive on the crust of this poor earth; instead he develops his so-called "private logic," pursuing his own objectives regardless of the hardships this may inflict on others. Confining the criminal, however, only takes him off the streets for a while, it does not alter his criminal tendencies. If anything, his crime pattern may become more confirmed, and his only interest will be to continue it in a more successful way, which means without being caught.

How can one influence the value system of individuals who display their own unfortunate and frustrated childhood by inflicting harm and hardship on others? Unfortunately, our psychotherapeutic methods, so often successful with other types of psychological difficulties, usually fail here. Since the criminal refuses to identify himself with the society in which he lives and to follow its laws, he is usually not interested or prepared to change his life style. Providing him with experience in a different way of living is sometimes helpful. Colonies for delinquents exist in some European countries, and reports from these show encouraging results. Group therapy which includes discussions of value systems (10) has also been successful in some instances where individual therapy has failed. The difficulty is to persuade the criminal to join such a group. He usually refers to group therapy as "just talk," indicating that he is not ready to change his pattern of life. It is common knowledge, however, that the majority of criminals give up their delinquency later in life, but usually not until they have wasted their best years.

Sometimes a prisoner reforms as a result of reading a book. For instance, a burglar, 38 years old, who had spent about half of his life in jail, wrote to my father, after reading his book, *Understanding Human Nature* (6), that he would like to seek his help on his release from prison. After their initial conversation, my father employed him as janitor in our country home. While he never betrayed our confidence in the following years, he did need guidance. Thus, on the first day of his employment, he was sent to fetch ten raspberry bushes at a nursery. He returned with twenty, reporting gleefully that the nurseryman had made a mistake. In a friendly manner he was informed that the nurseryman certainly would appreciate having the extra ten raspberry bushes returned, and that this would contribute to good business relations in the future. There was no recurrence of relapse. When in 1938, the Nazi occupation of Austria compelled many of our friends to flee, our janitor assisted them with many technicalities, and the only way in which he gave evidence of his former aggressiveness was when, to the amazement of our friends, he turned up with a collection of bed-bugs and stuffed them into the furniture before a Nazi official moved in.

To sum up: to make the delinquent a part of the community and to help his development should be the aim of our work with criminals.

Our prisons today are also filled with narcotic addicts. The drug most frequently used is heroin. In the last decade, however, we have been faced with a new development. Youth has taken to expressing protest through the use of hallucinogens, chiefly marijuana and LSD. It should not be forgotten that we expect intelligent youngsters to devote themselves to the improvement of our society, and it can be rightly said that an adolescent who never expresses protest against the so-called "establishment" may be lacking in promise in comparison with those who do. The danger lies with those who continue to protest without an adequate program of action. We know that the continued use of marijuana, LSD, and other hallucinogens represents an escape from the challenges we all have to face. Among the chronic users of hallucinogens many are seriously affected mentally. Several of them have been so before they started to take drugs and are schizophrenic. The remainder represent transient adjustment difficulties. These are the ones who finally realize that they are in need of help, and for whom psychotherapy is strongly indicated. When they are first seen, it is sometimes difficult to arrive at a correct diagnosis, because the habitual use of drugs may so confuse their thinking processes that these youngsters may talk and look like chronic schizophrenics. The most promising patients are those who state that they realize they have come to the end of their rope and that they must change. During therapy, they should be shown that they are fighting society indiscriminately, as they so often do, and in this way obstructing their growing-up process.

Not only delinquents, however, but youth in general today feels useless and unrelated to the so-called "establishment" which regulates their lives through patterns of education which are sometimes too rigid, sometimes not rigid enough, through compulsory military service—and in other ways — without, in many instances, holding out any hope of a promising manhood. Consequently protest movements are not lacking, but are, for the most part, too unstructured to bring about real progress. Also, while "hippie" culture stresses "love" as opposed to war and violence, it is doubtful that the way of life it advocates will benefit its young adherents in the long run. For instance, while one may sympathize with many aspects of student rebellion, it is difficult to condone the needless destruction of records and scientific papers which happened at

Columbia University in the spring of 1968. Growing alienation of the young people will sometimes bring about a complete inability to function. In this case they must be helped to regain self-esteem, the absence of which is often only superficially veiled by their protest activities. Since many of them are gifted and highly intelligent, efforts at reorientation are usually promising, either through individual or group therapy. Constant emphasis must be laid on a realistic approach to the world, on the fact that we are all aware of the absence of idealism in many of our power structures, and, finally, on the necessity of being united in our effort to meet the threat which the development of atomic weapons and other modern means of warfare represents. On the other hand, let us not forget that when our youth clamor for "salvation through love," and protest against violence and the entrenched political and economic power structures, they also point up many of the false values prevalent in our present-day society.

Patients who suffer from neuroses exhibit a very different pattern. They appear to accept the laws of society and the obligations these entail, at the same time trying to escape from them by hiding behind neurotic symptoms. They follow a "yes . . . but" pattern, excusing their inability to function because of their neurotic handicap. Take the so-called post-traumatic neuroses, for instance (1, 3). These give us a great deal of understanding of the process of symptom formation, and possibly also, therefore, of their prevention and treatment. After a major or minor injury, a patient may develop a whole cluster of mental and psychosomatic symptoms which cannot be explained by the injury alone. These usually make it impossible for him to continue in his previous occupation. I remember the case of a housewife who fell down from a ladder while opening a kitchen cabinet. She bumped her head slightly but did not lose consciousness and gave no other evidence of physical injury. However, a few days later, after the small bump on her head had disappeared, she developed recurrent nightmares, during which she dreamed she fell from a ladder, waking up in a fright, trembling and perspiring, and with heart palpitations. She could not get enough sleep, and was unable to get up in the morning to make breakfast for her family of four, or to do any housework. An examination of the family situation revealed that she had been involved in a long struggle, trying to induce her family to give her a helping hand with the housework. She had become alienated from her husband and daughters by constantly accusing them of not helping her. She had lost all interest in her work and in being a wife and mother, an attitude which made her whole life pattern disintegrate. The disruption caused by her family difficulties was expressed symbolically through her post-traumatic neurosis. This could have developed only after the woman had given up hope of influencing her family by other means. In her case, it was clear what direction psychotherapy had to take. The family was invited in and plans were worked out to establish better cooperation among its members to relieve the mother of the feeling of being an unwilling slave. The family proved understanding, and the symptoms of her anxiety neurosis gradually subsided.

It is not always possible to bring about a reconciliation between the patient and his environment. There is, for example, a large number of such post-traumatic neuroses which occur among persons dissatisfied with their working conditions, financial or otherwise. Similar reactions may be found among members of the armed services, who are opposed to the military aims, particularly when the general morale is low. It is well known that the incidence of post-traumatic neuroses varies considerably among different units, and depends a great deal upon the ability or inability of the leadership to convince the men that everything possible is being done to insure their safety and welfare.

Other neurotic patients are overwhelmed by unreasonable fears, fears which can pertain to a great variety of situations. The most frequent symptoms are fear of crossing an open place, of being confined in an enclosed space, of riding in a train or plane, of heights, and in children, school phobia. Particularly when dealing with children suffering from school phobia, a great deal of patience must be shown during therapy, in an effort to return them to school. In most cases, school phobia represents the reaction of a child accustomed to dominate its parents, in particular the mother, and who therefore experiences the necessity of greater independence and maturation as a threat. Such over-dependency has usually been fostered by the mother, who herself may be insecure, or may have other reasons for tying the child to herself. This situation demands prompt intervention, since, if left unattended, the conditions may become chronic, and the child may succeed in staying out of school in spite of the insistence of the truant officers, and continue its neurotic style of life into adulthood. Such a child is likely later to suffer from work phobia, and only be able to carry out work assignments under great tension. In therapy, an effort must be made to enlarge the child's horizon in order to make him realize that his problems are not of a private nature but pertain to the whole value system of society, and that he, by isolating himself, is the main sufferer. The prognosis in such children is favorable, unless, as happens in rare instances, the school phobia is an expression of a more sweeping thought disturbance, as is the case in childhood schizophrenia.

Though the symptomatology of other neuroses differs, they have one common characteristic, namely, that the patient tries to escape from dealing with important issues by finding neurotic solutions based on his own so-called "private logic." Adler pointed out many years ago that in order to understand the meaning of neurotic symptoms, one should ask the patient what he would do if he suddenly were freed from his liability, that is, his fear of crossing an open place, his compulsion to repeat certain acts over and over again, or his obsession with particular thoughts. The patient's answer will give the clue by revealing which of his obligations in the three main aspects of his life—work, social relations, and sex—he would be able to fulfill if freed from his neurotic impediment. It is usually fear of failure in one of these areas which opens the door to his retreat. His fight against the logic of society and his pattern of life involving "overtime work without pay," so to say, results in much suffering for him, and may induce him to turn for help through psychotherapy.

In many psychotic patients one also finds a lack of awareness and understanding of human values. This is caused by the unrealistic thinking of such patients. The judgment of the schizophrenic is often distorted by his hallucinations and delusions. In manic-depressive psychoses, the patient's approach is determined by his mood swings.

I would like to take up first some of the difficulties encountered in dealing with schizophrenic patients. Only a small percentage of them is ever hospitalized. Those who are, are either patients who are dangerous to others or to themselves, or who have no family, or family substitute, to take care of them if they cannot manage by themselves. Those who are not hospitalized have many diagnostic designations—borderline schizophrenics, ambulatory, mild, incipient, pseudoneurotic, pseudo-psychopathic, or schizo-affective. They have much in common with non-psychotic patients, in particular with the so-called schizoid personality. All display inability to establish normal human relations, and are usually painfully aware of this difficulty, often begging the therapist to help them make friends. Here is the point at which the therapist must try to make up for the patient's inability to create an adequate environment of his own. For instance, placing him in a group or social club (8) made up of people with psychologic difficulties can give him valuable training and experience, in an atmosphere in which his social awkwardness or occasional aggressive statements will be tolerated. It is of the utmost importance, of course, that the group leader be experienced in dealing with the specific difficulties of schizophrenics. The necessity of providing the schizophrenic with a substitute and protected environment, through which he can begin to make up for his lack of social experience in the past, is generally accepted. If sufficiently improved, he will be able to move into a more normal environment. Let us not forget that we all need, and make constant use of advice, encouragement or criticism, provided for us by our family and friends, who really serve as the psychotherapists of the average, normally adjusted individual. It is through them that we feel the pulse of society and are kept aware of the demands, ideals, and values, as well as of the pitfalls, of mankind.

Much is gained if the schizophrenic patient is able to work and hold a job. We all need to feel that we are useful to society. This desire is expressed even by the child who says he wants to be a truck driver, fireman, or policeman when he grows up and it is a danger signal if an adolescent declares that he never gave a thought to what he wants to become, for it indicates he is trying to perpetuate his childhood role and feel free from obligations. The psychotic, too, will not make a better adjustment until he feels that he can be useful (4, 11). In most instances, it is necessary to provide him, at first, with a sheltered environment at his place of work. This can often be done by placing the patient with a friend of his family who understands his difficulties. At present there are also several day hospitals where such patients can be trained to work and workshops, such as the Altro workshop in New York City, where patients are screened by experts and then given suitable work assignments. There are also regular jobs which may represent to the patient a compromise between his limitations and the normal expectations of society—certain clerical jobs, for instance, which allow him to work behind a screen, separating him from the public and making him feel protected, almost as if he were in a hideout or retreat (2).

Sexual adjustment is also beset with difficulties for the schizophrenic. Man can attain full satisfaction with his sexual partner only if he places him, or her, on a level equal to, or even higher, than himself. The isolation in which the schizophrenic lives prevents such adjustment and, consequently, his sexual life is often in a chaotic state. He fears being neglected or abused, and reacts to his sexual impulses as if satisfaction concerned him alone, without consideration of his partner. To him, sex becomes something like an indoor sport, and his chief aim usually is to prove his masculinity if a man, or seductiveness if a woman, about which, in either case, doubt is felt by the patient. These aims are often represented in a system of delusions. Nevertheless, marriage is sometimes entered into by even severe schizophrenics, and should not necessarily be discouraged, when contemplated. Usually both partners have psychologic difficulties of one kind or another. It is important that both are aware of these before they marry. If they are, there will be greater incentive to help each other and to be permissive. If, on the other hand, the family or the patient conceal past and present psychologic difficulties from the partner, he or she will feel deceived, and will tend to be uncooperative as soon as difficulties arise. As would be true in any marriage, the feeling of having been intentionally misled is likely to remain and to disrupt the relationship.

With the manic-depressive, difficulties appear during the depressive phase, when the patient cannot face going to work, seeing friends, and feels unworthy of his sexual partner. He may condemn life in all its aspects as not being worth living or working for, when he is depressed; when elated, he may feel that everything has been achieved and that one could not live in a better world than the present. It is understandable that a depressed patient for whom everything has lost its value may be contemplating suicide. The therapist must be aware that this danger will continue as long as the patient negates commonly accepted values. In mild depressions, moral support and reassurance to the patient that he will be able to overcome his depression in due time, as well as discussion of his condition with his family will be of great help. In more severe depressions, psychotherapy can be used only as an adjunct to drug and shock treatment, or, particularly if the patient is so disturbed that he does not even listen, is of no avail at all. In the latter case, no time should be lost in treating the patient with the newly available antidepressant drugs, or, if the suicidal threat persists, with electroshock.

It is questionable if relapses of the manic-depressive psychoses can be prevented through psychotherapy administered during or after a psychotic breakdown. In many cases, however, the patient undoubtedly becomes better able to deal with his mood swings when adequately prepared for them, and if enabled to gain some perspective on his irrationality during those episodes. It may be mentioned that a drug, lithium carbonate, has recently shown promise of being able to control and even prevent the recurrence of manic-depressive attacks.

Finally, in attempting to understand the function of value systems in psychotherapy (9), it is essential that the therapist not lose perspective and adopt a rigid attitude toward man's changing ways of life. What may pass for good form in one age and one milieu, may not necessarily do so in another. For instance, during long periods of history, the highest manly ideal was physical strength and the ability to kill off as many as possible of one's enemies. Our sexual mores, too, are changing, particularly as a result of the progress made in the field of birth control. We are also now witnessing a great wave of dissension aroused by the attempts of religious organizations to control in detail the conduct of their members. What a mistake, for instance, it would be to try to convince an ultra-modern composer, painter, or sculptor that he must first change his artistic style in order to come to terms with his psychological difficulties. Time will take care of such developments, weeding out what proves to be of no permanent value. Innumerable other examples could be cited as warning to the therapist against the danger of imposing his value system in minor details upon patients whose way of life may differ from his own. No one is omniscient, and the therapist should not play God and be inflexible in assessing values in a changing world.

In conclusion, let me quote the well-known categorical imperative of the philosopher Kant—"Act as if the maxim of your action were to become the foundation of general law." Individual Psychology has much in common with this principle formulated by Kant. Alfred Adler's concept of Social Interest, in particular, opens our eyes to the many challenges in the fields of psychology, psychiatry, psychotherapy, philosophy, and social work, and should serve as a guideline in our efforts to improve human society.

REFERENCES

1. Adler, Alexandra, "Post-traumatic Neuroses in War and Peace." *Indiv. Psychol. Bull.*, 4(1944-45), pp. 75-78.

2. Adler, Alexandra, "Problems in Psychotherapy." *Amer. J. Indiv. Psychol.*, 12(1956), pp. 12-24. Reprinted in K. A. Adler and Danica Deutsch (eds.), *Essays in Individual Psychology*. New York, Grove Press, 1959, pp. 177-179.

3. Adler, Alexandra, "Two Different Types of Post-traumatic Neuroses." *Amer. J. Psychiat.*, 102(1945), pp. 237-240.

4. Adler, Alexandra, "Office Treatment of the Chronic Schizophrenic Patient." P. H. Hoch and J. Zubin (eds.). *Psychopathology of Schizophrenio*. New York, Grune & Stratton, Inc. 1966, pp. 366-371.

5. Adler, A., *Social Interest* (1930). New York, Capricorn Books, 1964.

6. Adler, A., *Understanding Human Nature* (1927). Greenwich, Conn., Premier Books, 1965.

7. Adler, A., *What Life Should Mean to You* (1931). New York, Capricorn Books, 1958.

8. Bierer, J. and Evans, R. I., *Innovations in Social Psychiatry*. London, Avenue Publishing Company, 1969.

9. Dreikurs, R., "Psychotherapy as Correction of Faulty Social Values." *J. Indiv. Psychol.*, 13(1957), 150-158.

10. Papanek, Helene, "Charles in Ethical Values in Group Psychotherapy." *Int. J. Grp. Psychother.*, 8(1958), pp. 435-444.

11. Shulman, B. H., *Essays in Schizophrenia*. Baltimore, Williams & Wilkins, 1968.

SOCIAL INTEREST
AND SOCIAL CONFLICT

Helene Papanek

Many of Alfred Adler's disciples now living and working in this country belong to the generation born in Vienna around the turn of the century. We were teenagers during World War I. We became friends of Adler's children and studied under him before he left Austria in 1926. As adults we experienced Austrian Fascism and the beginnings of Nazism in 1938. By different routes, at different times, with more hardship or less, we settled in this country around 1940.

Why the biographical introduction? The terrible impact of World War I struck our adolescent minds, open and impressionable. We saw the misery and destruction brought by war. We became deeply convinced that there was only one way out of that misery, that only one thing could save us from a recurrence—a development of social interest (3, 5), *Gemeinschaftsgefühl*, directed toward all our fellowmen, toward the community *(Gemeinschaft)* of man. Nationalism, prejudice, discrimination became the arch-enemies. Our lives would henceforth be meaningless unless we could help to foster social interest and weaken all the divisive forces that drive men to destroy each other. Fascism, Hitlerism, World War II, all strengthened our conviction that *Gemeinschaftsgefühl* means survival; social interest "signifies cohesion with our life, the affirmation, the conciliation with it" (1, p. 25). We want to be useful, in Adler's sense; "By useful I mean in the interest of mankind generally" (2, p. 78).

Psychiatrists and psychotherapists in their daily professional lives promote individual human growth and the full function of the individual. If we succeed, we also derive satisfaction from the knowledge that when an individual patient is helped, his family, and sometimes the older and the rising generations may also profit. We try to prevent emotional sickness in our patient's children, and, we hope, help to make the patient a more useful member of society. This gives our professional efforts some significance. However, we have sometimes blinded ourselves to social conditions which contribute to the individual's psychological malfunctioning.

During the last decade new social trends have developed across America and intruded themselves forcibly into the daily routine of psychotherapy. In the past our private and clinic practice brought us into contact mainly with the educated white patient of lower or upper middle class status. We now meet the uneducated, the poor and the disadvantaged. We are beginning to learn from our experience with the unmotivated, unsophisticated patient. Nobody at present can teach us how to reach these people, who in many ways think and communicate differently from us, because nobody knows much about them. In addition to the poor white, black, and Puerto Rican, we are confronted with the black educated middle class patient. New problems emerge in the therapeutic relationship.

Culture is , after all, a set of prejudices of which one is not aware. The educated Western man has one set; the patient of a different cultural background has another. This gap can only be bridged by social feeling. "Social feeling remains throughout life, changed, colored, circumscribed in some cases, enlarged and broadened in others until it touches not only the members of [the individual's] own family, but also his clan, his nation, and finally, the whole of humanity" (4, p. 46). If social feeling remains circumscribed and limited to family, clan or nation, the sense of belonging can come into conflict with social feeling. Instead of humanitarian identification, a racial or national identification develops and unending misery can result. In the life style of each individual strands of experience within his family constellation are interwoven with strands from his community or from his nation, from his culture or from the subculture in which he and his family live. Only if he really believes in our common humanity can the therapist combine ruthless honesty towards himself with empathy and understanding for his patients. The therapist needs insight into his own prejudices and unrecognized preconceptions, and "outsight" into those of his patients.

Group psychotherapy has always been my preference for patients from a different socio-economic or racial background. It seems to me that recognized or unrecognized social or racial antagonisms come into sharper focus in the group situation than in individual therapy. The group provides a more flexible setting, where hostility, resentment, conflict and crisis come to the surface. The therapist has an opportunity to find an optimal tolerance level for these tensions and to help group members strike a creative balance between cooperation and group cohesiveness on the one hand and self-assertion on the other. Self-assertiveness means awareness of the difference between self and others; cooperation and group cohesiveness mean awareness of a common humanity above and despite these differences (7).

Ann, a 28-year-old Negro single nurse, started treatment with me on the recommendation of another patient, a white nurse who worked with her. Ann first indicated that overweight was her motive for seeking therapy. She was a tall, heavy, big-boned, well-dressed black woman with attractive dark, negroid features. After a few individual sessions, she joined a therapy group upon my advice. The group consisted of seven white people of both sexes who were approximately the same age. Occasionally Ann had individual sessions, usually because she requested them. She attended group psychotherapy regularly, and after one year, therapy was terminated by mutual agreement.

Ann's case history exemplifies the challenge faced by a white therapist working with a black woman. It all started with a white patient's recommendation. This patient told Ann that the well-known Negro author, Claude Brown, had written much about his friendship with my husband, Ernst Papanek. From Brown's book, *Manchild in the Promised Land* (6), Ann could see that my husband was free of any prejudice against Negroes, and consequently she felt she could trust me, in spite of our different racial backgrounds. Very soon after therapy started, we discussed openly whether she could have confidence in me. She believed me when I said that I had suffered under the malevolent, destructive onslaught of racial prejudice in Europe, that I felt only hatred for all prejudice and a firm commitment to fight against it. Ann was then able to confess that the real reason she wanted treatment was not that she was fat, but that she feared insanity. This fear had started quite suddenly, she said, four years previously. She felt guilty because she had gossiped about a girl friend's sister who was confined to a mental institution. Ann was sure that the girl friend, a nurse who worked in the same hospital with her found out about this "betrayal" and became her relentless enemy. She thought everybody at her place of work was aware of her misdeed and that she would eventually lose her job. These fantasies were multiplied and elaborated so that she became convinced that people in buses, in subways, and on the street were also talking about her contemptuously. Meeting imaginary accusations and threats wherever she went, she finally told her father about her panicky feeling. Her father, an educated man and a leading figure in the black community, advised psychotherapy.

For the purposes of this paper I want to focus upon the patient's life style, its development within the family constellation and within the social setting. Ann's cognitive map was influenced by experiences within her family and within her society. Why did she come to feel like a hunted creature in a hostile world?

Ann grew up in New York City, the youngest of three siblings. Her "parents were completely different." The father had a master's degree in Negro history and was a man proud of his black heritage. He called his daughter, "Blackie," a term of endearment. The mother was quiet, subdued, a hard-working domestic helper. The father left the family several times and then returned. He made the separation final when Ann was 14 years old. He went to live with another woman and her children by a previous marriage who had come up from the South to join Ann's father. He remained friendly with his wife and their children and continued to visit them. Ann reciprocated occasionally, but she became upset when she saw her father with his new family. She pitied her abandoned mother, with whom she lived until she was 25. But it was to her father that she talked about her intellectual interests.

Ann had always been closer to her father. She admired his education, his intelligence, his pride in his race. She loved his strength and manliness. His attachment to two families was accepted by Ann's mother, by their friends and neighbors. There was great warmth, genuine friendliness and concern among all members of this complicated familial network.

Ann's resentment against her father, her confused value judgments and conflicting loyalties were projected onto the therapist. After telling me about her past and present family situation, she said, "Sordid, isn't it?" It is hard to know how much this question reflected her assumptions about white people's value judgments and how much they reflected her own conflicts and confusions. My belief is that Ann felt hopeless and defeated in her attempts to differentiate right from wrong, good from bad, important from unimportant, real from pretended, truth from prejudice. In her confusion, unable to arrive at any solid evaluation of the world on which she could rely, she developed paranoid ideation under stress.

Three incidents during therapy brought this into sharp focus. As the only black patient in the group, she first tried to deny completely that any prejudice could exist among the white members. One day she became very angry because a female patient had not greeted her. In her rage she divulged her fear of being rejected or despised by the others. She was sure that as whites they must feel superior and reject her blackness. They responded with frank statements of what they liked or disliked in Ann. Some group members did not like Ann because she seemed haughty or aggressive and had a loud voice, being big and tall and apparently very sure of herself. Others liked her frankness and intelligence.

A few weeks after this incident, Ann's pathology revealed itself openly. A white, married doctor of 45 had been very solicitous of Ann and had praised her for her conscientious, intelligent work as a nurse. Once or twice he had taken her home in his car, since they lived in the same neighborhood. Not only did Ann think she was in love with this man, but she became convinced that he was in love with her, wanted to live with her and perhaps to marry her. She saw signs of his affection in the way he greeted her and smiled at her. Ann was living in her own small apartment at this time. She broke her lease, packed her belongings, put her furniture in storage, signed a lease for a larger apartment, and paid two months' security. She planned to live temporarily with her mother until the doctor had furnished the new apartment. He knew nothing about all this. Ann awoke as from a dream, suddenly finding herself alone in her empty, desolate apartment. She telephoned me, asked for an emergency session, and told the whole story. She had mentioned to the group several times how pleased she was by the doctor's praise, but that was all we had heard about the relationship.

As a supportive emergency measure I helped her cancel the new lease immediately, so that she got half the advance payment back. The whole episode was discussed in the group. At this point Ann was quite aware of the dreamlike nature of her expectations. Questioned as to what she based her belief in the doctor's amorous intentions on, she laughed and said, "He took my elbow once when we crossed the street." Any suggestions that this wish-fulfilling fantasy might have something to do with the doctor's racial background was vigorously denied by her. She agreed that she had been impressed by his status and age, but not at all by his being white.

The last episode was shortly afterward directed against me. After returning to her mother's house, she called me on a Sunday and told me that she had two sleepless nights, that she felt tortured and panicky, and awakened her mother several times to ask for reassurance. She said she was very angry at me. She was sure—"well, more or less sure"— that I had called the hospital superintendent and the grocer where she usually shopped and had warned both of them not to trust her because she was "unreliable and crazy." We talked on the phone for a while, and I tried to reassure her, scolded her good-naturedly for the notion that I had nothing better to do than go about warning all these people, complete strangers whose names I did not even know. What sort of opinion did she have of my trustworthiness and moral standards? Ann started to cry. She felt relieved and confessed how hard it was for her to trust me or any white person, how much she wanted to find out whether white people could be trusted at all.

After this episode Ann's therapy progressed smoothly. She and another female group member were able to discuss their competitive feelings, openly explaining that each of them felt more competitive as an educated, professional woman representative of her own race. Ann lost 50 lbs. and introduced her tall, very good-looking boy friend to the group shortly before she terminated therapy. They were a strikingly handsome couple. During the two year follow-up period Ann apparently has been doing very well in her work and relations with people. She has had no paranoid relapses although her weight does go up and down.

Ann referred her friend Lillian to me—a pretty, petite, 31-year-old, single, Negro nurse. When Lillian started therapy with me, the problem presented was that she had been anxious, upset, depressed, and confused for many years. Partly, these symptoms centered about her problem concerning her 3-year-old illegitimate son, Billy. Lillian's family had their home in another city, and the little boy lived there with Lillian's widowed mother. Lillian and her younger brother had been brought up by their mother as religious Catholics.

Like Ann's family or even more so, Lillian's family was strongly achievement-oriented, with middle class aspirations and values. Lillian's parents had both held well-paid secretarial jobs. Her father died when Lillian was 19 years old; the mother had been receiving a pension since her retirement.

As a young girl Lillian had learned to play the piano and had studied toward a master's degree in public health nursing while working in a hospital. Her out-of-wedlock pregnancy was a terrible shock to her and her family; it was the worst possible insult to their religious and middle class convictions. Though her mother has always been "a calm, sweet lady," ever since Lillian's early childhood she has made her feel "there was something wrong with the girl." Since her mother believed only in physical, not mental troubles, she took the little girl from doctor to doctor, and they assured her that everything was fine with the child. When Lillian was eleven years old, she realized that "mother was looking for a daughter, but I was never the right one." She had no idea what was wrong. Her father seemed to have recognized this subtle rejection; he kept telling Lillian that she had a "nice mother" who just expected "instant obedience."

Lillian's relationship with a Negro twelve years her senior started after her father's death and had been going on two years when she became pregnant. Her brother was engaged to be married; they arranged for the wedding to take place before Lillian's pregnancy showed. She had always known her boy friend did not intend to marry her.

To all appearances, this "shameful pregnancy" served several purposes. It proved to her mother and brother she could do as she pleased and disregard the values imposed by family and religion. It also proved to Lillian herself and to her family that she really was "no good," as her mother had always expected her to turn out.

Lillian had always been far above average intelligence. She was an ambitious, successful student, received much encouragement from her teachers and was the recipient of scholarships for undergraduate and graduate studies. Though she grew up in the ghetto and hardly encountered any white people until she went to college and nursing school, she, like Ann, denied the possibility that she had ever felt inferior to or resentful of white people. In contrast to Ann, she thought blacks never should have intimate or sexual contact with whites and should strive for their own educational and cultural betterment.

Actually, and consciously, she had firmer and more restrictive beliefs and values than Ann, e.g. that her pregnancy was God's punishment for sinful sexual relations, that abortion would have been a mortal sin which she could not even contemplate, and that it is wrong to have sexual desires, to show anger or strong emotion. She could not cry after her father's death, but in her dreams at night he returned.

Lillian joined an otherwise all-white therapy group. Her relationship to me had none of the usual ups and downs, but was continuously dependent, sometimes submissive. She never doubted my superior knowledge, my friendly intentions toward her, or my acceptance of her. She asked for reassurance and guidance and received it. For example, I assured her that she could bring her little boy to New York City without endangering her job. There is no doubt that Billy had been severely traumatized in infancy by changing foster parents, and when his grandmother finally agreed to take him, by her too. Since coming to New York Billy had been in psychotherapy and attending classes in a therapeutic preschool setting. His psychological prognosis is still doubtful. Lillian was quite aware of this, and it contributed to her depression and guilt feelings. During treatment Lillian at times overcame her fear of sexuality and had relations which made her feel happy and guiltless for a while. But these erotic attachments were short-lived. She felt that no man could accept Billy the way she wanted him to and her fear that he "would neither be the right man for her nor a good father for Billy" always caused a break.

During therapy the problems of racial identity remained covert most of the time. Lillian's passive acceptance of "her place in a white society" (of which she was unaware) came out twice during group sessions. At one early meeting she was able to talk about her shame and guilt at having an out-of-wedlock child. One of the patients, in the role of assistant therapist, spoke for the group before anyone else responded, "We don't judge you; we admire your courage in having the child." Nobody jumped on the "we," though Lillian seemed taken aback by it and stopped talking. I questioned the "we" as meaning "we white people;" I said it sounded condescending. Lillian then was able to express how terribly depressed and confused she had been after giving birth.

Another incident may also be interpreted either within the transactional, person-to-person framework or from a social viewpoint, revealing as it did Lillian's self-image as a second rate citizen, vulnerable to attack and obliged to be especially "good" to be accepted. One group member's undue tardiness or truancy from group sessions was discussed. He used rationalizations, excuses and other obviously dishonest maneuvers to explain his behavior, thus annoying everybody in the group. At one point I, along with others, raised my voice to make a point. The moment I showed anger, although it was obviously anger toward the provocateur and I did not even look in Lillian's direction, she suddenly said very apologetically: "Oh, I'm so sorry you're angry. It won't happen again!" She seemed to feel that she was attracting anger which really was directed elsewhere. We thought Lillian must be speaking to her mother, not to me. But perhaps Lillian, as a black, was also used to serving as scapegoat for white anger. Was Lillian's self-effacing attitude, and her life style of suppressed emotion due to her family constellation, or was it a result of exposure to racial prejudice? Both interpretations should be kept in mind.

I have already mentioned that Lillian regarded her illegitimate pregnancy as a punishment for sinful sex relations. During therapy she became involved with a black man who seemed in every way eligible for marriage. He had a good job; he accepted Billy; he was fond of Lillian and admired her intelligence. Lillian was unable to make up her mind, since she did not feel sexually attracted to him at all. She postponed her reply to his marriage proposals but agreed to sexual relations in order to hold on to him. Liking him less and less, she finally broke it off, with guilt feelings on two counts: about sex, and about not giving Billy a father. Months later I went on a long summer vacation. When I came back, she was in a state of acute anxiety.

She thought that she was punished again, that is, pregnant, because there was a "fluttering in her stomach" and some loss of urine during coughing or exertion. Five months had passed since she had had intercourse, and she had been menstruating regularly. She had been too frightened to consult a doctor. Here was an educated woman, a nurse, in a state of panic. I promptly relieved her fears with my assurances, and sent her to a gynocologist, who found no pregnancy nor any somatic abnormality. Her anxiety seemed nearly as irrational as Ann's paranoid ideation. Onset and relief were sudden, "like waking up from a bad dream."

Lillian's basic pathology, I believe, bears similarities to Ann's deep-seated insecurity, developed within an unpredictable society that has strong undercurrents of race prejudice. Lillian and Ann seem to have lacunae, blanks, missing parts in their interpretation of the world around them and in their self-images. The self-image one creates for himself is strongly influenced by other people's response to one's self. Children, even those who grow up in the homogenous atmosphere of a ghetto, are aware of those "others" who live outside. Their self-image is shaped by their family which is their immediate environment and later by their neighborhood and schools. It is also influenced by the white society surrounding them. Their parents directly or indirectly make them aware of "the other society." Then when they come in close contact with this heterogeneous society with conflicting values and subcultures, the constancy of their self-image is threatened. At the same time they have to come to terms with a confusing, contradictory outside world. Ann, who grew up in New York City, handled this by alternating between denial of any racial problem and sudden bottomless suspiciousness of the white world. Lillian's world had collapsed with the traumatic experiences of illegitimate sex and pregnancy. She clung to the values and judgments of her family. She had nothing to take their place. If she rejected her own background, her race and her religion, she would have no place of her own and would lose her identity completely.

Sometimes it seems impossible to strive for a consistent viewpoint, for integration of experiences in a society which is itself contradictory, dishonest and confused in its value judgments. The result may be denial of conflicts and deep-seated anxiety, self-doubt and doubts about others.

Did Ann and Lillian lack some tools which would have enabled them to cope with stress and anxiety? I would answer this question in the affirmative. I omit other examples of my two patients' confused way of thinking, which appeared in therapy sometimes as bizarre, at other times as delusional. Each time recovery was rapid; interpretation, confrontation with reality, and reassurance, all most often from group members, had an immediate effect. It was like telling them, "Don't you see that your responses are unreal and inappropriate? Don't you remember what you know so well?" All this was founded upon the following assumptions:

1. Psychotherapy with patients belonging to a racial minority should not be "color blind," nor should it assume consonance where dissonance exists. Prejudice, overt and covert, fears and expectations arising from the possibility of prejudice, must be discussed honestly, courageously and tactfully. We have to recognize that people are different, for personal and/or social reasons. Discussion of these differences can only be therapeutic, if "different" does not mean superior or inferior. It is the obligation of therapists to be aware of differences and to exert leadership in helping patients become aware of them. If we, as therapists, neither feel condescension toward a person who is different, nor fear him because of his "strangeness," we thereby influence group members to feel and behave the same way.

2. To be able to work through and reach beyond the barriers separating people is a most gratifying experience for everyone involved. Racial barriers, especially today in New York, and especially for those who have lived through the Nazi holocaust, are terrible and frightening. It should not happen here, neither to white through black bigotry, nor to black through white bigotry.

3. Even if one tries to bridge over or neutralize racial conflict within the microcosm of psychotherapy, it is a deeply satisfying experience to prove to oneself and to others that a common human bond does exist despite race, differences of heritage, and militant prejudice.

REFERENCES

1. Adler, A., "Der Aggressionstreib," in Adler, A., Furtmüller, C., and Wexberg, E., eds., *Heilen und Bilden,* 2nd ed. Munich, Bergmann, 1922, pp. 18-25.
2. Adler, A., *Problems of Neurosis* (1929). New York, Harper Torchbooks, 1964.
3. Adler, A., *Social Interest* (1930). New York, Capricorn Books, 1964.
4. Adler, A., *Understanding Human Nature* (1927). Greenwich, Conn., Premier Books, 1954.
5. Ansbacher, H. L., "The Concept of Social Interest." *J. Indiv. Psychol.,* 24(1968), pp. 131-149.
6. Brown, C., *Manchild in the Promised Land.* New York, Macmillan, 1965.
7: Papanek, Helene, "Bridging Dichotomies Through Group Psychotherapy." *J. Indiv. Psychol.,* 20(1964), pp. 38-47.

FAMILY THERAPY: A COMPARISON OF ADLER AND SATIR

Miriam L. Pew

With the burgeoning interest in family therapy, new approaches to this form of treatment, originally developed bp Adler are appearing. Satir's conjoint family therapy (5) represents one such development. The basic theoretical assumptions underlying Satir's conjoint family therapy and Adlerian family therapy will be briefly described; these assumptions and the two methods of family therapy will then be compared and contrasted.

Satir's Conjoint Family Therapy

Some basic theoretical principles underlying Satir's conjoint family therapy include the concept of the identified patient (IP). He is the symptom bearer for the family and distorts his own growth in an effort to alleviate and absorb his parents' marital pain. Selection of an IP in a family may be related to a combination of factors such as ordinal position, constitutional features and the parents' perception of the child's characteristics, i.e. whether such characteristics are given a positive or negative valence in a given family. The child's physical appearance, age or sex may be crucial variables. However, the IP role does not necessarily remain the same; it may be shared successively by younger siblings as a result of therapy or sometimes as an accompaniment to normal growth and development. Becoming and maintaining oneself as an IP involves a two-way transaction. Satir emphasizes how an IP victimizes his parents, making many demands and exploiting his pitiful position. Homes become geared to the demands of the patient since the parents are as helpless in taking a stand against the IP as the IP is in taking a stand against the parents.

Another cornerstone of Satir's theory is the construct of family homeostasis introduced by Jackson (12). The family behaves as a unit, acting to maintain balance through repetitious, circular and predictable communication patterns. Family homeostasis can be functional at some periods of the family cycle and not at other periods. The dysfunctional family with an IP might maintain a relatively stable homeostasis over a long period of time.

The family as a system is summarized by Watzlawick, Beavin and Jackson (17, p. 148) as follows:

> Human interaction is described as a communication system, characterized by the properties of general systems: time as a variable, system-subsystem relations, wholeness, feedback and equifinality. . . . Limitation in general and the development of family rules in particular lead to a definition and illustration of the family as a rule-governed system (17, p. 148).

Jackson explains that *rule* means the stabilization of relationship definition and the relationship can be symmetrical or complementary.

Satir uses "system" a little differently, emphasizing (1) there is more likely to be a stupid child in families that value intelligence, (2) crazy children are more common in families that value normality, (3) sickness occurs in health-oriented families, and (4) badness occurs in goodness-oriented families. Satir states that every piece of behavior makes sense, given the premises by which the individual operates and the system of which he is a part.

Dysfunctional systems are closed systems, change is feared and the uniqueness of the individual is ignored. If the therapist becomes essential he becomes a part of a closed system. An individual is dysfunctional when he has not learned to communicate properly and this is related to low self-esteem.

Communication theory is important to Satir's approach. Two levels of communication are emphasized: the denotative level, i.e. the literal content of the message; and the metacommunicative level, a message about a message. When the denotative and metacommunicative levels agree, a congruent message is being sent. When the receiver becomes part of an unsatisfactory interaction, the message is incongruent and a "discrepancy" results.

Double level communication does not necessarily lead to symptomatic behavior but under certain conditions, especially with children, the situational effect referred to as the "double bind" may be produced. Three conditions are necessary for a "double bind;" first, repeated double messages over an extended period of time; second, the messages must come from persons who have survival significance; third, the child must be conditioned at an early age not to ask clarifying questions.

A seeming contradiction in Satir's theory is her intentional use of ambiguous language (which she defends as the language of emotions and of meaning) and her stated goal that the therapist should be a "model of communication."

Creativity, flexibility, risk taking and a basic optimism are attributes a therapist should have according to Satir. Also, he should be a fully functioning person, able to say what he thinks, feels, sees and hears; one who is open to what another person thinks, feels, sees and hears. A therapist behaves differently from other family members by encouraging democratic virtues. Each person has a turn, minority views are accepted; everyone is encouraged to make compromises for the welfare of the group.

In family therapy Satir uses a modified funnel type of communication, i.e. the members tend to speak to one another but not for long periods and she interprets, clarifies and redefines what occurs by considering the effect of the past on the here and now.

An important technique in Satir's approach is the structured interview, a family life chronology, i.e. a history-taking process. The cast of characters is carefully delineated beginning with the parents' courtship. Bringing the discussion up to the present is accomplished by obtaining a description of a typical day.

Since Satir believes in the potential for change, she expects this from the family and feels most therapy should be relatively short-term, from three to twelve months. Treatment can be terminated when family members can complete transactions, identify accurately their own feelings and those of other family members, disagree, make choices and learn from practice. They must be able to send clear, congruent messages. Briefly, treatment is completed when eveyone in the family can use the first person "I" followed by an active verb and ending with a direct object.

Adlerian Family Therapy

Adlerian family therapy is based on the assumption that it is therapy for the child but counseling for the parents. The child's immediate goals are identified with his life style. The family constellation is a forceful, current reality. When present family relationships change, the child is not only better able to cope with the existing problem situation, but with life itself.

Psychotherapy for parents would involve reconstruction or reorganization of personality or life style. This is seldom necessary in family therapy since most parents are able to utilize simple, common sense advice toward the objective of changing parent-child relationships. This is characteristically provided in public family counseling centers geared to families with younger children (8). Adlerians are likely to utilize a variety of adjunctive approaches including group therapy for adults and for adolescents, psychodrama, music therapy, marital counseling and individual psychotherapy.

While Satir's model of therapy is based on the family with a schizophrenic child, the Adlerian model has a much more general orientation and application and is based on the assumption that appropriate family interpersonal relationships evolve from the same principles of equality, mutual respect and democracy regardless of the personalities of the individual members.

Adler named his school Individual Psychology (*individuum* means undivided or indivisible) emphasizing his holistic, organismic concept of human behavior. Since he considered an understanding of the uniqueness and indivisibility of the individual essential, the construct referred to as Life Style is basic to the theory (5). Life Style is the consistent theme, the child's conception (however mistaken) of how to find belonging, first in the nuclear family and later in society.

The basic philosophy is socioteleological; all living things move and every movement has a goal. Human behavior is impossible to understand without taking into consideration the goal of the individual and his social milieu.

An individual's private logic (6), or biased apperception, justifies his mistaken behavior and prevents him from seeing that many of the disappointments and difficulties in his life are the logical consequences of mistakes in his life style. Our experiences are created to a large extent by our expectations.

Social interest or *Gemeinschaftsgefühl* is Adler's term for the fully functioning, healthy individual's sense of belongingness not only in his immediate society but his embeddedness in all of mankind and his sense of being part of the total cosmic evolutionary process (3). Thus mental health is related directly to degree of social interest. Dreikurs (7) states that a man's ability to cooperate may be regarded as a measure of the development of his social interest. The greater the development of social interest, the better the relationship between the individual and the human community. This is Adler's "ironclad logic of social living."

In Adlerian theory much emphasis is placed on the dynamics of inferiority feelings. Behavior can be seen in terms of a balance between social interest and inferiority feelings. All humans experience, justifiably, biological, cosmic and social inferiorities, but only the latter tends to separate people. The basic urge is to find belonging by participation, but a child, feeling socially inferior, may, instead, seek self-elevation in relation to others. The two responses to experienced inferiority feelings are to compensate or to withdraw. Adler's best known construct, the inferiority complex, is the individual's final conclusion of hopelessness.

Adler enumerated three life tasks inherent in human community living—work, love and friendship to which Dreikurs and Mosak (9, 10, 14) have added a fourth, getting along with oneself, and a fifth, the spiritual. The work task may be fulfilled to the exclusion of one or more of the life tasks. The love task requires the highest cooperation because mutual respect between two people of the opposite sex is essential. Adler's concept of the "masculine protest" (4), an outgrowth of a male-dominated, authoritarian society, is still useful in considering inequality between the sexes. Getting along with oneself requires the "courage to be imperfect" (13).

Childhood family constellation and atmosphere are cornerstones for

165

Adlerian diagnosis (16). Ordinal position and how the siblings organize themselves and influence the parents is considered crucial. Pampering or neglect, being extreme examples of lack of respect for the dignity of the child, are given careful consideration (2). Since the family is the child's first community, the atmosphere of the home which is set by the parents helps to account for the individual's value system. Values and traits shared by siblings reflect the family atmosphere while striking differences in character, talent or interest reflect the competition between the siblings which ultimately is a reflection of the competition between the parents.

Adlerians feel that traditional, autocratic child rearing practices are obsolete and that new principles of parent-child relationships based on mutual respect must be taught. Thus the Adlerian therapist is primarily an educator whether he is working in a one to one relationship, as a group leader or as a counselor in a family education center.

Theoretical Similarities

Both points of view are interpersonal, transactional and social with a basic optimism and a belief that people can change. Jackson's concept of homeostasis is comparable to the Adlerian emphasis on the fact that change in attitude and subsequent behavior on the part of one or more family members results inevitably in a change in relationship and in change in attitude and behavior on the part of other family members. Both groups tend to avoid "standard psychiatric nomenclature" preferring to concentrate on the interactional aspects of behavior. No emphasis is placed on the so-called psychosexual development. Instincts are not considered causal. Both view the family as the basic learning context for the developing child and agree that children's behavior is firmly rooted in parental expectations. Dysfunctional families are viewed as groups of discouraged people with low self-esteem. The Adlerian view that emotions "cause" behavior only insofar as they energize behavior and are dependent variables created by the individual for the purpose of helping him reach his goal would seem to coincide with Satir's statement that people are not prisoners of their feelings. There is agreement that any behavior makes sense from the point of view of the behaver, given his premises and the milieu within which he is operating. His mistaken behavior makes sense when viewed with the bias of the behaver. Satir states that no behavior is irrational while Adlerians refer to understanding a person's private logic. Neither uses the concept of the "unconscious" but prefers to discuss levels of awareness on a continuum. Both groups underplay chemical or hereditary explanations for behavior, emphasizing clear communication and viewing therapy as an educational process avoiding the sin or pathology context. Both see behavior as goal directed toward survival, growth and belonging although Adlerians emphasize the latter.

Theoretical Differences

Satir states that parents provide the blueprint in the child's development while Adlerians insist on including the child's own perception of his situation and his jockeying with siblings thus emphasizing ordinal position and family constellation. Satir is impressed with the power of the parents over the children while Adlerians tend to view as equally important the power of the child on the parents and the effect children have on one another. Both schools recognize the importance of constitutional factors but Satir seems to omit the child's perception as an intervening variable. Although both groups look at symptom production as a mistaken way of finding a place in the family, Satir emphasizes the importance of symptoms as an attempt to alleviate marital pain while Adlerians see symptom production related to sibling interaction as well as interaction with the parents.

Although Adlerians refer to the uniqueness of the individual, problems of family units are thought to have much in common and are not as unique as Satir would seem to make them.

Satir's work is admittedly "marital therapy" in a family setting since she views children's misbehavior as an attempt to reduce marital pain. Adlerian family counseling could more appropriately be called family therapy since it does bring about a change in the child's basic misconceptions and a change in parental behavior.

The Palo Alto group's communication theory is more elegantly developed. Satir seems to emphasize the capacity to experience pleasure as a major criterion of mental health while Adlerians emphasize *Gemeinschaftsgefühl*.

Although Satir talks about an individual in the family playing the role of IP, in fact, it seems she considers the marriage as the IP. Adlerians would not look at either the marriage or any individual as an IP but would look at the family as a whole functioning unit.

Dreikurs[1] does not agree with Satir's explanation of family therapy:

> Effective influence on the children does not depend on the relationship of the mates, provided mother—since she is around most—does not use the children against the father or does not let him use them against herself. Very few people realize to what extent the children decide the role they want to play, and then stimulate the appropriate reaction in their parents.

Similarities in Methods

At Palo Alto, families are seen "privately," but even that is tempered by the family's knowledge of the tape recorder and observers on the other side of the one way glass. Also, supervisors may enter the session at any time. So the public aspects of Adlerian family therapy with its co-therapists is not in sharp contrast to Satir. Of course, Adlerians also do private family therapy. Entire families are seen by both groups although Adlerians, in the centers, often see parents and children separately unless the children are adolescents. Both disciplines spend more time in talking with the parents than with the children. Psychological testing is not relied on to a major extent by either group.

Both types of therapists are extremely active, hopeful and directive; they reveal a basic respect for the clients and underplay the "fragility" of people. These therapists depend on their ability to explain people to themselves; the Adlerian tendency is more direct in that the therapist constantly considers the purpose of behavior. Both therapists repeat, restate, and reemphasize points, and give reasons for arriving at conclusions. An individual's symptoms and fantasy life are not of much interest to these therapists. They avoid the roles of God, Mother or Judge but lean heavily on encouragement. This type of therapist dares to reveal himself and has the "courage to be imperfect" (13).

Both schools believe that all family relationships have positive points which can be encouraged. Democratic virtues are stressed; sameness is not favored, rather appreciation for individual differences is expressed.

Interviews have a definite structure which families appreciate because it gives them hope that problems can be solved. Critics of both groups think the structure tends to provide pat answers to please the therapist.

Satir repeatedly states that she favors the word "connecting" when discussing an individual becoming more a part of the group. It is interesting that Adler used this word when referring to his concept of cure. "As soon as the patient can *connect* himself with his fellow man on an equal and cooperative footing he is cured" (4, p. 260).

Both think in terms of relatively short periods of therapy. Adlerians would agree with Satir's criteria for termination although they might not spell it out as specifically.

Differences in Method

Greater structuring is evident in the early phases of Satir's therapy where Adlerians, although they too have a structure, have a tendency to move more rapidly into therapy spending less time on history and manifesting more concern about the here and now. While life style recreation is used for adults and teenagers, the immediate, short term goals are emphasized with younger children. Although Satir has ostensibly moved away from the Freudian triangle, in the family group she tends to deal with each child as if he were an only child and underplays the relationship between the children.

Adlerians tend to avoid lengthy discussion concerning absent people who are "important others" but both groups are careful to get the complete "cast of characters." Adlerians incorporate not only relatives but teachers, school counselors, play room workers, psychodramatists and music therapists.

Therapeutic goals for the two groups are similar but expressed in different terms. Satir refers to family pleasure and pain; Adlerians favor terms such as harmony, cooperation and mutual encouragement. Both groups aim for individual responsibility but Adlerians stress the establishment of order in the home.

Specific recommendations are more common in Adlerian family education centers not only for the purpose of educating the family being counseled but to disseminate basic principles of parent-child relationships to the audience. Satir tends to focus on improving the over-all communication process.

Summary

Satir's conjoint family therapy and Adlerian family therapy have been compared and contrasted on a theoretical basis, as well as from the standpoint of the function of the therapist and the process of therapy. Satir's family therapy is designed for the family with a schizophrenic child. Adlerian therapy is not as well-knit a process, which presents some disadvantages in attempting to compare it with other schools but from a pragmatic point of view, it allows for more imagination and creativity in the therapeutic process.

Satir's model of man is similar to the Adlerian model. The therapists of both schools show more similarities than differences, and the differences are more those of emphasis than of basic conviction. There is much in Satir's theory and practice that is closely related to Adlerian theory and practice, yet Satir does not recognize any historical kinship to Individual Psychology.

It seems both schools fall into Maslow's third force in psychology, exhibiting holistic, phenomenological, teleological, field-theoretical and socially-oriented approaches.

FOOTNOTE

1. Personal communication.

REFERENCES

1. Adler, A. and Associates, *Guiding the Child (On the Principles of Individual Psychology)*. London, Allen & Unwin, 1930.
2. Adler, A., *The Problem Child*. New York, Capricorn Books, 1963.
3. Adler, A., *Social Interest* (1930). New York, Harper Torchbooks, 1964.
4. Adler, A., *What Life Should Mean to You* (1931). New York, Capricorn Books, 1958.
5. Ansbacher, H. L., "Life Style: A Historical and Systematic Review." *J. Indiv. Psychol.*, 23(1967), pp. 191-212.
6. Ansbacher, H. L., "Sensus Privatus versus Sensis Communis." *J. Indiv. Psychol.*, 21(1965), pp. 48-50.

7. Dreikurs, R., *Fundamentals of Adlerian Psychology*. Chicago, Alfred Inst., 1950.

8. Dreikurs, R., et al., *Manual of Adlerian Family Counseling*. Eugene, Ore., Univ. Oregon Press, 1959.

9. Dreikurs, R. and Mosak, H. H., "The Tasks of Life: Adler's Three Tasks." *Indiv. Psychologist*, 4(1966), pp. 18-22.

10. Dreikurs, R. and Mosak, H. H., "The Tasks of Life. II. The Fourth Life Task." *Indiv. Psychologist*, 4(1967), pp. 51-56.

11. Dreikurs, R. and Soltz, Vicki, *Children: The Challenge*. Des Moines, Ia., Meredith Press, 1964.

12. Jackson, D. D., "The Question of Family Homeostasis." *Psychiat. Quart. Suppl.* (Part 1), 31(1), (1957), pp. 79-90.

13. Lazarsfeld, Sofie, "The Courage for Imperfection." *J. Indiv. Psychol.*, 22(1966), pp. 163-165.

14. Mosak, H. H. and Dreikurs, R., "The Life Tasks. III. The Fifth Life Task." *Indiv. Psychologist*, 5(1967), pp. 16-22.

15. Satir, Virginia, *Conjoint Family Therapy: A Guide to Theory and Technique*. Palo Alto, Cal., Science & Behavior Books, 1964.

16. Shulman, B. H., "The Family Constellation in Personality Diagnosis." *J. Indiv. Psychol.*, 18(1962), pp. 35-47.

17. Watzlawick, P., Beavin, Janet H. and Jackson, D. D., *Pragmatics of Human Communication: A Study of Interactional Patterns, Pathologies and Paradoxes*. New York, Norton, 1967.

LOGICAL AND NATURAL CONSEQUENCES

Maurice L. Bullard

The expression, "natural consequences," was popularized by Dreikurs in his early writings on child training (2). He wished to apply in a positive way the time honored folk-wisdom traditionally referred to as "suffering the consequences."

Unfortunately, his "natural" consequences as practiced by parents were not always natural. More often they were simply parental counteractions of family rule violations. It mattered not to them if the rules were arbitrary and the judgment biased and subjective.

This conflict of limitation imposed by the narrowed concept "natural" consequences as opposed to the more popular and inclusive general consequences became even more apparent when Dreikurs introduced his concept of the four goals of children's misbehavior (3). He identified the nature and intensity of these *short range* purposeful misbehavior goals in terms of attention-getting, power, revenge, and display of inadequacy (1, 2).

In practice it was apparent that the loosely conceived natural consequences were at times effective learning devices and at other times very obstructive. In their more inept usage they not only inhibited learning but actually increased resistance and defiance.

Upon closer observation it was found that all consequences were consistently effective with children not exhibiting any of the four goals of misbehavior and with those having the mild goal of attention-getting. It was equally apparent some kinds of consequences were effective in the goals II, III, and IV of power, revenge, and display of inadequacy; and yet other consequences contributed to and intensified these latter goals. As a result counselors were admonished not to use "natural consequences" for these three goals. But astute observers noticed that natural consequences occurred to the children in these goals in spite of the intentions of adults and often led to beneficial results.

The occurrence of natural consequences in the face of a strong power struggle is illustrated by an incident in which the parents opposed the smoking of their teen-age son. He retaliated with fury by smoking several cigars. His ensuing sickness can best be described by the saying, he "turned pea green." Following this experience any kind of tobacco was nauseating to him.

This was natural consequences in its most direct form. If the parents had placed something in the tobacco to induce such sickness and he had learned of it, he would have resented it highly, and probably have turned to goal III, the revenge stage. This incident reveals the most significant aspect of true natural consequences, the utter detachment of those involved. In this case, the parents didn't make the boy sick. In this situation even a vengeful boy would hardly have associated the consequence with parental attitudes or actions. This dissociation in natural consequences is true for all goal levels.

Of equal importance is the realization that natural consequences are not *used;* they *occur.* Simple examples surround us daily. A dropped object falls; rain soaks us; a hot iron burns. The action and reaction are automatic with little justification for resentments; so it is with the psychological aspects of *natural* consequences.

In the training of counselors and teachers a paradox was occurring in which incidental natural consequences were effective and yet the counselors were being taught not to use them in goals II, III, and IV. No one seemed to seriously study the elements of the problem or to propose a solution until the writer defined the problem and suggested a course of action. A clear distinction was to be made between the *natural* consequences and the contrived or unnatural consequences to be referred to as *logical* consequences.

Logical Consequences

Logical consequences as a learning experience are more involved than natural consequences. Since the elements are less well defined, the various aspects will be presented in detail (4).

In general, logical consequences are the resultant actions following violation of man-made rules or situations. The enforcement of the subsequent action is usually not inherent in the violation but comes from the pressures of an individual or a group. This introduces the human element not contended with in natural consequences. In turn, the more automatic and logical the consequences, the more they resemble natural consequences. The less related and illogical the consequences, the more unreasonable they appear, being completely unusable in goals II, III, and IV.

An example of logical consequences is found in this handling of a situation: a boy is detained in the house on a Saturday morning until the customary room clean-up is completed.

In this case the consequence is logical because it is closely related to the situation, has accepted precedent, can be terminated at will, carried out without words, does not discriminate, and is free of emotion. But even with all of these qualities it has no relation to natural consequences. A boy can have just as much fun with his playmates on the ball field with a cluttered room as with a neat room. Only mother's will enforces the logical consequences. The consequences are logical to the boy only to the extent which he subscribes to the reasonableness of them. In the strong goals of power, revenge and display of inadequacy, logical consequences can be used only with caution if at all.

Some Principles of Logical Consequences

1. The consequences must be *logical*. As obvious as this truth is, it probably is the most violated aspect of logical consequences. The lack of logic is usually in favor of the adult, a situation especially resented by teenagers. Punishments are notorious for their lack of relatedness to the violation. An example of illogical consequence is the case of the boy who had his bicycle locked up because he watched television too much.

2. The severity of consequences must be appropriate to the violation. One father dropped his small son's toys in the furnace each time he found them left out all night.

3. The rule being violated must have general and reasonably long time acceptance, especially in the eyes of the one experiencing the consequences.

4. The rules must apply equally and fairly to all.

5. The rules must relate to and stem from the social order and not from the capricious whims of adults.

Other Considerations

Sincerity is essential in utilizing both natural and logical consequences; lack of it destroys a trust relationship. Empathy should prevail with no sense of winning as the consequences become effective. Social interest would dictate a mild feeling of regret that the lesson of consequences was necessary. Consequences carried out in anger become retaliation. Words are not part of the consequence process. Laughing at the individual or his situation nullifies benefits of both natural and logical consequences.

The addition of the logical concept has increased the elements which must be understood in using this as a corrective device. However, this does not make the use more difficult. These influences become usable where they were previously unusable, especially in the strong goals of misbehavior.

To facilitate their use it is strongly recommended that in casual conversations with pupils, as in class councils, the generalized term "consequences" be used omitting reference to natural and logical. These are diagnostic adjectives for personal use.

With practice, the distinction becomes automatic and is no burden on the practitioner whether he be counselor, teacher, or parent.

REFERENCES

1. Bullard, M. L., *Goal Recognition.* Corvallis, Oregon Community Parent-Teacher Education Centers, 1960.
2 Dreikurs, R., *The Challenge of Parenthood* (1947), 9th ed. Des Moines, Iowa, Meredith Press, 1962.
3. Dreikurs, R., *Psychology in the Classroom* (1957). New York, Harper & Row, 1968.
4. Dreikurs, R. and Soltz, Vicki, *Children: The Challenge.* Des Moines, Iowa, Meredith Press, 1964.

GROUP PROCEDURES
IN THE CLASSROOM

Bernice Grunwald

Talking with school children has too often been conducted as one-way communication. The teacher talked and the child either listened or tuned out the teacher. Conducted on a one-to-one basis, the discussion placed the teacher, or confirmed her, in an authoritarian role, removed the teacher-child or child-child problem from its social context, and failed to utilize the influence of the peer group in the solution of the problem. Beginning with the assumption that all problems are social problems, Adler, in his *Erziehungsberatungsstellen,* introduced group discussion with children, parents and teachers (1). Later, Spiel introduced the group discussion into the classroom in his Individual Psychology Experimental School in Vienna (4), and while the method has been extensively used by Adlerians (2)[1], it did not make great inroads in American education until Glasser (3) decribed the method in his recent book.

Group discussion involves a group of people talking and thinking together about some problem or topic. It is different from a conversation in that it has direction; it examines problem areas; it deals with feelings; it analyzes cause and effect of behavior; and it faces unpleasant facts which normally are ignored or sidetracked. It is a democratic interchange of ideas guided by the needs of the group.

Through group discussion children develop better interpersonal relationships. Difficult tasks seem lighter when we have shared our ideas, aspirations, problems and anxieties. This is especially true for the children who discover that they are not alone in their predicament, that others have the same or similar problems. As the child experiences interest and support from others, he becomes supportive himself. Thus, he begins to change his values, attitudes and behavior pattern. This may influence his entire life because he learns constructive ways of handling frustrations and of working through upsetting problems.

Group discussions are probably the most effective means by which a teacher can integrate all children into one class for a common purpose. Through well directed group discussions, the teacher may succeed in raising the morale of the group and changing the atmosphere in the class from one which is charged with hostility and antagonism to one of harmony and mutual understanding and concern, without which a teacher can not teach effectively.

Teachers may ask, "Can young children understand the dynamics of their behavior? Isn't it a waste of time which ought to be devoted to the teaching of subject matter? Won't the children talk forever in order to avoid school work?" Many teachers see no value in such discussions; some would like to try them but feel that they cannot afford the time. I cannot share the pessimistic attitude that some teachers exhibit. Talking things over has strong therapeutic value for everyone. The value lies not only in the content of the discussion but also in the pure freedom to talk without being hushed up or ridiculed. Children have a need to talk, and as yet have little opportunity to discuss the things that really matter to them.

Talking is a sharing medium. The child who cannot share himself is usually a lonely child, one who is constantly on guard, afraid of being hurt. To him sharing means giving of himself, and since he only sees himself as being on the receiving side, he cannot participate in a discussion on a give and take basis. The withdrawn child will withdraw from participation in group discussion as he withdraws from almost all participation.

In group discussion, the immediate focus is on the problem as it affects everyone, and not on the individual child. The child who fears to speak up because he may say the wrong thing—the thing which may meet with disfavor by the group will not speak up either. He will not risk being a failure. The show-off may withdraw from participation as soon as he realizes that he cannot put on a show.

Many children would like to participate in the discussion, but they do not know how, for at home they are either the ones who give orders and rule, or the ones who must obey orders without questioning them. They have never experienced a friendly discussion.

Initiating Class Discussions

With such a variety of problems, how can a teacher unite the class into a friendly, outgoing and constructive discussion? When does she begin training her students toward this end? Group discussion must start as soon as the teacher becomes acquainted with her class. She may start on the first day of school. Such a discussion might concern the decorating of the classroom; planning the activities for the first week; a get-together party with another class, etc. It must be a topic toward which most children have an attitude and would respond if asked to voice an opinion. Gradually the teacher may bring up problems for discussion concerning order in the corridor and in the washroom. This, too, is a problem which concerns everybody, but it incorporates the necessity to arrive at a conclusion and a decision. Later, the decision must be evaluated for its effectiveness. If the decisions the children made were ineffective, new and better ones must be decided on.

A teacher must encourage children who consistently remain quiet to take part in the conversation. To such a child, she may say, "What is your opinion, John? We would like to know how you feel about this problem." A teacher should never ask for suggestions or advice from a child unless she is prepared to take his words seriously.

After two or three weeks, when the children have already achieved some idea of how to conduct a discussion, the teacher may bring up a problem which concerns specific children, although she may avoid using their names. She might say, "You have been wonderful with your suggestions. It has helped me a great deal, and I should like you to know that I appreciate your efforts. I am wondering if we could discuss some of the problems people have, mine or yours. We could help one another by talking things over. The students of my previous class did it often, and they found it very helpful. What do you think?" If the children do not understand, she may say, "I am thinking of people who have difficulties in getting along with others, doing their work in school, getting here on time, being orderly, disturbing the class, and so on. I am sure you understand now what I mean. I think that we could help children who have such difficulties if we talk about them in a manner which would not make these children feel that we criticize them, but that we are interested in helping them. Sometimes, you may talk about something I don't do quite the way I ought to be doing it. Teachers have difficulties, too, and I would be very grateful to you if you could help me." In most instances, the children will understand what the teacher is after, and will agree to such discussions.

If the teacher feels that her class is not ready to discuss a problem which concerns a classmate, she may bring up a problem which one of her former students had, or she may use a character from a story in which the latter has difficulties in social adjustment. Almost every story lends itself to such a discussion. Let us follow a discussion of a story prepared by the teacher.

"Carmen was in second grade. She was a very smart girl according to everyone who knew her. She liked to go to school but she did not do any work in class. She spent most of her time drawing, getting out of her seat, talking to her neighbors. This made the teacher angry and she often scolded and punished Carmen for her behavior. The parents were also very angry with her; they could not understand why she behaved that way since they were always very good to her; they gave her everything she asked for."

TEACHER: "What do you think of Carmen?"

CHILD: "Well, she sure doesn't act right."

TEACHER: "What do you mean?"

CHILD: "She is not nice."

TEACHER: "Could someone explain why she doesn't act right and isn't nice?"

CHILD: "She should be doing her work in class just like everyone else."

TEACHER: "Yes, she should, but she doesn't. Why doesn't she?"

CHILD: "Maybe it is too hard."

TEACHER: "Do you believe that the work is too hard for Carmen?"

CHILD: "Maybe it isn't."

TEACHER: "How do we know that the work isn't too hard for her?"

CHILD: "It said that she is smart and that everybody said so."

TEACHER: "That's right. She could do the work easily, yet she is not doing it. Let's see if you could figure out why she isn't."

CHILD: "I think she is just stubborn and has to have her own way."

OTHER CHILD: "I think that Carmen is spoiled."

TEACHER: "What do you mean?"

CHILD: "Well, she gets everything she wants."

TEACHER: "Is that bad?"

CHILD: "Well, if you get everything all the time, you want everything all the time, and if you can't have it, you get mad."

TEACHER: "Larry said a while ago that he thinks Carmen has to have her way. How would this have anything to do with her not doing the work?"

CHILD: "I mean, that she isn't going to do the work because she wants to do only what she decides she wants to do."

TEACHER: "How do other children feel about Carmen having to have her own way?"

CHILD: "Well, on the playground, she never plays a game with us unless we play what she wants to play."

TEACHER: "Now, why is it so important for Carmen to have her own way?"

CHILD: "I still think that she is spoiled."

TEACHER: "What does Carmen get out of having her way?"

CHILD: "She wants to be the boss."

TEACHER "Why is it so important for her to be the boss? Try to think about my question, and also try to see if you can find something that she gets out of behaving as she does."

CHILD: "Yes, she gets a lot of attention."

TEACHER: "From whom?"

CHILD: "From her parents. They give in to her."

TEACHER: "What else do they do? It may seem to some that what she gets is unpleasant, but I wonder."

CHILD: "They scold her."

TEACHER: "That's right. Isn't this also attention? Look how she is keeping her parents busy with her. Who else gives her this kind of attention?"

MANY CHILDREN: "The teacher."

TEACHER: "Yes, the teacher. As we see, Carmen keeps many people busy. Now, let us see if Carmen could get attention in a different way. I mean, in a pleasant way."

CHILD: "I think she could."

TEACHER: "How?"

CHILD: "If she is smart she could do good work and get attention."

TEACHER: "Yes, I think you are very right. She could also be a helper to the teacher. Every teacher needs help, and Carmen could be of great help to her."

TEACHER: "You see how well you could help Carmen understand her problem. I am sure that you could help equally well someone in our class who is having difficulties. Maybe there is somebody here who has Carmen's problem. I hope this child will feel free to talk about it next time when we have a discussion."

This is but one example of a group discussion with children. A resourceful teacher will find ways and means of bringing up problems for discussion which will invariably apply to some child in the class. In time, the children will discuss the problems John or Mary has. In time, the teacher will be able to withdraw more and more, and ask occasional questions, so as to keep the discussion going and to the subject.

A teacher must be a good listener. She must sit with the children not, as some do, behind the desk, doing some paper work while the group discussion is in progress. If the teacher gives her full attention, the children will do likewise. If the teacher observes listlessness, she may invite the child to voice an opinion concerning the topic of discussion, or she may ask the speaker to stop until everybody pays attention.

As teachers, we must not use discussions to express merely our own ideas. This usually results in "preaching," and is not a discussion. Preaching may be necessary occasionally, but if overdone, the children stop listening and really do not know what has been said. At the end of the week, the teacher may have an evaluation of the week's progress for discussion. Thus, the children learn where they have planned well and where they need to improve.

Some Guidelines for Group Discussion[2]

1. Classroom discussions should be set up for a specific time each week. In this way children can rely upon a scheduled opportunity to discuss their problems, and they can plan ahead for this. Except for problems which must be handled immediately, specific problems should be held over until this time when children can expect that they will be brought up. A benefit of this procedure for the teacher is that she is not

cast in the role of "fireman" during the remainder of the week.

2. The duration of a session is a function of the age of the children, the time of day, the time of year, and other such variables. However, there should be a scheduled beginning and ending time.

3. Preferably the children should be seated in a circle.

4. As illustrated above, it is frequently advisable to talk about a child or about classroom behavior without identifying the child or children. The teacher can construct a fictitious case centering about a problem which actually exists in the class without mentioning any names. The children may know who is involved, but use of names should be avoided unless the child referred to identifies himself as, or as being like, the fictitious character.

5. Occasionally the teacher may find it necessary to take the students into her confidence with respect to a particular child whom most of the children dislike for some reason. Some kind of errand can be formulated for getting this child out of the classroom while the others are discussing his situation. The major emphasis here must be, "How can we help this child to feel that he belongs to the group?" Usually the children will express negative feelings toward the child in question, but the teacher should keep wondering aloud, "How can we help this child?", as well as "Does he do this because he's really mean (stupid, cruel, or however is he usually labeled by the group), or because he feels he can't get recognition or attention in any other way?"

Generally, if the pattern of the discussions has been established, children will forward ideas as to how this child can be helped to get recognition through constructive activity. It is also remarkable how they will go out of their way to refrain from reacting negatively to such a child's provocations after such a discussion. Essentially the emphasis here is not in making the child special but in removing his specialness by attacking the question of "How can we help him to become a member of the group?"

Once a pattern has been established in which the children bring up their own problems for the group to discuss, the above may be unnecessary except in extreme cases of revengeful or severely discouraged children.

6. When misbehavior is being discussed, and the teacher feels that interpretation is necessary, the emphasis should be upon the four goals of misbehavior (2). The child's need to belong, to be liked, and to be valued by others are other foci. In all instances, the positive attributes of the child rather than his misbehavior should be emphasized. The teacher's efforts should be directed toward encouraging the children to express these goals in their own words. Interpretations should only be made when it would seem that they will not come forth through questioning.

Goals are generally only understood by children when they are expressed in functional terms or in terms of activity or movement. Goal I (attention getting) may be expressed as "He did it because he wants the teacher to fuss over him, to pay attention to him." Goal II (power seeking) can be represented by sentences such as, "He did it to prove he was the boss and could do anything he wanted without anybody stopping him." A statement like, "He did it to get even because he thinks everybody is against him and wants to hurt him," can describe Goal III (revenge taking), while "He wants everyone to leave him alone" can characterize Goal IV (display of inadequacy).

7. The teacher should refrain from contradicting or speaking critically of any child's offering, even if it is wrong, punitive or negativistic. The best way to handle such statements is to ask others what they think of it, whether they agree or disagree and why. Usually such statements are refuted very quickly without the student involved feeling censured or criticized.

8. Children should not be permitted to humiliate one another. If a hurtful statement is made, other children can be asked what they think of it. If they tend to agree with the humiliating statement, the teacher might inquire, "Do you really think he's just mean (stupid, a bully, etc.) or do you think there might be another reason for what he's doing?" thus leading them to the goal of the misbehavior and laying the groundwork for remedial action.

Types of Discussion

A versatile method, the group discussion may be employed for many purposes. In addition to the discussion of the problems of individual children, it can serve as a vehicle for discussing the problems of the group, of teacher-children problems, and of administration-children problems. Extended to issues beyond the classroom, the discussion can be related to the challenges and problems of living. Many teachers find the method useful for planning the classroom use and decoration as well as for the planning of studies and assignments. Others see the method as being uniquely suited for teaching subject matter, especially when "factophilia" (5) is replaced with thinking, imagination, evaluation, opinion, and creative problem solving.

Whatever the goal of the discussion, the opportunity to participate in discussion which is related to individual and group destiny is in the tradition of the democratic town meeting. Once children discover that they can speak openly and freely discuss their views with the knowledge that they will be accepted and respected even if they are wrong, the barriers come down and a spirit of cooperativeness and helpfulness emerges. The feeling of responsibility for oneself and one another, the feelings of worth and equality which develop reflect the *Gemeinschaftsgefühl* which the Adlerian teacher strives to install in her partners in the educational enterprise.

FOOTNOTES

1. Several of the writer's papers on classroom discussion have been distributed by the School of Education, School Psychological Services, University of Oregon. The method has been taught to teachers by Mosak at the Teacher Development Center, Rockford, Illinois, Public Schools as part of a Title III project.
2. I am grateful to Dr. Loren Grey and Dr. Harold H. Mosak for their helpful suggestions in the preparation of this section.

REFERENCES

1. Adler, A., *The Problem Child.* New York, Capricorn Books, 1963.
2. Dreikurs, R., *Psychology in the Classroom* (1957). New York, Harper & Row, 1968.
3. Glasser, W., *Schools Without Failure.* New York, Harper & Row, 1969.
4. Speil, O., *Discipline Without Punishment.* London, Faber & Faber, 1962.
5. Winthrop, H., "Scientism in Psychology." *J. Indiv. Psychol.,* 15(1959), pp. 112-120.

REMINISCENCES OF A CHILD PSYCHOLOGIST

Blanche C. Weill

I first met Dr. Adler in the fall of 1926 at a dinner for him at the home of Professor Harry A. Overstreet in New York. I was then working toward my doctorate at Harvard University Graduate School of Education. In that one evening, indeed in that one hour at dinner, I received a basic education in what Adlerian theory could mean for children, parents and teachers. As a result I traveled the following summer to Vienna where I had an analysis with Adler and attended daily classes in theory. We had opportunities for observation in various clinics in the city. Later when Adler came to New York City, I again had the opportunity to study with him.

I had already found an excellent basis for work with children from Dr. Maria Montessori with whom I had studied in Rome and in California, and had opened schools at her request which specialized in educating children with physical and mental impairments or behavioral and emotional problems. Montessori methods and Adlerian insights proved to be a most felicitous combination.

For the purposes of this paper I have decided that children themselves are their own best spokesmen, and so of Adler's chief theses—(1) social feeling, (2) courage in the face of difficulties, (3) desire for power (what used to be called "the masculine protest"), and (4) the individual's goals, constructive or non-constructive, or, as Adler phrased it, "plus or minus," I have chosen to illustrate the last—goals and their motivation. The stories are drawn from my experiences in public and private schools in Michigan, New York and California, and occasionally in children's homes or in my own office. It should be remembered that in all behavior there is movement toward a goal. There may also be more than one goal for a specific behavior.

Two Boys of Equal Ability

The first two children were boys of the same age, eleven, and with identical I.Q.'s of 76. One was tested in the morning, the other in the afternoon. In neither case did I engage in therapy, although there was some give and take during the testing sessions. My recommendations were based upon the tests and upon my observations during the testing. The first boy's history showed that he had first been tested in the first grade, at which time he was given an I.Q. in the mid-nineties. From then on his I.Q. steadily declined. He had come from a broken home and had been moved about often. He had lost all confidence in people, exhibited little interest in anything, and reiterated that people were "no good," and that he hoped he would be able to "get back at them." My recommendation in his case was to place him in an environment among people he could trust; otherwise I feared for his future.

The other boy had always been a slow learner but did have an absorbing interest in maps and geography that impelled him to learn to read and to achieve far more than his I.Q. would have suggested was possible. "I like to know about other countries. Maps are fun." he said. For him, my prognosis was favorable.

A Non-Reader

The third child was a pretty child of ten who was in a public school where I did volunteer work. She was in the fifth grade, pleasant to everyone, and she did well in some of her school work, especially arithmetic, but she had never learned to read. It was the policy of the school to promote each child yearly, regardless of achievement. The family had moved to the city two or three years previously from a French-Canadian enclave in Florida. The tests she had had never resulted in an I.Q. less than 127. Physical examination had shown no eye or other defects. The school term was half over and her class was thinking about promotion to the sixth grade.

One day I said to her, "Well, it's getting near the end of the term."

"Oh," she said, "do you know whether I'll pass?"

"Of course not," I answered. "How could you do sixth grade work when you can't read?"

She began to cry. "But I have always passed."

"This time you won't," I answered.

"Oh, how can I ever look the other girls in the face. Will you help me if I work and work?"

"Of course," I said, and then it all came out. She had thought it a grand joke to play on her family to pretend she was doing her homework at night when they all sat around the table, but no one had ever thought to see if she knew her lessons. She had felt very smart to be able to fool them all.

"If I fail the exams next month, will you help me during vacation so

I can take them again at the opening of school? I know I can pass them."

I told her I would help her, and she began to work ceaselessly. She quickly learned how to sound a new or long word phonetically, and then we began reading together a not-too-easy book about a French girl who was a sort of Joan of Arc. I would let her read until she got stuck and then would help just a bit until she got the word and went on. She so enjoyed that book that she asked to take it home nights and weekends.

She did not quite make the grade in reading by the end of the school year, but read many books during vacation and passed with flying colors at the special examination she was given at the opening of school, and so was able to go on with her friends into sixth grade.

A Handicapped Child

A child was carried in by his mother to the little school my sister and I had opened in California. He was six years old. His mother also carried a pair of crutches.

"If only you can get him to use these," she said, "I'll ask for nothing more."

The youngster was not afraid of being left with us, but crawled about, looking at everything. Then he explained to me, pitifully, "My nurse dropped me when I was a baby, so I can't walk." His legs were withered.

I put him in a comfortable chair and asked if he'd like to paint or draw. He agreed, and I laid the materials on a little table he could manage. Suddenly he dropped to the floor, crawled into a little conservatory off the main room and started to shut the door, saying, "I'm going in here and I'll shut the door and lock it, and you'll never see me again."

"Sorry," I said, "but there is no lock on that door." However he banged it shut. I signaled the other children to pay no attention. Before long the conservatory door opened, the child crawled to his chair, managed to pull himself up on it and painted quietly. No one acted as if he had been noticed. I stopped briefly to see his painting and said how nice it was.

Then came a change in activity. The children put away the materials on which they had been working, and one of them noticed the crutches, which had been left standing against the wall, and began trying them out. Then another and another child wanted a turn. This was more than Charles could stand. They were *his* crutches. He went for the boy who had them. I explained to everybody that they really were Charles' and that he should have them, though he could always share them if he wanted.

That was all that was needed. He, who had refused to touch the crutches before, now was proud to find that he could do what the other children did on them and that he was no longer different. Also he could do the other children the favor of allowing them to use the crutches. He was intrigued to find the children trying new tricks on them which he could imitate, and he could even devise new tricks himself.

His mother was delighted and reported further that the temper tantrums she had not mentioned before had now almost disappeared at home. He no longer needed to vent his rage on a world that had no place for him.

A Semi-Blind Child

Another boy was also in our school, brought in by his parents. The child, almost twelve, had been born with one-sixteenth of normal nerve connections and was also almost blind. He was eager to try anything that could help him. I sent for a large-type book for the semi-blind, gave him the Montessori sandpaper letters and taught him, as we had taught the other children, to run his fingers over them gently, thus actually writing the letter as he sounded it, so he could connect the shape with the sound and at the same time prepare his arm and finger muscles for writing. We took him to the moveable bar in the play yard. At first we had to hold his fingers over the bar so he wouldn't fall, but soon the fingers got stronger and he could not only hold his own weight, but could turn and twist on the bar.

Then he found the piano. He touched the keys lovingly. Before we could realize it, he was playing tunes by ear. He came to me radiant, saying, "I can play the same tune no matter on which key I start." Next he discovered the scales. Meanwhile the reading and writing were going ahead.

With all their love and concern for this only son (there was one much older sister), none of his family ever realized that this child needed to be treated as an individual. At home we found that he had no place to call his own. His bed was a couch in his sister's room. He had part of one drawer in her bureau for his clothes and a few hooks and hangers in the closet. He had no shelf anywhere for his pet belongings.

When Tom stayed with us for a couple of weeks while his family was away, he had his own room and closet and bureau for the first time. During this visit he had all his meals with us, and his appetite improved. He had previously had lunch with us on school days, and was finicky about his vegetables. One day I suggested that he try the string beans. He looked at me and said, "At home no one cares what I eat. I could go out into the desert where there is nothing but sand and never get any food and it wouldn't matter, because God would take care of me."

I answered, "Yes, God takes care of us, and He gave us all our bodies as a kind of temple to worship him with, and our brains to take care of that temple so it can live and grow. That is why he provides us with our food." This convinced him and he became much less difficult about eating vegetables.

He made constant improvement and his eagerness to learn never ceased.

"My Father Can't Read"

With this child I must record a real failure, where the motivation to learn to read was completely lacking. That is, to read in English. I have never forgiven myself for not having tried to teach him to read Spanish. Maybe I might have got through to him. Jose, eight years old, was sent to us from a third grade in the New York public school. He lived with his father, grandmother and aunt. The father had been an oil-rigger in Venezuela and his wife had died when her first baby was born there. The father immediately brought the child back to the maternal grandmother and aunt and found work as a carpenter. The family was Puerto Rican and spoke almost no English. They all adored the child and when he had to go to school his grandmother took him by the hand and brought him to and fro four times a day. This was still continuing. The child had learned English from playing on the street, always with his grandmother's eye upon him. At school he understood small numbers and could write them and knew what they stood for. The tests given him were inconclusive, except that the non-verbal ones showed normal intelligence.

My first day with him went splendidly. I had the child an hour each day. His English seemed adequate. He was cooperative and friendly. He liked the sandpaper letters, and seemed to learn the sounds and even started to put together a vowel and one or two consonants vocally, always making a real word he knew. He would read them as I changed the consonants or the vowel, always a simple real word. But the next day he had forgotten everything. Sometimes by the end of the hour he would have forgotten what he had learned during the first part of the hour. Gradually, however, he became able to read phonetic material I prepared for him, and soon I brought him a little pre-primer with charming illustrations and he was able to finish it. Each day, though, the bulk of the previous day's work had been forgotten. There seemed little progress. I obtained another pre-primer, which used largely the same vocabulary as the first. He was very pleased. However, soon he became stuck on a word he had had before, but had forgotten. Instantly he reached for his first book, rapidly turned the pages until he came to the one on which this word had been introduced. He ran his eye down the page reading half-aloud until he came to the word, then picked up the new book and read the word there. He kept on using the first book as a dictionary. I realized that here was a boy whose intelligence was not deficient, but he still kept forgetting.

One day when he came in, I was writing a letter. "Would you like to know to whom I'm writing, Jose?" I asked. He said that he would. "I'm writing to your father. I know you want to be a builder like him and I know he'll want you to be able to read so you can make out blue-prints." (We had often talked of his beloved father's building jobs.)

He looked at me pityingly. "Dr. Weill, my father can't read or write. But he's a good workman. Me, I want to be a toymaker." (He had told me this before.) "My father will teach me, and I can make toys and paint them any color people want. I want to be like my father."

So then I understood. It was obvious that Jose felt that it was un-necessary for him to learn to read or write, and that I was wasting my time having him as a pupil, so we went to the principal's office and I told him that I was licked. Jose's family moved away soon afterwards.

A Mother Who Listened

I remember vividly the aftermath of a mothers' group in a crowded Harlem school where I had been talking about how important it was to take time to listen to a child when he came in, all excited about something, bursting to tell you, and that you must try never to be too busy to drop everything and listen to him. The following meeting the mother of a seven year old boy bustled in, bursting with importance. Before anyone could speak she broke out, "You were right about that listening. Yesterday I told my little boy to wait for me at a neighbor's as I was going out and might not be back in time to pick him up at school or get back before he did to unlock the door. The sun was shining and I wore my new hat. But just before three, a heavy rain began to fall. I rushed to my friend's house to pick up Johnny, but no one was there. I was furious, thinking of my new hat getting spoiled in the rain, and somehow laying it all on him for not being there, and I was going to give it to him good when he got in. I rushed home. The front door is always open and I was no sooner inside than I heard him calling to me from the stairs in front of our apartment. I was just starting to yell at him, when I suddenly thought, 'Child Study; Dr. Weill.' He ran down the stairs, seized my hand and snuggled up to me and said, 'I thought I'd better run home because no one was at Davy's.' So I picked him up and praised him for his good sense and he beamed. And I thought if I hadn't listened to him I'd have had him hurt and crying and I'd probably never have known why."

It is almost half a century since the Overstreet dinner, but Adler's statement that we must see with the child's eyes and hear with his ears remains valid (1). Only then can we understand his goals.

REFERENCES

1. Adler, A., *What Life Should Mean to You* (1931). New York, Capricorn Books, 1958.
2. Weill, Blanche C., *Through Children's Eyes: True Stories Out of the Practice of a Consultant Psychologist.* New York, Island Workshop Press, 1940.

TEACHERS ARE PEOPLE, TOO

Eugene W. Wade

It would seem to this author that one who is a teacher ought to find his self-esteem and significance through being useful to his students. He would use his talents to catalyze learning; he would work with his class in a common goal of understanding the subject matter; he would help them build their own ideas. Thus, he would share himself in a way that would be useful to the students and hence fulfilling to himself. However, this is not always the case. Some teachers have developed styles of life that involve controlling, dominating or using people (2). In the classroom these styles inhibit the learning process and are ultimately self-defeating to the teacher's goal of belonging and self-esteem.

Projecting the goals of childhood misbehavior as identified by Dreikurs (1, p. 26) into the adult profession of teaching, we can see more clearly some of the techniques which can be used to serve styles of life other than social usefulness.

Attention Getting Mechanisms

Here the essential element is being the star with the use of techniques for gaining and retention of the spotlight. Jokes are frequent; dress may be unusual. Words are used for shock value rather than for learning. Verbal delivery is designed to be sensational rather than for the purpose of facilitating learning. As the classroom becomes a stage for the display of the performer, others are excluded from the cast. Communication is concentrated in the teacher. Students are not permitted to share ideas with one another; they must talk directly to the teacher. Any other show-off who attempts to steal the spotlight is a threat to the star and is quickly extinguished. The traditional classroom in which the teacher is the central figure, provides the opportunity to actualize the mistaken goal of being a "somebody" by having a great deal of attention.

Power

One who searches for power and feels pride in his own power feels important as he directs the lives of other people. He feels significant as he tells others what to do. He is very sensitive to direction from others and often rebels and storms when he feels that an administrator is controlling him. He is the first to scream (justified or not) that his civil rights and professional freedoms are being violated.

Teaching provides a haven for one with the goal of power. One can be a dictator (enlightened or tyrannical) and still justify himself as a good teacher. Few roles remain in our twentieth-century society where excessive authority is permitted, but that of the teacher is one. Police, army officers, company executives, and the Ku Klux Klan have had their power and authority checked, but the teacher, for example, still has the right in some places to strike with a board, stick, or hand. Kings and nobility have been restrained by revolution and constitutions, but most classroom teachers have yet to feel either.

Teachers who need power, use it to crush "insubordination." If children behave only under threat of power, the monarchs dare not permit one child to "get away with anything." If one child can defy authority, the idea may spread. The monarch lives under constant threat of rebellion. He deals harshly in class with the child who disobeys. Obedience and respect are rewarded by this teacher.

Revenge

Revenge follows upon power. Revenge is hurting. Revenge is being unable to accept blame or a slight, or forgive an error. Revenge is hurting another more than one is hurt—to turn the receiving of pain into the inflicting of pain. And teachers sometimes have little ability to tolerate hurt. Slights from life can be avenged upon students. Punitive and excessive demands for homework, or homework over Christmas vacations, can serve the need for revenge. Failure of students at the end of the year can be the settling of the score. This retention can be the satisfaction of a year of resentment—resentment generated because the child did not learn or work or behave as the teacher had demanded. He did not fulfill the many needs of the teacher. How many tests are given in anger to punish students who did not conform to demands? Or, how many low marks serve to hurt?

Retention, tests, and marks are ostensibly tools for assisting learning. The long range goal of these devices is to uncover or report weaknesses in order that they may be remedied. The vengeful teacher takes these tools of learning and forges them into instruments of hurt.

Defeat

Another mistaken goal is that of defeat. To that extent which the teacher feels personal discouragement, he will hide from the requirements of effective teaching. These discouraged souls throw up their hands at their problems. They exude and radiate hopelessness.

In talking to a defeated teacher, one is filled with the emotion of giving up. Children in her room are too bad, too lost, too far behind, too emotionally disturbed, too far beyond help—so why try? Why attempt to make plans for changing the children? The end of the year is near, or the parents don't care, or the child doesn't care—so let's quit. These teachers have never even started! Expecting to fail, they seldom try.

In higher grades the discouraged teacher is a slave to the textbook—one is safe between those two covers. Personal stands, opinions, or creative thinking do not emanate from the teacher. Limits upon the behavior of students may not be set or adhered to with firmness. Requests for work, order, and quiet may be abused by the students. The fear of taking a stand and/or the overwhelming need to please and be loved may make a doormat of the teacher.

The following life style is included to illustrate its effect in teaching.

Being Better Than Others

Some people are comfortable in teaching because they can get a constant sense of being better than others. They avoid the competitive outside world where there are often reminders of their "inadequacy." (I put this in quotes because it is usually a felt inadequacy rather than a real inadequacy.) By being the teacher, they can structure the learning so that they can know more than others—the students. But some who strive to be first must work at it! These teachers admit no mistakes in their logic or performance and so continue to maintain their image. Students behave and ask no embarrassing questions; they uncover no areas of scanty knowledge in this teacher's classroom.

One who strives may use big words to impress himself (note the goal is to impress *oneself*). He may dwell at length upon the moral shortcomings of others and humanity—not out of concern but only to cast himself in better light. Students' inabilities are more likely to be noted than their strengths for the same reason. This teacher is mistake oriented—for his own good reasons.

Other aspects of this 'god' complex are the use of low grades, lectures on obscure topics during which the lecturer's knowledge of trivia shines through, and intolerance of ambiguity. He rarely says, "I don't know."

One who labors after vertical success (3) suffers the dual consequences of loneliness and fear; loneliness, because by using students and people to be better than, he cannot appreciate them as human beings; and fear, because he lives in dread of being found out as an ordinary being.

191

REFERENCES

1. Dreikurs, R., *Psychology in the Classroom.* New York, Harper & Row, 1968.
2. Mosak, H. H., "The Controller: A Social Interpretation of the Anal Character." This volume.
3. Sicher, Lydia, "Education for Freedom." *Amer. J. Indiv. Psychol.,* 11(1954), pp. 97-103. Also in Adler, K. S. and Deutsch, D., eds. *Essays in Individual Psychology.* New York, Grove Press, 1959, pp. 16-24.

THE EXTENSION AND IMPLEMENTATION OF ADLERIAN PSYCHOLOGY

Manford Sonstegard

Since the beginning, Individual Psychology—which became known as Adlerian Psychology after Alfred Adler's death, and sometimes is referred to as Teleoanalytic Psychology—has been applied in many fields. From a rather unobtrusive beginning in a medical setting in Vienna, it was first applied to the schools of that city. There Adler conducted clinics and counseled children and parents before groups of teachers. His primary purpose was the instruction of teachers in the understanding of children. Thus, probably for the first time, therapy and counseling were performed before a group. It seems reasonable that the psychological concepts that Adler formulated in working with children in the schools would be conducive to application in varied educational situations, and this has actually occurred.

It seems natural that Adler should introduce this innovation. He was a gregarious man who felt at ease beyond the confines of his office, and the approach in the schools was a professional extension of the social, philosophical, and psychological discussions held with innumerable friends in the coffee shops of Vienna which he frequented.

It is probably safe to say that in the school, rather than in his office, Adler arrived at many of the psychological formulations which eventually became a psychology of use rather than of possession (3), for Adler readily departed from conventional approaches if he believed innovations would result in therapeutic advancement. Thus, his formulations from the beginning were not static, but subject to change and new applications. These innovations must have been disconcerting for Freud, bound as he was to the objective and mechanical spirit of natural science which held sway in the nineteenth century. As a matter of fact, Freud had written a paper, "Project for Scientific Psychology," which opened with these words, "The intention of this project is to furnish us with a psychology which shall be a natural science: its aim, that is, is to represent psychical processes as quantitatively determined states of specific material particles and so to make them plain and void of contradictions (10)."

Adler's eventual break from the Freudian circle is understandable. That it was due entirely to differences in their personal temperament, as is sometimes implied, is an oversimplification of their differences. Soon after the turn of the century came the advent of a new era, an age that ushered in a new and different model of man. Adler, with his infinite ability to analyze, was probably among the first to sense revolutionary trends that would overthrow the old, erroneous model of man which began with the pronouncements of Copernicus. The break with Freud in 1910 which is referred to by Matson (13) as the "great departure" probably marks the general disengagement from psychoanalytic theory and therapy. The separation, viewed without attention to historic events, could be attributed exclusively, but erroneously, to differences in the personal temperament of the two men and to Adler's disagreement with the sexual derivation of Freud's theory of neurosis (3).

The Extension by Innovation

The courage and imagination which Adler demonstrated in his willingness to make use of various methods and approaches was apparently transmitted to his students and colleagues. The introduction of multiple psychotherapy is an example (9). In addition to facilitating therapy, it has also been demonstrated to be an effective method for training therapists. Multiple psychotherapy is only one of the methods developed in the vast expanse of Adlerian innovativeness. It appears that the followers of Adler are fully as ingenious and courageous as he was in making use of various methods and approaches. Dreikurs is probably the most widely known among the Adlerians in the field of education and he has made Adlerian Psychology in this area more exportable. This occurred largely through his proclivity for teaching and demonstrations of counseling children and parents before his classes.

This pioneering approach has since been adopted by other Adlerians. Where Adler relied almost entirely for his teaching upon the presentation of cases to be discussed through the interview method, the therapists in the United States incorporated psychodrama and music therapy into their regular therapeutic procedures. The training of students to become perceptive has been furthered, and the method of sharpening diagnostic skills has been taught in such a way that it can readily be communicated to students. This training disproves the notion that sensitivity is a talent and therefore cannot be acquired by others. It has been definitely demonstrated that sensitivity can be transmitted to students, thereby increasing their diagnostic skill.

A discussion of the extensiveness of Adlerian Psychology would be incomplete without some attention to approaches which are linked to theoretical assumptions, but are innovations in application rather than new principles. Throughout the United States and other countries, in numerous communities, Parent Study Groups are conducted by laymen trained in Adlerian methods of group leadership (14). In the schools, teachers trained in workshops and courses taught by Adlerians in universities and colleges are holding weekly discussions with their pupils (11) thereby helping them to learn how to manage their own affairs. Some teachers conduct small group discussions with high school or junior high school students using as a basis for their group sessions, Adlerian materials such as *Children: The Challenge* (7).

Group Approaches and Counselor Training

The application of group approaches to the education of counselors enrolled in the counseling practicum is a comparatively recent innovation. The procedure was started simultaneously in two separate universities about 1960 (4). The practice had its beginning with Alfred Adler who interviewed children and their parents before a group of teachers (2). This initiated a general trend of counseling parents and children in a group, a procedure used by Adler and his associates in counseling centers throughout Europe (1) and later in the United States (8, 12, 15).

In line with this development, we are supervising counselors in a group and in counseling before a group. During graduate study, in the prevalent system of supervision, the counselor usually has little opportunity to experience working as a member of a group. More often, he finds himself competing with his fellow graduates for grades as well as for approval from his professors. He generally counsels an individual child or student in the seclusion of the counseling room, perhaps observed through a one-way screen and discusses the sessions individually with the instructor, usually with a tape recorder playing back the interview. He is afforded little opportunity to exchange his ideas and perfect his counseling techniques through interaction with a group of his colleagues, observing his actual counseling.

In our approach, the student, acquiring knowledge and skill in counseling in a group setting of his peers, experiences feedback of inestimable value from the observations and the questions of his colleagues during and after each counseling session. As students observe and participate in the counseling and discussion of all cases, they are confronted with a wide range of problem situations, thereby increasing their understanding and insight and further developing their skills. Each student counselor, as he counsels before the group and instructor, thus contributes to the learning experiences of each member of the group, as he in turn learns from them.

195

The practicum groups may consist of ten to twelve graduate students. The majority of them have had several years of teaching experience and some have worked as counselors. For the sake of obtaining free professional help, parents volunteer to be counseled with their children in front of the students. Also, many feel that they are making a contribution to the education of counselors.

The first meeting of the practicum group is devoted to a discussion of the techniques and procedure. Some basic principles of effective interviewing are presented and explained to the students who are advised to follow a set routine, in order not to overlook pertinent material (16). Once they become confident and experienced, they do not need to follow a rigidly structured interview pattern, since they then develop their own style and can proceed with greater freedom. It is advisable to interview the parents first while the children remain outside under supervision (5). The parent, usually the mother, is first asked to state her problems. After she has spontaneously related her problems and the reasons she came for help, the counselor assumes an active role. The first important lesson which the student has to learn to detect is what we call a "gold mine," a statement which indicates important latent material to be brought out. The counselor has to know how to ask opening questions. Those which can be answered by "yes" or "no" usually close the door instead of opening it. The second important lesson is to respond to every statement by the parent about what the child is doing wrong with the question, "And what did you do about it?" When one knows the parent's reaction to a child's misbehavior or disturbance one can recognize its purpose and the transaction which exists between child and adult.

The practicum student is taught to structure his further inquiry if the parent begins to repeat what he has already reported. It is essential to ascertain first the routine of the average day, because in the interactions during getting up, getting dressed, meals, the full impact of the child's and the parent's roles becomes apparent. We must discover how the child does in school, how he gets along with friends, or if he has none. Then we proceed to explore the family constellation—the sequence of birth and the characteristics of each child, since the behavior of every child is correlated with the behavior of the others. The sibling who is most different from the problem child is usually the most important person in his life. He is the main competitor who, by his success, may have discouraged the deficient child and thus contributed to his failure. Usually the "good child" is the real problem (1, 2) and then the problem has to be ascertained, the situation which fostered it, and the role of parents and relatives, especially of grandparents, in giving the child a wrong picture of himself and of his rights and possibilities in life.

After all the information has been obtained, the counselor candidate attempts a tentative interpretation of the nature of the difficulties and their origin. Then the parents leave the room, and the children enter. The discussion with the children should be short and to the point. By this time, the counselor should already have some idea about the possible goal of the child's disturbing behavior. Well formulated questions permit a disclosure which, if correct, brings about a "recognition reflex" (6). A short discussion with each child, and particularly with the "problem child" ensues, evoking an expression of their ideas and an explanation of their "private logic" and of alternatives to their behavior.

Finally the parents return to the counseling room. They are told about the interview with their children and whether it has verified the tentative diagnosis or suggested other evaluation. Then, the counselor explores the point at which the parents would find it easier to change their approach and thereby improve their faulty relationships with the child (5). The starting point for a change may not be the problem for which the parents originally came for help. As they succeed in one conflict area, although it may be less significant, they can gain confidence to tackle more difficult problems. The suggestions made to parents should be in line with the new principles which have been developed for coping with the child's problems in a democratic setting (7). They are designed to extricate the parents from the undue demands of their children, to enable them to be a match for their children's nonconscious schemes, to establish a relationship of mutual respect and order. This instruction may take more than one session.

The next step in the practicum is a demonstration of the counseling technique by the instructor. The demonstration puts into focus the principles explained in previous sessions. It may involve a parent and all the children of the family or a teenager. The parent is interviewed before the practicum group. The instructor asks first if he may be permitted to interrupt the interview from time to time for the purpose of instructing the group which is primarily concerned with educating counselors. This request is always granted. The parent becomes interested in and benefits from the discussion with the students. Interview and discussion usually lasts one or one and one-half hours. The interview of the children is also interrupted, but not before the instructor has asked the youngsters if he may do so.

Counselors who have been trained in groups and in counseling before a group of their colleagues are prepared to develop a more extensive counseling program in the public schools. Such a program will be described to illustrate a holistic approach to elementary school counseling. The principles which Adler initiated in the schools of Vienna and those perfected by Adlerian psychologists since that time have been implemented by this writer. The elementary school children who are in need of psychological help are referred to the counseling department by the teachers. The youngsters may be counseled individually or in groups. The parents of the children being counseled are invited to join in a

197

group which usually meets in the evenings so the fathers may participate. The procedure followed is identical to that followed by Dreikurs (8) and Sonstegard (15) in the Community Child Guidance Centers. The only difference is that the children do not attend the parent group meetings since they are interviewed and counseled during the school day. The teachers attend the parent group counseling sessions and sit in when the child is counseled during the school day whenever feasible.

When it is not possible for the teacher to leave her classroom to be present when a child from her classroom is being counseled, other arrangements to help the teacher understand the child's behavior have to be made. This is handled in two ways. The counselor may have an individual conference with the teacher to explain to her the purpose of the child's behavior and discuss with her what might be done to redirect the child's mistaken goals. This is effective, but time consuming. A much more efficient procedure is to hold a seminar with a group of teachers after the children are dismissed for the day.

The seminar approach has many advantages. Teachers who have not referred children for counseling that week may attend, thus learning from the cases being discussed. Teachers whose children are being counseled learn from other cases being discussed. The teachers begin to help each other not only in the understanding of child behavior, but by relating the procedures they found that work in redirecting a child's mistaken goals. The seminars may go beyond the discussion of specific cases to a discussion of general principles of understanding children which they can apply in the classroom. The seminars thus become a team effort by teachers and counselors in providing more intensive and extensive help for the children who are not living successfully in school. The team approach is extended further. Where there are health, reading, and speech problems, the specialists in these areas meet with the counselor and teachers during the seminar.

The principals may attend the teacher seminars. The principals are invited to become a part of the children's group counseling sessions and are welcome at the individual counseling of a child or parents. When attending the group or individual counseling it is understood that they are not attending in the role of principal and anything that transpires during the sessions does not concern them directly when they return to their office. The primary objective is to provide the principal with a clear understanding of the counselor's role and function. Since principals can be the guiding force of a counseling program, it is important that they know the procedure used by the counselor, and this they may observe. However, to function adequately as leaders of the program they must have some knowledge of the theoretical formulations upon which the program is built. To achieve this objective the counselor holds periodic seminars with the principals during the school year.

The description of the implementation of Adlerian principles of psychology in a public school district has of necessity been brief. Initiating the program requires the involvement of administrators, teachers, parents, and specialists such as speech and remedial reading teachers, and school nurses. Obtaining the commitment of large numbers of people working toward an all-inclusive counseling program calls for organizational skill by the counselor (17).

REFERENCES

1. Adler, A., *Guiding the Child.* New York, Greenberg, 1930.
2. Adler, A., *The Problem Child.* New York, Capricorn Books, 1963.
3. Ansbacher, H. and Rowena, eds., *The Individual Psychology of Alfred Adler.* New York, Basic Books, 1954.
4. Dreikurs, R. and Sonstegard, M., "A Specific Approach to Practicum Supervision." *Counselor Educ. and Supervision,* 6(1966), p. 23.
5. Dreikurs, R., et al., *Adlerian Family Counseling: A Manual for Counselors.* Eugene, Ore., Univ. Oregon Press, 1959.
6. Dreikurs, R., *The Challenge of Parenthood.* New York, Duell, Sloan & Pearce, 1964.
7. Dreikurs, R. and Soltz, Vicki, *Children: The Challenge.* New York, Duell, Sloan & Pearce, 1964.
8. Dreikurs, R., "Our Child Guidance Clinic in Chicago." *Indiv. Psychol. Bull.,* 3(1943), pp. 14-19.
9. Dreikurs, R., "Techniques and Dynamics of Multiple Psychotherapy." *Psychiat. Quart.,* 24(1950), pp. 788-799.
10. Freud, S., *The Origins of Psychoanalysis: Sigmund Freud's Letters.* New York, Basic Books, 1954.
11. Grunwald, Bernice, "The Application of Adlerian Principles in a Classroom." *Amer. J. Indiv. Psychol.,* 11(1954), pp. 131-141.
12. Kramer, Hilde C., "The First Child Guidance Clinic and Its First Patient." *Indiv. Psychol. Bull.,* 2(2), (1942), pp. 32-37.
13. Matson, F. W., *The Broken Image.* New York, George Braziller, 1964.
14. Soltz, Vicki, *Study Group Leader's Manual.* Chicago, Alfred Adler Inst., 1967.
15. Sonstegard, M., "A Center for the Guidance of Parents and Children in a Small Community." *Amer, J. Indiv. Psychol.,* 2(1954), pp. 81-89.
16. Sonstegard, M., "A Rationale for Interviewing Parents." *The School Counselor,* 12(1964), pp. 72-76.
17. Sonstegard, M. and Dreikurs, R., *The Teleoanalytic Approach to Group Counseling.* Chicago, Alfred Adler Inst., 1966.

AN APPLICATION OF
ADLERIAN CONCEPTS
TO SCHOOL PSYCHOLOGY

Marven O. Nelson

During recent years, school psychology has become one of the most rapidly growing fields of professional psychology. More and more school systems have begun to employ one or more full-time school psychologists to work with children, teachers, and parents in order to facilitate the process of education. While the greater concentration of school psychologists has been in the larger school systems of metropolitan and suburban areas, many of the more rural school systems have shown increased interest in making use of the special skills that psychologists have to offer.

Along with the rapid growth in the employment of school psychologists, there has also been a change in the functions which school psychologists have been expected to perform. Gradually, the school psychologist has moved from being a testing technician, who was involved mainly in giving the Binet and various other tests to discover the I.Q. and to evaluate achievement, to being a psychological consultant, a diagnostician, a member of the mental health team, and sometimes, a psychotherapist.

In these newer and expanding roles that school psychologists are expected to play, there are ever increasing demands for the kind of services that require quick diagnostic judgment and consultation based on less than three interviews with the child. Therapy, if it is done at all, must be done on a very short term basis, since the number of referrals make longer term therapy impractical and since it is generally understood that schools are not responsible for treatment other than what can be done as a part of the regular school procedure. With these kinds of demands it is necessary for the psychologist to have the kind of theoretical orientation that will help him to make valid judgments on the basis of limited contacts. Both psychoanalysis and stimulus-response learning theory seem much too involved in the elementaristic aspects of personality and learning to serve the school psychologist well under the pressures of his load of cases. An approach is needed which is capable of detecting the pattern of personality on the basis of small samplings of behavior, of recognizing the errors which exist in the pattern, and of formulating valid recommendations for correcting the errors.

Individual Psychology

The Individual Psychology of Alfred Adler has provided a theoretical orientation which can serve the school psychologist well. Its value for school psychology was demonstrated by Alfred Adler himself in more than thirty child guidance clinics which he established in Vienna prior to 1934 (4). After World War II, several of the clinics were reopened and Individual Psychology was taught in the Pedagogical Institute of Vienna by Oskar Spiel (15). In the United States, the Alfred Adler Mental Hygiene Clinic under the leadership of Danica Deutsch, and the Alfred Adler Institute, led by Helene Papanek, have provided classes in Individual Psychology aimed at helping teachers in New York City to learn better methods of dealing with children in the classroom. Recently, the services of the clinic have been extended to provide demonstrations of Adlerian techniques within the public schools. Under the leadership of Dreikurs, the principles and techniques of Individual Psychology have had wide acceptance among teachers and parents in many areas of the country (9, 10).

Adler gave the following description of how he was able to gain an understanding of the child which he endeavored to help:

> When I first take up the case history of a difficult child, my aim is always to discern the basic underlying factors, which are the goal and the guiding idea around which the whole life-style has been developed and organized. Once we have an understanding of that, we can see that everything which has occurred did not necessarily have to occur (from the objective point of view) but that it was merely one of the possible things that could happen under the circumstances. We can then go so far as to put ourselves in the place of the patient and feel, think, and act with him. We can transpose ourselves into the role that the child has played and make the honest admission that under the some conditions, with the same picture of the world and with the same erroneous goal of a personal superiority (that is from the child's subjective point of view), we ourselves would have taken practically the same course of action. With this approach we lose much of our inclination to judge and condemn, and that is a fortunate loss.
>
> What is most important is that we are enabled to see the connection of all the surface phenomena with the essential inner core, the life-style of such a difficult child. We come to understand that the disturbing behavior is related to and grows out of a particular conception, or misconception of life and that the whole personality is a unity which shows the same direction of movement at whatever point it is observed (6, pp. 3-4).

201

Early Recollections

One of the "points" to which Adler attached great importance for gaining an understanding of the life-style of the person was the earliest recollection (1). This first recollection, he felt, indicated the person's fundamental view of life and the first crystallization of his attitude. It represented the starting point for the person's development. Though he recognized that the first recollection was more of an interpretation than a correct record of actual facts, Adler pointed out that what was altered or imagined was also expressive of the person's goal. This real or imagined recollection could be used to discover the individual's law of movement which, if discovered, would be confirmed in other forms of expression in the life of the person. Thus, the earliest recollection would help to understand the private world of the individual and give some indication for appropriate treatment.

Adler recognized the value of using the early recollections of children in his work in the schools: "We can ask a class to write their earliest recollections: and if we know how to interpret them, we have an extremely valuable picture of each child (8, p. 75)."

Use of the early recollections has become a fundamental part of the psychological examination of children in the writer's work in school psychology. Early attempts to use the technique proved so helpful that it has come to be used with nearly every child examined. The technique has many points to commend it. Besides serving as a "one glance" view of the child's starting point of personality development, it has great practicality of convenience. It can be used as a natural part of an interview situation without the obtrusiveness of formal testing; only a few minutes are required for the inquiry and response; and, except for the very young children who have difficulty understanding the request for the first memory or recollection, most children seem to enjoy entering into the discussion of their recollections. While other examination techniques are generally used in addition to the early recollections, the responses obtained from this technique have generally served as a "key" to unlock the meaning of the information gained through other means.

Connie, a thirteen-year-old girl in the 8th grade, gave me the following recollections:

> *First recollection:* "When my sister was home, we had lots of fun. She took me horseback riding. She took me to the city and we did a lot of stuff."
>
> *First recollection about mother:* " . . . I know, she used to teach, and I didn't like it because she was never home."
>
> *First recollection about father:* "He used to bring me things from the office—little things the company put out—toys, etc."
>
> *First recollection about brother:* "He used to take me to baseball games."

In attempting to analyze these recollections[1], it seemed that the following points were evident:

1. In three of the recollections, there was an emphasis on personal pleasure provided by others: "Sister took me horseback riding . . . ;" Father " . . . used to bring me things . . . ;" Brother " . . . took me to baseball games." Thus, it appeared that Connie placed particular value on receiving from others.

2. In two cases, Connie recalled sports activities: horse-back riding and baseball. She seemed to have considerable interest in athletics with possible masculine identification.

3. Mother was recalled as being absent from the home and involved with other children (teaching). Mother was perceived as not paying attention to Connie and as separate from the rest of the family in a blameworthy way. Difficulty between Connie and her mother seemed likely in that the recollections emphasized the idea that mother had withheld herself from Connie.

4. Members of her family, and possibly other people as well, were valued in terms of what they had given to, or withheld from, Connie.

Birth Order Position

One of the important factors which Adler considered in attempting to understand the life-style of the child was the birth order position:

> It is a common fallacy to imagine that children of the same family are formed in the same environment. Of course there is much which is the same for all children in the same home, but the psychological situation of each child is individual and differs from that of others because of the order of their succession (5, p. 96).

On the basis of insights gained from Adler's principles of birth-order position, the exploration of the family constellation has become routine in the examination of children referred to this psychologist. The following was learned about Connie's family:

Connie was the youngest of three children. A sister, age 23, was married, and her brother, age 19, was away at college. The family had recently moved from a city several hundred miles away because the father had been transferred to an office in New York City. The mother was employed as a teacher in a nearby school.

Connie was referred to the psychologist by one of her male teachers who complained that she tried to monopolize his time by talking about her problems. Since she often talked of difficulty with her parents, he felt that she should be seen by the psychologist.

During the interview with the psychologist, Connie complained that she had nothing to do at home. Since the family had moved and her brother and sister were no longer home, her parents did not do enough things with her. However, she did note that she played miniature golf and bowled with her father each week. Her main complaint was her mother whom she professed to dislike. She said that she and her mother never did anything together except housework; and she complained that her mother would not let her wear the clothes she wanted to wear. She stated that she wished her mother were not around. She kept wishing that the family were back in the house where they had formerly lived. She said that most of the good times she had had were when they lived in that house. Connie stated that she thought it would be much better to be a boy. If she were a boy, she could do more things like having a "hot rod," etc. Her desire in this direction seemed demonstrated by a somewhat masculine hair cut and an awkward masculine posture and movements.

In describing the youngest child of a family, Adler had the following to say:

> All other children can be dethroned, but never the youngest. . . . He is always the baby of the family, probably the most pampered, and faces the difficulties of a pampered child. But because he is so much stimulated and has many chances for competition, he often develops in an extraordinary way, runs faster than the other children, and overcomes them all. . . . And yet, the second largest proportion of problem children comes from among the youngest, because all the family spoils them. A spoiled child can never be independent . . . (8, p. 150).

Connie seemed to fit the role of the pampered youngest child who had been spoiled by the other members of her family. Her attitude that she must be entertained by others reflected her lack of independence.

Connie's Dreams

Adler often used the dreams of his patients to gain an understanding of their life-style (3). He stated:

> The so-called conscious and unconscious are not contradictory, but form a single unity, and the methods used in interpreting the "conscious" life may be used in interpreting the "unconscious" or semi-conscious" life, the life of our dreams. Only by considering dreams as one of the expressions of the style of life may an adequate interpretation of them be found (6, pp. 211-212).

When it is possible, the dreams of children are obtained during their interviews. Connie reported the following dreams which she said she had had on several occasions: "It is about the house where we used to live. Something comes—something big like a dinosaur. I used to run down the stairs and hide. It used to kill people; but it never got me. It was just the sensation of it coming; but it never got me."

When asked for her associations, Connie associated the "house where we used to live" with the people around it: "They were nice people and I knew everyone." With "dinosaur," she first associated it with "something you read about;" but later she related it to the company for which her father worked: "It is the symbol of the company."

Analysis of Connie's dream suggested the following points that gave further understanding of her life-style:

1. The dream was oriented toward an idealized past—"the house where we used to live." The association of the "house" with the "nice people" of childhood experience suggested something of her desire for a dependent relationship. Already, her first recollections had suggested her tendency to value people in terms of what they did for her.

2. A destructive force, the "dinosaur," destroyed other people; but Connie was spared by hiding. Thus, as in her early recollections, there seemed to be a lack of social interest. The thrust of her concern was the saving of herself by an escape technique: she neither attempted to help the others who were being killed nor did she stay to defend herself.

3. The "dinosaur" was associated with her father, since it represented the company for which he worked. In actuality, her father, by way of the company, had "destroyed" the relationship Connie had had with the "nice" people she knew. The company had forced the parents to move to New York leaving behind her sister, brother, and friends.

4. Connie's early recollections and her description of her family suggested however, that Connie was really very fond of her father, and, further, she had some fantasy of the mother leaving so she could have father to herself[2]. This fantasy may have reflected a wish that "Father would get rid of everyone but me." The "dinosaur" had "killed other people; but it didn't get me." It seemed likely that Connie's tendency to identify with her father, her awakening sex interest, and her exploitative desires converged in this dream.

Connie's dream seemed to illustrate Adler's statement that "The supreme law of both life-forms, sleep and wakefulness alike, is this: the sense of worth of the self shall not be allowed to be diminished" (7, p. 4). The selfish, exploiting tendencies of Connie were underscored in her memories, her description of her family, and in her dreams.

Adlerian Principles and the House-Tree-Person Drawings

One of the most basic principles of Individual Psychology is reflected in Adler's statement that, "All the behavior of a human being fits into a unit and is an expression of the individual's style of life" (7, p. 4). This principle has been used in interpreting the drawings of children. Application of the principle to Connie's drawings reveal a pattern of attitudes and reactions similar to that revealed by other techniques.

When asked to produce the drawings of the HTP test, Connie drew a small house with no chimney, no ground line, and very little detail. The picture of the house (Fig. 1) was less than 2 x 1½ inches in size; and the only detail, other than the outline of the walls and roof, were four small windows and a U-shaped figure which represented a door. The picture was drawn on 8½" x 11" paper; and it was placed slightly to the left of the center of the sheet. Her "tree" (Fig. 2) was a "key-hole" tree with talon-like roots, and it was drawn much larger than the "house." The first "person" drawn was a girl, by request of the psy-

Figure 1. *House* drawn for the HTP Test.

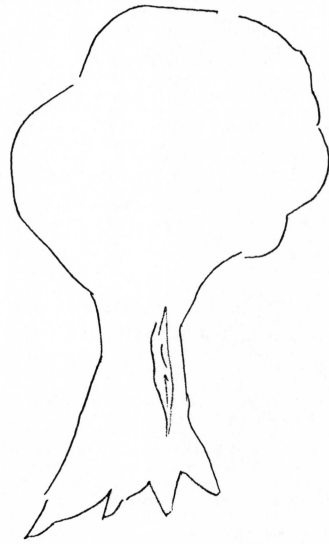

Figure 2. *Tree* drawn for the HTP Test.

Figure 3. *Person* drawn for the HTP Test. (left)
Figure 4. *Girl* drawn for the HTP Test. (right)

chologist. However, the girl turned out to be the same figure as the boy, except that it was given a dress and long hair.

During the inquiry regarding her pictures, Connie stated that the house was a big one, that it was white, and that it had a picture window in front. If the house were her own, she would like to have the side bedroom because "it has a nice view and it is pretty." She said the house was a new one. Her "tree," she said, was 50 years old; and it had never been hurt. She said, "It stands out, but it is in the forest. It is bigger and better looking than the others." She stated that the tree was alive.

Of the picture of the "boy," (Fig. 3) she stated: " He is not a happy boy. He is not good; and he is in a gang with other hot-rods." The picture of the girl (Fig. 4) was described as, "About 16 or 17 years old, and not happy."

Connie's efforts to draw the "house" were constricted and lifeless as was her description of her home. The picture she produced was cold and empty. The lack of detail and the absence of ground-line pointed up her rejection and instability in relation to her home. Her drawing of the "tree" was less constricted; but it, too, was empty and immature for Connie's age. The manner in which it was drawn suggested that she was hostile, resistant, and rigid. Only in the drawing of the "boy" did she show any genuine interest or artistic quality. The figure of the boy was well proportioned, and, though lacking in detail, the rather clever use of line quality and the posture of the figure suggested more detail than was actually there. Connie seemed to "come alive" in this drawing.

Her drawing of the "girl," however, brought a return of her difficulty. In this figure, she had difficulty with proportion; and the figure was lacking in any feminine quality. The dress which she drew had a low neck-line that revealed the same masculine shoulders that were drawn for the boy. The girl appeared somewhat crude and immobile. It was not difficult to relate the picture of the girl to Connie's own awkward, masculine appearance; nor was it difficult to recognize in her interest in drawing the boy the same quality of interest which she had revealed in her early recollections and in her statement that she thought that it would be better to be a boy so she could do more things like having a "hot rod."

Connie's Life Style

The foregoing information, which was obtained in one interview with Connie, gave sufficient data to give a good view of her life style. It appeared that she had created for herself a life style which was similar to what Adler often described as the "pampered child." Of the pampered child, Adler said:

> He has been trained to expect that his wishes be treated as laws, and to receive without giving. He is granted a prominence without working to deserve it and will generally come to feel this prominence as a birthright. Others have been so subservient to him that he has lost his independence and does not know that he can do things for himself. His interest was devoted to himself, and he never learned the use and necessity of cooperation. When faced with difficulties he has only one method of meeting them, that is to make demands on others[3] (9, p. 16).

Connie's attitude toward other people was clearly one of dependence in which others were valued in terms of whether or not they met her demands. At no point did she show any genuine sense of responsibility for herself or social interest toward others. Her identification with her father and wish that her mother "were not around" appeared to be a wish to be pampered. Father had been seen by Connie as one who endeavored to meet her demands while mother had been seen as cold and indifferent. The demands for attention that she had placed on her teacher seemed to be an extension of her need to be pampered as she had been by her father. Her desire to be a boy, a reflection of her masculine protest, (5, 7, 8), seemed to be a part of her rejection of her mother whom she had seen as not meeting her needs to be pampered. Not only would she reject mother, but she would even reject being like her!

Consultation with the Teacher

Having gained some understanding of Connie through the techniques described above, a conference with her teacher was arranged. He was given a report on the psychologist's findings in which her life-style was described as observed through her interview responses. Her dependency needs and her goal to be treated as a very special person were explained. This was then related to her behavior with the teacher which was aimed at using him to fulfill her goal. Thus, her attempts to monopolize his time, lingering in the classroom when other children had left, and wanting to talk about her home problems all took on greater clarity of meaning when viewed from vantage point of an understanding of her life-style.

In order to help the teacher manage his problem with Connie, some suggestions were offered as to how he might respond to her attempts to monopolize and involve him. The objective was to use the real life setting of the classroom to help her to understand some of the erroneous aspects of her life-style and to encourage her to make appropriate changes. During the next few weeks, an occasional conference with the teacher was held in order to give him some support in his efforts to respond appropriately in his work with Connie.. The psychologist also interviewed her on a few occasions in order to get an impression regarding her improvement.

Within a period of a few weeks, Connie showed considerable improvement in her attitude and behavior. She made fewer demands for the exclusive attention of the teacher and she appeared to relate better to her peers. She began to show greater interest in her academic work and seemed more self confident and relaxed than previously. The degree of improvement was such that it was concluded that further therapeutic measures were unnecessary.

Some Implications of the Method

It is recognized that the therapeutic steps taken in the case of Connie did not exhaust all of the possibilities for action. The problem of time and the large number of children waiting to be seen by the psychologist made it quite important to cooperate with the teacher in the case. But the approach had certain advantages other than the economy of time.

1. It kept the treatment in a natural setting within the framework of regular school environment.

2. The use of the teacher in solving the problem was an opportunity to build a cooperative relationship between the psychologist and the teacher.

3. It helped the teacher to learn how to manage children with similar problems.

4. The follow-up interviews with Connie and her teacher provided an opportunity to observe any signs that might indicate that further therapeutic steps should be taken. Such steps might have involved a conference with both Connie and the teacher present or a conference with Connie and her parents. Had it been necessary, a series of such conferences would have been used. If those measures had been tried unsuccessfully, she would have been referred for psychotherapy. The type of psychotherapy preferred would involve other members of her family in therapy sessions.

FOOTNOTES

1. While Nelson refers to these as recollections, many Adlerians would treat them as reports. For the distinction between these two treatments, see Mosak (12). —Ed.

2. For Adlerian interpretations of the Oedipus Complex, see Adler (2), Lazarsfeld (11), and Powers (14).

3. A more complete discussion of the "getting personality" may be found in Mosak (13).

REFERENCES

1. Adler, A., "Erste Kindheitserrinerungen." *Int. Z. Indiv. Psychol.* 11(1933), pp. 81-90.

2. Adler, A., "The Neurotic's Picture of the World: A Case Study." *Int. J. Indiv. Psychol.,* 2(3), (1936), pp. 3-13. Also in Ansbacher, H. L. and Rowena, eds., *Superiority and Social Interest.* Evanston, Ill., Northwestern Univ. Press, 1964, pp. 96-111.

3. Adler, A., "On the Interpretation of Dreams." *Int. J. Indiv. Psychol.,* 2(1), (1936), pp. 3-16.

4. Adler, A., *The Problem Child.* New York, Capricorn Books, 1963.

5. Adler, A., *Problems of Neurosis* (1929). New York, Harper Torchbooks, 1964.

6. Adler, A., "A School Girl's Exaggeration of Her Own Importance." *Int. J. Indiv. Psychol.,* 3(1), (1937), pp. 2-12.

7. Adler, A., *Social Interest* (1930). New York, Capricorn Books, 1964.

8. Adler, A., *What Life Should Mean to You* (1931). New York, Capricorn Books, 1958.

9. Dreikurs, R., *Psychology in the Classroom* (1957). New York, Harper & Row, 1968.

10. Dreikurs, R., and Soltz, Vicki, *Children: The Challenge.* New York, Duell, Sloan & Pearce, 1964.

11. Lazarsfeld, Sofie, "Did Oedipus Have an Oedipus Complex?" In Adler, K. S. and Deutsch, D., eds., *Essays in Individual Psychology.* New York, Grove Press, 1959, pp. 118-125.

12. Mosak, H. H., "Early Recollections as a Projective Technique." *J. Proj. Tech.,* 22(1958), pp. 302-311.

13. Mosak, H. H., "The Getting Personality, a Parsimonious Social Interpretation of the Oral Character." *J. Indiv. Psychol.,* 15(1959), pp. 193-196.

14. Powers, R. L., "Myth and Memory." This volume.

15. Spiel, O., *Discipline Without Punishment.* London, Faber & Faber, 1962.

CONTRIBUTIONS OF ADLERIAN PSYCHOLOGY TO SCHOOL CONSULTING

Don Dinkmeyer

The Need and the Setting

It is increasingly apparent that teachers require a type of professional assistance that enables them to function more effectively with the child who is difficult to teach. The present provision of specialists in pupil personnel services who diagnose and develop reports or who develop a therapeutic experience for the child outside of the classroom, is often not a solution for the concerns of the teacher.

The teacher is concerned with practical problems. She asks, "What do I do when he wanders from his seat, annoys other children, starts fights, and even sulks and refuses to move his pencil when kept after school? It is interesting to know that he has low ability, a bad home situation, and should be treated as an individual; but specifically, what do I do?"

Specialists in pupil personnel services often spend extensive time in diagnostic appraisal only to summarize in psychological language what the teacher has already suspected. Furthermore, recommendations are often developed in the office without any consideration of the teacher's capacity to execute such recommendations. In some instances, children are referred to counseling with little expectation that the counselor and teacher will communicate. Occasionally it is even suggested that if the child's behavior becomes more difficult the teacher should take this as a sign of improvement. This type of assumption is not easily accepted by the teacher who has a large group of children to educate. The type of assistance that teachers have received has made them suspicious that psychology has little to offer the harried teacher. Occasionally, it has encouraged them in desperation to adhere to authoritarian practices, even though this tends to increase the conflict and reduce the communication with the child.

212

A possible solution to the communication gap between counselors and teachers exists in a new approach to consultation:

> Consulting is the procedure through which teachers, parents, principals, and other adults significant in the life of the child communicate. Consultation involves sharing information and ideas, coordinating, comparing observations, providing a sounding board, and developing tentative hypotheses for action. In contrast to the superior-inferior relationship involved in some consultation with specialists, emphasis is placed on joint planning and collaboration. The purpose is to develop tentative recommendations which fit the uniqueness of the child, the teacher, and the setting (2).

This approach has long been advocated by leaders in the field of counseling (7, 8, 9, 10).

A national committee of the American Personnel and Guidance Association identified consultation as one of three major responsibilities of the counselor (1). The three responsibilities were described as counseling, consultation, and coordination. However, little can be found in the literature which suggests procedures for school consultation. The failure of counselors to consult effectively with teachers can probably be traced to two factors:

1. Lack of understanding of a rationale of human behavior which enables them to comprehend the purpose of a child's behavior and develop hypotheses regarding corrective actions.

2. Inability to develop a program which structures their role as a consultant who collaborates in contrast to a crisis manipulation.

The Consultant Relationship

The consultant relationship is based upon mutual trust and mutual respect. The teacher comes with a problem which requires additional professional skills and insights. The consultant recognizes that he cannot solve the problem without the complete collaboration of the teacher. There must be an alignment of goals and purposes. This can only be established as educational jargon is deleted and they communicate their perceptions clearly.

The consulting relationship is collaborative, a joint venture in which both contribute to understanding the problem and developing solutions. An atmosphere for cooperative problem-solving must be developed. This is not a superior-inferior relationship, and the teacher must be made aware that she has something to contribute to the consultant through 1) her access to daily observation of the child; 2) feedback regarding the efficacy of the ideas. The consultant has no one else who can provide this information and without it meaningful consultation is impossible.

It is apparent that well educated counselors are effective in listening to students and in promoting self understanding and decision-making. However, work with teachers frequently deteriorates to advising and vague generalizations. To use this valuable professional time well, the counselor must listen, be empathetic, and focus on the teacher's perception of the situation. He hears what is said and not said, while noting the tone and affect. He is concerned with what the teacher believes about children, and this child specifically. He is more concerned about how she converts her belief into transactions with the child. He helps her to clarify what the child's actions and her actions mean.

While the relationship with teachers is similar to the counseling relationship, it is also a teaching relationship. There is a concern for helping develop principles which can be applied to other situations. The truly effective consultant helps the teacher build her competencies. Skilled consultation may result in fewer referrals from a teacher as she understands the specific application of principles.

Propositions for Understanding Behavior

Adlerian psychology has some specific contributions to make to the school consultation. The increased interest of teachers in Adlerian procedures indicates the efficacy of these procedures for use with classroom problems (3, 4). Teachers find the procedures effective in meeting the challenge of the child who resents typical attempts to secure his cooperation.

The consultant process immediately takes on new meaning in terms of the conceptualization of man as an indivisible, social, decision-making being whose psychological movements and actions have a purpose. The consultant is less concerned with the pattern that emerges from the data. He is interested in how the passive resistance in the classroom relates to the child's aggressive behavior on the playground. Perhaps both are indications that the child is interested in controlling others and believes the best way he can do it in school is through forcing the teacher to notice him. He always searches for the relationship between the data.

The following assumptions are basic to consultation:

1. *Behavior is goal directed and purposive.* Consultation time is not lost in attempting to determine the causes of the behavior. Too many of the causes (i.e. physical handicap, broken homes and poverty) are beyond the capacity of the school to change. In contrast to looking backward to determine a cause, focus is on the "here and now" behavior and understanding the goal. If Johnny is not working at mathematics, one should not start a lengthy child study. The focus is on the consequences of not accomplishing math. The consultant is always interested not only in what the child does, but more specifically, what do peers, parents and teachers do about the refusal to work? Dreikurs made a major contribution to school consultation in his description of the four goals of misbehavior: attention-getting, the struggle for power, the desire to retaliate, and the display of disability (4).

The teleoanalytic approach is a unique contribution to school consultation. While different in theoretical premise, it is similar to the behavioral approach in its emphasis on the consequences of the behavior (6).

2. *Motivation can be understood in terms of striving for significance.* The striving receives direction from the child's uniquely conceived goal or self-ideal. The emphasis then is on how the child is seeking to be known. There is less concern with what he is doing and more with the direction in which he is moving. The child's refusal to cooperate in the classroom which results in punishment and penalties may not make immediate sense. However, if it enables him to become known by his peers as one who dares to challenge the teacher, it may help him to establish a reputation. If the child is to be changed, a method of helping him increase self-esteem in relationship to the peers must be found. The consultant team is always questioning how does this behavior help him to be known?

3. *All behavior has social meaning.* Behavior is always understood in terms of its social context. Thus, the consultant must rely on the teacher's classroom observations. He requests that anecdotes be kept, which describe the action of the child, reaction of others, and the response of the child to these reactions. This enables the team to infer social meaning and establish tentative hypotheses. The consultant comes to the classroom to observe and here the teleoanalytic frame of reference enables him to record observations he shares with the teacher. The consultant becomes another pair of eyes for the teacher.

The following anecdote provides data for consultation: "As Bill came to the front of the room to give his report, Jack got up to sharpen his pencil. The teacher ignored Jack, but Dave and Sam laughed. The teacher corrected all three of the boys."

The anecdote shows the social rewards Jack receives. Adlerians recognize that social striving is not secondary, but primary. It is not suggested that decisions about the meaning of behavior should be made from one anecdote, but several may reveal a pattern.

4. *The individual is understood in terms of his phenomenological field.* We are not concerned with how the events appear externally, but seek out the meaning the events possess for the individual. This enables the consultant to recognize that the teacher may be operating from a model in which she sees herself as a source for all information and controls. This will certainly affect recommendations if the teacher is afraid to make a mistake or permit the child to learn from the consequences of misbehavior. Too many professional recommendations do not result in changes because the consultant does not understand the teacher's frame of reference. Until the verbal message that is sent by the consultant is the same as that received by the teacher, and vice versa, no communication or consultation will have transpired.

This principle obviously applies to understanding the child's private logic. The child who believes "It is safer to withdraw than try and fail;" "I am not as able as others;" or "I only try if I can be perfect" will function on the basis of these assumptions, regardless of their validity. The consultant's training in this specific rationale of human behavior enables him to "guess what the child is thinking." Guessing in the right direction is an acceptable procedure in establishing hypotheses, and is always presented to the child in a tentative fashion for confirmation. The disclosure of goals is discussed extensively by Dreikurs (4).

5. *The individual has the capacity to assign personal meanings to experiences, to decide.* Adler was the first to call our attention to the biased apperception. This principle is particularly important insofar as it cautions against any simple stimulus-response interpretation of behavior. It recognizes that the teacher cannot predict the child's response to her behavior. Behavior is more than reactive; it is creative. On one occasion the child is kept after school, and he immediately gets to work and completes his assignments. The next time he is kept he refuses to pick up the pencil. He had the capacity to decide how he will respond. However, the teacher can learn to observe her response to his behavior and his responses to correction in order to understand the behavior. The meaning of the psychological movement will become apparent. She will recognize that the child has this capacity to choose ultimately. Once this is acknowledged, then choice can be utilized as a therapeutic agent insofar as the teacher is willing to permit the child to experience the natural and logical consequences of his behavior (5).

6. *Failure to function relates to the psychodynamics of discouragement.* The extremely discouraged individual, teacher, or child assumes he cannot function or that it is not worthwhile to function or that he will fail or that if he succeeds, others will only demand more. He does not even attempt to see alternatives. He believes he is not as capable as others and refuses to accept his inevitable imperfections.

Changes in human behavior are based on alterations in concepts, beliefs, attitudes, and expectations. Corrective efforts must be directed toward altering the individual's anticipations, the strongest human motivations.

Consultation cannot be a theoretical exchange but must be planned to alter specific behaviors. The focus is on action by the child which will change the individual's opinion of self. This may require manipulation of the environment so the child receives different feedback.

"Bill's transfer to school was preceded by a lengthy letter describing him as incorrigible. The new principal decided to treat Bill as if he could function. He did not wait for him to earn a place through misbehavior, but he gave him a responsible job and relayed his anticipation that Bill would succeed. Bill was confused at first, but in the new environment found he could be recognized for active-constructive behavior".

However, the process of encouragement is difficult, and the child is often better equipped to discourage the adult than the teacher is to encourage.

7. *Belonging is a basic need.* Man can only be actualized as he finds his place and belongs to someone, or something. Fear and anxiety, often cripplers of the learning process, arise out of the fear of not being acceptable.

The school often generates the environment for the feeding of the neurotic process. Demands are set high, standards are frequently irrelevant to individual differences, and the teacher is perceived as primarily concerned with diagnosing mistakes or liabilities. Teachers do not use the potential power which comes from involvement and belonging, and in many instances even work to suppress social development not directly related to academic progress. They are often at war with the socially powerful students.

When the significance of belonging is recognized, various sociometric procedures can be used to identify social needs. Corrective procedures then might consist of revised seating, new study groups, group discussion, or group counseling. The focus then would be on activities which facilitate belonging.

8. *Adlerians are less concerned with what a person has than what he decides to do with what he possesses.* The schools are overconcerned with testing and the accumulation of data. This preoccupation with identification of traits and abilities has led to many studies of underachievement.

Frequently the test data in the school records provide only the skeleton, and do not reveal anything of importance for the teaching process. Pupil personnel records, to be functional, should acquaint one with the child's attitudes, beliefs, motives, and convictions. There should be data which help to clarify his purposes and interests. The data may consist of anecdotes, autobiographies, sentence completion forms, and other procedures which permit access to his private logic. Each teacher should be required to describe "what works" with this child.

This brief excerpt from a case may clarify some of the practical applications of Adlerian psychology in school consultation.

Action	Analysis
Mrs. Smith contacted the consultant regarding Jane, a second grade student. The complaint centered around the child's causing a disturbance in the classroom and failing to work up to ability. The consultant, after listening to the general complaint, asks the teacher to de-	Attack a specific problem, not generalities.

217

Action	*Analysis*
scribe the situation which she finds most difficult.	
Mrs. Smith: Well, if she is given an assignment, rather than doing it she first visits with 5 or 6 children in the room.	
Consultant: What do you usually do about this?	Seek to clarify. Focus on the psychological movement and the transaction between teacher and child.
Mrs. Smith: I usually say, "Jane, get busy and take your seat."	
Consultant: What does Jane do?	
Mrs. Smith: In a few minutes she's back in the same pattern. She never seems to be bothered and readily recognizes she shouldn't do this.	
Consultant: It seems teacher and Jane have an agreement about their roles—Jane misbehaves and you remind her. Is it possible she does this to get your attention?	Seek to identify the child's purpose.
Mrs. Smith: That's probably true!	
Consultant: Do you have any idea of what might be done differently when she gets out of her seat and starts wandering around the room?	Consultant seeks teacher's perceptions and her collaboration.
Mrs. Smith: I've thought about ignoring her, but I feel this is not fair to the other children to ignore her when she is disturbing them; and if they enjoy her company everything gets out of hand.	Teacher poses first potential solution.
Consultant: You feel ignoring wouldn't change the situation in this case?	
Mrs. Smith: No, Jane enjoys people too much.	
(At this point the teacher was encouraged to explore other remedies. After some exploration, the consultant poses ten-	

Action   *Analysis*

tatively a new procedure).

Consultant: I wonder how you
would feel about giving Jane a
choice about whether she'd
rather sit in her seat when
there's work to be done, or if
she'd rather stand up.

Mrs. Smith: That might work.
I've never thought of that!

Consultant: My idea is that fre-   Utilize the therapeutic agent of
quently with children like Jane   choice and the child's capacity to
we are forced to react to her.   decide by changing the conse-
I'm wondering if, instead, we   quences.
could get her to cope with you
by giving her a choice. The
next time in a private conference you could pose to her the
alternatives of working at her
seat or standing for the morning. This must not be relayed
as a punishment, but as a
choice.

(At this point the teacher and
consultant explore other examples of misbehavior. Emphasis
is placed on observing closely
times when Jane is functioning
and commenting positively. Consequences are to be balanced
with encouragement).

This transcript from a consultation situation provides a snapshot of
the consulting procedure with teachers.

The Consultant Process

Adlerian psychology makes a specific contribution to the actual consultant process through:

1. a focus on dynamics and psychological movement rather than
   upon labels and static entities.
2. a concern for the pattern of behavior, the life style, or characteristic pattern of responses.
3. a recognition that misbehavior and failure to function convey a
   non-verbal message.
4. awareness that the consequences of the behavior point to the
   purpose.

219

5. analysis of the relationship and interaction between teacher and child.

These principles influence the type of information collected from the teacher and the child. They give direction to the consultation interview.

REFERENCES

1. ACES-ASCA Committee on the Elementary School Counselor, *Preliminary Statement*. Minneapolis: American Personnel & Guidance Association Convention, April, 1965.

2. Dinkmeyer, D., "The Counselor as Consultant: Rationale and Procedures." *Elem. Sch. Guid. Couns.*, 2(1968), p. 187.

3. Dinkmeyer, D. and Dreikurs, R., *Encouraging Children to Learn: The Encouragement Process*. Englewood Cliffs, N. J., Prentice-Hall, 1963.

4. Dreikurs, Rudolf, *Psychology in the Classroom*. 2nd ed., New York, Harper, 1968.

5. Dreikurs, R. and Grey, L., *Logical Consequences*. Des Moines, Iowa, Meredith Press, 1968.

6. Krumboltz, D. and Hosford, R. E., "Behavioral Counseling in the Elementary School." *Elem. Sch. Guid. Couns.*, 1(1967), pp. 27-40.

7. Oldridge, B., "Two Roles for Elementary School Guidance Personnel." *Personnel and Guidance*, 43(1964), pp. 367-370.

8. Patouillet, R., "Organizing for Guidance in the Elementary School." *Teachers Coll. Rec.*, 58(8), (1957).

9. Smith, H. and Eckerson, L. O., *Guidance Services in Elementary Schools: a National Survey*. Wash., D.C., U.S. Govt. Print. Off. 1966.

10. Wrenn, C. G., *The Counselor in a Changing World*. Wash., D.C., American Personnel & Guidance Association, 1962.

A BALANCE OF POWER

Wilmer L. Pew

A state of warfare exists between children and adults in our society. This condition is, in part, basic to and directly analagous with the current conflicts that exist between other subgroups in our country.

Maria Montessori predicted this state of affairs during her exile in India and gave top priority to the resolution of conflict between youth and adults. Fifteen years ago, Kelley and Rasey (6) prophesied that we would need to learn to live together in peace by 1970 or perish. Recently Whitney Young said, "The nation is in a critical period. . . . The cause of this state of affairs is the adult value system—and the adults who make it. And, consequently, the total rejection by our young people of adult values begins in the family. We are experiencing severely strained relationships between parent and child at every level of society" (10). And later, ". . . . this tiny globe that we are all privileged to inhabit has become so shriveled and so diminished that every man is in fact every man's next door neighbor. In our enforced intimacy with other human beings, our most precious possession is friendship with other human beings . . . our choice is clear: We must either learn to live together as brothers or we shall surely die together as fools."

Dreikurs has commented on "the increasing evidence of psychological warfare in our schools because the traditional superiority of adults over children is rapidly disappearing . . . in line with the declining supremacy of the white race." He talked of a dual rebellion in schools with large Negro enrollments because of the drive for equality of black with white as well as young with old.

One of Clark's most telling arguments in the social science brief presented to the U.S. Supreme Court which tipped the weight toward integration was the evidence that segregation was as harmful to white children as it was to blacks. Yet a decade later, there is little evidence that much integration has occurred in our schools.

It is of considerable interest that Kelley, Dreikurs and Clark all speak from a foundation in Adlerian psychology, thus sharing a similar model

221

of man and a similar attitude toward children. In classrooms and in families throughout our nation children are still treated as inferiors, as second-class citizens. And, as with the blacks, this attitude is not always consciously malicious but is fostered in the minds of well-meaning but uneducated people. There is a pervasive, perverse prejudice against children in our society and, like most prejudices, the people who carry and propagate it often are unaware of their deep-seated bias. Now prejudice can only occur in human relationships when some people are designated as inferiors and others as superiors. And, in the words of the popular song from "South Pacific" prejudice must be carefully taught. The basis for parent-child inequality must begin in the home or perhaps even in the hospital. Montagu has pointed out (in a speech in St. Paul, Minnesota, January, 1968) the fact that immediately after birth this nine month old human already is equipped with the capacity to make meaningful contributions to the welfare of another human being, his mother. Yet we whisk him away to a strange place called a nursery apparently because there is no nursing taking place there. And the child is denied his opportunity, by suckling at his mother's breast, to facilitate the third stage of labor, to minimize maternal hemorrhage and to ameliorate the congestion in his mother's breasts.

Or think of the way we continue to separate the child from his mother. Have you ever tried to get a puppy away from a fiercely maternal Scottie during the first few days? We say that separation of the baby and his mother are "good" for both but with what evidence? We treat the infants in the nursery as if they were all identical blobs completely ignoring Aldrich's years of painstaking observation to the contrary (2). So the lack of respect for the dignity of the individual begins early. The human infant is born with an innate capacity for social interest, with an ability to be a cooperating, contributing human (1). A mother, breast feeding with her child, is one of the best examples of human cooperative interaction. But picture the scene which all too often occurs in our "modern hospitals." As the partially drugged mother-to-be is wheeled, on a cart, toward the delivery room, a disinterested nurse or nurse's aide, who is only concerned with filling in a blank on a chart, says "You don't want to nurse your baby, do you?" and accepts any grunt as a negative. If by some administrative error the mother happens to start out nursing her baby, she is discouraged at every hand by doctors, nurses, well-meaning visitors and other mothers who are usually successful in persuading her to give up the process before the milk ever comes in on the fourth day. After all, it's much more convenient to give the baby a bottle in the "nursery."

Following this initial denial of the rights of the infant, the denial of his basic humanness, we continue to underestimate his capabilities. If we make a man feel that he is truly inferior, we will no longer have to force him to accept inferior status, for he will seek it himself. It hardly seems accidental that we keep our children out of school during the prime learning years, namely the ages from two to five. It has been shown that two year olds can be taught to operate electric typewriters, to take dictation, and to read with understanding. Now I am not suggesting that we teach our two year olds to use electric typewriters but this well-documented study gives us some idea of just how capable small children can be.

It has been said that our educational system in this country with its great emphasis on sub-mediocrity, takes creative, imaginative, alert and spontaneous children and turns them into rather dull, stupid adults. If there is any validity in such a statement, those who are truly interested in the growth of our children toward a goal of cooperative, contributing citizenship must take a hard look at the basic assumptions about children and about education. If the school is somehow different from life, we had better ask what is wrong with the school.

One assumption about the members of minority groups, is that they must be kept in their place or they will overrun us. For the last two or three millenia, in Western society, we have had an accepted tradition of child rearing which was in many ways quite appropriate for the autocratic society in which they were to live. It was Chisholm (4) who warned that ". . . the education of children has always been controlled largely by tradition—the effect usually has been to try to prepare children to live acceptably in a previous generation." This is reminiscent of a recent phrase about hurrying into the future with our eyes on the rear view mirror.

Chisholm goes on to say, "Non-cooperation has been taught by many teachers by not allowing children to help each other in school. The impression is commonly firmly made on children's minds that knowledge is an asset, not for use for common good, but to be hoarded for one's own competitive use."

Children were in a slave-master relationship with adults just as all other human relationships were those of inferior to superior. Women, religious and racial minority groups and labor found themselves in similar circumstances. Recognizing the failure of autocratic methods of child rearing with all the humiliations of reward and punishment and misinterpreting Dewey, Spock and Gesell, many parents and teachers contributed to the pendulum's swinging far to the other side, in our so-called "progressive" classrooms and families to what might better be called a state of anarchy. Children were permitted to run roughshod over their former masters, and chaos ensued. But the slave had tasted license, if not freedom, and the old order could not be restored. So we have seen a child-centered society, "Parents on the Run" (3), teachers ill-prepared to deal with the new relationship between children and adults. The old ways were no longer working and there was little a-greement on what the new child rearing approaches should be. We are

223

still in this state of interregnum today. There is no generally agreed upon way to raise children. Many of us find the old punitive, humiliating methods repugnant but we do not know what else to do.

It is interesting to note that Montessori solutions and Adlerian solutions for this state of affairs are often subject to the same kinds of attack. It is said we are too permissive; we let the child do what he pleases; we don't demand respect. All of these things may occur in the misuse of Adlerian or Montessori principles. But these two schools of thought have one very definite concept in common—the necessity for establishing order. What many people fail to understand is what Maria Montessori demonstrated so beautifully. Given a reasonable environment and minimal interference from adults, small children normally prefer order and will establish their own order.

The second point we have in common is covered in the term mutual respect. As adults we do not automatically have or deserve the respect of children any more than we automatically get respect from any other human beings. We have to earn the respect of children and this is accomplished only if we are willing to respect them. Now this respect business sounds good, but how do we do it? And isn't just loving a child enough? It seems that many very disrespectful things are done to small children in the name of love. We neither respect a child nor show our love when we do things for him that he can do for himself.

We neither respect a child nor show our love when we pity him and feel sorry for him.

We neither respect a child nor show our love when we interfere in his disagreements with other children.

We neither respect a child nor show our love when we talk at him or talk down to him.

We neither respect a child nor show love when we overpower him punitively, either by physical effort or words.

What is more, whenever we overpower a child, just as when we overpower any other human in an inferior position, we teach him to admire power and to train himself for the day when he can overpower us. Misguided behavior on the part of small children for the purpose of demonstrating power is appearing much earlier and the struggle is more intense. Even ten years ago mistaken behavior on the part of small children was most commonly for the purpose of simple attention getting. We seldom saw, as we do today, one, two and three year olds tyrannizing their parents. The power-drunk toddler is *not* the exception today and parents are at a loss in dealing with him. Punitive measures only reinforce the child's conviction that power and revenge are the ways to find his place. And soon we see full-scale warfare and mutual retaliation.

So now we are back to the balance of power. Is this the only choice in our families, in our classrooms, in our communities? I think not. And the only other alternative is *not* anarchy. There is a middle ground between autocracy and anarchy. This way, democracy, is far more difficult for parents and teachers and far more rewarding.

In a democratic classroom or family there are no superiors and inferiors although there are juniors and seniors in varying degrees. Each human is accorded equal dignity and respect and each human is expected to contribute what he can. Decision making becomes a shared process, often more cumbersome and time consuming. The primary purpose of the family and of the classroom group becomes learning to live together, cooperatively and constructively, as equals. With increasing freedom (not license) comes increasing responsibility. The ultimate goal is for each child, within the limits of his developmental status, to learn to become responsible for his own behavior. A child growing up in such an atmosphere respects himself sufficiently to resist any outside efforts to return him to the position of an inferior. He also learns to respect the rights of others. He learns to live as an equal among equals. He is truly free to remain a creative, imaginative, spontaneous human.

Just as he feels no need to emulate the slavish, "mature" adults he sees around him, the child growing up in a democratic setting feels no need for conformity. Equality does not imply sameness. This is another area where Montessori and Adlerian principles are attacked with the same mistaken premises. I repeat, "Equality does *not* imply sameness." George Bernard Shaw said: "Do not do unto others what you would have others do unto you; their *tastes* may be different."

Many of the same people who complain about a Montessori classroom or an Adlerian inspired democratic classroom because they think there is not enough structure, not enough order, turn right around and say that these approaches are so limited that the individuality of the child is stifled; he is not free to express his basic libidinal and aggressive drives (whatever they are); his "dependency needs" are unmet. One can easily detect the peculiar logic. But such arguments are not meant to be logical; they are psychological and based on deep, sincere bias about human nature (whatever that is) and about the natural inferiority of children. People who argue psychologically, in this manner, have also, often unwittingly, provided fuel for those who wish to proclaim the *naural* inferiority of women, the *natural* inferiority of non-Aryans, and the *natural* inferiority of blacks.

I have become convinced that there are not nearly as many *facts* about human nature and human behavior as many of our factophilic experts (9) would lead us to believe. And even apparent facts can be looked at in different ways. For example, it appears to be a well established fact that blacks score lower on standardized I. Q. tests than whites . . . *but* 25% of blacks score *higher* than the average white so this group could be classified as whites . . . and 25% of whites score lower than the average black so, as far as I. Q. is concerned, that group of whites could be classified black.

Statements of "fact" which begin as follows:

> Two year olds are . . .
>
> Blacks can't . . .
>
> Women always . . .
>
> Boys will be . . .
>
> Children do . . .
>
> Infants don't . . .

should be considered as highly suspect.

Piaget (8) has investigated the mistakes which children make in solving simple problems. He has made many statements about the cognitive capacity of small children. Recently, Mehler and Bever (7) have demonstrated that one of the capacities Piaget found absent in 4 year olds actually was present in younger children, then lost and then regained. Newly born infants who can swim during the first few weeks seem to lose this capacity and then regain it at a later age.

Ponder, if you will, the following question: What would our society be like if every person treated every other person as if he were doing the best he could, given his particular, unique perceptions and circumstances? Ours is a mistake-centered society. We are highly skilled at recognizing, emphasizing and pointing out the weaknesses in our fellow human beings. Very few humans have developed the skills of encouraging other humans. But, like Adler, I choose to believe that change is possible.

FOOTNOTES

1. Personal communication.
2. See Elam's paper. This volume.

REFERENCES

1. Adler, A., *Social Interest* (1930). New York, Harper Torchbooks, 1964.
2. Aldrich, C. A. & Aldrich, Mary, *Babies are Human Beings*. MacMillan, 1936.
3. Beecher, W. & Beecher, Marguerite, *Parents on the Run* (1955). New York, Agora Books, 1966.
4. Chisholm, B., "Can People Learn to Learn?" In *World Perspectives*. New York, Harper, 1958. Ch. 14.
5. Clark, K. B., *Dark Ghetto*. New York, Harper & Row 1965.
6. Kelley, E. C. & Rasey, Marie I., *Education and the Nature of Man*. New York, Harper, 1952.
7. Mehler, J. & Bever, T. G., "Cognitive Capacity of Very Young Children. *Science*, 158(1967), pp. 141-142.

8. Piaget, J., *The Child's Conception of Number.* New York, Humanities Press, 1952.
9. Winthrop, H., "Scientism in Psychology," *J. Indiv. Psychol.,* 15 (1959), pp. 112-120.
10. Young, W. M., Jr., "Tell It Like It Is," *Soc. Case Work,* 49(1968), pp. 207-212.

INDIVIDUAL PSYCHOLOGY
AND BAHA'I

Erik Blumenthal

The major principles of Individual Psychology may serve as a guide for the treatment of our subject.

Man is goal-directed. His thinking, believing, perceiving, anticipations, and behavior are directed toward goals of which he is mostly not conscious. Each person strives toward the goal of perfection for the optimal realization of his capabilities. Those who believe in a consciously planning force, one which is generally called God, "the most brilliant manifestation of the goal of completeness" (23, p. 275), want to come closer to and to resemble His image.

A further goal is man's endeavor to belong, to find his place. Man is a social being with innate social interest.

Different from these positive goals are negative goals such as excusing our shortcomings, getting attention, retaliating, and proving one's superiority. Between these negative and positive goals resides what we call the life style, which includes the mistaken goals for the future. The positive goals indicate that man is both a developing creature in need of being educated, as well as a social being, dependent upon others and carrying responsibility toward others. Thus, the concept of social interest moves into focus (5).

Basically, all people have equal worth, although this social equality is not often recognized (16). This equality causes us to see others as brothers rather than competitors. Others are fellow-beings whom we respect if for no other reason than that they are human.

Man is a totality, an undivided whole. The many uncountable parts of man, *e. g.* his body, his soul and spirit, his conscious and unconscious self, are no more than superficial attempts to attain a better understanding of man.

Man is a decision-making creature. The consequences of this realization is that man is fully responsible for what he does as well as for

228

what he does not do. Man bases his decisions on the relative freedom he has in forming and training his views. This occasionally leads to the formation of mistaken convictions. However, he behaves in accordance with these opinions "as if" (31) his views were correct. In other words, facts are of secondary importance. Man makes, in the truest sense of the word, his own experience.

Individual Psychology is a psychology of use rather than a psychology of possession. It is less important what qualities or potentialities man has than for what purpose and how he uses what he is and what he has.

The recognition of the tremendous power of our expectations leads to the optimism of Individual Psychology. If we expect success, we are more bound to move in the right direction than when we anticipate or fear failure. The optimist experiences more good things than does the pessimist.

The goals of Individual Psychology is for the individual to attain the highest self-realization, to shed prejudices, "to synthesize personality and community" (30), to strengthen the sense of responsibility and to replace latent feelings of hatred and suspicion through mutual good will. These goals can be realized through new teachable methods in education (4, 15, 19, 28).

Before we turn to our major subject, it might prove helpful to present a summary of the relationship of Individual Psychology to religion.

Adler and Religious Belief

Adler says, "The idea of God and its immense significance for mankind can be understood and appreciated from the view point of Individual Psychology as concretization and interpretation of the human recognition of greatness and perfection, and as commitment of the individual as well as of society to a goal which rests in man's future and which in the present heightens the driving force by enhancing the feelings and emotions" (23, p. 276).

Adler's benevolent and positive attitude toward religion can be discerned in many of his works. He says that "the Bible, to be sure, is a wonderful work which one can constantly read and reread with astonishment at its perspicacity, after one's judgement has matured" (6, p. 182). However, Adler did not apply his positive feelings in this respect only but "always liked to find himself in cooperation with religion" (12). No wonder then that we find far-reaching acceptance of Adler, especially noticeable in the obituaries appearing in religious newspapers at the time of his death (29). Adler's attitude toward religion was intellectually similar to that of Freud, but lacked the latter's pungency and polemic. Adler could not believe in anything that could not be attested through science. He could not believe in the irrational of the supernatural or a personal God. He observed that "Whether one calls the

229

highest effective goal deity, or socialism, or, as we do, the pure idea of social interest . . ., it always reflects the same ruling, perfection-promising, grace-giving goal of overcoming" (23, p. 278). For those who believe in God, "God cannot be proven scientifically. He is a gift of faith" (23, p. 277).

Adler's recognition of the value of and the necessity for religion refers primarily to the past. Forecasting the declining importance of religion in the future, he writes, "Should, or could mankind have waited until it rose through scientific illumination to the active recognition of the unavoidable necessity for brotherly love and the commonweal, and thereby also to the active recognition of the correct relationship of mother and child, the social lawfulness in the cooperation of the sexes, and the interest in others' labor? Such spiritual and psychological clarification, which leads to the most profound recognition of interconnectedness, which closes all doors to error and proves that virtue is teachable, has not as yet become realized by many. Religious faith is alive and will continue to live until it is replaced by this most profound insight and the religious feeling which stems from it" (23, p. 279).

The thus proclaimed priority of science over religion appears also in the following quotation: "It is not my office, nor have I ever conceitedly taken it upon myself, to praise or criticize movements which, like Individual Psychology, have the well-being of all mankind in view. And I cannot suppress my feeling of awe and reverence for the great accomplishments of such movements. But Individual Psychology must use only purely scientific methods, must remain a pure science . . ." (23, p. 280). This objective position of Adler made it possible for him to distinguish between religion and the church even though he never expressed it explicitly. The fact that an increasing number of people defend against religion is not due to its essence but results from the perceived contradictions between religious creed and the church's power structure, as well as from the frequent misuses of religion (23, p. 279). According to our terminology, it would have been clearer if Adler had spoken of the power apparatus of the church rather than of religion.

Individual Psychology as Applied to Religion

1. *Man as a goal-directed personality.* According to general opinion, teleology dates back to the old Greek philosophy (Diogenes of Appolonia, Socrates, Aristotle). The Christian theologians of the early Christian era and of the Dark Ages regarded the world as an existence arrangement in which everything was directed toward an ultimate goal. The concept of God dates back much further, as for instance Job's, "You have set a goal" (Job 14:5) or "The Lord made everything for a definite purpose" (Sprüche, 16:4). While science depended little on teleology, the latter was never abandoned in religion. On the contrary, teleological explanation in religion has been elaborated over the centuries. In modern re-

ligion the orientation of the individual toward an infinite goal is of utmost significance. This includes his strivings for his personal development as well as the striving of mankind toward the achievement of paradise on earth.

In Bahá'i religion the meaning of the individual's earthly life is not limited to the development and preparation of his soul for the next, the intellectual life. Very specific, concrete life goals are expressed by 'Abdu'l-Bahá, the son of the founder of the religion.

These should be your goals:

1. To show compassion and goodwill to all mankind.
2. To render service to humanity.
3. To endeavor to guide and enlighten those in darkness.
4. To be kind to everyone, and show forth affection to every living soul.
5. To be humble in your attitude toward God, to be in constant prayer to Him, so as to grow daily nearer to God.
6. To be so faithful and sincere in all your actions that every member may be known as embodying the qualities of honesty, love, faith, kindness, generosity, and courage (1, p. 74).

Education, which is always oriented toward a specific goal, plays such an important role in this modern religion, founded about a century ago, that it is being referred to as the "religion of education." One can discover numerous quotations from the holy writings of the Bahá'i in which one can observe the emphasis placed upon the circumvention of the finality of untrue and negative goal-setting and moving toward the "purity of motive." In order to achieve this purity of motive, Individual Psychology can make a major contribution through its addressing itself to the question of man's goal-directiveness.

2. *Man as a social being.* Love of fellow-beings is one of the two life tasks to which every higher religion, i.e., religion of revelation, wants to lead man. At the beginning of the Old Testament (1:4,9), Cain's stubborn question alludes to it. Since the dawn of time man has attempted to apply the so-called Christian love in everyday life. The realization of this human goal could be greatly accelerated if the principles of Individual Psychology were applied to differentiate between deed and doer. One can reject the socially unacceptable behavior of a person without the latter feeling that he is rejected as a fellow being. Generally when we fail to distinguish between deed and doer, it is because our social feeling is not yet fully developed.

In the Bahá'i religion it is pointed out that we should regard people who demonstrate socially unacceptable behavior as either infantile, ignorant or sick. We then have no aversion toward them because of their imperfections. On the contrary, we feel called upon to help them either to gain more knowledge, to receive protection and guidance, or to undergo psychotherapy.

231

3. *Man as socially equal partner.* Individual Psychology postulates the equality of human life which should not be confused with equality of achievement (14). Adler speaks of the former as "the law of equality of all human beings" (6, p. 191).

All higher religions teach us to see the other as a fellow-being, a brother or companion (24). However, contemporary man cannot divorce himself easily from his autocratic past. The Bahá'i teachings make explicit such demands as:

"All men are equal before the law" (1, p. 154).

"Neither sex is superior to the other in the sight of God" (1, p. 161).

"Daughters and sons must follow the same curriculum of study" (2, p. 170).

"In the estimation of God there is no distinction of color" (2. p, 41).

Whatever man uses to differentiate himself from others, be it the difference in race or nation, class or education, age or sex, intelligence or size of bank account or even church or sect, it cannot be right. Equality between the sexes is a demand of modern times. 'Abdu'l-Bahá points out that in the past the world was ruled by force and that man dominated the woman."But the pendulum is swinging. Force ceases to rule and intellectual creativity, intuition, and the ability to love and to be helpful, characteristics formerly associated with woman, gain in importance. Therefore, the new era will be less of a masculine era but will be more permeated by womanly ideals. In other words, it will be an era of equality between man and woman" (20). Therefore, today we should stress the training and education of girls more than we have in the past, especially since they will be the mothers and teachers of the coming generation.

A further point of commonality between Individual Psychology and Bahá'i religion is their attitude toward solution of social problems. Alexander Muller said, "The economy functions not according to its own laws but according to the psychological disposition of its members" (25, p. 71). The *Paris Talks* inform, "One of the most important principles of the teachings of Bahá'u'lláh is: The right of every human being to the daily bread by which he exists . . . The arrangements of the circumstances of the people must be such that poverty will disappear" (1, p. 151). Zabih stresses the point that "As human beings we must know that we can enjoy our own well-being and happiness when we are striving for the happiness of others" (32, p. 166). Zabih's statement is reminiscent of Adler's concept of social interest.

4. *Man as an undivided whole.* Man lives on various levels. Some body functions follow physical and chemical laws. Next, the body is subject to biological laws. On the next higher level, man has external senses and the strength of movement in common with other animals. The inner senses and the development of psychological and intellectual concepts puts him on the human level.

"Each step is dependent upon the previous step; however, it is not terminated by it. 'Man always has alternatives.' In modern religion it is thus expressed: 'Man is in the highest degree of materiality, and at the beginning of spirituality; that is to say, he is the end of imperfection and the beginning of perfection. He is at the last degree of darkness, and at the beginning of light . . . He has the animal side as well as the angelic side . . ." (3, p. 272).

Man can make himself master of his feelings. He can strive for self-realization and understanding or he can be dominated by his emotions and passions and make his heredity, upbringing, drives or instincts responsible for it. In doing the latter, he does nothing more than downgrade himself to the animal level. This is unworthy of man not only according to Individual Psychology but as Bahá'u'lláh said, "It is in no way permitted to surpass the boundaries of one's own position and rank must be strictly guarded. That means that all that was created should be regarded in the light of the rank which was attributed to it (8, p. 12)."

'Abdu'l-Bahá wrote in a letter to August Forel, "It requires courage to admit to oneself that one did not behave in 'a manner worthy of man.' And then the concept of dualism is very convenient: 'The spirit is willing but the flesh is weak.' One considers himself as a tool of strange powers, as for instance good and bad, God and devil, reason and emotions, consciousness and unconsciousness, 'two souls live, oh, in my heart.' " In this kind of superstition we are split into two I's which constantly fight each other, so that we can never reach inner peace (16, 18). The fact is that man is a whole, a unit, capable of deciding between right and wrong, to be objective or subjective, to think, to feel, and to act. "The choice of good or evil belongs to the man himself" (3, p. 289).

5. *Man as decision-making being.* It takes considerable courage to forego excuse-making and to admit one's own responsibility. If we were to decide upon a new attitude toward individual responsibility and to accept it for what it is, namely a wonderful task which can aid our growth, then the required courage would no longer be so great because we could then see that our excuses limit our freedom. Whatever degree of courage is required, faith and an understanding of the principles of Individual Psychology can help us acquire it. "The source of courage and power is the spreading of the word of God and the steadfastness in his love" (10, p. 14). Let us consider the three tasks of life (7, p. 17).

Work and occupation. Even when we are forced by circumstances to choose a profession for which we are not exactly suited, it is still up to us to decide upon a proper attitude toward it. One can find something positive in everything if one so wishes. 'Abdu'l-Bahá says, "The man who makes a piece of note-paper to the best of his ability, conscientiously, concentrating all his forces on perfecting it, is giving praise to God. Briefly, all efforts and exertions put forth by man from the fullness of his heart is worship, if it is prompted by the highest motives and the will to do service to humanity. This is worship—to serve mankind and to minister to the needs of people. Service is prayer. A physician ministering to the sick, gently, tenderly, free from all prejudice and believing in the solidarity of the human race, he is giving praise" (21, p. 99).

Love and marriage. Many subconscious decisions are made in this area. Dreikurs has described in detail how the choice of a partner is made and how we can decide on the proper attitude toward the partner. His *Challenge of Marriage* (13) is one of the best examples of the application of Individual Psychological principles. He shows how these principles can be of assistance to people who already are aware of them through their religion.

Outlook on life. This third life decision appears not to correspond with Adler's life task of friendship and companionship. Outlook on life is, however, only the broad term in the frame of which religion is to be understood. Religion was not regarded by Adler as an independent life task because he considered it as only temporary. Religion was defined as "a tie between man and God and man and man." This latter aspect of religion is what Adler had in mind when he spoke of the life task of friendship and regard for one's fellow-beings. One would have to add that the concept of outlook on life is so inclusive that it includes the attitude toward nature, matter, art (25), morals (25), and oneself (18, 26).

6. *The secondary importance of facts.* Our own person appears very small and unimportant when we compare it with political, industrial, and social facts. We may then get the feeling of helplessness and tend to believe that everything depends upon circumstances. However, Confucius said 2000 years ago, "Every individual is responsible for the rise and fall of the whole world." And Albert Einstein once said, "He who thinks that his life as well as that of his fellow-beings is without significance is not only unhappy but unworthy of his life." Modern religion always stresses the importance of the individual. It is forbidden, according to Bahá'i, to humble oneself before other human beings, to consider oneself inferior. Each one is God's creation and as such he cannot be inferior, for this would be criticism of God's work.

It is our decision how we evaluate ourselves and how much value and power we attach to external circumstances and to the people around us. Even though it may not always be easy and sometimes even impossible to see immediately the meaning of life, a person who has the conviction of his own importance can still give it meaning.

7. *Individual psychology as a psychology of use.* It is difficult to eradicate the opinion that man is a product of his heredity and of his environment. As I have pointed out in an unpublished paper about twins (11), most of current research on twins stresses that heredity or environment are the main factors in their development. The fact is that each man

possesses many abilities as well as great strength but most likely only develops a small portion of his potential. What is important to the Adlerian, therefore, is what he does with his potential. Bahá'u'lláh also adopts a religion of use rather than possession, writing, "Oh Son of Spirit, I create thee rich; why dost thou bring thyself down to poverty? Noble I made thee; why dost thou abase thyself?" (9, p. 13). Bahá'i emphasizes repeatedly the strength which man carries within himself, strength which he has not yet realized. What matters is how and for what purpose man uses his potential. Since he has the choice between egocentric and altruistic, he can use his potential for either. On the altruistic level science serves progress for mankind; on the egocentric level, science is an ally in the lust for power. On the altruistic level religion serves to unite mankind; on the egocentric level, it serves to separate people.

8. *Optimism as rational-emotive force.* There is a wonderful English saying, "If you think you are beaten, you are." Life's battles don't always go to the stronger or faster man, but sooner or later the man who wins is the one who thinks he can. In religion we speak of the force of faith, as for instance that faith can move mountains. Our expectations, which are among the strongest psychological forces, not only influence our own movements but can also influence others. Experiments with placebos confirm that confidence in medication is increased by patients' confidence in their doctors who also had confidence in the medication. Thus, "forces" freed by faith proved greater than chemical and biological forces.

Optimism, Adlerians say, is important because it produces movement toward the good through expectation of the good. Bahá'i expresses it as follows, "One should always look for the good and not for the bad. When man has ten good qualities and one bad one, observe only the ten good qualities, and ignore the one bad one. However, if he has ten bad qualities and only one good one, observe only the one which is good and not the ten bad ones."

9. *Man as a conscious being.* Man should examine himself, and this self-understanding is an important demand of religion. Bahá'u'lláh says, "It is a true loss for man if he spends his days in complete ignorance of his true self" (10, p. 15). The question is not only one of greater self-understanding but as Muller states, man "must also be inclined always to question and to search, to recreate himself and the world, and to understand the world better. He must strive for the ability to distinguish the significant from the insignificant, the genuine from the false" (25, p. 28). One of the main demands of religion is that all men should search independently for the truth. According to Bahá'u'lláh, " . . . we must be willing to clear away what we have previously learned, all that would clog our steps on the way to truth. We must not shrink if necessary from beginning our education all over again" (1, p. 137). This ed-

ucation to awareness—Gebser (22) speaks of awareness intensification
—is also expressed in another religious demand of Bahá'i—"Prejudices
of any sort must be relinquished." Individual Psychology formulates
this principle as, "We must learn not to live by prejudice and preference, but according to our true self, directed by our intellect" (25, p.
42).

Conclusion

In the application of Individual Psychological principles in religion,
the importance lies in their being applied in the service of mankind
rather than in determining which contributes more. I can think of no
better ending than to quote Sperber (27) who summarized Adler's contribution, saying, "The Individual Psychological philosophy is older
than any psychology and science. Partially it is contained in each religion. To sort it out and to provide the scientific basis is the everlasting
merit of Alfred Adler, the philosophical physician."

REFERENCES

1. 'Abdu'l-Bahá, *Paris Talks*. Wilmette, Ill., Bahá'i Publ. Trust, 1951.
2. 'Abdu'l-Bahá, *Promulgation of Universal Peace*. Wilmette, Ill., Bahá'i
   Publ. Trust, 1922.
3. 'Abdu'l-Bahá, *Some Answered Questions*. Wilmette, Ill., Bahá'i Publ.
   Trust, 1954.
4. Adler, A., *The Education of Children*. Chicago, Gateway, 1970.
5. Adler, A., *Social Interest*. New York, Capricorn Books, 1964.
6. Adler, A., *Understanding Human Nature*. New York, Permabooks,
   1949.
7. Adler, A., *What Life Should Mean to You*. New York, Capricorn
   Books, 1960.
8. Bahá'u'lláh, *Gleanings from the Writings of . . .* Wilmette, Ill., Bahá'i
   Publ. Trust, 1963.
9. Bahá'u'lláh, *The Hidden Words*. Wilmette, Ill., Bahá'i Publ. Trust,
   1949.
10. Bahá'u'lláh, *Worte der Weisheit*. Frankfurt-am-Main, Bahá'i Verlag,
    1965.
11. Blumenthal, E., *Die Bedeutung des Ältersunterschieds von Zwillingen*.
    Diplomarbeit am Institüt für Angewandte Psychologie, Zurich,
    1966.
12. Bottome, Phyllis, *Alfred Adler: Apostle of Freedom*. New York, Van-
    guard Press, 1957.
13. Dreikurs, R., *The Challenge of Marriage*. New York, Duell, Sloan &
    Pearce, 1946.
14. Dreikurs, R., "The Impact of Equality." *Humanist*. 24(1964), pp.
    143-146.

15. Dreikurs, R., *Psychology in the Classroom.* New York, Harper & Row, 1968.

16. Dreikurs, R., *Social Equality: The Challenge of Today.* Chicago, Regnery, 1971.

17. Dreikurs, R. & Mosak, H. H., "The Tasks of Life I. Adler's Three Tasks." *Indiv. Psychologist,* 4(1), (1966), pp. 18-22.

18. Dreikurs, R. & Mosak, H.H., "The Tasks of Life II. The Fourth Life Task." *Indiv. Psychologist,* 4(2), (1967), pp. 51-55.

19. Dreikurs, R., Grunwald, Bernice and Pepper, Floy C., *Maintaining Sanity in the Classroom.* New York, Harper & Row, 1971.

20. Esslemont, J. E., *Bahá'u'lláh and the New Era.* Wilmette, Ill., Bahá'i Publ. Trust, 1952.

21. Ferraby, J., *All Things Made New.* London, Allen & Unwin, 1957.

22. Gebser, J., *Ursprung und Gegenwart.* Stuttgart, Deutsche Verlags-Anstalt, 1949.

23. Jahn, E. & Adler, A., "Religion and Individual Psychology." In H. L. Ansbacher & R. Ansbacher, eds., *Superiority and Social Interest.* Evanston, Ill., Northwestern Univ. Press, 1964. pp. 271-308.

24. Mosak, H. H. & Dreikurs, R., "The Life Tasks III. The Fifth Life Task" *Indiv. Psychologist.* 5(1), (1967), pp. 16-22.

25. Muller, A., *Du sollst ein Segen sein.* Schwarzenburg, Switz., Gerber-Buchdruck, 1954.

26. Neufeld, I., "Application of Individual Psychological Concepts in Psychosomatic Medicine." *Amer. J. Indiv. Psychol.,* 11(1955), pp. 104-117.

27. Sperber, M., *Alfred Adler—der Mensch und seine Lehre.* Munich, Bergmann, 1926.

28. Spiel, O., *Discipline Without Punishment.* London, Faber & Faber, 1962.

29. Thune, N., *Religion und Minderwertigkeitsgefühl.* Leipzig, Author, 1950.

30. Wexberg, E., *Individual Psychology.* London, Allen & Unwin, 1929.

31. Vaihinger, H., *The Philosophy of "As If."* New York, Harcourt, Brace, 1925.

32. Zabih, M., *Die Lösung der sozialen Fragen.* Stuttgart, August Schroeder, 1949.

AN ADLERIAN CONCEPTION
OF POLITICS

Leo Rattner

The investigation of social behavior is the proper province of Individual Psychology. Adlerian psychology is not concerned with the isolated individual but tries to comprehend man in his social relatedness. From this premise, it is but one step to the study of man's political behavior and the institutions he creates to express his political ideals. The rationale for such a study is inherent in Adler's progressive, evolutionary system of thought.

Adler himself was fully aware of such a connection. Towards the end of his life, he stated in an article in the *Internationale Zeitschrift für Individualpsychology* that "A psychological system has an inseparable connection with the life philosophy of its formulator" (3, p. 446). That life philosophy, for Adler, was democratic socialism. As a student and young physician, Adler was openly identified with the goals and ideals of the Austrian Social Democratic movement. Subsequently, he withdrew from active participation in political affairs. He recognized that Individual Psychology could not be tied to any political movement, and he strenuously resisted the efforts of some of his followers to make Adlerian psychology the handmaiden of a left-wing political organization. But he never lost his interest in the cause of social betterment. In one of his final statements about Individual Psychology, he expressed his hope for the future thus: "I have always endeavored to show that Individual Psychology is the heir to all great movements whose aim is the welfare of mankind" (3, p. 463). The spirit of social idealism and humanitarian concern was still as much an integral part of his mature appreciation of life as it had been in his earlier days.

Thus, even though Individual Psychology has no active connection with politics, its system lends itself readily to a better understanding of the political process. Politics is concerned with people and the ways in which they interact with each other. To understand politics, we must understand the institutions that human beings create to rationalize their political beliefs and ideals. Finally, politics is concerned with the distribution of power in a society, and this is specifically the province of Individual Psychology. All political behavior occurs within a social context. The psychologist who is concerned with the well-being of individuals and society, cannot arbitrarily decide to withdraw into the realm of pure science, and leave to others the political arena. If we agree with Pope that "the proper study of mankind is man," then we cannot neglect the fact that man is primarily a political animal. It therefore behooves the psychologist to help shed whatever light he can on the strange and complex ways in which human beings conduct their political affairs.

The Political Process

The field of politics has not been completely neglected by psychologists. Almost forty years ago, Laswell (7) wrote a pioneering study in which he attempted to show how pathological personality types are attraced to politics. Several years later, Reich (8) tried to explain the nature of fascism on a narrow psychoanalytic basis. But these attempts were isolated. It seems as if psychologists retreated from contact with the rough and dirty world of politics, generally leaving it to historians and political scientists to explain politics. The few attempts at psychological interpretations were done by non-psychologists who had no connection with the mainstream of psychological thought.

Let us begin our analysis with a brief description of the political process. Political movements are composed of individuals who have in common certain goals and expectations. These movements are generally hierarchically structured, with an elite group holding leadership positions, and a large mass of followers providing the soldiers, as it were, with which political pressure and influence can be exerted. In our age of mass movements it comes down to a simple arithmetic equation: the greater the number of followers, the more power the movement represents or aspires to. Generally, a supreme leader represents the movement to the public as well as to its followers. While he may not make all policy decisions by himself, he has the power to speak for the movement and to dramatize its goals and ideals.

Political movements often represent economic interests, though nationalistic demands are currently just as likely to provide the sparkplug for political action. Yet it would be a mistake to assume that a movement can progress only if its economic or nationalistic demands are well represented by the leadership. The function of the leader is greater than that. He must articulate the psychological needs of his followers and create an emotional bond that is based on the promise of satisfying these needs. He has to be leader, prophet and mass psychologist simultaneously. It can safely be stated that in modern times great political movements have succeeded only if they had the charismatic leadership that combined the essential qualities mentioned above.

The Political Leader

To understand the leader, then, is to understand a good deal about the movement and its followers. However, psychological studies of great leaders have been few and far between. Fromm (6) and Eriksen (5) did some pioneering work in analyzing the childhood and personality development of Adolf Hitler. But, generally, the field was left to biographers who proved to be more or less competent amateur psychologists. No psychological school has made as yet a determined effort to incorporate political psychology into its structural system.

Adlerian psychology, however, is in an advantageous position to pursue just such a goal. More than Freudian psychology, it emphasizes the social nature of man, the plasticity and purposefulness of his behavior. It sees man as an antagonist to the social process. It views society and culture as providing a variety of life styles and life chances[1], from which the personalities of the leader and the followers can emerge.

To analyze a leader, then, by Individual Psychology means to understand his personality and his life style. In the case of Adolf Hitler, for instance, we might go along with Fromm and Eriksen who stressed the particular configuration which makes for an authoritarian personality—a harsh, critical father and a pampering mother. We would certainly emphasize the strong inferiority feelings that resulted from such a childhood and view them as basic ingredients in a pathological personality development. But our analysis would not stop at this point. It would proceed to emphasize the tendency to overcompensation in Hitler's personality, the "drive" to be strong, powerful, masculine. We would interpret his lust for power as a desire to escape from infantile feelings of helplessness and powerlessness. We would understand his drive to dominate not only Germany but the whole world as a characteristic expression of his lifestyle. The adolescent and the grown-up Adolf Hitler who was considered a "nobody," and who probably thought of himself in such terms, had to become God-like in order to erase the memory of his earlier failures.

Yet it can rightly be argued that other people grow up under similar circumstances as did Hitler and do not become leaders of mass movements. Evidently, it takes more than just an unhappy childhood to become a leader. For one thing, the time has to be right for the emergence of a leader and a mass movement. It has to be sufficiently out of joint to permit a revolutionary movement to flourish. But the leader is the central figure who galvanizes great masses of people into collective action. Contrary to Marxist dogma, his personality contributes a great deal to the success of the movement. He must have a number of essential qualities without which it would be impossible to succeed. He has to be a shrewd judge of other people's personalities. He should be a brilliant orator who appeals to the emotions and not to reason. He must be a strategist who knows when to advance and when to retreat. He must understand the strength and weaknesses of his opponents. But above everything else, he must know the mind of his followers and be able to arouse them to passionate convictions. He must be in tune with the "collective psyche"[2] of a large group of people. He is the mass psychologist par excellence.

The Leader and His Followers

It is the followers from whom he draws sustenance and strength, and to whom in turn he imparts hope for the future. These followers are originally an amorphous mass in the modern nation state. They come from all strata of society, but they share the feeling of being left out, dispossessed, taken advantage of. They have feelings of inferiority and resentment whose origins lie in the social and economic structure of society. Like all individuals they want to escape from the feeling of inferiority, and this is where the leader steps in. He shows them a way out of the hopelessness and despair of their situation.

The leader can identify with the feelings of inferiority, oppression and resentment. What is more, he can articulate these feelings and he can promise relief from them. He practices a kind of mass catharsis the workings of which is as yet poorly understood. The first objective is to arouse hatred of a visible enemy who is deemed responsible not only for economic hardships but for emotional suffering as well. It helps if one can give a collective name to the enemy and thus make him easily identifiable: e.g. Jews or Communists or the Establishment. The problem thus becomes a relatively simple one. All that stands in the way of successful compensation, that prevents a large mass of people from becoming strong, masculine, powerful, is a highly visible group which controls the levers of power. Eliminate that group, the leader says or implies, and you will have power for yourself. Furthermore, only the leader knows the correct way of attaining such a goal.

The leader presents himself to his followers as a modern magician. He promises instant success in curing their emotional ills. He is going to transform them from outcasts into a chosen people. Like Moses, he will lead his followers into the Promised Land. But while the children of Israel had to wait forty years for their deliverance, the true believer of the modern mass movement is not asked to wait that long. All he has to do to achieve instant success, is to transfer power to the supreme leader and to follow his leadership unquestioningly. The road to power is based on the abnegation of individual self-determination. By a process of seductive propaganda, the followers of a mass movement are asked to relinquish critical thinking, rationality and individuality, and to propel the leader into national power by the sheer mass of their weight as blindly obedient soldiers of the movement.

This unwritten contract between leader and followers is the basis of their psychological interaction in the modern mass movement. Intuitively, the leader knows the mind of his followers; he knows how to express and to channel their frustrations, fears and resentments. Moreover, it is generally understood that the leader knows best, that the mass of followers must forego all critical reasoning and judgment. All decisions, all power must be left to the supreme leader. "Leader, command, we obey you," was one of the most ringing slogans that exemplified this spirit at the mass meetings of the German Nazi Party before and after it achieved political power.

Thus, there is no mystery about the leader-follower relationship. They share a common psychological makeup. They are of a similar type, an identical social character, as Fromm put it. Expressed in individual-psychological terms, we would certainly emphasize the common basis of an authoritarian personality structure. The leader must be understood not as the exceptional individual but as the embodiment of a social character type. He is the person who can best articulate the frustrations and resentments of a large group of people. He feels as insecure as they do, but he knows a way to overcome these feelings of inferiority. He assumes the role of the all-knowing, all-powerful father who asks his obedient children to suspend judgment on his leadership until he has made good on his promises. Like a modern-day prophet he is deemed infallible, and quite often he comes to think of himself as being unable to make any mistakes. The vision of his God-likeness sustains him and his followers in periods of crisis. It is the strongest bond between them, and the psychological basis for the certainty of the ultimate success of the movement. The leader cannot fail because then they would all have to recognize themselves as failures. Out of such intangible psychological realities, great political movements are born and propelled to success.

The perceptive reader will undoubtedly have realized that most of the preceding analysis is based on the example of Nazi Germany. The recognition of this fact, however, should not induce us to dismiss the German experience as irrelevant for ourselves. What happened in Germany has happened with minor variations elsewhere, and is still happening all over the globe. There is seemingly no dearth of power-hungry leaders and would-be leaders who are prepared to bring disaster upon all of us if it furthers their ambitions, as Sinclair Lewis pointed out some thirty years ago in *It Can't Happen Here*. We too have had our share of demagogues who wanted to pervert and corrupt our political institutions. What prevented them from ultimate success was the vitality of our institutions which provided people with enough psychological stability to let them escape from ultimate despair. We must therefore turn to a brief analysis of the political institutions if we want to comprehend fully the political process as it appears in the psychological perspective.

The Concept of Democracy

In his famous list of possible governments, Aristotle designates democracy as only one form of government among many others, and not necessarily the best one at that. Individual Psychology, however, does not hesistate to affirm that for modern man democracy is indeed the best form of government. We choose democracy not only because we realize that we cannot live and work in the oppressive climate of a totalitarian dictatorship, but because we also recognize that the premises of a political democracy are basic foundations for Adler's system of thought. In modern times, it is primarily in a democracy where Adler's *Gemeinschaftsgefühl,* "social interest" (2), can develop and prosper.

Having made a value judgment for democracy, let us state categorically that this does not mean support for a particular political party or uncritical acceptance of democracy as such. We realize that our system of government is imperfect and can stand many improvements. Democracy is for us a beginning and not an end. Political democracy especially does not seem to imply economic and social democracy as well. We still have too many instances of exploitation and domination of one group by another. Democracy rests on the ideal of equality (4). As long as inequality and discrimination exist, we cannot speak of a truly democratic society. As Adlerians we must be sensitive to the fact that no political creed, no ideology, no belief in a millenium can justify exploitation of man by man. We have to speak out against any fancy rationalizations that deny equal rights to religious and ethnic minorities, to women and to children. The ultimate test of a democracy is whether it offers genuine participation to all classes and social groups in the affairs that determine their lives. Anything less than that is a hindrance to social cooperation and an obstacle to the development of a mature *Gemeinschaftgefühl.*

The Adlerian concept of democracy, then, does not seem to fit any present-day society. This is true insofar as we think of democracy *sub specie aeternitatis*—"in the light of eternity." Complete democracy is an ideal of perfection towards which we must constantly strive. Adlerian psychology states unequivocally that the individual must adjust to his society. But this adjustment must be a creative process. It cannot and does not mean uncritical acceptance of the status quo. Rather it means that we must work within a given social reality with the aim of transcending it, that we must ceaselessly strive to improve our *Gemeinschaftsgefühl* in all social endeavors. Individuals as well as social groups must learn to cooperate better before the premises of a democracy can be more fully realized.

Thus, we are now in a position to provide a specific Adlerian definition of politics. Politics is concerned with the distribution of power in a society. It determines at any given historical moment who is inferior and who is superior on the social scale. Politics gives meaning to social life, defines goals for groups as well as individuals. But, ultimately, politics is the area where *Gemeinschaftsgefühl* is constantly tested, and we have to judge the effectiveness of institutions, movements, leaders and followers not by standards of national grandeur and glory but by the simple yardstick of whether they further or inhibit social interest. This, in a nutshell, is the Adlerian conception of politics.

The Psychologist and Politics

In conclusion, we have to say a few words about the role of the psychologist in the political process. As evidenced by the introductory statement, Adlerian psychology does not permit its practitioners to function in isolation from social reality. It demands from the Individual Psychologist a commitment to the health of society as well as individuals. Its inherent logic demands active participation in the political process, rather than passive endurance which is often disguised as "scientific objectivity." The Adlerian psychologist cares deeply about what kind of society we live in, and he has the duty to speak out when he sees the basic values of freedom, autonomy and self-determination threatened by political movements and institutions.

The psychologist has a responsibility to speak out when irrational forces tend to disrupt the orderly process of society. He must defend rational values in an increasingly irrational world. He must identify pathology in the political process, whether it is manifested in the person of the leader or the movement he represents. Psychology can help remove myths from politics. Basically, we must try to understand politics and political movements the way we understand individuals with neuroses and psychoses. We can point out what is healthy and we can emphasize what is abnormal. Political psychology must be a bastion of truth, rationality and reason in a world increasingly threatened with destruction by the irrational forces of fear, hatred and rampant nationalism.

Politics, we stated previously, is the area where the struggle for power is worked out with universal implications. More than any other psychological school of thought, Adlerian psychology presents us with tools for a rational understanding of the political process, and justifies our demand that social interest be the basic yardstick by which the mental health of political leaders, movements and institutions be measured.

FOOTNOTES

1. The term was coined by Max Weber.
2. This phrase is used metaphorically, not as an Adlerian construct.

REFERENCES

1. Adler, A., *Understanding Human Nature* (1927). Greenwich, Conn., Premier Books, 1965.
2. Adler, A., *Social Interest* (1930). New York, Capricorn Books, 1964.
3. Ansbacher, H. and Rowena, eds., *The Individual Psychology of Alfred Adler* (1956). New York, Harper & Row, 1964.
4. Dreikurs, R., *Equality: the Challenge of Our Times.* Chicago, Ill., Author, 1961.
5. Erikson, E. H., *Childhood and Society.* New York, Norton, 1963.
6. Fromm, E., *Escape from Freedom.* New York, Rinehart, 1941.
7. Laswell, H., *Psychopathology and Politics.* New York, Viking Press, 1960.
8. Reich, W., *The Mass Psychology of Fascism.* New York, Orgone Inst. Press, 1946.

THE PSYCHOLOGY OF PREJUDICE

Lewis Way

It is only in the past two decades that the problem of prejudice has been given careful scientific study—a study sparked off by the experience of Nazism and by the realization of the almost limitless evil which indulgence in prejudice can let loose. It was in 1950 that Adorno and his co-workers published a monumental work upon the subject (4). Other social scientists, such as Allport (5), were engaged in similar enlightening research. Subsequent years have seen no lessening of the problem's importance. As peoples of different races and different cultural backgrounds become intermixed, social and economic difficulties of adjustment are constantly arising, and such peoples are increasingly required to learn what Adler called "the art of living together."

In seeking to define the nature of prejudice, the above writers have pointed out that it is a state of mind not necessarily to be equated with ignorance. Although some prejudiced persons may be ignorant, the ranks of the prejudiced may also contain others who appear to be very well informed. Moreover, all persons are to a greater or lesser degree ignorant, since as Adler put it, no person can possess the Absolute Truth. Ignorance, or the holding of a false belief, is therefore no criterion of prejudice, since all beliefs must be considered in the light of a set of "guiding assumptions." Such assumptions, however, are, even when erroneous, necessary and useful, since a person who refrained altogether from making assumptions and eschewed all beliefs from fear that these might be mistaken would be without orientation to the world. However, in the relativist and pragmatic outlook of Individual Psychology, the usefulness of such assumptions and beliefs is held to depend upon their remaining flexible. When a person finds this belief is in contradiction to the facts, he must be ready to correct or modify it accordingly, and thus to bring himself more in harmony with reality.

In this view, the person who is to be called prejudiced is to be defined as one who holds to inflexible assumptions. He considers himself in possession of the Absolute Truth which Adler pointed out as being logically impossible for any one human being to possess. The difference between the person to be called tolerant and the person to be called prejudiced would thus seem to be a matter of degree, the degree to which, in any specific assumption, flexibility of adjustment to reality can be shown. The tolerant may not be tolerant on all points. There are certain areas of belief where even a person considered generally of a tolerant disposition remains inflexible, and other such areas where a person considered as prejudiced appears to be open-minded. Given this proviso, we shall proceed to consider the general nature of prejudice as a matter of mental flexibility.

Whoever has argued with a person prejudiced upon a certain subject will probably have found that the appeal to reason is useless. The appeal to reason has, rather, the opposite effect to that which the reasoner desires. The cause of this is fairly obvious. The better the arguments brought against the prejudiced person's point of view, the more incontrovertible the facts used to enlighten his ignorance, the more threatened he feels, and the more obstinate he becomes. We may therefore consider prejudice as stemming from a feeling of insecurity. Were he to agree to relinquish the belief in question, he would forfeit those assumptions which had previously guided his conduct and find himself floundering in a sea of uncertainties. Allport has conducted experiments which show this very clearly. "In all cases of character-conditioned prejudice," he writes, "underlying insecurity seems to lie at the root of the personality" (5, p. 396). He and his associate, Kramer, put the following question to the subjects of their investigation: "To what extent would you agree with the proposition: the world is a hazardous place in which men are evil and dangerous?" Those who agreed most with this proposition turned out to be those who were most prejudiced (6, pp. 9-39).

If it belongs to a person's fundamental assumption about life that the world is hostile and dangerous, we may expect that person to be of a generally prejudiced disposition, even though, in matters that do not touch the security of his life style, he may prove open-minded. Where such prejudice exists, the next logical step is for such a person to ask where security can be found. The prejudiced person answers with that mental inflexibility which we have characterized. Safety lies in clinging to the established order of things. The rules, laws, and conventions which govern social life should never be broken. The accepted beliefs should never be questioned. An unconventional person becomes in his eyes a dangerous traitor to the whole Establishment. An unorthodox opinion becomes a threat. "The prejudiced person," says Allport (5, p. 404), "leans on external institutions." Adorno (4) remarks that such a person lays great emphasis upon outward conventionality and is censorious of anyone who does not conform to social rules. For this reason, it may often look as if such a person were the staunchest upholder of social values, always speaking in the name of the public good. To a superficial observer, it might almost seem that such a person were the exponent of that social interest which is one of the chief tenets of Individual Psychology.

The problem of social conformity was not raised during the life-time of Adler, and probably owes much to the studies of Riesmann in *The Lonely Crowd* (14). But it was a frequent criticism of Adler that he advocated "adaptation to the community," and that his theory was conformist in character. This appears to be the place to draw a firm distinction between Social Interest and social conformity. Conscious of the criticism that might be leveled against him that he was proposing "mere adaptation to existing mores," Adler was always careful to qualify his statements upon social interest with a phrase borrowed from Spinoza— *sub specie aeternitatis*. Social interest, as he expounded it in all his books, meant working for the permanent good of humanity as a whole as far as the individual, whose judgment is naturally fallible, can understand that good. Such a definition will include the many rebels, reformers, martyrs and others who refused to accept the established order of their time and worked to achieve a better order. By contrast, the attitude of the social conformist, which we are here seeking to define, is that of a person who clings for safety to the existing status quo and who usually places the welfare of some sectional interest above "the good of the whole." Of movements other than Individual Psychology, Adler wrote "Other movements which have made the community the guiding aim of their endeavors must show chapter and verse to prove that the good of the whole is safeguarded not only in their words or in their intentions, but in their deeds. When it is a question of effects lying in the remote future, a judgment is not always easy, since nobody can boast of possessing the absolute truth. I would regard as valuable any tendency whose final aim guarantees the good of the whole" (3, p. 64).

One of the least disputable truths established by Individual Psychology is that feelings of insecurity often give rise to symptoms of aggression. Just as it is possible to mistake the prejudiced person's conformist attitude for one of social interest, it may be possible to overlook the aggressive side of his character. On the surface, all that we see is a person who is loyal, hard-working and devoted to the interests of whatever group or society of which he is a member. He may be conscientious in fulfilling his obligations, of absolute rectitude and integrity, and full of qualities that win one's admiration. "In a study of anti-Semitic girls," Allport tells us, "they appeared to be charming, well-adjusted and entirely normal girls. That is what the ordinary observer would see. They were polite and well-adjusted to their friends. But, looking deeper, (with the aid of projective tests, interviews, and case histories) these girls were found to be very different. Underneath the conventional exterior, there lurked intense anxiety, much buried hatred towards parents, destructive and cruel impulses" (5. p. 397).

This concealed aggression under a conventional exterior is well brought out in an anecdote told by Spiel. "In one of our classes we had a ten-year-old boy who was polite, tidy and a good worker. For weeks he was regarded as an exemplary pupil. But on one occasion during the weekly discussion hour he came out with the following proposal: the teacher should secretly give one or two boys instructions to provoke other children to mischief during the break. The evildoers should then be severely punished. None of us would have dreamed that this particular boy was capable of making such a proposal" (17, p. 92).

Prejudice and neurosis thus appear to spring from the same psychological root—a fundamental insecurity, probably in both cases originating in childhood. But their manifestations are rather different. Allport's girls were outwardly quite normal, and the little boy just quoted, who harbored such aggressive designs of planting crimes upon his schoolmates, appeared at first to be an exemplary pupil. The difference between neurosis and prejudice thus appears to lie in the means which the subject uses to meet his fundamental feeling of insecurity. The neurotic, who values himself as inadequate, counters the feeling by openly and aggressively asserting his superiority. He stands alone, opposing the claims of his own personality to the whole environment which seems to deny them. He must triumph over everybody or else he deems himself defeated. But the prejudiced person does not pit his own personality against the whole world in this fashion. Instead, he seeks to ally himself with others of a kindred nature. He finds his defense against insecurity by identifying himself with a set of extreme opinions or by taking refuge in a group. He becomes a loyal, obedient, and often very competent servant or supporter of such a group. While he thus purchases his feeling of security by conformity to the group, he at the same time finds an outlet for his aggression by attacking the group's enemies.

A typical example of the prejudiced character, arising both from individual childhood and later social experience, is provided by the autobiography of Rudolf Hoess, the Commandant of Auschwitz, and the man directly in charge of the massacre of two million Jews. Written in prison while he was awaiting execution, it bears all the marks of authenticity and is especially valuable in furnishing a clear and factual summary of his childhood.

Hoess, in the first place, was an eldest child. Adler (2, ch. 8) has indicated that, in the sibling hierarchy, the position of the eldest child is the one most likely to lead to authoritarian attitudes. For a period of time, the eldest child is also the only child and the center of the parents' attention. When a second child is born he is, in Adler's terminology, "dethroned" from his central, kingly position, and sees the mother preoccupied with the needs of the infant. This experience may fill him with a deep sense of betrayal, pessimism, and disappointment. He does, however, remain the eldest, the strongest and the most responsible of the siblings, and, as such, he tends to ally himself with his parents' authority against his younger rival. He may thus develop that ambivalent attitude towards authority which Allport noticed in the prejudiced character, namely, an outward veneration for the parents coupled with a deep inner resentment against them for their apparent betrayal. Austerity, conformity, pessimism, suspicion and envy may be the marks of such a character. Although Adler does not claim that this is the only possible pattern of development in eldest children, it is, in his view, a likely one in the context of our particular society. One might tentatively suggest that it would be of interest to Individual Psychology to establish by research how many of those recognized as prejudiced were in fact eldest children.

Hoess's kingship was prolonged for five years—that is to say, for the whole of that crucial period when the child is making his first orientation to the world and forming those attitudes which will color all his future interpretations of experience. Thereafter, two sisters were successively born. His deep disappointment over these events would have been intensified by the length of time in which he had come to regard himself as the family center, while the five years lead which he had over the other members of the family would also have increased his sense of leadership and authority. "My two sisters," he says, "were very attached to me, and were always trying to establish a loving and sisterly relationship, but I never wished to have much to do with them. They have always remained strangers to me" (10, p. 33).

Mortification at his dethronement caused him to turn away from human beings, and he describes himself as a solitary child who poured out his affection upon animals.

Towards his parents, Hoess maintained the intense veneration of the eldest child. "I had been brought up to be respectful and obedient towards all grown-up persons, regardless of their social station. It was constantly impressed upon me in forceful terms that I must obey promptly the wishes and commands of my parents, teachers, and priests, and that nothing must distract me from this duty. Whatever they said was right. These basic principles in which I was brought up became part of my flesh and blood. Yet love," he adds, "the kind of love that other children feel for their parents, I was never able to give them. Why this should have been so, I have never understood" (10, pp. 32-33).

Allport has stressed the fact that an authoritarian education fails to meet the child's needs for affection. In households where "a relationship of power rather than of love prevails . . . it is often difficult for the child to identify fully with the parents, because his affectional needs are not met. He learns through imitation, coerced by reward, punishment and reproof. He cannot fully accept himself and his failings, but must be ever on guard against slips from grace. In such a family situation, a child never knows where he stands. A threat hangs over his every step" (4, p. 398).

So strict an upbringing naturally produced in the child a compulsive, puritan conscience. "A spot that I found particularly attractive was the large reservoir that supplied the town. Water had an irresistible attraction for me, and I was perpetually washing and bathing. This passion for water remains with me to this day" (10, p. 30). This incipient wash compulsion and oppression which this child suffered from an authoritarian education where, to quote Allport again, "a threat hung over his every step," is brought out in another remark: "I developed into a solitary child and was never happier than when playing alone and unobserved. I could not bear being watched by anybody" (10, p. 30).

As a boy, Hoess was devoutly religious. The Catholic Church was another symbol of infallible authority. With this devotion, he also came nearer to his father, "My father had taken a vow that I would be a priest, and my future profession was therefore already firmly laid down. My greatest passion was to hear my father speak of his experiences on active service, and to listen to his descriptions of battles against rebellious natives, and his account of their lives and customs and sinister idolatries. I listened with passionate enthusiasm when he spoke of the blessed and civilizing activities of the missionaries, and I was determined that I would one day be a missionary" (10, p. 32).

But the Catholic Church also betrayed him. It was the crisis of his adolescence to discover that his priest had recounted to his father some trifling misdemeanor which he had committed, thus breaking the seal of the confessional. "My faith in the sacred priesthood had been destroyed," he says, and he turned away from the Church as he had turned away from his parents. Subsequent events unfolded for him in a way that does not need too much quotation. World War I broke out when Hoess was only fifteen. He disguised his age in order to join the colors—an indication, perhaps, that he still found his home life unsatisfactory. "I had an implicit and unusual confidence in my captain," he tells us. "He became, so to speak, my soldier-father, and I held him in great respect. It was a far more profound relationship than existed between myself and my real father" (10, p. 38).

After a military career distinguished by bravery and efficiency, Hoess returned to the chaos of a defeated Germany. One may readily imagine how the almost total collapse of law and order, the economic inflation, the demoralization of life in towns like Berlin, would affect one who depended so entirely upon external authority. Hoess enlisted in the *Freikorps*, a savagely reactionary organization engaged in maintaining order through lynching. His activities as a member led to a ten year prison sentence for his part in the murder of a "traitor" to the organization. Upon leaving prison, order had once more been established in Germany, and Hoess was determined not to be drawn into any further political activities. "During the long years in my cell, I had come to one conclusion. There was for me only one object for which it was worth while working and fighting, namely, a farm run by myself, on which I should live with a large and healthy family. This was to be the aim and content of my life" (10, p. 38).

Accordingly, Hoess joined a cranky puritan organization, called the *Artamanen,* dedicated to a healthy, tough life on the land. But like many of his generation, who, since their teens, had lived a life of violence and excitement, Hoess could not settle down. "The temptation of being a soldier again was too strong" (10, p. 64). In 1933, he joined the NSDAP as an SS Man. In Hitler he found that father-figure which had been missing from his life since he had lost his "soldier-father" in the War, and in the Nazi organization he found a substitute for the authority of the Catholic Church. His farm and his animals were not enough without this.

Hoess was a physically brave man, an honest, truthful and efficient executive. He asked nothing for himself, and he was a good husband and father. But at no point in this unhappy career, was he able to resist authority. He does not present the picture of a maladjusted individual such as one is accustomed to see in the case of the neurotic. Indeed, the very conformity of his type ensures a measure of outward social adjustment. The only detectable symptoms of maladjustment in Hoess might seem to lie in his cold relationship with humanity due to his childhood dethronement and, from the age of fifteen, to his acclimatization to scenes of violence and brutality, and in certain compulsive and puritanical tendencies due to an over-scrupulous conscience. But such considerations are wholly inadequate to account for the crimes for which he was condemned. Nor can he be considered a "sadist," which obtrudes an irrelevant sexual element into the picture. He claims to have intensely disliked his official duty to attend floggings and executions and to have sought every pretext to avoid witnessing them. There is little reason to doubt his word, if only because a strict regard for honesty is a feature of his overscrupulous character. What stands out in such a person is his lack of any insight into himself coupled with lack of identification with the feelings of others, and his absolute dependence upon and obedience to a superior authority. Hoess had always to ally himself with some group, whether it was the Church, the Army, the *Freikorps,* the *Artamanen* or the SS, and the danger of such characters appears to lie less in their savage instincts than in their conformity.

If we are not to speak in terms of sadism, we are however obliged to attempt some further explanation of the callousness and cruelty of which human nature is evidently capable in pursuit of some ideal. One clue, noted by Adler (1), may lie in the proneness of persons with insecure life styles to overgeneralize. The more the assumptions of such persons suffer contradiction from reality, the greater becomes what was earlier referred to as their mental inflexibility. They must seek everywhere for material which will lend support and justification for these assumptions. This may sometimes result in the most fantastic elaborations. For a McCarthyite, the most trivial incident becomes evidence of a Communist plot. A fall in the value of shares on the Stock Exchange becomes evidence for the Nazi of a world-wide Jewish conspiracy of international financiers. This tendency to overgeneralize, which strongly resembles the mechanism of paranoia, ends by dividing the whole world into sheep and goats. Anyone who is not wholly of the opinion of the prejudiced person is regarded as an enemy. This attitude places severe restrictions upon such a person's ability to understand and to react correctly to events and to other people. He sees others no longer as particular individuals, in all their variety and uniqueness, but as examples of a collective stereotype. He stereotypes them as fellow-travellers, crypto-Fascists, bourgeois intellectuals, or members of some race or profession which he happens to dislike. The normal person also makes use on occasion of stereotypes. If, for instance, he is told that he is to meet an American business man, he has some notion in advance of the "type" to expect. The American will probably not resemble a French professor or a Tibetan monk. But when the actual individual is met, he may differ in many respects from the ready-made picture of an American business man. The normal person then quickly rearranges his ready-made picture to conform to the reality. It is the inability of the prejudiced person to make this adjustment that accounts for his mistakes, and his mistakes, of course, increase his feeling of insecurity and render him still more prejudiced.

In all times when people feel threatened, even those who are normally of a tolerant disposition may show a tendency to fall back upon stereotypes. Thus, in wartime, when a nation's very existence is threatened, all Germans immediately become Huns or Nazis in the eyes of their enemies. In wartime the members of the opposite collectivity are no longer thought of as individuals, and this makes possible their indiscriminate destruction. Those who dropped the atom bomb on Hiroshima were ordinary, decent American pilots, not in any way sadistic, not people who took a delight in inflicting suffering, but the enemy was "the Jap" in his collectivity, and the act could thus be done without compunction. The substitution of a stereotype for a concrete individual is a psychological process which has the obvious function of the self-preservation of the group (12).

The theory of the stereotype would seem to be of assistance in explaining man's inhumanity to man on the cognitive side. The view of the enemy is narrowed down from a concrete reality to a mental abstraction. But this narrowing appears to be accompanied by a corresponding phenomenon which I would like to refer to as "a narrowing of the empathetic field." Long ago, at the Salpêtrière, Janet noticed among his hysterical patients a phenomenon which he referred to as "a narrowing of the visual field" (11). Some of his patients suffered what he termed a "dissociation" between focal and peripheral vision. They were able to distinguish objects that lay only straight ahead and were "blind" to anything that lay beyond this range. In *The Neurotic Constitution*, Adler sought to explain such phenomena as a result of very high goal-concentration. The hysteric, with his well-known emotional lability and his aptitude for converting psychological states into physical symptoms, was able to see only straight ahead towards his goal, and was impervious to all that lay outside that goal. In Adler's view, such symptoms were an example of what he called the use of "organ-jargon."

A similar phenomenon appears to occur in the case of the prejudiced person. It is possibly not without reason that a fanatic is referred to in common parlance as "blind," and a sectarian movement as "narrow." The effect of high concentration upon a goal seems to render a person blind to all subsidiary considerations. This would seem to be true in the case of the actions of even a normal individual. In some moment of great urgency—say, when a man is called upon to rescue others from a burning building—he may become impervious to every other fact, including regard for his own safety. This narrowing of the faculties in order to achieve a certain goal may result in heroism as well as in cruelty, in both of which extreme qualities the human race appears to be preeminent.

In the case of the prejudiced person there appears to be not only an ideational narrowing which transforms the opposing individual into a stereotype, but also an empathetic narrowing due to high goal-concentration, which puts this individual outside the range of normal human feeling. Such empathetic narrowing is of quite usual occurrence in normal life (2, p. 60). In ordinary life, we are obliged to explain to a child that a moth, whose wings he is experimentally burning in the flame of a candle, is a sentient creature like himself. We have to expostulate with the peasant who is driving his mule with blows, for he has not yet identified himself with what the animal may be suffering. In many primitive tribes, the tribe considers that it alone is human, and the sufferings of an enemy tribe are without reality. In a society in which class distinctions are very strongly marked, such as in the European 18th Century, readers of social history will probably have been struck with the callousness with which some aristocrats, known to have been in all other respects both benevolent and enlightened, treated the sufferings of the poor. It has been noted that execution crowds seldom show emotion. The faces in the crowd express neither horror nor pity. In an account of a lynching at Maryville, Missouri, in 1931, of a Negro whom the mob tied to the roof-tree of a small wooden school-house where he had allegedly raped and murdered the woman teacher, and then burned alive, Raper records, "While the building was in flames, the 'News

Press' reporter saw standing by his side, intently watching the burning, one of the deputies who had brought the prisoner from the courthouse to the mob. 'Isn't this an awful thing to watch?' the reporter commented. 'Yes,' said the deputy, 'but it just had to be'" (13, p. 421). Doubtless, such would have been the only comment of those who witnessed medieval witch-burnings.

Bettelheim has illustrated the working of the stereotype from his own experiences in a concentration camp (9, pp. 218-220). "Both Jews and SS guards," he explains, "behaved as if psychological mechanisms comparable to paranoid delusions were at work in them. . . . During my camp experiences I was impressed by the unwillingness of most prisoners to accept the fact that the enemy consisted of individuals, not just of so many replicas of one and the same type. Yet they had enough close experience with some SS to know of great individual variations" (9, p. 221). In the same way, "the anti-Semitic SS had to see the Jew as a very dangerous person, and, in so doing, applied psychological mechanisms much like those that accounted for the prisoners' distorted view of the SS. The SS could not see themselves waging a war of extermination against a helpless minority. In order to justify their treatment of prisoners, they had to believe in a powerful and threatening conspiracy. Whenever Jews approached the guard on the basis of their stereotyped picture of the SS, the guard dealt with them on the basis of his stereotyped picture of the Jew" (9, pp. 225-6).

The theory of stereotypes formed under conditions of stress or insecurity seems to offer the best explanation of those extremes of human behavior known as sadism or heroism. The result is a narrowing of the field of consciousness both on the intellectual and empathetic plane, so that the opponent is no longer perceived as "real," with a consequent inflexibility of adjustment. Even of the SS, Bettelheim tells us that "many were quite dangerous, some were cruel, but only a few were actually perverted, bloodthirsty or homicidal" (9, p. 224). In social psychology, as in the psychology of the individual, the creation of stereotypes results in a clinging to an in-group's narrowly conformist ideology with a corresponding intensified aggressive attitude towards out-groups. All such groups tend to find their security in authoritarian leadership and doctrinal orthodoxy. "The adult Doukhobor has virtually no capacity for self-direction and no confidence in his ability to make decisions. Inevitably, he must turn to some authoritarian figure from which he expects support and guidance in all affairs of importance. . . . It is very important to be loved by the leader and by other members of the community. . . . It is not enough for the Sons of Freedom to know that Sorokin loves them: they must have a photograph of him" (16, p. 141). "Most of their hostile feelings are projected on to the non-Doukhobor population and the Government, whose malice, vindictiveness and venom are, according to Doukhobor belief, boundless. They continually see themselves surrounded by enemies who are bent on their destruction, and the wildest and most improbable tales of persecution gain acceptance" (16, p. 139).

In the same way, "to the observer, the Jehovah's Witnesses seem to have made hate a religion. Whatever else the Witnesses believe, they do feel that the whole world is arrayed against them and they respond with resentment, hatred and bitterness. They believe that they owe the world nothing, for it is evil and not in any sense a part of the divine purpose" (18, p. 145). Yet, in their original home in Russia, the Doukhobors locked themselves, their wives and their children to their wooden house and set fire to the building, preferring to burn themselves alive rather than submit to authority, and we have the account of Hoess of the marytrdom of the Jehovah's Witnesses under his charge in Auschwitz. "Eicke frequently sentenced them to be flogged because of their anti-disciplinarian behavior. They underwent this punishment with a joyful fervor that amounted almost to a perversion. They begged the Commandant to increase their punishment, so that they might the better be able to testify to Jehovah. After they had been ordered to report for military service, which, needless to say, they flatly refused— indeed they refused to put their signature to a military document— they were condemned to death by the Reichsfuehrer SS. When told of this in their cells, they went almost mad with joy and ecstacy, and could hardly wait for the day of execution. They wrung their hands, gazed enraptured at the sky, and constantly cried 'Soon we shall be with Jehovah. How happy we are to be chosen!' A few days earlier they had witnessed the execution of some of their fellow believers, and they could hardly be kept under control, so great was their desire to be with them. Their frenzy was painful to watch. They had to be taken back to their cells by force. When their turn came, they almost ran to the place of execution. They wished on no account to be bound, for they desired to raise hands to Jehovah. Tranformed by ecstacy, they stood in front of the wooden wall of the rifle range, seemingly no longer of this world. Thus do I imagine that the first Christian martyrs must have appeared as they waited in the circus for the wild beasts to tear them to pieces. Their faces completely transformed, their eyes raised to heaven, they went to their death" (18, pp. 88-9).

Summary

The matter of prejudice is here discussed in the light of the findings of other authors. The conclusion is offered that prejudice, whether in individuals or in groups, arises from feelings of insecurity not always or immediately recognizable to the investigator. It is suggested that the prejudiced and the neurotic have different methods of meeting their fundamental feeling of insecurity, and that, in the case of the prejudiced, the method requires a measure of outward normalcy in respect of the conventional standards of the group with which he identifies.

Prejudice is viewed as a failure in mental flexibility, resulting in the creation of stereotypes and incapacity to adjust to reality. It is characterized by conformity to the orthodoxy of an in-group and its authoritarian leadership and by aggressive tendencies towards out-groups. It is suggested that this will make for a connection between such extremes of behavior as cruelty to opponents and heroic self-sacrifice for an ideal.

REFERENCES

1. Adler, A., *The Neurotic Constitution*. London, Routledge and Kegan Paul, 1917.
2. Adler, A., *Understanding Human Nature* (1927). Greenwich, Conn., Premier Books, 1965.
3. Adler, A. and Jahn, E., "Religion and Individual Psychology," in Ansbacher, H. L. and Rowena, eds., *Superiority and Social Interest* (1964). London, Routledge and Kegan Paul, 1965, pp. 271-308.
4. Adorno, T. W., and others, *The Authoritarian Personality*. New York, Harper, 1950.
5. Allport, G. W., *The Nature of Prejudice*. Cambridge, Mass., Addison-Wesley, 1954.
6. Allport, G. W. and Kramer, B. M., "Some Roots of Prejudice." *J. Psychol.*, 20(1946), pp. 9-39.
7. Ansbacher, H. L. and Rowena, eds., *The Individual Psychology of Alfred Adler*. New York, Basic Books, 1956.
8. Bettelheim, B., "Individual and Mass Behavior in Extreme Situations." *J. Abnorm. Soc. Psychol.*, 38(1943), pp. 417-452.
9. Bettelheim, B., *The Informed Heart*. New York, Free Press of Glencoe, 1960.
10. Hoess, R., *Commandant of Auschwitz*, trans. by C. FitzGibbon. London, Weidenfeld and Nicholson, 1959.
11. Janet, P., *The Major Symptoms of Hysteria*. New York, Macmillan, 1920.
12. Knebel, F. and Bailey, C., *No High Ground*. London, Weidenfeld and Nicholson, 1960.
13. Raper, A., *The Tragedy of Lynching*. Chapel Hill, N. C., North Carolina Univ. Press, 1933.
14. Riesman, D., *The Lonely Crowd*. New Haven, Conn., Yale Univ. Press, 1950.
15. Rose, A., *The Roots of Prejudice*. New York, UNESCO, 1951.
16. Shulman, A., "Personality Characteristics and Psychological Problems," in H. H. Hawthorne, ed., *The Doukhobors of British Columbia*. Vancouver, B. C., Univ. of British Columbia, 1955.
17. Spiel, O., *Discipline Without Punishment*. London, Faber and Faber, 1962.
18. Stroup, H. H., *The Jehovah's Witnesses*. New York, Columbia Univ. Press, 1945.
19. Way, L., *Adler's Place in Psychology* (1950). New York, Collier, 1962.

BLACK PRIDE AND
SOCIAL INTEREST

Harry P. Elam

A transformation has taken place in the black communities of America. This is most dramatically borne out by the way the concept and meaning of "black" has been elevated from a connotation of opprobrium into an idea of honor. This pride in blackness has been exaggerated proportionately to the depth of humiliation associated with blackness in white America. A black man is one who is striving to define and to achieve a sense of positive identity with other black men and women. This current phenomenon is the black response to de facto white separation. It is also a movement within the American social field, to establish black dignity. Hopefully, black dignity can be established through emphasis on the importance and value of black culture, history and power. A black culture, defining and stressing black values, needs, and objectives will create a conscious sense of positive black identity. There has always been a negative black identity.

The current transformation has a momentum that comes from the lower economic levels and moves upward to the middle class. The relevance of the transformation is found in the fact that the black community had to face the fact that the "white liberal" really was often a patronizing, pseudo-intellectual, and the white civil rights workers were marginal to white society. The white liberal and white civil rights worker frequently identified a person from the black community as somebody to be helped from a sense of goodness, but also out of a feeling of superiority.

A community that feels itself besieged tends to unite. All economic classes in Black America today feel besieged, with the result that unity of race is proving more powerful than the division of class. The growth and expansion of sentiments of black consciousness and pride, therefore, should come as no surprise. The surprise is that it took so long to come. Black Pride and consciousness, in some form, are the absolute prerequisites to black equality. The purpose of this paper is to examine some of the purposes and goals of this crescendo of awakened Black Pride.

Background

Historical

The Black American has never been permitted the luxury of forgeting that he is black. Uprooted from preliterate and literate cultures of Africa and shipped to America in chains; finally emancipated from slavery, and not quite a free man; he became, because of his high visibility, a member of a lower caste. This social position was allotted to him by a rigid and absolute social system. However, the social system was rigid and absolute only in its application to the black man. All other immigrant groups could eventually move out of the lower caste.

Historically, and until recently, the numbers of Black Americans were mainly in the South, where the established, traditional customs and reactions to this group were those directed to an inferior caste. Today, approximately half of the Black American population is in the northern part of the United States. Approximately two-thirds are in and around urban areas.

The Experience of Inferiority

The experiences of the black American, his high visibility, and particularly the stigma of color, with an enforced inferior caste position on the American scene, are all a part of this historical perspective. In the process of identification, the black child becomes aware of the caste status assigned to the group with which he identifies himself. He begins to learn about the inferior status to which his group has been assigned (10). He notices that his group is usually isolated from the more privileged members of the wider society. This intensifies and reinforces deep feelings of inferiority. In the evolution of this socially-determined caste role, the individual and his group were expected and it was demanded, that the role and concept of "being black" be the common reference point when dealing with the dominant society. Black was equated with inferiority, thus reinforcing a negative identity (11).

The Social Field and Black America

In the south, white aggression and the social patterns which permit it, are forms of social control. They are instruments for keeping the black man "in his place" and for maintaining the superior position of the white caste. In the urban north, black communities often appear to be occupied countries, analagous to colonial outposts, with colonial police (black and white), keeping an eye on "the natives," retaining and putting them in their place. Thus, control by the superior caste over the inferior caste determines movement in the social field and the position each has. Historically, this is not, nor has been, peculiar to any specific section of the country. It is all-pervasive with differences of control being more apparent than real.

Patterns of Black Response to the Inferior Social Role Behavior in Relation to "Whitey"

The black man, individually and as a group, has created and developed many patterns of response to this enforced social role. Among the responses are self-depreciation or playing the role; developing a "white folks manner," or playing it cool; moving away from a member or members of the superior caste; distrust; withdrawal; humor; a feeling of "in-group" cohesiveness, since all are in the same boat; telling whites what they want to hear; the "dignified" black man, and many other examples.

Playing the role. The pattern of self-depreciation or playing the role is one where the black man depreciates himself or his group. It must be remembered that deference is *demanded* of him and is not freely given. By "playing the role" and acting in a self-abnegating, servile manner, his survival is assured.

Playing the role involves not only the observable, servile exterior that is demanded, but also encompasses a psychological process. It is a process of active mental withdrawal. The person playing the role must present the expected exterior. He must constantly be aware mentally of maintaining the position of affirming the white man's ideas, wishes and expectations. By showing his lack of contrary intent, ideas, individuality or disagreement, he acts in a way that is expected of his inferior role. This mental role playing is heightened, particularly when physical encounter is unavoidable. After all, from his inferior position, he is dependent on "the man" for a job and/or recommendations for a job.

Another example of playing the role that has also been developed to an exaggerated degree is playing on the vanity of whites by telling them what they want to hear. Closely studying white people and psychologically marking the circumstances in which they are susceptible to influence is part of the response pattern. In addition to giving the impression that the black man knows his place, another purpose of playing on this vanity is to put the black man in control of a given situation.

Playing it cool. "Playing it cool" or developing a "white-folks" manner, insures a passive exterior. The expectation is that this submissiveness and passivity is freely and automatically given. Again, this is a response that has assured survival.

Humor. Humor is another creative way in which physical and psychological oppression has been made bearable. Humor permits one to be superior by making molehills out of mountains. One can laugh at "Whitey" and feel superior. Humor also permits laughter to be directed towards the superior-caste, either individually or the group. Examples from Jeering and Taunting Rhymes (5) are:

A bushel o'wheat, a bushel o'sand,
Ah'd rather be a nigger than a po'
white man.

> *　　　*　　　*

I had a baby and its eyes are blue.
It can't be mine, Cap'n, it must be you.

> *　　　*　　　*

They asked me why the nigger move;
I'm gonna tell you the reason why:
The grasshopper eating up everything,
So it's nigger move, or die.

> *　　　*　　　*

Humor is used as a way of compensating for inferior status transcending the inferior role. Humor, as a pattern of response, has been developed to an exaggerated art form in the black community (6). Certain similarities between Jewish wit and black humor can be explained by the fact that both evolved under analagous conditions. This permits a momentary feeling of superiority by which the participant elevates himself above those around him.

The "dignified black man." The "dignified black man," a patriarchal figure, is one whose speech and actions are not stereotyped. His role is that of being "the exception." It is further colored by education or by developing special skills or qualifications. His dignity, more often, comes from the superior caste and not from the inferior caste. His position is analogous to the only male in the family constellation, where the other children are female. In assuming the "dignified" role, this man takes on the values and attributes of the patriarchal model. This model is important since it is the ideal for which the "dignified" black man is striving. This characteristic is partly an imitation of the paternalism that he finds in his social field.

The "shiftless." Along this same line, one common stereotype of the black man was that he was childlike and irresponsible. Examples of the shiftless stereotypes are to be found in the various forms of passive resistance. These are quitting a job without giving notice, slowness in doing a job, affecting indecision while working, and deserting families. This resistance is effective as evidenced by the fact that the superior-caste member shows his annoyance. A show of disinterest, the lack of attention and distrust are further forms of passive resistance. The past experiences of the black man in dealing with whites, justify the distrustful attitude that he takes, and the "inferior behavior of the black man reinforces the white man's feeling of superiority."

Special Black Institutions

Moving away physically and having contact only when it is absolutely necessary, assures the black man some respite from continuously playing the expected role. It serves two additional purposes. One purpose is to give the idea that he "knows his place," thereby reinforcing a survival pattern. The other purpose is to imply that in many instances, particularly in the labor market, his availability as a source of cheap labor, makes the dominant caste dependent on him. An example of this in rural areas is share-cropping and tenant farming. In urban areas, examples are to be found in the many menial jobs as clean up men, washroom attendants, and house cleaners.

Distrust, with its high degree of suspicion, produces a response of being perpetually on guard for any threat to survival. It literally states that in his dealings with whites, the black man is in an armed camp and must be ever on the alert to flee, thus assuring survival. Potential danger is always present.

The feeling of cohesiveness, resulting from the common inferior social role, has been highly developed around certain social institutions. Examples are the church, as a *social institution,* and certain fraternal and social organizations. The purpose of this is to reinforce a "feeling of belonging."

The evolution of black institutions like the church, and certain fraternal, benevolent and social organizations was in response to white patterns of behavior. These institutions were created within the more or less isolated world of the black man. Historically, the church, as a formal or organized institution, was founded out of protest (9). It gradually took on the role of an effective agency in accommodating the black man to his subordinate position. This history, and its lack of championing the ideals of the black militant, is one of the reasons why he has accused the church of fostering inferiority. Despite that role, the Protestant, black church was the one outstanding institution in the black community over which it had control. It offered a vehicle for community feeling and cooperation.

Mutual aid and benevolent societies, often in connection with religious organizations, grew out of attempts at social cooperation. Cooperation for mutual aid in times of crises, as sickness and death, became a part of rural folkways. Later, fraternal and social organizations, devoid of the religious connections, began to be a part of this cooperative endeavor.

It is of interest to note that aside from the purely religious nature of the church and fraternal organizations, the community used them as vehicles for cooperation and contributing to the good of the black community. Although these institutions grew out of the result of enforced segregation, the black community, thus separated, worked together for the common good of its members.

The organization and growth of mutual aid associations and fraternal societies were in response to forces that relegated the black man an inferior role. These various organizations, founded in response to this imposed role, were concerned with the social welfare of their members.

The Dual Role of the Black Man

The creation and development of survival techniques have produced a remarkable capacity to function in a dual role. One is the inferior role he is forced to play in his interpersonal relationships with the white world, the other is the "real black man" as he appears in his interpersonal relationships with his own group.

A look at this apparent dichotomy reveals that the black man possesses the same creativity for dealing with the social field, from a position of alleged inferiority, as others who find themselves similarly placed. Examples of this kind are found in children's and adolescents' dealings with their parents; women's relationships to men; a Catholic minority dealing with a Protestant majority and vice versa; the Jew dealing with the Gentile society, etc. On the current, contemporary scene, this is probably best exemplified by the action of students in their relationships to teachers. This amounts to defiance and revolt against a "white supremacy" system that teachers have created for themselves.

When the need to play the role has passed, another personality emerges. This is the "real' personality, since acute restraints and expectations do not color the interpersonal relationships. The environment and social field is now different. It is now a much more democratic social field, shared by "equals." Thus the response is different.

The durability of the group, despite an imposed inferior-caste position, was strengthened not only by its instruments for survival, but from a common base-line of destructive experiences. In addition, group mores and folkways produced general values which may have preserved the sense of inferiority. On the other hand, these had not only survival values but were also mechanisms of compensation for inferiority.

The Adlerian Explanation of Caste-Conflict

An inferior-caste role implies that a superior-caste maintains a supra-ordinate position. It does so by its will to enforce its superiority, and by active domination. Adler (2) has described these interactions as associated with characteristics of the masculine role in our society. Our culture, despite its evolutionary democratic process, is still mainly masculine-oriented. One result is an emphasis on the importance of the male and of the masculine ideal. This privileged group, men, is thereby guaranteed certain advantages which permit them to dominate women. "Thus the dominant male assumes advantages and directs the activity of women to the end that the more gratifying and pleasurable aspects of life will always pertain to the males" (2, p. 105). (It is to be remembered, however, that male dominance is not innate to the masculine role).

A review of the history of the origin of masculine dominance shows that this is a phenomenon which does not occur naturally. This is indicated by the numerous laws which are necessary to guarantee legally this domination to men. "The triumph of man was simultaneous with the subjugation of women, and it is especially the evidence in the development of the law which bears witness to this long process of subjugation" (2, p. 107).

Male dominance occurred chiefly as a result of constant battles between primitive people. In the evolution of these societies, as man assumed the more prominent role as warrior, he finally used his newly won superiority in order to retain the leadership for himself and to promote his own ends (2). Concurrent with this development was the development of property and inheritance rights which became a basis for masculine domination.

A similar review of the history of white domination, on the domestic scene, reveals that this was established by a series of laws that relegated the black man to an inferior-caste position. These legal maneuvers, in effect, stated that a black skin would ultimately be equated with inferiority and that of an inferior-caste for all time. The implementation of these laws and the attitudes preceding them are all the more remarkable when the history behind founding the colonies is put into perspective. Colonial subjects, who themselves had been in an inferior-caste position, now made laws, based on color, to raise themselves to a supraordinate position. A black skin became the symbol and the justification for discrimination. A creative way of elevating this symbol to a supraordinate position is the current slogan, "black is beautiful." This, too, is a method of compensating.

In contrast to this supraordinate position associated with the masculine role is the alleged inferior position of women. When we compare this to the inferior-caste role we see similarities. Not only does the superior male assume that his superiority is natural, he further supposes that his position is a result of the inferiority of women. This prejudice results in the concept of the feminine role being passive, obedient, servile, subordinate, humble, and less intelligent (12).

There is a similarity between the current black protest, indeed, the protest of all minority groups, and the Adlerian concept of the masculine protest of women. The black protest moves in a similar manner to that of women who find themselves with strong feelings of inferiority because of circumstances within the social field. These circumstances strive to assign an inferior position to women overtly and covertly.

The woman had several alternatives in her protest. First, she could become more "masculine," developing masculine attitudes and attempting to choose activities which are usually considered the privilege of men (2). In the black community a similar role is played by some men, who would speak out against injustice, who would not play the inferior role and who spoke out for their constitutional rights. When they asserted this masculine role, they were branded "trouble makers and agitators." These methods are similar to the methods used by the suffragette movement, namely, an open rebellion from an imposed inferior position.

The second alternative was to accept, with resignation, the imposed, inferior position. This woman went through life exhibiting an incredible adjustment, humbleness, and obedience (2). A similar role of adjustment is found in the black community. An example is seen in a black man who "knew his place." This also permitted the person to be dependent and even irresponsible, e.g., "Let the Boss-man do the worrying."

The third alternative was for the woman, in her inferior role, to have the conviction that the only worthwhile contributions that can be made are within the context of a masculine role (2). She is convinced of the inferiority of women, and approves of the privileged position of the· masculine role. An example of this is the black man who has contempt for himself and all members of his group. In its most dramatic form, we see it in the person who passes for white. Consequently, the superior-caste role is idealized and exaggerated. This is seen when the role of "Tomming" is played. This self-debasement and self-abnegation further subjugates the inferior-caste relationship. The result is a special position demanded for the superior-caste.

The value of the increasing awareness of pride in and consciousness of being black has an analogy in psychotherapy. It gives the individual and the group fresh courage; creativity on the positive side for cooperation both in the group as well as outside the group. It helps to focus attention on the group and helps it to understand that its problems are not exclusive but are community problems as well. It helps the group to feel that it is important and has definite contributions to make to the common good. If equality is the basis for therapy, then the current awareness of black pride provides much in creating an equalitarian social field in which cooperation can take place.

An American Dilemma: The Democratic Ideal

The general changes now occurring in American society, at many points, touch various institutions and institutionalized concepts. One highly visible ·institution that is being challenged is the inferior-caste system, as it applies to Black Americans. As a feature of our social order, automatic prestige associated with a superior-caste position is passing. Democratic practices based on reciprocal rights and duties are growing. The transition period is not an easy one and threatens the prestige of those who consider themselves superior to the lower caste groups—women, children, and blacks.

The Search for Identity

"The ability to identify must be trained, and it can be trained only if one grows up in relation to others and feels a part of the whole" (4, p. 136). A person from the inferior-caste has trained himself to identify with his group, and also shares in its comforts and discomforts. Whenever a common chord is struck between the individual and a member of his group, there is an understanding of feeling, social interaction, and identification.

A child develops an idea about himself and the problems of life by freely utilizing inferences from experiences as well as the influences of the world about him. The interpretation that the child gives to himself of the world about him determines the way he feels, thinks, and acts. His goal of superiority, the strength of his feeling of inferiority, and the degree of his social feeling and their relationship to each other all contribute to the nature and extent of social feeling.

For the black child and his family, since African historical tradition did not survive, it was difficult to develop a pride in established customs, mores, and traditions. From the American experience evolved an orally transmitted folk-culture including local mores and traditions, folk songs, dance forms, and a church. The folk-culture church, while serving as an instrument for identity and cooperation also fostered a feeling of inferiority. Thus, the whole black culture evolved and developed from a position of subjectively felt inferiority. Currently, black militants are trying to change the folk-culture, which fosters the inferior role.

The person or group, when in an inferior position, will find ways of improving this position. The inferiority feelings that accompany this position lead to compensatory efforts to improve one's position. An example of this is the way a child, from an inferior position, deals with his mother by putting her into his service. He may do this by passive behavior, playing the role of the model child, being very polite and playing on the mother's vanity. This is seen also in the male-female relationship, where the woman, from the inferior position, plays on the vanity of the man to improve her position.

A developing sense of community and a new consciousness in black people have been influenced by many factors. Among these are the heightened "democratic ideal" which was given new impetus by World War II; rapid communications; the concept of self-determination and the sentiments expressed in anti-colonialism. Another dimension that has affected and brought "group identification" into sharper focus has been the failure of "integration." Integration meant assimilation on the terms of the superior-caste. The illustration of "school bussing," is a case in point. The common mass of black people was not eligible for this assimilation. For the "grass roots," there were two or three events that helped the sense of pride and community to crest. These were, the concept and meaning of Black Power, the assassination of Martin Luther King, and the candidacy of George Wallace for President of the United States.

Given the framework of the contemporary scene, the black man began to move psychologically from his inferior-caste position. He began to use a new way of compensating—submissive behavior and passive rebellion changed to open defiance.

Black Consciousness: Its Psychological Forms

When the different manifestations of Black Consciousness, Black Pride and/or Black Militancy are analyzed, several patterns of behavior emerge. Each serves a purpose.

The more common behavior used to compensate for inferior feeling is to contribute. This implies a sense of belonging and a sense of community, which is trained or potentially can be trained to make contributions. This sense of cooperation for the community, in Adlerian terms, is called Social Interest.

The majority of Black Americans are developing a genuine interest in and for members of their ethnic group. This produces a positive identification within the individual and the group. From this identification emerges a heightened awareness of the need between group members for cooperation and for the contributions that each person makes to the group. A feeling of worth and value replaces inferiority feelings and the individual and the group begin to see life from an optimistic view point. This is reinforced because of the "knowledge and the feeling of being valuable," instead of being isolated and discouraged.

Some Black Americans react by withdrawing and believe that because of their color, no contribution to the common good can be made. This behavior resembles that of the neurotic. The neurotic withdraws from making positive contributions and feels that "he is entitled" to a special place. He expects to be appreciated, without having to make any contributions to the group. His degree of cooperation is stifled. To safeguard his self-esteem and to provide excuses for failing to himself and to others, he arranges his neurosis. This is done by such devices as expecting the worst and thereby insuring his failure; exaggerating the self-ideal (seen in idealizing the position of the dominant-caste); hostility to the dominant-caste; hostility towards self, because of color; reinforcing anxiety and thereby assuring defeat in any potential contribution, etc.

Adler's position is that neurosis is an evasion of the tasks of life and one of life's tasks is solving the problems of communal life. When we analyze the behavior of the neurotic, we see that he uses many devices to avoid making a contribution. Efforts toward cooperation and the benefit of others is missing.

A third type of behavior manifested by some members of the Black group is similar to that of the psychotic. They isolate themselves from and make no attempt to participate with any other ethnic group. Like the schizophrenic, they solve the problem by creating their own private logic and rules. If we follow their logic, everything makes sense. On the

267

other hand, private logic is at odds with common or community logic. An example is the view point that the solution to communal problems is to have massive repatriation of the Black American to Africa. Still another example is the suggestion that the Black American should be resettled in one or two States.

Compensatory behavior expresses itself also in a manner similar to that seen in the sociopath. An outstanding example is the black who oppresses other blacks. Instead of contributing, he moves to the useless side of life and shows his contempt for the whole system by preying on his fellow men. In the context of the example used, oppression of other blacks is a compensatory mechanism for overcoming the inferior-caste position and the discouragement that has been experienced. He finds justification for his actions from numerous encounters and incidents of his life. He is of the conviction that this is the only way to survive. By this behavior, he identifies with the aggressor.

Group Defiance and the Changing Self-Image

As a reaction against the alleged inferior role, Black Americans began to revolt, moving from submissive behavior and passive rebellion to open defiance. Examples of this current defiance are found in music, poetry, drama, and literature. However, the most dramatic example is to be found in the behavior of Black Militants.

Black Militancy, whether appealing to the emotions or projecting a philosophy for action, brings to the community one alternative for moving them from a position of weakness. In a militant, racist society, where power, dominance and color are the sine qua non for being in a superior position, the potential always exists for transforming passive rebellion into an active process. Black Militancy is one of these processes. From such concrete examples as the destruction of property and real estate, which generally is not owned by the black community, riots, fires, and sniping, although these are the actions of a discouraged group, nevertheless show the group that it also possesses power. This makes it possible for the group or a member of the group to change its feelings of inferiority and its inferior image towards a more positive ideal. The group process affects the total group, as well as each member.

Each of the above mentioned clinical types makes a contribution to the whole. The effect of the "normal" type is to bring about greater co-operation and contribution to the group's common good. The development of the group and its common welfare is its goal.

The "neurotic," with his exaggerated self-ideal, acts as a catalyst in the community. He does this by demanding special privileges that are his "by right." He insists on the right to be placed in a special position, without reciprocal contribution and cooperation to the common good. An example of this is the Black Studies Curriculum, with the proviso that only Black teachers are equipped to teach the courses. This example fits the neurotic tendency to create a certain emotional state by which a victory can be secured. By shutting out the unconquerable "others," he has maintained his superiority. This example is one of the themes running through current Black Students' campus protests. Despite the neurotic thread that runs through these examples, they do much to create a positive self-image.

The psychotic has the conviction "that common sense and the way things work for others" will not work for him. When he makes this choice, he is now free to create and develop his own private logic. He turns black into white. This is expressed in the idea that only the black community has made a positive contribution to the common good.

If the goals of psychotherapy are considered, there are techniques for using Black Pride and consciousness as one uses therapy. This is relevant since in each instance we are dealing with inferiority feelings, low self-esteem and a negative self-image.

Summary

The social field is responding to forces that produce change. Some results are seen in the steady change in the status of women and adolescents. However, the guiding ideal remains the supraordinate position of the masculine role which represents power and domination. Personal power and domination over others is the goal of racism. It matters not whether the racism is white or black.

Physical and psychological power and domination of an inferior-caste is the bed-rock of white racism. The potential exists, from the will to be superior, for a form of black racism to develop. On the other hand, when Black consciousness is used for contributing to Black Pride and to the community and the common good, this potential for racism is minimized. The Black man, who truly has pride in his blackness, can rebel against his inferior position and demand equality. If he has social interest, this does not permit replacing one superior group with another. Having been useful to and genuinely interested in his own group, he can now, with continuous training, cooperate with a group for the overall good of the community, neighborhood, city, and Nation.

REFERENCES

1. Adler, A., *The Practice and Theory of Individual Psychology* (1925). Paterson, N. J., Littlefield, Adams, 1963.
2. Adler, A., *Understanding Human Nature* (1927). Greenwich, Conn., Premier Books, 1965.
3. Ansbacher, H., "The Concept of Social Interest." *J. Indiv. Psychol.*, 24(1968), pp. 131-149.
4. Ansbacher, H. L. and Rowena, eds., *The Individual Psychology of Alfred Adler.* New York, Harper Torchbooks, 1964.

5. Brewer, J. M., *American Negro Folklore*. Chicago, Quadrangle Books, 1968.
6. De Carava, R. E. and Hughes, L., *The Sweet Flypaper of Life*. New York, Hillard Wang Press, 1967.
7. Dreikurs, R., "Group Psychotherapy and the Third Revolution in Psychiatry." *Int. J. Soc. Psychiat.*, 1(3), (1955), pp. 23-32.
8. Dreikurs, R. et al, *Manual of Adlerian Family Counseling*. Eugene, Oregon, Univ. Oregon Press, 1959.
9. Frazier, E. F., *The Negro Church in America*. New York, Schocken Books, 1966.
10. Frazier, E. F., *The Negro in the United States*. Rev. ed., New York, Macmillan, 1957.
11. Kardiner, A. and Ovesey, L., *The Mask of Oppression*. New York, Norton, 1951.
12. Weisstein, Naomi, "Woman as Nigger." *Psychol. Today,* 3(5), (1969), pp. 20-22, 58.

MYTH AND MEMORY

Robert L. Powers

Adler's psychology provides an approach to the understanding of the function of myth in culture which until now has remained largely unexplored. By an examination of this approach this paper will show the usefulness of Adler's ideas to those whose study of man locates them outside the usual confines of psychology in such fields as anthropology, sociology, or history, including history of religions.

Review of Past Efforts

The effort to relate psychological studies to an understanding of cultural productions such as myth is, of course, anything but new. Both Freud and Jung offered interpretations of myth consistent with their psychological theories regarding the more private human creations, especially dreams and fantasies. But in fact the effort to understand mythology as "projective" material is much older even than modern psychology.

O. A. Piper (25) has shown that in the period of Eighteenth Century Rationalism, when many thinkers regarded myths only as "erroneous-interpretations of nature, due to faulty reasoning (Spinoza, Hobbes), to priestly deceit (Lord Herbert of Cherbury), or to the inevitable exaggerations concomitant with oral communication (Hume)," at least one German classical scholar was putting forward a quite different view.

Christian Gottlieb Heyne (1729-1812) "explained the myth as the language by which primitive man described his inner states, particularly his reaction to those features in his environment by which he was particularly impressed" (25, p. 778). Piper shows the influence of Heyne in a tradition that leads to Ernst Cassirer and, through Schelling, to Tillich.

The contributions of Freud and Jung to the discussion of this relationship between "inner states" and outward, including mythological,

271

expression are by now well known and familiar. For Freud the myth is a disguised retention of repressed self-knowledge, in which the conflict between instinctual demand and cultural requirement is dramatized with the use of elaborate symbols (15, 16). For Jung the myths are expressions of archetypal images, developed in the course of the evolution of the human species, and retained in the "shape" of the psychic component of our biological inheritance. As such, they represent "forces that are beyond logical justification and moral sanction; they are always stronger than man and his brain. Man believes indeed that he molds these ideas, but in reality they mold him and make him their unwitting mouthpiece" (20, p. 42).

Freud and Jung and their followers have had an undeniable influence on the thinking of workers in other fields, and even those who oppose their ideas often find it necessary to take them into account. Nevertheless, the interpretive usefulness of their conceptions to an understanding of the ways in which the myth functions in the life of a given society has been called into serious question. As early as 1926 Malinowski was moved to complain, not without some asperity, against

> . . . the psychoanalyst who has come at last to teach us that the myth is a daydream of the race, and that we can only explain it by turning our back upon nature, history, and culture, and diving deep into the dark pools of the subconscious, where at the bottom there lie the usual paraphernalia and symbols of psychoanalytic exegesis (22, p. 99).

Ernest Becker, an anthropologist who has done extensive interdisciplinary research in psychiatry, is representative of those who bring this line of criticism up to date. Becker dismisses Jung's "archetypal unconscious" in a passing reference (8, p. 164), but his reaction to the effort to apply Freud's "view of instinctive man" to cultural studies involves an extensive critique of what Becker calls "the straight jacket in which Freud has held social scientists" (7, p. 133).

If Freudian psychology is being so roughly driven from the field of cultural studies, Adlerians might well be excused for hesitating before the risks involved in trying to take its place, were it not for the striking invitation Becker offers when he goes on to say:

> We shall make no real progress in social science until we accept the symbolic nature of human striving upon which Adler . . . insisted long ago. We have not yet swept out the darkest Freudian terminological corners, which continue to hobble the analyses of our best thinkers (7, p. 134).

Adler's Views on Mythology

Although Adler gives only occasional attention to mythology in his writings, he makes it clear that his understanding of it is quite different from either Freud's or Jung's.

Writing in 1912, shortly after his formal break with Freud, and just after his fateful encounter with Vaihinger's then newly published *The Philosophy of 'As If'* (29), Adler says:

> In the psychological life of the neurotic we find the inclination to stylize experiences and persons in the environment to a very pronounced degree, exactly as we find it in primitive thought, mythology, legend, cosmogeny, theogeny, primitive art, psychotic productions, and the beginnings of philosophy. In this process phenomena which do not belong together must, of course, be sharply separated by abstractive fiction. The urge to do this comes from the desire for orientation which, in turn, originates in the safeguarding tendency. This urge is often so considerable that it demands artificial dissection of . . . even the self into two or several antithetical parts (1, p. 248).

Taken by itself, this early statement could be misunderstood as a depreciation of the cultural works of primitive man, identified as they are here with neurotic functioning and "psychotic productions." Closer reading, especially considering the context of the recent rift in the Vienna group, reveals its broadside to be directed not against primitive man's efforts to orient himself in the world, but against the psychoanalytic penchant for locating intrapsychic conflicts between "antithetical parts" of the self.

Be that as it may, it does seem endlessly necessary to remind readers of the quarter-century of development in Adler's psychology which followed his 1912 study of the neurotic character. In 1927 Adler referred to primitive cultural institutions again, this time more positively, but an astute reader will note the continuing quarrel with Freud:

> We understand now that all the rules of the game—such as education, superstition, totem and tabu, and law—which were necessary to secure the existence of the human race, had first of all to do justice to the idea of a community (1, p. 130).

By 1933 when, together with Ernst Jahn, a German Lutheran minister, he produced a book on *Religion and Individual Psychology,* Adler was writing more sympathetically of primitive religions, "in which animal figures symbolized the goal of superiority," than of the modern naturalism which he saw as emerging

> . . . when man no longer sees himself as the center of world events and is satisfied with a more meager concretization, with the recognition of causally acting forces of nature as the image of highest strength. Individual Psychology, which has not till now attempted to extend its investigations and insights into this area, would by the essence of its view be forced to regard such an unpremised, mechanistic view as an illusion inasmuch as it is without goal and direction, just like drive psychology, which is cut from the same cloth (3, pp. 276, 277).

As important to our purposes here as the development in Adler's stated views on mythology and other religious phenomena is his movement away from any sharp distinction in theory between the ways in which "neurotic" and "normal" maintain the unity and consistency of personality. As the concept of the "life style" came more and more to be elaborated Adler was moved to amend the emphasis of his 1912 work. So, in 1930 we find him saying this:

In the narrowness of the 'abnormal' frame of reference the variety, the change of phenomena, and the adaptation to new life problems and demands of the day are excluded. But to some extent such exclusion, and therefore such repetition, is found in everyone. Contrary to the view of many recent characterologies, what we call *character* is the always repeated way, the guiding line, the way in which one behaves towards the problems of life on the strength of one's style of life. The style of life itself can come about only through the exclusion of forms of expression which are less suited, and through a kind of abstraction. It is exactly the same with regard to style in painting, in architecture, or in music. We could understand neither a healthy nor a sick person, if we had not comprehended, consciously or unconsciously, his habitual, always repeated forms of expression. Any experience and concept formation always occurs under the necessity of exclusion. But the nervous individual formulates his style of life more rigidly, more narrowly; he is nailed to the cross of his narrow, personal, noncooperative fiction, as I explained originally in 1912 in my book *The Nervous Character* (1, p. 279).

From this it can be seen that the "primitive thought, mythology, legend, cosmogeny, theogeny, (and) primitive art" referred to earlier reflect an "inclination to stylize experience and persons in the environment" which is part and parcel of human "experience and concept formation," that is, our formulations of our styles of life. The neurotic life style is not only more rigid and more narrow; it is also distinguished for being more "personal" and "noncooperative," that is, for failure "to do justice to the idea of community." The important point is that the same process which gives rise to mythology is, according to Adler, found in everyone; and further, that primitive, no less than contemporary, concept formation, in order "to secure the existence of the human race, had to do justice to the idea of a community," which is something the neurotic logic fails to do.

We are seeing that, as the concept of the life style came to be more elaborated by Adler, his respect for mythology came also to be more openly acknowledged. The following passage, newly translated by Ansbacher (5, p. 192), is from 1933:

> Our knowledge of the individual is very old. To name only a few instances, the historical and personality descriptions of the ancient peoples, the Bible, Homer, Plutarch, all the Greek and Roman poets, sagas, fairy tales, and myths, show a brilliant understanding of personality. Until recent times it was chiefly the poets who best succeeded in getting the clue to a person's life style. Their ability to show the individual living, acting, and dying as an *indivisible* whole in closest context with the tasks of his sphere of life rouses our admiration for their work to the highest degree (2, pp. 32-33).

Life Style

This concept of life style, so central to Adler's later thinking, is not easy to define. Shulman (27), comparing Allport's concept of the "proprium" to Adlerian concepts of life style, finds agreement between Allport and the Adlerians, but not without noting some differences among the Adlerians themselves. Some hold that the term is to be restricted to the characteristic movement or *leitmotif* discerned in an individual's behavior (Sicher, Dreikurs). Others extend it to include the convictions shaping the individual's phenomenological world, convictions including self-concept, self-ideal, environmental evaluation, and ethical convictions (Mosak).

Ansbacher, in a recent "Historical and Systematic Review" of the concept, essays the following summary definition:

> For Adler life style represented the organismic ideas of the individual as an actor rather than a reactor; of the purposiveness, goal-directedness, unity, self-consistency and uniqueness of the individual; and of the ultimately subjective determination of his actions (5, p. 191).

The present writer, in teaching at the Alfred Adler Institute of Chicago, has devised his own image of the way an individual's life style develops. It is as if the situation of each child were that of being born into the middle of the second act of a play, and having to ad lib his way into the action. To do this he has to "size up" the situation and his place in it (his "role" in the "play") by asking (and deciding), "What's going on here? What kind of a world is this? What kind of person am I? What must I do, and what must I become in order to get in on things?" And so on. Neither the questions nor his answers take this explicit form, however. They are played out in movement amongst the others, first by trial and error, later in a more finished performance to which he adheres as to a well rehearsed role. The quality of his objective—for example, either to be a prima donna who would like to force everyone else into supporting roles, or to be a member of the cast whose attitude is, "The show must go on"—determines our labelling him either neurotic or normal.

If there is merit to this image, it is in showing the *social* function of the life style, as well as the subjective, fictional, symbolic character of its composition. It tries to take into account an observation of Dreikurs that "the desire to become part of the group, i.e. to relate functionally to their world, is basic to all human beings, and even their physiological and more self-centered psychological desires and urges become subservient to it" (10, p. 3). The individual must be understood as much in his social context as in his indivisible uniqueness. Adler says it this way: "Individual Psychology regards and examines the individual as socially embedded. We refuse to recognize and examine an isolated human being" (1, p. 2).

In the "Review" by Ansbacher, mentioned above, we are presented with some strong evidence for supposing that in 1929 Adler adopted the term, life style, from his colleague Folkert Wilken. Wilken had been a student of the pioneer sociologist Max Weber, for whom life style was a descriptive concept referring to the characteristic way of life of a whole social class (5, p. 196 ff.).

Ansbacher also mentions the position taken by Rothaker, a contemporary German scholar, who, in discussing the problems of cultural anthropology, "maintains that cultures *are* life styles, emerging from a more primitive state of life-communities *(Lebensgemeinschaften),* and possibly developing into a higher state of cultural styles" (5, p. 202). In the same place we read of another German, "Johannes Neumann, an Adlerian psychotherapist, (who) in a special connection made the analogy that culture is to the larger group what life style is to the individual" (5, p. 202).

If what we are seeing here is a confluence of sociology, cultural anthropology, and Individual Psychology in approaches to a unified science of man, it is a development which Adler predicted in 1933. In a chapter on "The Psychological Approach to the Investigation of the Style of Life," he refers on one page both to the "individual, perpetually comparing himself with the unattainable ideal of perfection," and to "each cultural epoch form(ing) this ideal for itself from its wealth of ideas and emotions" (2, p. 37). On the next page we find even more striking analogies between individual and social group:

> The sense of inferiority, the struggle to overcome, and social feeling—the foundations upon which the researches of Individual Psychology are based—are therefore essential in considering either the individual or the mass. . . .
>
> But just as other civilizations under the pressure of evolution drew different conclusions and followed wrong courses, so does every single individual (2, p. 38).

The next chapter, "The Tasks of Life," begins: "At this point Individual Psychology comes into contact with sociology" (2, p. 42).

Myth and Memory

Everything that we have said so far in this paper leads up to and is meant to justify our raising a question and testing a thesis in a rather rough, initial, and exploratory way. Our necessarily modest beginning may, however, serve to invite further investigation by more competent researchers into the usefulness of Adlerian principles for cultural analysis.

The question is this: If, as Neumann suggests, culture is to the society as life style is to the individual, can the unity and self-consistency of a culture be investigated and delineated by methods analogous to those employed in the psychological investigation and understanding of a life style? Our thesis is that this can be done if it can be shown that myth is to culture as the early childhood recollections are to life style. The remainder of the paper will try to show that this analogy between myths and the early recollections holds.

According to Adler we can expect to find "just as many forms of memory as there are forms of the style of life" (2, p. 205).

> (The individual's) memories are the reminders he carries about with him of his own limits and of the meaning of circumstances. There are no

'chance memories': out of the incalculable number of impressions which meet an individual, he chooses to remember only those which he feels, however darkly, to have a bearing on his situation. Thus his memories represent his 'Story of My Life'; a story he repeats to himself to warn him or comfort him, to keep him concentrated on his goal, and to prepare him by means of past experiences, so that he will meet the future with an already tested style of action (1, p. 351).

Although Adler believed that *any* memory retained by the individual, whether from early childhood or from the more recent past, whether accurate as to the historic facts or mixed with fantasy, could reveal the style of life, he stressed the importance of the first memory, and believed the "theme" of the life style to be more clearly illuminated by the earliest recollections retained. Perhaps his most startling observation in this connection, amply confirmed in the present writer's clinical experience, is the following:

In so far as (the individual's) style of life alters, his memories also will alter; he will remember different incidents, or he will put a different interpretation on the incidents he remembers (1, p. 351).

Using Adler's method, Dreikurs has shown the importance of the early recollections for psychiatric diagnosis (9), and Mosak has demonstrated their usefulness as a "projective technique" (23). Mosak points out that according to Freud incidents of "infantile sexual conflicts or traumata . . . were repressed but were revealed in disguised form in the patient's early recollections," whereas for Adler the "selective factor" leading to the retention of early memories "was not repression but rather consistency with the individual's attitudinal frame of reference, the life style" (23, p. 302).

Following Mosak, then, we may say that Freud provides a "repressive" theory of memory, Adler an "expressive" one. They are quite different. Any analogy between myth and memory will be expected to produce equally differing understandings of myth.

Freud, as is well known, and as we have already noted, made the analogy, using his repressive theory. He refers at one point to the early recollections of the patient as "the phantasies in which he has shrouded the history of his childhood, just as every race weaves myths about its forgotten early history" (16, p. 377).

This is followed by some rather murky speculations about the content of certain "primal phantasies" which are necessary to the development of the neurosis, but which may not be available to the individual from his own personal and direct experience. In that case, according to Freud, they are available as "a phylogenetic possession" and "the child in its phantasy simply *(sic)* fills out the gaps in its true individual experiences with true prehistoric experiences" (16, p. 380).

Whatever may be thought of the scientific value of this rather oracular utterance, it does help toward understanding the turns Freud was willing to take in applying his repressive theory to the interpretation of myth, more especially the myth which had so much importance for him, and to which his name is now so firmly related:

> If the *Oedipus Rex* is capable of moving a modern reader or playgoer no less powerfully than it moved the contemporary Greeks, the only possible explanation is that the effect of the Greek tragedy does not depend upon the conflict between fate and human will, but upon the peculiar nature of the material by which this conflict is revealed. There must be a voice within us which is prepared to acknowledge the compelling power of fate in the Oedipus. . . . And there actually is a motive in the story of King Oedipus which explains the verdict of this inner voice. His fate moves us only because it might have been our own, because the oracle laid upon us before our birth the very curse which rested upon him. It may be that we were all destined to direct our first sexual impulses toward our mothers, and our first impulses of hatred and resistance toward our fathers; our dreams convince us that we were. King Oedipus, who slew his father Laius and wedded his mother Jocasta, is nothing more or less than a wish-fulfillment—the fulfillment of the wish of our childhood. But we, more fortunate than he, in so far as we have not become psychoneurotics, have since our childhood succeeded in withdrawing our sexual impulses from our mothers, and in forgetting our jealousy of our fathers. We recoil from the person for whom this primitive wish of our childhood has been fulfilled with all the force of the repression which these wishes have undergone in our minds since childhood. As the poet brings the guilt of Oedipus to light by his investigation, he forces us to become aware of our own inner selves, in which the same impulses are still extant, even though they are suppressed. . . . Like Oedipus, we live in ignorance of the desires that offend morality, the desires that nature has forced on us, and after their unveiling we may well prefer to avert our gaze from the scenes of our childhood (15, p. 308).

Freud argues for this interpretation by pointing to the universality of incest taboos, and concluding that there would be no need for such taboos if incest were not a real danger to human community. But then it becomes necessary to show why mankind has everywhere resisted this danger and erected taboos against it. For an Adlerian the answer would have to be sought in purely social motives. But Freud cannot allow the independence of social motives, and so must make another speculative appeal to phylogeny:

> In 1913, under the title of *Totem und Tabu,* I published a study of the earliest forms of religion and morality in which I expressed a suspicion that perhaps the sense of guilt of mankind as a whole, which is the ultimate source of religion and morality, was acquired in the beginnings of history through the Oedipus complex (16, p. 341).

Perhaps. Then again, perhaps not. And if not, then "the ultimate source of religion and morality" will have to be sought elsewhere than in "the sense of guilt of mankind as a whole." It may even be found in a "desire for orientation," as Adler called it, peculiar to a symbol using creature whose instincts are too poor and formless to serve the purposes of adaptation in the face of the uncertainties of an always changing social and symbolic environment.

An Expressive Theory of Myth

Freud asks how it is that *Oedipus Rex* can still move us now "no less powerfully than it did the contemporary Greeks." His answer ("the only possible explanation") is that we both—fifth century B.C. Athenian, and twentieth century "Modern"—find ourselves in the same psychic predicament. We and they, with every man born into civilized society, have had to weather the same storm of conflict in putting down our natural urgings toward incest and parricide during the course of our psychic development. Because we have succeeded in this only tenuously, and then only "in so far as we have not become psychoneurotics," Oedipus strikes a responsive chord in those still living urgencies, stirring them to uneasy movement beneath the surface of the repressions by which they are bound.

But must we grant so much about human nature in order to answer so little a question about the enduring charm and fascination of a classic play? The question as Freud has posed it really raises a broader question from which it will not do to be distracted: How is it that all the culture of ancient Greece, and perhaps especially of Periclean Athens, whether reflected in the drama or in sculpture, in architecture or in statecraft, has still so much power to move us, to inform our imaginations, to guide our reflections on ourselves and on our institutions? Must we assume that the whole story, from the Trojan war to the Macedonian conquest, is one long diagrammatic key to an understanding of our psychosexual development and psychopathologies? Somehow, one thinks we must not.

If an "expressive" theory is to demonstrate a more adequate conceptualization it must reverse the Freudian argument and show that the power of the myth does not depend "upon the peculiar nature of the material" but rather upon the *purposes* for which the material is chosen and the convictions which the peculiar *use* of the material can be seen to dramatize.

To do this an expressive theorist would have to show how the same legendary themes (the "material" of the myth) have been used at different times in history, under the conditions of different cultural convictions about the nature of man and of human social order, with recognizably different results. In this way he would be able to interpret the myth by analogy to his interpretations of the early childhood recollections of the individual. He would expect to see that, just as the individual human being orders his experience and takes a direction for the development of his life by the purposive recollection of certain childhood incidents experienced within the context of his given (but subjectively perceived) family constellation, so the culture is ordered and guided in its development by the purposive recollection of the myth within the context of its given (but only relatively understood) historical situation.

279

There is at least one parade example available to us in which these expectations of an expressive theory can be justified. Both Homer (17, Books I & III) and Aeschylus (4) recount the myth of Orestes, and the themes of the myth (the "peculiar material") are in all essential respects the same for each of them, even though almost five hundred years separates them in time. Nevertheless it is clear upon even the most superficial reading that their respective handling of those themes is so thoroughly and fundamentally different that, if only the names of the characters were changed in either one of them, the modern reader might be hard put to recognize the relationship.

For Homer, writing against the background of a social system dominated by a masculine aristocracy of gods and nobles[1], the story of Orestes illustrates in a direct and uncomplicated way the dependence of honor upon vengeance. The autocratic social order rewards those who serve it and punishes those who ignore or attack it. Aegisthus—in "going beyond that which was ordained," taking the "wedded wife of the son of Atreus" and killing "her lord on his return" from the Trojan war — invited and deserved the revenge of Orestes who, in his turn, proved himself worthy of "renown" by killing this killer of his father, and by killing "his hateful mother" as well (17, Books I & III). The point here is perfectly clear: Agamemmon, the hero of the Trojan war is good. Aegisthus, his murderer, is bad. Clytemnestra, his wife, is decent enough, but being only a woman is easily led astray by the "guileful Aegisthus" until "at last the doom of the gods bound her to her ruin" (17, Book III). Orestes is best of all for avenging his father's murder. As Jaeger says, " . . . Telemachus in the *Odyssey* has an apt model to imitate during his training as a man. The obvious pattern for him to follow was Orestes . . ." (19, pp. 32-33).

For Aeschylus the matter is not nearly so simple. Writing against the background of the new Athenian democracy, within living memory of the defeat of Persia and the overthrow of the tyrants[2], he is part of a generation whose task it was to develop and maintain social structures and forms appropriate to the ideals of freedom and equality. In times of rapid social change from autocratic to democratic organization, a central problem (as we are continually having to learn in our own age and generation) is that of establishing norms and procedures of common civic justice on a historical foundation of traditional inequality, hitherto dominated by ideas of vengeance, reward, and punishment.

It is said that hard cases make bad law, but it would be better to say that for Aeschylus (and for present day Americans) hard cases expose the inadequacy of outmoded legal and social systems.

So it is that for Aeschylus the story of Orestes illustrates the unending and unbounded horror that ensues when vengeance stands in the place, and bears the name, of justice. Atreus is cuckolded by Thyestes, his brother. In revenge for this Atreus tricks Thyestes into eating the cooked flesh of two of his own children, and so drives him into unwitting sacrilege and subsequent madness. In revenge for this monstrous crime Aegisthus, the youngest (and only surviving) son of Thyestes, plots the murder of his cousin Agamemmon, the son of Atreus, Aegisthus seduces Clytemnestra, the wife of Agamemnon, and makes her a partner to his plans. Clytemnestra has her own motives, however. In revenge for his having sacrificed their daughter Iphigenie, in order to gain a favorable wind at the time of the embarkation for the Trojan war, it is she (not Aegisthus) who kills her husband. In revenge for her having murdered his father it is now the turn of Orestes, the son of Agamemnon and Clytemnestra, who is given a command from Apollo to murder his mother. The Furies (Erinyes), ancient divinities pledged to revenge murdered parents, now seek the life (or, at least, the wits) of Orestes. Apollo comes to the defense of Orestes (and so, into conflict with the Furies), having commanded the murder which has offended them.

Revenge among men has finally issued in a conflict between divinities. Aeschylus reconciles this conflict before a court of mortals in the final situation of the trilogy, and it is wonderful to see how he makes every detail and sub-theme of the drama contribute to and depend on this final reconciliation. The forum in which it is all resolved is not just any court of mortals, to be sure, but one which is representative of the new Athenian democracy. This is the point. It is Athens and Athenian democracy which according to the *Oresteia* of Aeschylus is capable of adjudicating disputes even between the gods and of transforming the Furies into the Eumenides, the "Kindly Ones," by the use of reason and persuasion instead of revenge.

The expressive theory would hold that, in the case of the myth of Orestes, it is this point, this purpose which moves us "no less powerfully than it moved the contemporary Greeks" for whom Aeschylus wrote his plays. The "peculiar nature of the material" is important only in that it presents the hardest case possible in testing the conviction that democracy is capable of resolving those conflicts which autocracy could only compound. We may even be so daring as to suggest, on this approach, that this is a large part of what makes Homer so much duller for us in comparison to Aeschylus. The claims of autocracy, and the assumptions of masculine and aristocratic superiority no longer ring true for us, "in so far as we have not become psychoneurotics," and "the peculiar nature of the material," as Homer handles it, has no great power to move us in this instance, remaining just that for us as we read him: peculiar.

The expressive theory can also show that, just as the myth of Orestes changed as it moved from the hands of Homer to those of Aeschylus, so the myth of Oedipus changes as it moves from the plays of Sophocles (28) to the analyses of Freud. The expressive theory is even prepared to maintain that if Freud's argument about the myth seems plausible to us now, it is largely because it is Freud's Oedipus which we carry in our minds when we turn to Sophocles. Freud has done for the twentieth century A.D. what Sophocles did for the Athens of the fifth century B.C. Just as no Athenian after Sophocles could be expected to think of the Oedipus legend in quite the same way as it had been thought about before the appearance of *Oedipus Rex, Oedipus at Colonus,* and *Antigone,* just so none of us can think of Oedipus except in connection with the complex to which the name Oedipus is now so firmly connected in our minds. The Oedipus Complex has become the very form of the myth for our times, and by means of it many still hope to answer the ancient imperative of the oracle: Know Thyself.

According to Freud, Oedipus is a victim, the representative as such of all of us, victims "because the oracle laid upon us before our birth the very curse which rested upon him." If he is a sinner, if we are all sinners—if, indeed, "as the poet brings the guilt of Oedipus to light . . . he forces us to become aware of our own inner selves," and to know ourselves as guilty "of the desires that offend morality"—then he and we and all men are sinners *because* we are victims, "guilty" precisely and only in that we are victims of "the desires that nature has forced upon us." In fact, on such a view "guilt" is a word which has lost its meaning, along with any others that imply self-determination and responsibility. The victim is not a sinner in hope of redemption. He is the butt of a pointless and cruel joke which once it is exposed, he can only despise, and from which he can only hope, stoically, "to avert (his) gaze."

This is the view of Freud, and it is perhaps the key to the understanding of psychoanalysis, but it is certainly not the key to the understanding of Sophocles, at least not "the only possible key."

The Oedipus of Sophocles is of course a victim too. But this Oedipus makes himself a victim because he is a "sinner" and not the other way around. His pride and quick temper, and his own high opinion of himself at the expense of others, work both to fulfill and to reveal the curse of the oracle, as Lazarsfeld (21) and Atkins (6) have both shown in earlier Adlerian critiques of Freud's interpretation.

But neither is that the end of it. At the risk of entering upon a pedantic dispute, it must be pointed out that, as one old professor was fond of saying, "Nothing, gentlemen, throws quite so much light upon the commentaries as a reading of the text."

Freud thought that in the *Oedipus Rex* it was the intention of Sophocles to elaborate "the pious subtlety which declares it the highest morality to bow to the will of the gods, even when they ordain a crime" (16, p. 340), and that this pious intention protected Sophocles from seeing what he was really doing. In this Freud was simply and plainly wrong. Oedipus never bows to anyone, god or man, right to the end. "No god will speak for me," is almost his final line. He leaves the stage raging and balking to the very end. As for the preposterous notion that Sophocles did not know what he was doing we can do no better than to repeat an observation of Adler, made of psychoanalysis in another connection, that it "really betrays a want of the sense of intellectual shame" (2, p. 218).

The intent of Sophocles should, indeed, be described as devout, but his piety is not expressed in and should not be mistaken for theodicy. There is no justifying the ways of God to man in the *Oedipus Rex*. What there is instead is the celebration of a man's endurance through the worst that he had feared, and wonder and awe at that endurance. His greatness emerges as something in himself, not in his circumstances and not in his "fortune." And the same is true of his difficulties: they were not in his circumstances either. The effort to flee them by leaving Corinth revealed them in Thebes.

A first rate classicist may speak for us. Werner Jaeger's chapter on "Sophocles and the Tragic Character" (19, pp. 268-285) should be required reading for anyone in need of a corrective to Freud. Here is just a glimpse of it:

> (Sophocles) does not passively accept the unavoidable suffering sent by God, which Greek lyric poets had from earliest times lamented; and he has no sympathy whatever for the resignation of Simonides, who concluded that man must forfeit his areté (That special glory or beauty or nobility peculiar to the nature of a thing—R.L.P.) when cast down by inescapable misfortune. By making his tragic characters greatest and noblest of mankind, Sophocles cries Yes to the fateful question which no mortal mind can solve. His characters are the first who, by suffering by the absolute abandonment of their earthly happiness or of their social and physical life, reach the truest greatness attainable by man (19, p. 283).

There is one more point, important to our purpose here. In writing the *Oedipus at Colonus*, twenty years or so after the *Oedipus Rex*, Sophocles reveals another aspect of his intentions. Just as Aeschylus showed Orestes fleeing to Athens for justice, Sophocles shows Oedipus received by the Athenian king, Theseus, who grants him a final resting place in the sacred grove of the Eumenides, "the kindly ones" we met in the *Oresteia*. It is as if to say, "The myth of Oedipus is for Athens to understand and to receive. It is here that true greatness in man is honored among men."

Oedipus endures, we said earlier, and there is wonder and awe at his enduring. For Sophocles this enduring makes him the model of Man, enduring every handicap and every calamity of fate and of his own making, and by enduring, overcoming. Oedipus has become not only victim and sinner, but also saint. And by offering himself to and for the Athenian land which received him in mercy and protected him from all further exploitation at the hands of his own ambitious relatives and countrymen, he became both priest and victim on behalf of others, passing into death without dying, "in a passing more wonderful than that of any other man."

Aeschylus argued for Athens the just. Sophocles, the contemporary of Aeschylus and his acknowledged successor, is saying that Athens the just is Athens the blest. If the story of Oedipus move us "no less powerfully than it moved the contemporary Greeks," may it not be that we desire to have in our communities and in the structure of our societies the same high dedication to justice, mercy, and reconciliation which was the vocation they sought to serve as free men? And may it not be that "the peculiar nature of the material," the theme of incest and parricide, is chosen to show, here again in the hardest case possible, how in a just and humane community even the worst sins into which we might fall could not exclude us from humanity, and so cannot exclude us from redemption? If this is not "the only possible explanation" for the effect of the Greek tragedy upon us, it is at the very least as plausible as Freud's.

Some Confirming Evidence

It now remains for us only to show that the thesis put forward here can find support in the writings of those whose competence it is to study the myths of peoples in their living cultural contexts. In this our first obligation is to acknowledge a possible objection from this quarter to our choice of the Orestes myth as a central example.

It is true, as we have demonstrated, that Homer and Aeschylus "remember" the myth differently, and that the societies for which they write were prepared to make use of the myth just as differently in the task of self-understanding and in the affirming of common goals or ideals. It is also true however, as Eliade (12) reminds us, that all the Greek myths that have survived have come down to us as literary works, and not as religious beliefs: "not a single Greek myth has come down to us in its cult context" (12, p. 158).

Our argument is only that there is an analogy between myth and memory, as there is between culture and life style; and that myth serves (and expresses) the unity and uniqueness of a culture just as memory serves (and expresses) the unity and uniqueness of a life style. The distinctions between cult and culture, and the questions which may be raised regarding continuity or discontinuity in the historical movement or development from one to the other are fascinating, and they beg to be explored. They do not however appear to affect our case.

On the night of December 24, 1968, the first three men ever to speak to the earth from the moon read twelve verses from the Biblical myth of the creation. There was no question of a "cult context" for the event. The material read was at least as much "literary work" as "religious belief" for most of those who heard it. Still, it is hard to imagine a more universally recognizable way they could have communicated to "Western Culture" and its global relatives and descendants the belief in the goodness of "the good earth" they were addressing. The "valorization"

(Eliade) of a *new beginning* in human history, the era of space exploration, was also clear in this recital of our mythical account of what occurred "In the beginning. . . ."

If this myth can be seen to have still so much power in "modern" times, there seems no good reason for supposing that the Greek myths of "classical" times are wholly different in their use or in their effect from those of the "archaic" world of which Eliade says that

> . . . every act which has a definite meaning—hunting, fishing, agriculture; games, conflicts, sexuality—in some way participates in the sacred. . . . The only profane activities are those which have no mythical meaning, that is, which lack exemplary models (11, pp. 27-28).

Werner Jaeger supports us here when he points out that

> . . . the later Greeks also held to the *paradeigma*, the *example for imitation,* as a fundamental category in life and thought (19, p. 34).

There may be other objections which we are unable to anticipate here. Initially, however, there does appear to be some scholarly support for our contention that there is an analogy between myth and memory, as there is between culture and life style.

To illustrate this we have set out below five statements of Alfred Adler previously cited in this paper, concerning the nature and function of memory. Following each of these we have put one or two statements concerning the nature and function of mythology, which should be seen to offer striking parallels. The authors of the statements regarding myths are authorities in various fields: Eliade, in History of Religions; Jaeger, in Classical Studies; Malinowski, in Anthropology. Mark Schorer, the biographer of William Blake, is quoted from a passage chosen by the editor of the recent symposium, *Myth and Mythmaking,* as providing "so far as we know, as complete and concise a view of current usage of the term (myth) as recent literature affords" (24, p. 354).

1) There are "just as many forms of memory as there are forms of the style of life" (2, p. 205).

> *Jaeger:* A myth is the expression of a fundamental attitude to life. For that reason, every social class has myths of its own (19, p. 61).
>
> *Eliade:* . . . we have to approach the symbols, myths and rites of the Oceanians or the Africans . . . with the same respect and the same desire to learn that we have devoted to Western cultural creations, even when those rites and myths reveal "strange," terrible or aberrant aspects. But now, it is no longer for the psychologist to interpret these, by showing how such nocturnal aspects are inseparable from the profound dramas enacted in the unconscious:[3] this time the symbols, myths, and rituals have to be judged as cultural values—in the final analysis as the privileged expressions of the existential situations of peoples belonging to various types of society, and impelled by historical forces other than those which have shaped the history of the Western world (13, p. 10).

2) The individual's "memories are the reminders he carries about with him of his own limits and of the meaning of circumstances" (1, p. 351).

> *Schorer:* A myth is a large, controlling image that gives philosophical meaning to the facts of ordinary life; that is, which has organizing value for experience (24, p. 335).

> *Eliade:* We are at last beginning to know and understand the value of myth, as it has been elaborated in "primitive" and archaic societies— that is among those groups of mankind where the myth happens to be the very foundation of social life and culture. Now, one fact strikes us immediately: in such societies the myth is thought to express the *absolute truth,* because it narrates a *sacred history;* that is, a transhuman revelation which took place at the dawn of the Great Time, in the holy time of the beginnings. . . . (13, p. 23).

3) "There are no 'chance memories': out of the incalculable numbers of impressions which meet an individual, he chooses to remember only those which he feels, however darkly, to have a bearing on his situation" (1, p. 351).

> *Malinowski:* Myth fulfills in primitive culture an indispensable function; it expresses, enhances, and codifies belief; it safeguards and enforces morality; it vouches for the efficiency of ritual and contains practical rules for the guidance of man. Myth is thus a vital ingredient of human civilization; it is not an intellectual explanation or an artistic imagery, but a pragmatic charter of primitive faith and moral wisdom (22, p. 101).

4) "Thus his memories represent his 'Story of My Life'; a story he repeats to himself to warn him or comfort him, to keep him concentrated on his goal and to prepare him by means of past experiences, so that he will meet the future with an already tested style of action" (1, p. 351).

> *Malinowski:* . . . the really important thing about the myth is its character of a retrospective, ever-present, live actuality. It is to the native neither a fictitious story, nor an account of a dead past; it is a statement of a bigger reality still partially alive. It is alive in that its precedent, its law, its moral, still rule the social life of the natives (22, p. 126).

> *Eliade:* Being *real* and *sacred,* the myth becomes exemplary, and consequently *repeatable,* for it serves as a model, and by the same token as a justification, for all human actions. In other words, a myth is a *true history* of what came to pass at the beginning of Time, and one which provides the pattern for human behavior (13, p. 23).

5) "In so far as (the individual's) style of life alters, his memories also will alter; he will remember different incidents, or he will put a different interpretation on the incidents he remembers" (1, p. 351).

> *Malinowski:* One of the most interesting phenomena . . . is the adjustment of myth and mythological principle to cases in which the very foundation of such mythology is flagrantly violated. This violation always takes place when the local claims of an autochthonous clan . . . are overridden by an immigrant clan. Then a conflict of principles is created, for obviously the principle that land and authority belong to those who are literally born out of it does not leave room for any newcomers. . . . The result is that there come into existence a special class of mythological stories which justify and account for the anomalous state of affairs. . . . (T)he myths of justification still contain the antagonistic and logically irreconcilable

facts and points of view, and only try to cover them by facile reconciliatory incident, obviously manufactured *ad hoc* (22, p. 117).

Conclusion

The importance of Adlerian psychology for cultural studies and a
general social science, seen already by Ernest Becker, may be expected
to be more and more widely recognized in the days ahead. Malinowski's rejection of psychoanalysis is echoed not only by Becker, but also,
as we noted above, in Eliade's impatience with "profound dramas en-
acted in the unconscious." But it would be hard to know how they could
object to the confirmation of their own researches available in Adler's Individual Psychology. Eliade appears to be reacting, not against psychology, but against Freudian and Jungian speculations concerning
phylogenetic psychic inheritances, when he argues for an interpretation
of myths independent of the psychologists.

Jacobi, an authoritative interpreter of Jung, uses the expression "individual mythology," which he attributes to Kerenyi, to argue for the
"magic power" of the archetypal images to produce not only the myths
but also their "impressive parallel(s)" in private psychic productions
(18, p. 47). It is apparently against this kind of thinking that Eliade
sets his own views, for example in the following:

> But modern man's "private mythologies"—his dreams, reveries, fantasies,
> and so on—never rise to the ontological status of myths, precisely be-
> cause they are not experienced by the *whole man,* and therefore do not
> transform a particular situation into a situation that is paradigmatic. In
> the same way, modern man's anxieties, his experiences in dream or im-
> agination, although "religious" from the point of view of form do not, as
> in *homo religiosus,* make a part of a *Weltanschauung* and provide the basis
> for a system of behavior (14, p. 211).

But the "private mythologies" of a man's early childhood recollections are in fact "experienced by the whole man," and do transform
particular situations into situations which are paradigmatic, as Adler
showed by explicating their relationship to the style of life. They are a
man's expressive symbols of the personally apprehended frame of reference which maintains a unity in all his movement, and they are his own
most reliable touchstones for growth in accordance with his own unique
life style. As such they do in fact "provide the basis for a system of behavior" which colors his every act and gesture. They represent that by
which he manages to remain the same person through all the changes
and chances of this mortal life, as well as that which guides his striving
to exceed himself, whether in the direction of the neurotic fiction of personal superiority or in the direction of social interest and self-transcend-
ence. As such they reveal even "modern man" to be a closer relative of
"homo religiosus" than might otherwise have been supposed.

Of course it may be difficult and even impossible for us moderns to
see the myths which shape our culture. It is only possible clearly to dis-

cern the myths of others (which will include those we believe ourselves to have "outgrown"). Our myths are the "absolute truth" by which we see, and so their mythological character remains out of our direct line of sight. But there is enough movement and upheaval in all our institutions today for significant glimpses of them to be caught, even if the experience is jolting. Consider, for example, how the foundations of a liberal democratic tradition are shaken by both radical and reactionary dissent against the cherished value of dissent. Again, consider how precariously ecclesiastical organizations previously modelled on the myth of a divine monarchy experience "renewal," as they struggle to accommodate to democratic assumptions and ideals[4]. Consider also how "liturgical reform" excises odious references to "non-believers" from public prayers as the realities of pluralism render the claims of religious imperialism not only intolerable but also absurd and incredible. We may be tempted to smile cynically at current efforts to justify, by a new use of Western religious mythology, the fostering of "ecumenical" relationships between formerly hostile sects. Pope John XXIII is said to have embraced the leaders of a Jewish delegation with the cry, "I am Joseph, your brother!" (His baptized name was Guiseppe.) In Malinowski's words, we may be struck only by "facile reconciliatory incident, obviously manufactured *ad hoc.*" Nevertheless, our survival as mankind may depend on the success of just such efforts, made on an ever-widening scale.

If it is true as the expressive theory suggests, that every man creates the cosmos anew for himself in the poetry of his own mind, in the subjective apperceptions of his own fictive convictions (subject always, of course, to what Adler called "the iron logic of communal life" (1, pp. 127 ff); and if men live by this creating, and cultures rise and grow and change by it; then it may be that we are in a little better way able to understand the force and weight of the medieval principle, *credo ut intelligam,* and to begin to believe that it is the very business of our lives to believe, whether we believe it or not. There is no way to "see through" belief, in other words, as the repressive theory hopes to do. It is belief, conviction, which enables us to see through the pandemonium of experience to whatever view of the world we may creatively attain, even if it is an impoverished belief in "repression," and our only purpose were to demonstrate that there are no purposes at all.

Summary

The unsatisfactory character of previous psychological interpretations of myth is noted. Adler's views on mythology are reviewed and similarities are noted between his understanding of human communal development and his delineation of the individual development of life style. Early recollections are seen to be the key to interpreting life style, and an effort is made to show that myths provide an analogous key to the interpretation of culture. This view is compared and contrasted to others, especially Freud's interpretation of the Oedipus myth, which is found to be untenable. Scholarly support is found for the Adlerian method of interpretation, and Adler's importance for a unified study of man is predicted. Finally, implications for the understanding of contemporary social and religious movements are indicated.

FOOTNOTES

1. Athene disguises herself as a man, Mentor, in order to guide Telemachus (17, Book I). cf. Jaeger (19, p. 10): "Homer's gods are an immortal aristocracy"; and Eliade (12, p. 149): "Homer . . . composed his poems for a specific audience: the members of a military and feudal aristocracy."
2. Aeschylus was perhaps fifteen years old at the time of Marathon, and it may be that he himself took part in the decisive battle at Salamis. cf. Podlecki, *The Political Background of Aeschylean Tragedy* (26) for a full and interesting discussion of scholarly research and opinion on this subject.
3. But see also our discussion of this point in the "conclusion."
4. One hears of a new Roman Catholic parish named "Christ Our Brother." A few years ago it would have been "Christ the King!"

REFERENCES

1. Adler, A., *The Individaul Psychology of Alfred Adler*. Ansbacher, H. L. and Rowena, eds. New York, Basic Books, 1956.
2. Adler, A., *Social Interest* (1933). New York, Capricorn Books, 1964.
3. Adler, A., *Superiority and Social Interest: A Collection of Later Writings*. Ansbacher, H. L. and Rowena, eds. Evanston, Ill., Northwestern University Press, 1964.
4. Aeschylus, *The Oresteian Trilogy*. Transl. with an introduction and notes by Philip Vellacott. Baltimore, Penguin Books, 1959.
5. Ansbacher, H. L., "Life Style: A Historical and Systematic Review." *J. Indiv. Psychol.*, 23(1967), pp. 191-212.
6. Atkins, F., "The Social Meaning of the Oedipus Myth." *J. Indiv. Psychol.*, 22(1966), pp. 173-184.
7. Becker, E., *The Birth and Death of Meaning*. New York, The Free Press of Glencoe, 1962.
8. Becker, E., *The Revolution in Psychiatry*. New York, The Free Press of Glencoe, 1964.
9. Dreikurs, R., "The Psychological Interview in Medicine." *Amer. J. Indiv. Psychol.*, 10(1952), pp. 99-122.
10. Dreikurs, R., *Psychology in the Classroom*. New York, Harper and Row, 1957.
11. Eliade, M., *Cosmos and History: The Myth of the Eternal Return* (1949). New York, Harper Torchbooks, 1959.
12. Eliade, M., *Myth and Reality*. New York, Harper Torchbooks, 1968.
13. Eliade, M., *Myths, Dreams, and Mysteries* (1957). London, Havill Press, 1960.

14. Eliade, M., *The Sacred and the Profane: The Nature of Religion.* New York, Harper Torchbooks, 1961.
15. Freud, S., *Basic Writings.* New York, The Modern Library, n.d.
16. Freud, S., *A General Introduction to Psychoanalysis* (1924). Garden City, New York, Permabooks, 1953.
17. Homer, *The Odyssey.* Transl. with an Introduction by W. H. D. Rouse. New York, The New American Library, 1949.
18. Jacobi, Jolande, *The Psychology of G. G. Jung.* London, Routledge and Kegan Paul, 1962.
19. Jaeger, W., *Paideia: The Ideals of Greek Culture.* Vol. I (1933). New York, Oxford University Press, 1945.
20. Jung, G. G., *Modern Man in Search of a Soul.* New York, Harcourt, Brace & World, Inc., 1933.
21. Lazarsfeld, Sofie, "Did Oedipus have an Oedipus Complex?" In K. A. Adler & Danica Deutsch, eds., *Essays in Individual Psychology.* New York, Grove Press, 1959, pp. 118-125.
22. Malinowski, B., "Myth in Primitive Society" (1926). In *Magic, Science and Religion,* Garden City, New York, Doubleday Anchor, 1954.
23. Mosak, H. H., "Early Recollections as a Projective Technique." *J. Proj. Tech,* 22(1958), pp. 302-311. (Reprinted in C. S. Hall and G. Lindzey, eds., *Theories of Personality: Primary Sources and Research,* New York, John Wiley & Sons, Inc., 1965.)
24. Murray, H. A., ed. *Myth and Mythmaking.* New York, George Braziller, 1960.
25. Piper, O. A., "Myth in the New Testament." In L. A. Loetscher, ed., *Twentieth Century Encyclopedia of Religious Knowledge.* Grand Rapids, Mich., Baker Book House, 1955, pp. 778-781.
26. Podlecki, A. J., *The Political Background of Aeschylean Tragedy.* Ann Arbor, Mich., The University of Michigan Press, 1966.
27. Shulman, B. H., "A Comparison of Allport's and the Adlerian Concept of Life Style: Contributions to a Psychology of the Self." *Indiv. Psychologist,* 3(1965), pp. 14-21.
28. Sophocles, *The Theban Plays.* Transl. with an introduction and notes by E. F. Watling. Baltimore, Penguin Books, 1959.
29. Vaihinger, H., *The Philosophy of 'As If': A System of the Theoretical, Practical and Religious Fictions of Mankind.* Harcourt, Brace & Company, 1925.

BEAUTY'S ROSE:
SHAKESPEARE AND ADLER
ON LOVE AND MARRIAGE

D. D. Carnicelli

From fairest creatures we desire increase,
That thereby beauty's rose might never die.
—William Shakespeare

Some day soon it will be realized that the
artist is the leader of mankind on the path
to the absolute truth. Among poetic works
of art which have led me to the insights of
Individual Psychology the following stand
out as pinnacles: fairy tales, the Bible,
Shakespeare, and Goethe.
—Alfred Adler

Like Freud and Jung, the other two members of the great triumvirate of modern psychology, Alfred Adler freely admitted that our modern scientific knowledge of the ways in which men think, feel, and behave has existed from time immemorial, embodied for the most part in the historical and personal narratives of ancient people and in the writings of the poets, and that psychology remained a "harmless art" until philosophy took hold of it and transferred general philosophic laws to the study of human behavior (1, pp. 32-34).

In the past half century the philosophical and psychological analysis of man has gained such widespread currency that all too often we forget the basic historical fact that every great psychologist has taken great pains to point out—that the poet, as Adler himself remarked, through divination or intuitive knowledge "until recent times . . . best succeeded in getting the clue to a person's style of life," for he above all had "the ability to show the individual living, acting, and dying as an indivisible whole in closest connection with the tasks of his environment" (3, p. 329). Moreover, the student of literature who turns to Adler's writings is delighted by the refreshing ease and grace with which he accepts the instructive and even the therapeutic value of poetry, for that acceptance squares with the time-honored critical principles that poetry is at once didactic and psychologically cathartic (1).

Aristotle, for example, discussed the emotionally cathartic effects of tragedy on the beholder, and the notion that poetry is *utile et dolce,* useful and delightful, was a commonplace of literary theory until the end of the eighteenth century. Equally interesting is the extent to which Adler understood the operation of the creative mind itself. He noted, for example, that while much of what we call poetic inspiration is the result of intuitive understanding of human nature, even more of that talent can be traced to the poet's sympathetic bond with the community of man and to his general interest in mankind. Consequently, instead of rejecting the findings of the poets and philosophers as alien to the spirit of modern scientific inquiry, Adler put those discoveries to the service of Individual Psychology. It is therefore not at all surprising to observe him citing often from the poets and philosophers when formulating the principles of Individual Psychology.

Now a full discussion of Adler's knowledge and use of literature can hardly be undertaken here, but it may nevertheless prove interesting to take one small aspect of the question and analyze it with a view to establishing a point of contact between Adler's view of man and the view of man found in the work of great poets. Let us limit our field of focus somewhat and consider Shakespeare's sonnets, for they contain some fascinating attitudes toward love and marriage, attitudes which bear sharp resemblances to Adler's general views on the subject and, more particularly, to his central principle of *Gemeinschaftsgefühl,* or social interest.

The parallels are there, and they are strong ones indeed. One word of warning may be necessary, however: in pointing out these parallels I do not suggest for a minute that we call into question the validity or originality of Adler's psychological observations, or that Adler's attitudes toward love and marriage were in any way "derived" from Shakespeare. I do not even suggest that Adler was intimately acquainted with Shakespeare's sonnets, though the English poet's work had been known to the German-speaking world at least since August Wilhelm Schlegel's great translation at the beginning of the nineteenth century. But the correspondences between the two thinkers do point out the extent to which great and creative minds share an understanding of basic truths about human nature. What I should like to demonstrate is that Adlerian principles of Individual Psychology are in many instances in perfect harmony with those of Shakespeare, particularly with respect to the nature and scope of human life.

It is not far from the mark to say that the Adlerian can turn almost at random to any page of Shakespeare and find corroborated there many of the basic principles of Individual Psychology. I am suggesting, too, that we attempt to establish contact between the behavioral sciences and the humanities once more, for each has much to teach the other. Throughout his career Adler never lost contact with literature and philosophy, and in fact those two disciplines were often absorbed into his scientific observations and provided reinforcement for those observations. There are numerous references to Shakespeare in his writings: his analysis of phobia, hypochondriasis, and melancholia makes reference to *Hamlet* (3, p. 320), as does his discussion of the inferiority complex (1, pp. 106-107); his analysis of the plight of the second child (3, p. 380) and his study of the duality of obedience and defiance refer to *Macbeth* (3, p. 66). Had we world enough and time, we could cite numerous other examples of direct use of Shakespeare by Adler and of correspondences in world outlook between the two.

Most interesting of these correspondences, however, is that dealing with the question of love and marriage. Readers of Shakespeare's comedies, for example, are struck by the resemblances between Adler's definition of love and marriage and the central themes and dramatic resolutions found in those plays. Adler remarked that "Love with its fulfillment, marriage, is the most intimate devotion towards a partner of the other sex, expressed in physical attraction, in comradeship, and in the decision to have children. It can easily be shown that love and marriage are one side of cooperation—not a cooperation for the welfare of two persons only, but a cooperation for the welfare of mankind" (2, p. 263). It is precisely this sort of belief that permeates a comedy such as *The Tempest*, in which love between social equals, stripped of wasteful and destructful lust and aimed at "issue" or procreation, becomes the dominating *leitmotif*. Shakespeare's lifelong insistence that love, marriage, and sexuality are inseparable human activities can in fact be traced throughout his work, and most especially in the comedies, which end for the most part with a demonstration of spiritual and psychological concord between man and man, between man and society, and above all with a concord between the sexes that leads to marriage, procreation, and harmony. But nowhere in all of Shakespeare's work are these ideas more clearly and more concisely set forth than in the sonnets, and it is to these that we should turn for an understanding of the correspondences between Shakespeare and Adler.

The 154 sonnets which make up Shakespeare's collection are a small world unto themselves; they treat, in capsule form, moral and psychological issues so profound and so complex that the reader must often admit that the "scanty plot of ground" that is the sonnet simply cannot embrace them and that they require fuller treatment in the broader fields of comedy and tragedy. Indeed, the reader comes away with the feeling that the sonnet provided an excellent proving ground for ideas which Shakespeare was to take up in greater detail and depth in his plays. Because they are eloquent microcosms of Shakespeare's thinking on important issues, they should be of particular interest to the Adlerian. They contain, among other riches, provocative discussions of the destructful and wasteful nature of erotic love and promiscuity[1], as well as analyses of the revitalizing, socially useful power of non-erotic love, the latter of which has been labelled *agape,* "Platonic" or "Christian" love, depending on the critical or philosophical orientation of the reader. It must be emphasized that in putting the sonnet to the service of such a broad range of moral and psychological problems, Shakespeare used the sonnet form in a totally original way, for his own contemporaries were writing highly stylized and mannered sonnets in imitation of the fourteenth-century Italian poet, Petrarch. These Elizabethan sonnets in imitation of Petrarch were polished, lifeless "anatomies" of the suffering of the rejected lover. They glorified an ideal of romantic, self-destructive love which had little to do with any real passion for a woman and even less to do with marriage and socially useful sexuality.

Of particular interest to Adlerians is the group of seventeen sonnets that opens the collection and that considers the place of love, marriage, and procreation in the well-ordered life. These poems are addressed to a "Mr. W. H.," whose identity has been the subject of much head-knocking among literary scholars. Whether he was Henry Wriothesley, Earl of Southampton, as some maintain, or William Herbert, Earl of Pembroke, as others insist, is really irrelevant to our purposes here; what does matter is that he was an exceptionally handsome, well-born, talented young man, exactly the sort of person who, according to Shakespeare, should have married and fathered children. But for reasons unknown to us the young man refused to marry, to propagate "beauty's rose," and the poet's duty appears to be to urge him to marry and to analyze the reasons for his refusal to do so. Shakespeare's argument to the young man is perfectly consistent with Adlerian views of avoidance of marriage: the young man has apparently nailed himself to what Adler called "the cross of his narrow, personal, non-cooperative fiction" (3, p. 279) by his fear of coming to the test of marriage and by his lack of social feeling.

The task of marrying and procreating is—as Adlerians need hardly be reminded—one of the three great tasks of life, the other two being the achievement of a sense of communal life and the finding of socially useful life's work. Both Shakespeare and Adler seem to agree that the greatest obstacle to achieving marital and sexual happiness is a sense of egotistical superiority that renders the individual incapable of performing these vital domestic and social functions. Shakespeare bluntly accuses the young man time and again of exactly this sort of egotistical superiority, and much of what the poet says to the young man serves the very purpose served by the modern Adlerian therapist—that of describing the life-style in the hope that self-knowledge will bring about confrontation and resolution of the problem. The reward that Shakespeare holds out to the young man is the promise of immortality and the joy that comes when personal, subjective needs and the demands of society for procreation are reconciled and harmonized. In a sense the sonnets on marriage become a series of hymns to the glories of love, marriage, and procreation and a reaffirmation of the joy that man can derive from those most human of activities. Let us now look at the first of these sonnets:

> From fairest creatures we desire increase,
> That thereby beauty's rose might never die,
> But as the riper should by time decease,
> His tender heir might bear his memory;
> But thou, contracted to thine own bright eyes,
> Feed'st thy light's flame with self-substantial fuel,
> Making a famine where abundance lies,
> Thyself thy foe, to thy sweet self too cruel.
> Thou that art now the world's fresh ornament
> And only herald to the gaudy spring,
> Within thine own bud buriest thy content
> And, tender churl, mak'st waste in niggarding.
>> Pity the world, or else this glutton be,
>> To eat the world's due, by the grave and thee.

"Beauty's rose," or excellence, should be propagated by the young man, but he is narcissistic and behaves perhaps as does the pampered child (as is suggested by the phrase "tender churl"); he refuses to submit to the demands of humankind that he reproduce his own excellence, and self-centeredness prevents him from seeing that there is "something larger" than himself, as Adler described it (2, p. 264). In being "contracted" to his own "bright eyes," he is obviously in love with his own beauty, and the deep irony here is that in trying to preserve his beauty by keeping it to himself and pursuing his "guiding self-ideal" he actually brings about his own extinction instead (2, p. 280). Shakespeare insists on a further irony, that the young man makes "waste in niggarding" since in refusing to marry he cheats himself and society at large. Compare this with Adler's statement that "with man, one method of surviving is to have children." What seems to be operating here is a natural justice; built into the scheme of things, Shakespeare implies, are immutable laws by which those who work in harmony with Nature are rewarded and by which those who contravene Nature are punished. Readers of Shakespeare's plays know full well how this natural morality is demonstrated time and again, particularly in tragedies such as *King Lear* and *Macbeth*. The young man's violation of Nature lies in the fact that he refuses to accept his role as husband and father—an attitude which Adler would have viewed as a form of masculine protest as well as a sign of defective social feeling.

There are other correspondences: Adler noted that the fear of growing old and the fear of death "will not terrify the person who is certain of his immortality in the form of his children and in the consciousness of his having contributed to the growth of civilization (1, p. 66), and this is the very point that Shakespeare underscores in Sonnet 2, which also argues that procreation defeats Time and brings about emotional rejuvenation in the parent, who is able to enjoy vicariously through his offspring the joy and loveliness of his own youth:

> When forty winters shall besiege thy brow
> And dig deep trenches in thy beauty's field,
> Thy youth's proud livery, so gazed on now,
> Will be a tottered weed of small worth held:
> Then being asked where all thy beauty lies,
> Where all the treasure of thy lusty days,
> To say within thine own deep-sunken eyes
> Were an all-eating shame and thriftless praise.
> How much more praise deserved thy beauty's use
> If thou couldst answer, "This fair child of mine
> Shall sum my count and make my old excuse,"
> Proving his beauty by succession thine.
>> This were to be new made when thou art old
>> And see thy blood warm when thou feel'st it cold.

Sonnet 3 picks up this very notion and extends it:

> . . .
> Thou art thy mother's glass, and she in thee
> Calls back the lovely April of her prime;
> So thou through windows of thine age shalt see,
> Despite of wrinkles, this thy golden time.
>> But if thou live rememb'red not to be,
>> Die single, and thine image dies with thee.

Adler noted elsewhere that it is "a dismal prospect to realize that our mistakes and blunders, our lack of social feeling in love, can lead to our exclusion from everlasting existence on this earth in our children and in our cultural achievements" (1, p. 61). The horror of the death of a childless man reverberates through virtually every single one of the sonnets on marriage:

> . . .
> Then how, when Nature calls thee to be gone,
> What acceptable audit canst thou leave?
>> Thy unused beauty must be tombed with thee,
>> Which, used, lives th' executor to be.
>
> (Sonnet 4)

. . .
Then what could death do if thou shouldst depart,
Leaving thee living in posterity?
    Be not self-willed, for thou art much too fair
    To be death's conquest and make worms thine heir.
              (Sonnet 6)
. . .
  So thou, thyself outgoing in thy noon,
  Unlooked on diest unless thou get a son.
          (Sonnet 7)
. . .
Be as thy presence is, gracious and kind,
Or to thyself at least kind-hearted prove:
    Make thee another self for love of me,
    That beauty still may live in thine or thee.
           (Sonnet 10)

Sonnet 12 argues that man's defeat at the hands of Time is inevitable since man himself is part of a natural order that is itself totally at the mercy of Time; only "breed," procreation, can defy Time and assure man of immortality under these circumstances:

When I do count the clock that tells the time
And see the brave day sunk in hideous night,
When I behold the violet past prime
And sable curls all silver'd o'er with white,
When lofty trees I see barren of leaves,
Which erst from heat did canopy the herd,
And summer's green all girded up in sheaves
Borne on the bier with white and bristly beard;
Then of thy beauty do I question make
That thou amongst the wastes of time must go,
Since sweets and beauties do themselves forsake
And die as fast as they see others grow;
    And nothing 'gainst Time's scythe can make defense
    Save breed, to brave him when he takes thee hence.

The voice we hear in these sonnets, then, is a clear one. It celebrates marriage and procreation as the sole method by which man can defeat Time and mortality. It speaks eloquently of the need for the young man to dedicate himself to something larger than self-love, for self-love is ultimately a form of personal and social death. It speaks, in short, the language of social interest, and the Adlerian is invited to savor the sonnets himself. And yet the very intensity and fervor of Shakespeare's voice, the concern the poet seems to have felt for the young man who would not or could not submit himself to some larger, socially useful goal, has evoked much indignant commentary for its alleged homosexual overtones, and to "demonstrate" this homosexuality some critics have adduced the very sonnets we have been discussing, along with a more ambiguous sonnet, number 20, as evidence. The charge originated in the middle of the nineteenth century, and it made the rounds without a full airing until Samuel Butler articulated it in his edition of the sonnets (1899). Its most eloquent exponent in more recent years has been the English critic, G. Wilson Knight, who insists that the poems show "bisexual integration," or a world view that is both masculine and feminine and that has its origins in the poet's homosexual love for the young man (8). Among American critics Leslie Fiedler is the foremost champion of this reading of Shakespeare (5, 6)[2].

Now the charges made by these critics are serious ones, and they must not be passed over lightly by anyone interested in the question of love and marriage in Shakespeare's sonnets. Interestingly, we need go no farther than Adler's own observations in the nature of the homosexual personality to refute these assertions. Adler noted that "homosexuality is the miscarried attempt at compensation of persons with a distinct inferiority feeling, and corresponds in its disturbed social activity to the patient's attitude toward the problem of society," and that homosexuality is a revolt against the demands of social life (3). Clearly both these conditions apply to the young man himself, and we might conclude with some justification that the refusal to marry is understandable in the light of his homosexual inclinations. This view is somewhat tenable, though I for one could not subscribe to it wholeheartedly; but to ascribe these sentiments to the poet himself is another matter entirely since in appealing—even if in the most endearing terms—to the young man to marry, Shakespeare is asking the young man to accept his masculinity and his responsibilities to mankind. Far from being an expression of homosexual interest in the young nobleman, the series of sonnets on marriage stands as an impassioned appeal that the young man reject the self-love, fear, doubt, and pride that stand in the way of his fulfilling one of the three great tasks of life. Furthermore, as many commentators have rightly pointed out, it is inconceivable that a poet with homosexual interests would beg his beloved—on at least seventeen separate occasions!—to marry and have children. Adler himself would have argued that if the young man's refusal to marry was based on homosexual propensities, then rejection of that homosexuality would have to begin with an attempt to develop social feeling. If Shakespeare's urging amounts to anything, it amounts to an attempt to develop precisely such social feeling in the reluctant young man. The conjectures of these critics are therefore highly subjective and impressionistic, and they can easily be refuted by close reading of the Shakespearian text and by a sensible application of Adlerian principles. Fortunately, historical inquiry has also helped to curb the excesses of such critics. We now know, for example, that both the Earl of Southampton and the Earl of Pembroke had passionate love affairs with ladies of the Elizabethan court and that these affairs brought down upon their heads a good measure of Elizabeth's disfavor. There is little reason, therefore, to believe that these young noblemen were anything but heterosexual.

Let us, however, look at the sonnet that has given rise to so much speculation and wild conjecture; it is number 20 in the series, following shortly after the group devoted to marriage and procreation:

> A woman's face, with Nature's own hand painted,
> Hast thou, the master-mistress of my passion;
> A woman's gentle heart, but not acquainted
> With shifting change, as is false women's fashion;
> An eye more bright than theirs, less false in rolling,
> Gilding the object whereupon it gazeth;
> A man in hue all hues in his controlling,
> Which steals men's eyes and women's souls amazeth.
> And for a woman wert thou first created,
> Till Nature as she wrought thee fell a-doting,
> And by addition me of thee defeated
> By adding one thing to my purpose nothing.
>> But since she pricked thee out for women's pleasure,
>> Mine be thy love, and thy love's use their treasure.

An early editor of Shakespeare, George Steevens, remarked in 1780 that he found it "impossible to read this fulsome panegyrick, addressed to a male object, without an equal measure of disgust and indignation." Let us look at the poem with a more objective and clinical eye and ask ourselves what illumination Adlerian psychology can bring to it. What, first of all, does the poem *say?* Once we have made necessary allowances for the hyperbolic language of passionate friendship that we find so often in Renaissance poetry, it seems to say something of this sort: You have all the beauty of a woman, without all the defects of character usually attributed to women; in fact, so intense is your beauty that you generate love and admiration in both men and women. Nature herself intended you to be a woman, but stunned too by the intensity of your beauty, she inadvertently added male genitals at your creation. (Shakespeare notes, significantly, "to my purpose nothing"). Since those genitals define your maleness, I may love you insofar as it is proper and natural for one male to love another (i.e. in friendship), and your sexuality ("use" is a common Elizabethan pun for the sexual act) must be reserved for women. What the poem seems to say with a fair degree of clarity is that the poet himself understood full well the difference between heterosexual and homosexual love and that he accepted the limits set on their relationship by Nature herself.

That the turning point of the poem is the addition of male genitals by Nature (lines 9-12) and that there is punning on the genitals and the sexual act in lines 13-14 is far from accidental, nor can it be attributed to mere salaciousness on Shakespeare's part. In point of fact the choice of the sexual organ as the central symbol of the poem is an excellent example of Adlerian "organ dialect," or the focusing of a complex psychological problem on a particular organ of the body and then allowing that organ to speak a symbolic "language" of its own. Shakespeare's poem is, after all, an attempt to define normal sexuality and to set proper limits upon its use. Since it is the genitals that define one's sexuality, Shakespeare seems to say, it is those organs that I must discuss when I talk about the limits Nature has placed on my love for you.

To be sure there is a minor element of homosexual interest on the part of the poet, as there is bound to be in the most normal of personalities, and psychologists have assured us of the prevalence and normalcy of such ambivalences. Those critics who insist on the heterosexual-homosexual dichotomy in Shakespeare's sonnets might well be answered by Adler himself, who believed that antithetical thinking—conscious and unconscious, remembering and forgetting, sleeping and waking—is highly characteristic of the primitive or neurotic character and that psychological processes should be homogenized into continua:

> In the thinking of primitive peoples and of ancient philosophers, we always meet this desire to put concepts in strong antithesis, to treat them as contradictions. The antithetic attitude can be illustrated very clearly among neurotics. People often believe that left and right are contradictions, that man and woman, hot and cold, light and heavy, strong and weak are contradictions. From a scientific standpoint, they are not contradictions, but varieties. They are degrees of a scale, arranged in accordance with their approximation to some ideal fiction. In the same way, good and bad, normal and abnormal, are not contradictions but varieties. Any theory which treats sleep and waking, dream thoughts and day thoughts as contradictions is bound to be unscientific (3, p. 229).

And, we might add, any reading of Shakespeare that insists on dichotomies such as that of heterosexuality and homosexuality is bound to miss the very understanding of the duality and multiplicity of all nature that makes Shakespeare a prince among poets. So, far from being an expression of homosexual interest in the young man, sonnet 20 is a shockingly honest—and, as is all too often forgotten, wryly humorous—affirmation that love between males is limited *by Nature* to friendship, though in point of fact that friendship, especially by Renaissance standards, may be tender and affectionate rather than gruff and back-slapping. This tenderness in male friendship is one of the major themes of the sonnet collection, and it is unfortunate that modern readers misunderstand it so often.

It is also enlightening to read Adler on the subject of friendship, for he understood fully its meaning and its power as both cause and expression of social interest. Adler asserted that social interest could actually be trained through friendship since "we learn in friendship to look with the eyes of another person, to listen with his ears and feel with his heart . . . Training in friendship is a preparation for marriage" (2, p. 277). This last statement is of primary importance to an understanding of the common ground between Shakespeare and Adler since, apart from the concern with love and marriage that occupies the first seventeen of Shakespeare's sonnets, the second most important theme of the collection is the healing, civilizing power of pure friendship. This is an idea which Shakespeare inherited in part from classical authors such as Aristotle and Cicero, but more importantly it is the idea which permeates all of his work.

As in so many other key matters, Adler is squarely in an honorable humanist tradition when he insists on the civilizing power of friendship. To the reader who is aware of this richly complex tradition and has traced it from Aristotle and Cicero through Shakespeare, Spenser, and Milton, Adler stands out as an eloquent twentieth-century spokesman for a seminal idea in western civilization, and it is reassuring to hear that idea articulated by a member of the scientific community, which all too often loses sight of its place in the history of ideas. Consequently, Adler's statement that "training in friendship is a preparation for marriage" strikes the historian of ideas with great force, for he is aware that our humanist tradition has consistently viewed marriage as a subdivision of the ethical virtue of friendship.

Montaigne's pronouncements on the subject are typical of that tradition, and they have the added advantage of having been spoken by one who was Shakespeare's contemporary:

> We do not marry for ourselves, whatever we say; we marry just as much or more for our posterity, for our family. The practice and benefit of marriage concerns our race very far beyond us. . . . A good marriage, if such there be, rejects the company and conditions of love (i.e. intense sexual passion). It tries to reproduce those of friendship. It is a sweet association in life, full of constancy, trust, and an infinite number of useful and solid services and mutual obligations. No woman who savors the taste of it . . . would want to have the place of a mistress or paramour to her husband. If she is lodged in his affection as a wife, she is lodged there much more honorably and securely (9, pp. 646-647).

What Adler called "the submission of the self to something larger" was conceived of by Shakespeare and his contemporaries as an indispensable precursor to the Concord—a key word in Shakespeare's thinking—that could exist between man and man, man and woman, adult and child, subject and ruler, and man and God. Friendship, then, the willingness to look at the world from the point of view of another, is to both Shakespeare and Adler the key to happiness in all human intercourse.

Shakespeare's work is many-faceted—rich, deep, beautiful, moving, complex, truthful—and I have done little more here than sample a very small fraction of that work for Adlerians in the hope that, despite differences of time, language, and social custom, they will be able to better understand how great minds often vibrate at the same frequency. As far as Shakespeare and Adler are concerned, there is really very little conflict between the two cultures of science and the humanities, and just as the literary scholar learns that Adlerian Individual Psychology sheds light on human conflicts as they are dramatized in Shakespeare's work, so can the Adlerian learn that Shakespeare's knowledge of the human condition is at one with Adler's. As a literary scholar who has entered the house of Adler, I am delighted and instructed by the great beauties I find there, and in return I invite the Adlerian to enter the house of Shakespeare, where the language is slightly different, but where the main concern—man, his happiness, his search for meaning in life—is very much the same.

FOOTNOTES

1. The sonnets cited are taken from the Penguin edition (4). For examples of Shakespeare's sonnets on destructive erotic love and promiscuity, see sonnets 56, 94, 95, 118, 129, 135, 138, 144, 147 and 151.
2. Appendix I of Hubler's *The Sense of Shakespeare's Sonnets* (7) contains some sound correctives to Fiedler (5, 6) and Knight (8).

REFERENCES

1. Adler, A., *Social Interest* (1930). New York, Capricorn Books, 1964.
2. Adler, A., *What Life Should Mean to You* (1931). New York, Capricorn Books, 1958.
3. Ansbacher, H. L. and Rowena, eds., *The Individual Psychology of Alfred Adler* (1956). New York, Harper & Row, 1964.
4. Bush, D. and Harbage, A., eds., *Shakespeare's Sonnets*. Baltimore, Penguin, 1961.
5. Fiedler, L., *Love and Death in the American Novel.* New York, Criterion Books, 1960.
6. Fiedler, L. "Some Contexts of Shakespeare's Sonnets." In E. Hubler, ed., *The Riddle of Shakespeare's Sonnets.* New York, Basic Books, 1962.
7. Hubler, E., ed., *The Sense of Shakespeare's Sonnets.* Princeton, N. J., Princeton University Press, 1952.
8. Knight, G. W., *The Mutual Flame.* London, Methuen, 1955.
9. Montaigne, M. de, "On Some Verses of Virgil," in D. M. Frame, trans., *The Complete Works of Montaigne.* Stanford, Calif., Stanford Univer. Press, 1957.

CONTRIBUTORS

Willard and Marguerite Beecher studied with Adler for two years before his death. As co-directors of their own agency for twenty-five years, they have provided service in parent-child guidance, adult counseling and group discussions; have worked in personnel and in schools; have lectured, taught and appeared on television and radio; have written articles for professional journals and co-authored three books: *Parents on the Run, Beyond Success and Failure,* and *The Mark of Cain: An Anatomy of Jealousy.*

Vytautas J. Bieliauskas was born November 1, 1920 in Lithuania where he received his education through A.B. degree in philosophy. His graduate studies in psychology included Universities of Kaunas, Tübingen and Munich. He received his Ph.D. degree from the University of Tübingen in 1943. Susequently he was faculty member at the University of Munich (1944-1948), King's College (1949-50) and College of William and Mary (R.P.I.) (1950-58). He joined the faculty of Xavier University (Ohio) 1958 and was named Chairman of the Department of Psychology in 1959. Besides his present position as professor and department chairman, Dr. Bieliauskas has been consultant to Longview State Hospital, Cincinnati, Ohio and to the Bureau of Catholic Charities of the Archdiocese of Cincinnati. He joined ASAP in 1964. He is a Fellow of APA, Society for Projective Techniques and Personality Assessment, and OPA. In 1968 he developed a training program for police community relations based upon Adlerian principles. This program has been in operation under special grants from the U.S. Department of Justice. In 1969 he was named president-elect of the Congress of International Catholic Association for the Study of Medical Psychology.

Rudolf Dreikurs was Professor Emeritus of Psychiatry at the Chicago Medical School, Director of the Alfred Adler Institute in Chicago, founder of the Alfred Adler Institute in Chicago, founder of the Alfred Adler Institute in Tel Aviv, Israel, and visiting professor at many universities, here and abroad.

He was a pioneer in music therapy and group psychotherapy, which he introduced into private psychiatric practice in 1929. He also originated the technique of multiple psychotherapy. A former student and collaborator of Alfred Adler, he developed specific technical procedures, based on Adlerian principles, in many fields of human relations. He published nine books and numerous papers.

Paul Rom studied in Leipzig and joined the Verein für Individualpsychologie in Dresden in 1930. He emigrated to France in 1933, served in the British Army, and now makes his home in London. He has been editor of the *Individual Psychology News Letter* since 1950. Among his publications are *La Paix des Nerfs* and *Alfred Adler und die wissenschaftliche Menschenkenntnis.*

Harold H. Mosak, clinical psychologist in private practice, is a Past President of the American Society of Adlerian Psychology. He has taught at Roosevelt University, the University of Chicago, and the University of Delaware. He is a consultant to several Veteran's Administration hospitals in Chicago, as well as to St. Joseph Hospital. He served as consultant in classroom management for the Teacher Development Center conducted by the Rockford, Illinois schools under a HEW Title III grant.

Erwin O. Krausz (1887-1968) was a co-worker of Adler since 1912. He received his Ph. D. in Austria and an M.D. from Rush Medical School of the University of Chicago. He served as a psychotherapist at the Student Health Service of The University of Chicago, was a consultant at Henrotin Hospital in Chicago, and maintained a private practice in psychiatry.

303

James Hemming, B.A., Ph.D., was a teacher, then became an educational psychologist working in education, industry and with youth. He is a member of the Television Research Committee, and trustee of the Community Development Trust. He participated in the field project for the modernization of methodology in primary education in Africa. He is a member of the Executive Board of the World Education Fellowship, and Chairman of the Education Committee of the British Humanist Association. His books include *Teach Them to Live,* 1948; *Mankind Against the Killers* (with the World Health Organization), 1956; *Problems of Adolescent Girls,* 1960; and *Individual Morality,* 1969.

Donald N. Lombardi received his Ph.D. from Fordham University. He is a Professor of Psychology at Seton Hall University in New Jersey and serves as Psychologist for the Essex County Juvenile Court and Youth House. He is also a Lecturer for the Alfred Adler Institute in New York City and is a Certified as well as a Licensed Private Practicing Psychologist.

Danica Deutsch was a student and co-worker of Alfred Adler in Vienna since 1912. She has been active in child guidance and psychotherapy for more than thirty years.
Mrs. Deutsch was one of the organizers in 1948 of the Alfred Adler Consultation Center (now The Alfred Adler Mental Hygiene Clinic) and has been its Executive Director ever since. She is interested especially in individual and group therapy, in the problems of the middle years and the aging, as well as in family and marital counseling.

Joseph Meiers, M.D., University of Berlin, 1925, is supervising psychiatrist, Alfred Adler Mental Hygiene Clinic and lecturer in psychiatry, Alfred Adler Institute, New York. He is a group therapist who has written on the origins and development of group psychotherapy, and its subspecies, intermediary-distantial therapy. He is contributing editor of *Group Psychotherapy,* a member of the International Society of Social Psychiatry, and historian of the American Society of Adlerian Psychology.

Adaline Starr is currently an instructor in the Department of Psychiatry at Northwestern University Medical School, a Consultant in Psychodrama to the N.U.M.S. affiliated hospitals, as well as to St. Joseph and Hines V. A. Hospitals.
She as a pioneer in the use of psychodrama in its application to the family. Her approach is an integration of Adlerian concepts with action techniques.
In addition to being a staff member of the Alfred Adler Institute, she is in private practice.

Asya L. Kadis was a psychologist who had been a member of the European Individual Psychology group since the 1920's. She later was a staff member of the Alfred Adler Institute and the Alfred Adler Consultation Center in New York. For the last part of her life she was coordinator for group therapy at the Postgraduate Center of Psychotherapy in New York.

Charles Winick, Ph.D., is currently teaching at the City College of the City University of New York, having previously been on the faculty at the Postgraduate Center for Mental Health Columbia University, MIT, and the University of Rochester. With Asya L. Kadis, Jack D. Krasner, and S. H. Foulkes, he is co-author of *Practicum of Group Psychotherapy* (1963). With Paul Kinsie, he wrote *The Lively Commerce: Prostitution in the United States* (1971). He has also written *The New People* (1968). He was co-recipient, with Asya L. Kadis, of the Flowerman Award of the Postgraduate Center for Mental Health.

Sofie Lazarsfeld joined the Individual Psychological Association in Vienna just after the first World War. Analyzed and trained by Adler, she helped from the beginning to establish guidance centers. She wrote and edited books and numerous articles promoting Adler's thinking. The best known is probably the book about male-female relations, *Wie die Frau den Mann erlebt,* which was translated into seven languages. In 1932 she helped Adler create the first international summer school. She has been in private practice since 1925 in Vienna, Paris and since 1941 in New York where she still practices as a certified psychologist.

Paul Brodsky was an associate of Alfred Adler and Oskar Spiel in the teaching of emotionally disturbed children in Vienna. Upon moving to the United States, he entered private practice in Los Angeles. He also served as Acting Director of the Alfred Adler Counseling Center of Los Angeles as well as Director of the West Hollywood Parent-Child Counseling Center.

304

Alexandra Adler is Clinical Professor of Psychiatry at New York University School of Medicine and a Diplomate of the American Board of Psychiatry and Neurology. She is also Medical Director of the Alfred Adler Mental Hygiene Clinic of New York City and Chairman of the Advisory Board of the Alfred Adler Institute of New York City. She is President of the Individual Psychology Association of New York and has been President of the American Society of Adlerian Psychology and of the International Association of Individual Psychology. She is the author of more than 80 publications.

Helene Papanek has been a practicing psychiatrist in New York City since 1949. She is dean and director of the Alfred Adler Institute of New York and a supervising psychiatrist at the Alfred Adler Mental Hygiene Clinic and the Postgraduate Center for Mental Health. A past president of the American Society of Adlerian Psychology, she has published widely on Adlerian psychology and group psychotherapy.

Miriam L. Pew, whose training is in nursing and social work, initiated and is director of a comprehensive community corrections center for Amherst H. Wilder Foundation in St. Paul, Minnesota. Stimulated by Rudolf Dreikurs she and her husband have been co-therapists on marriage and family therapy for more than a decade, founding several Marriage Education and Family Education Centers. They have conducted demonstrations and lectured in several countries.

Maurice L. Bullard, director of special services for the Corvallis, Oregon public schools is a life-long teacher, counselor, and administrator. During World War II, he organized the emergency industrial training for the Oregon State Department of Education and supervised the industrial training for the Northwest Henry Kaiser Shipyards. Since 1957 he has studied and promoted Individual Psychology. The Corvallis special classes for extreme behavior problems have won national recognition. The extensive parent-study groups have served as a model of their kind. He has actively promoted the Oregon Society of Individual Psychology known for its News Letter and distribution of educational materials.

Bernice Bronia Grunwald was born in Horodenka, Poland, and was educated in Vienna. She came to the United States in 1932. She received degrees in education from Pestalozzi-Froebel Teachers College and Roosevelt University in Chicago. For many years she taught children with behavior problems in the Gary, Indiana public schools. In addition to teaching at the Alfred Adler Institute and many universities, she is co-author of *Maintaining Sanity in the Classroom.*

Blanche C. Weill, born in 1883, received her doctorate in psychology from Harvard University in 1927. She was trained by Dr. Maria Montessori to work with the physically and psychologically handicapped child. She is the author of *Through Children's Eyes.*

Eugene W. Wade is an associate professor of education at Wright State University, Dayton, Ohio. After receiving his Ed. D. from Indiana University, he worked as a school psychologist until joining the W. S. U. staff in 1964. In addition to teaching, his consulting work helps teachers to see themselves through videotape, interaction analysis, and the Adlerian approach.

Manford A. Sonstegard, Professor of Guidance and Counseling at West Virginia, is a past president of the American Society of Adlerian Psychology. For two years he was advisor to the Ethiopian Ministry of Education and for one year acting director of the AID program there and in Eritrea. He also is a consultant to schools and family education centers in Delaware and Pennsylvania.

Marven O. Nelson, Ed.D., is chairman of the psychology department, Rockland Community College, Suffern, N. Y. and administrator of the Alfred Adler Mental Hygiene Clinic, New York City. A member of several psychological associations, he is Secretary-General of the International Association of Individual Psychology and Treasurer of the American Society of Adlerian Psychology. He is a licensed psychologist and certified school psychologist.

305

Don Dinkmeyer, Professor of Educational Psychology and Counseling at DePaul University, Chicago, received his doctorate from Michigan State University. He has a Certificate in Psychotherapy from the Alfred Adler Institute, Chicago. His work includes numerous published articles and books such as *Encouraging Children to Learn: The Encouragement Process* (with Rudolf Dreikurs); *Child Development: The Emerging Self, Guidance and Counseling in the Elementary School, Developmental Counseling and Guidance* (with Edson Caldwell); *Group Counseling: Theory and Practice* (with James Muro); and *Raising a Responsible Child: Practical Steps to Successful Family Relationships* (with Gary D. McKay). He is editor of *Elementary School Guidance and Counseling Journal,* a publication of the American Personnel and Guidance Association.

W. L. Pew is past president of the American Society of Adlerian Psychology and a staff member of the Alfred Adler Institute of Chicago. He is trained in three medical specialties—pediatrics, general psychiatry, and child psychiatry. He is currently a staff member of the Hamm Memorial Psychiatric Clinic in St. Paul and in that capacity works as a mental health consultant to Hamline University, Luther Theological Seminary and Northwestern Lutheran Theological Seminary. He and his wife, parents of five children, are founders of Pew, Inc., Consultants in the Technology of Human Relationships.

Erik Blumenthal, psychologist and psychotherapist, is President of the German Society for Individual Psychology as well as of the Swiss Society for Individual Psychology. He is lecturer on Individual Psychology at the University of Wurzburg (Germany) and at the Institute for Applied Psychology in Zürich (Switzerland). Born in 1914, he studied psychology at the Universities of Tübingen (Germany) and Zürich. He was trained in Individual Psychology first by Alexander Müller and Susanne Rolo, and later by Rudolf Dreikurs. His latest book is *Practice and Theory of Self-education.*

Leo Rattner received his Ph.D. in 1962 from the New School for Social Research in New York City. He is currently engaged in private practice in Forest Hills, N. Y., and also heads a small, low-cost clinic providing individual and group psychotherapy for the community.

Lewis Way, born in 1911, educated at Sherborne Public School, took a degree in Economics at Cambridge University, and thereafter studied psychology under Leonhard Seif of Munich and with Adler. He has always been interested in social applications of psychology. Among his publications are *Man's Quest for Significance, Adler's Place in Psychology,* and *Alfred Adler: An Introduction to His Psychology.*

Harry P. Elam, M.D., 1953 Loyola University, Chicago, is Director of Ambulatory Care, Department of Pediatrics, Rush-Presbyterian St. Luke's Medical Center Chicago. He is a certified Pediatrician and a Candidate in Psychotherapy at the Alfred Adler Institute of Chicago. He was formerly Medical Director of the Mile Square Health Center, Section of Community Medicine, Rush-Presbyterian St. Luke's Medical Center. Before coming to the Mile Square Health Center he was Medical Director, the Children and Adolescent Unit, Chicago State-Read Mental Health Center Department of Mental Health.

Robert L. Powers began his professional work as a priest in the Episcopal Church. An interest in counseling led to studies in psychotherapy at the Alfred Adler Institute of Chicago, where he was subsequently appointed to the faculty. Now a psychologist in private practice, he is President of the American Society of Adlerian Psychology. He is married, and the father of three children.

D. D. Carnicelli, who holds a doctorate in English and Comparative Literature from Columbia University, is Associate Professor of English at Lehman College of the City University of New York and a specialist in Elizabethan and Renaissance literature. In 1970-71 he was in England as Visiting Lecturer at the University of Kent at Canterbury. In addition to contributing articles to scholarly journals, he is the author of a study of Petrarchism in English Renaissance literature, published by Harvard University Press in 1971, and is currently working on a critical study of Shakespeare's sonnets and editing a rare Elizabethan translation of Machiavelli's *Discorsi.* His is married and the father of a son and a daughter.